PRAISE FOR *BEAUTIFU*

"I own every writing book ever written, and Linda Sivertsen has done the near-impossible: given writing itself a personality. There's a reason we all say yes to coming on her literature podcast–and to being excerpted about our writing processes in this book. I feel like I'm in the very best company. And. Good God, can this woman write! I love Linda's voice and her honesty. Her stories are cinematic, hilarious, heartfelt, and pitch-perfect—with energy and punch, so often lacking in nonfiction."

—**Terry McMillan**, #1 *New York Times* bestselling novelist of *Waiting to Exhale* and *How Stella Got Her Groove Back*, and eight other bestsellers

"*Beautiful Writers* is *The Artist's Way* for a new generation. The sheer number of years it took to compile all the wisdom in this book is staggering. I love it and think it will inspire many—not just to write, but to find the mystery and divine in their own creative journeys."

—**Tosca Lee**, *New York Times* bestselling author of *Iscariot* and *The Line Between*

"With her *Beautiful Writers Podcast* and now this book, Linda's created the salon we don't have anymore—where really interesting writers like the *A Movable Feast* kind of people: Ezra Pound and Hemingway and F. Scott Fitzgerald—are all comparing notes."

—**Patricia Cornwell**, #1 *New York Times* bestselling author (26 Scarpetta novels + nonfiction)

"This is a REALLY good book that will help a LOT of people . . . When I was a guest on the *Beautiful Writers Podcast*, I told Linda it was one of my all-time favorite interviews. After reading how she's masterfully interwoven her entertaining publishing stories with our interview excerpts, I feel the same way about being in this book!"

—**Steven Pressfield**, bestselling author of *The Legend of Bagger Vance*, *Gates of Fire*, and *The War of Art*

"Linda Sivertsen is someone everyone should know."

—**Martha Beck**, *New York Times* bestselling author of *The Way of Integrity*, an Oprah's Book Club selection

"This is such an original, encouraging, funny, and very helpful offering of a book. Anyone wanting to stoke their creativity will find nuggets of wisdom from many of our great writers and creatives, all wrapped in Linda's marvelous storytelling. I hope the book flies into a gazillion hands!"

—Elizabeth Lesser, New York Times bestselling author of Broken Open
and Cassandra Speaks, and cofounder of Omega Institute

"I stayed up all night reading Linda's stories. The fact that her path is landscaped with celebrities, movie stars, gurus, shamans, and astrologers—well, pop some popcorn, you're in for an entertaining ride."

—Allison K. Hill, CEO of American Booksellers Association

"If Linda's life were a movie, I'd call it a real-life, Hollywood female Horatio Alger story."

—Leeza Gibbons, Emmy-Award winning talk-show host, and New
York Times bestselling author of Take 2 and Fierce Optimism

"It doesn't seem possible, what Sivertsen has accomplished with this book: masterfully braiding three genres: memoir, self-help for writers and creatives, and wisdom from the hearts and minds of our most beloved authors and industry pros. Beautiful Writers is practical magic for any writer, aspiring or experienced. You'll feel a sense of belonging as it catapults your creativity and self-confidence and answers all your nitty-gritty questions from process to publishing. This book is a gift for readers and writers alike."

—Steph Jagger, bestselling author of Everything Left to Remember

"The perfect nudge and source of inspiration for anyone looking to pursue a career in writing. Linda Sivertsen weaves her personal story with pertinent, relatable anecdotes from literary greats, detailing all of the highs and lows that come along with authoring a book. She provides all the tools to help harness your greatness and silence that pesky doubting voice in your head. Beautiful Writers far exceeds just being a "how-to" guide for authors, and instead serves as a funny, relatable reminder to everyone on how deeply rewarding it is to follow your passions, trust your gut, and create."

—Brooke Baldwin, veteran journalist and bestselling author of Huddle

"*Can't put it down . . . I* must *put it down!* I want to keep bingeing this addictive book, but it also makes me itch to get up and write. Between the motivating personal insights from celebrity authors and Linda Sivertsen's own riveting path, *Beautiful Writers* is that rare combo: an instructive manual you want to bring to the beach. Wish I'd had it while I was writing my own book!"

—Laura Belgray, author of *Tough Titties* (2023, Hachette), founder
of Talking Shrimp, and co-creator of The Copy Cure

"Brilliant, engaging, and conversational, with a palpable enthusiasm that feels like a letter from home."

—Paul Williams, Oscar-, Grammy- and Golden Globe–winning Hall of Fame songwriter,
ASCAP President, and *New York Times* bestselling coauthor of *Gratitude and Trust*

"When I look back on my career as a top book publicist, literary agent, author of eleven books, and sister of bestselling author Debbie Ford, the one person I'd call my literary soulmate is Linda Sivertsen. Whether editing one of my books, recommending writing books that transformed my work, or sharing a technique or story with me that altered my thinking, it's Linda who has had the biggest influence on my writing career."

—Arielle Ford, bestselling author of *The Soulmate Secret* and former book publicist
to Deepak Chopra, Marianne Williamson, Wayne Dyer, and Neale Donald Walsch

"What a joy to read! I loved it. The conversational voice will make readers feel like one of Linda's many friends. The stories, both personal and universal to the creative process, are accurate, articulate, and deeply inspirational."

—Guru Singh, world-renowned yogi/spiritual teacher and author of *Buried Treasures*

"Linda Sivertsen is charming in the most magical sense of the word and this book is a flashpoint of enchantments. Writers you know and love open hidden doorways to pathways of inspiration and practical insight. Linda threads her own life story through the stories of others to illuminate from all directions what it means not just to write, but to transform yourself into a beautiful writer."

—Justine Musk, novelist, essayist, three-time TEDx speaker on creativity

ALSO BY LINDA SIVERTSEN

Lives Charmed: Intimate Conversations with Extraordinary People
Generation Green: The Ultimate Teen Guide to Living
an Eco-Friendly Life (with Tosh Sivertsen)
Your Big Beautiful Book Plan (with Danielle LaPorte)

BEAUTIFUL WRITERS

A JOURNEY of BIG DREAMS & MESSY
MANUSCRIPTS—with TRICKS of the TRADE
from BESTSELLING AUTHORS

LINDA SIVERTSEN

BenBella Books, Inc.
Dallas, TX

 BenBella Books, Inc.
10440 N. Central Expressway
Suite 800
Dallas, TX 75231
benbellabooks.com
Send feedback to feedback@benbellabooks.com

BenBella is a federally registered trademark.

Printed in the United States of America
10 9 8 7 6 5 4 3 2 1

Library of Congress Control Number: 2022935039
ISBN 9781637741030 (trade paperback)
ISBN 9781637741047 (ebook)

Editing by Vy Tran
Copyediting by Michael Fedison
Proofreading by Ashley Casteel and James Fraleigh
Indexing by WordCo Indexing Services
Text design and composition by Aaron Edmiston
Cover design by Linet Huamán Velásquez
Cover image © Shutterstock / Angela Zanin (typewriter) and perori (vines)
Interior vine images: Freepik.com
Printed by Lake Book Manufacturing

The wood used to produce this book is from Forest Stewardship Council® (FSC®) certified forests or recycled material.

Special discounts for bulk sales are available.
Please contact bulkorders@benbellabooks.com.

To Carol and Betsy: the keepers of my dreams.

CONTENTS

PART THREE:

Losing Your Religion: Handling Disbelievers and Haters (Even When That Hater Is You)

PART FOUR:

Birthing the Baby: Putting Your Work Out into the World

INTRODUCTION

"Beauty was not simply something to behold; it was something one could do."
~ Toni Morrison, *The Bluest Eye*

Dear Writer,

For as long as I can remember, I've wanted to write books. I'm guessing you can relate because you have stories too. World-transforming ideas tickling your brain. A unique perspective on a corner of life somehow overlooked. A tale that won't stop unfurling its chapters inside your mind. The dream, the ache to write, has been thrumming through your veins for longer than you can recall.

And yet, something—time, confidence, *life*—is holding you back.

I felt this frustration even before I knew it plagued most writers. Long before a turbaned guru stared deeply into my eyes and told me that writing was why I was here. But I'm getting ahead of myself. Except to say, I had no reason to think I could be a writer and was thus grateful for the nudge. My grades had me, and probably everyone else, convinced that I was most definitely not "book smart." Several humiliating interactions corroborated this, which I'll share in the chapters that follow.

Against all odds, I did write and sell my first book, which received generous national publicity. I may be the only author you know whose CNN segment aired while she was scrubbing toilets at Trader Joe's market, but publishing opened countless doors for me. Missteps and absurdity notwithstanding, over the next twenty-three years, I was able to write, ghostwrite, and co-author eleven books (including two *New York Times* bestsellers); more than forty magazine articles; and help birth hundreds of books as a coach. Meaning, I understand a thing or two about your ache.

I know what it feels like to pulse with a longing to write and publish and publish again and write some more, preferably soon, but most definitely before you die. Bestselling author Katherine Woodward Thomas and I used to joke about the inability to birth a book akin to being pregnant with a twenty-thousand-pound baby, ten years in gestation. Books unborn weigh on you.

I'm guessing some questions eat at your resolve and feel paralyzing: *Can I do it? I mean,* really *do it—start and finish an* entire *manuscript? And, if I ever do, could it be great?*

Great books changed you. You want to be great too.

It's scary to consider that you might not be able to fulfill your soul's calling—and perhaps equally terrifying to embrace that you are already great, fully capable of creating what you came here to create. As in, all is well. Or, as Hafiz wrote, "This place where you are right now, God circled on a map for you."

If what I just said leaves you suspicious, suppose we take the lofty spiritual perspective out of the equation and honor the reality of time. To paraphrase Ira Glass, host and producer of *This American Life,* as creatives, we have good taste. But there's a gap between knowing what we want to bring forth and being able to execute it in alignment with our vision. It takes time and a lot of work to close the gap, and many people quit before their work no longer disappoints them. But I believe simply being able to recognize quality and having the desire to get there means that you're an artist capable of seeing your work match your ambitions. You have that greatness within you.

I hoped as much about myself in 1991 when six books appeared to me all at once in a dream in the middle of the night (we'll get to that too). I flung my heart, enthusiasm, and lousy punctuation into two worlds—the New York publishing scene and Hollywood celebrity circles—that most find unattainable. Walled cities? Who says?! And who cares about walls when your visions are sky-high? Anyway, I lived on the "left coast," the magical sunny one. A place where everyone knows you only have to decide which reality to call your own. Just give me my grappling hook; I'm ready to scale those walls! Despite having no idea how to craft, structure, edit, publish, market, or promote my imagined books, I was *all* in!

BUT but but . . . you don't know how to write a book! And remember, you never even heard a full college English lecture because you were busy fooling with your hair. All your participles dangle. You can't even sing "The Preposition Song"!

Damn. The voice of resistance was loud. But screw the voice! I was on a mission from God. My first book would be finished in six—no, let's make it nine—months!

That's when I started studying what the greats—*like the people in this book*—had to say on everything to do with writing and publishing. I became obsessed. Books from geniuses like Julia Cameron, Anne Lamott, and Strunk and White gave me the confidence to keep writing. They taught me how to write a book proposal, get an agent, and understand the norms of publishing while bettering my grammar and syntax, and editing skills: my real-world practice, enthusiasm, and steady streams of submissions filled in the blanks. Without taking a single writing class, I saw immediate improvement.

That first book, *Lives Charmed: Intimate Conversations with Extraordinary People*, incubated for w-a-a-y longer than nine months before publication; I could have papered my bathroom with all the rejection slips it garnered along the way. I'll share the whole story on these pages, not to mention some outrageous, humorous, magical, behind-the-scenes-clawing-my-way-to-the-middle experiences. Stumbling blocks? I've fallen all over 'em. Face-plants? I've made 'em. Setbacks? Just as I hoped my first *New York Times* bestselling collaboration would dig us out of debt, my husband of nineteen years left me for another woman. His parting words, when I had a mere eight weeks to deliver eighty thousand additional words to my publisher, were: "*Have fun with your booooooks! That's all you ever wanted anyway!*" Oh, and my co-author went to prison. That was fun. So yeah, I've dealt with setbacks.

But delays and drama didn't single me out. Every one of the authors you're about to hear from has faced incredible setbacks:

- Steven Pressfield wrote for seventeen years before he sold a single piece.
- Seth Godin sent queries for hundreds of book ideas in one year—and was rejected by thirty publishers, twenty-five or so times each.
- Martha Beck was finishing her doctorate at Harvard with severe fibromyalgia that made it impossible for her to write or use her hands most of the time.

- Jillian Lauren claimed she'd kill herself if her first novel was rejected. It was. Thankfully, she didn't.

That's right: Many of the world's most beloved bestselling writers struggled every bit as much as I did when they were starting out. Who knew? If I'd been privy to their hardships, could I have jump-started my own writing journey? Taken a few shortcuts and saved myself some psychic pain? Surely someone must have compiled all those "best practices" before, right? I'd scan the shelves and ask every clerk during my visits to Vroman's, Barnes & Noble, or the Bodhi Tree Bookstore, but I never found the perfect guide. I'd get to the last page of a memoir or writing book, and, though I loved 95 percent of what I read, I'd think, *But where are the messy-middle details? Where are the stories about the things I'm experiencing?* From that curtailed perspective, it seemed like success came too fast for the writers of these books. The authors were struggling, and then, boom! They weren't. Success! *Whaaat?*

I wanted narratives to unfold cinematically and *show* me how my idols pushed past drama, rejection, hunger, and broke-ness to get beauty down on the page. I longed for the details of how they got their ideas and then busted through resistance and continued to deliver, day after day, year after year, book after book. A few authors would deliver, and I devoured their stories. And yet, because they were writing from lives and genres far removed from my own, I was left wanting more. Greedily, I wanted this type of play-by-play honesty from every author I loved.

Then one day, it hit me. If I launched a podcast on writing, I could ask bestselling authors those very questions myself! Publishing *Lives Charmed* had flung open the door to a fulfilling career as a writer and book coach that's enabled me to connect authors with agents, leading to many book deals and bestselling results. But through the podcast, I could learn things I had yet to experience.

I teamed up with bestselling author Danielle LaPorte as co-creators and co-hosts of the *Beautiful Writers Podcast*. We invited a few treasured author friends to come on air and talk about everything from breakout success to staying power. The show debuted at #6 on iTunes in October of 2015 and has remained on Apple's Top Literature (now Books) Podcasts list nearly every day since. When Danielle left the show, I pulled in former guests like Glennon

Doyle, Martha Beck, Robert McKee, Leeza Gibbons, and Dani Shapiro to come back on as co-hosts to help me interview writers penning bestselling fiction, memoir, thriller, self-help, creative nonfiction, and more.

The podcast struck an immediate chord. Listeners told us it felt like they were getting an MFA in creative writing by hearing guests like Tom Hanks, Arianna Huffington, Van Jones, and Maria Shriver give specifics on topics such as coaxing the muse; feeling worthy; embracing creative habits; wrangling time; conquering fear; overcoming jealousy; networking; discovering when to stop editing and press SEND; using different kinds of editors; wooing agents and landing book deals; handling disbelievers and haters; trying new marketing angles; and so much more.

Like me, our listeners were spellbound, for instance, when Anne Lamott, who came on to promote her seventeenth book, shared the prayer she says before she writes (also in these pages). Or when Marianne Williamson spoke of how *A Course in Miracles*—the book that started her writing career—seemed to physically stalk her until she finally picked it up. When Danielle and I interviewed Elizabeth Gilbert—whose name is eternally tied to the word "prayer" because of her genre-exploding memoir *Eat Pray Love*—I practically spat out my tea when she confessed how hard it was for her to pray. It was an admission none of us, Liz included, saw coming.

Fans reached out to say they couldn't get enough, would binge-listen for days, felt like they were having coffee with us, and pulled their cars over on the side of the road to take pages of notes. But they also wanted to review the information, again and again, get the stories and lessons distilled in an organized way, where the details could be easily digested, remembered, and returned to whenever needed. That's how this book was born.

You're about to gain access to all this writing magic, from granular to visionary, including gems never before heard on the podcast. These literary superstars will make you think, laugh, and shorten your learning curve. They'll help keep you in the game if—*make that* when—the going gets tough. Because, in case you haven't heard, the blank page can be a real A-hole. And the publishing world, worse.

I believe you were born to share your worldly tales in these complicated times. Let the fact that you want to write be enough of a reason. No one ever said it'd be all blue skies and calm waters, but I can promise you that the tips and stories in these pages will make it easier for you. (Hint: Publish when you're no longer bleeding. Write when you are.) Filled with heart-centered encouragement, street-smart advice, and accounts of insider success—and failure—to help you gain the courage to get your book, blog, or biz finally birthed into the world where it belongs, this is the writing book I always wanted to read.

In this labor of love years in the making, you'll find wisdom from many of the smartest, most generous, and beloved authors alive. No more dangerous driving for you note-taking listeners of the podcast. There will be no carpal tunnel syndrome on my watch! Your literary heroes are here, in all their humble honesty and effervescent humor, happy to inspire and entertain you with their decades of hard-won know-how. (Not sure who they all are? No worries! You'll find a brief bio by each author's name the first time their words appear—plus a complete list of Featured Authors, with the title of their corresponding podcast episode(s), in case you'd like to listen later, in the back of the book.)

As you'll soon discover, *Beautiful Writers* is part inspirational, part practical, and part writing memoir suspense story, filled with wild twists and mystical turns, just as they happened, and insights into the writing life few authors have the courage—or maybe good sense—to reveal. Blended throughout is a straight-from-the-trenches, true story about how a degreeless, clueless newbie who put six commas in every sentence turned herself into a career writer. If you're feeling out of your league or intimidated by what you don't yet know, my coming-of-career dreams, adventures, and misadventures will support you to find—and believe in—your own path while putting the wisdom of the greats in a vivid, relatable context.

No matter where you are in your process, I believe you can create and finish your masterpiece (or many of them). I've seen it over and over again—even for those of us who have "no business" dreaming so big.

If you have the ache, you have what it takes. Consider this book your official welcome to the Beautiful Writers Club.

I'm so happy you're here.

Write on!

PART ONE

Courting the Muse

The Work and Play Begin

Welcome! In this section, you'll be granting yourself permission. Tapping into grace and flow. Connecting to your why. Silencing mental bullies. Assembling rockin' resources that catapult your craft and your confidence. Harnessing time and quiet (easier than it sounds, but we have hacks!). Most importantly, you'll be aligning with your highest writerly guidance.

1

No Degree? No Problem

The Myriad Ways to Become a Writer

> "The human brain is special. It starts working as soon as you
> get up and it doesn't stop until you get to school."
>
> ~ Milton Berle

What if you have the ache to be an author but no credentials? No school newspaper bylines. No teachers calling you "gifted." No stellar grades in English. Or worse: you got *bad* grades; your papers returned covered in red ink. A teacher said you're *not* gifted.* A writing group sniggered at your early attempts.

Will a publisher tell you to "keep your day job"?

Does going to school for writing matter? Should you think about going back now?

If you're like me, you grew up in a community steeped in reverence for the university system. Perhaps you were indoctrinated over Cheerios with talk of extra credit, straight A's, SAT prep classes, and taking as many AP courses as

---

* To be fair, not every bookworm with a history of being teased as "Teacher's Pet" feels 100 percent ready to go public either.

your little brain could hold. The goal: to win over admissions counselors, even if you'd have to sell a kidney to afford tuition.

As trusted systems crash around us, nothing is assured. For me, a student who both loved and hated school, nothing ever was . . .

"Señorita Tisch!" Señor Gomez yelled across the Spanish II classroom. "You're one of my brightest students in all my classes, and yet you don't pay attention. You don't apply yourself! *Whyyyy?*"

Caught off guard, I froze in my chair, love notes I'd been scripting to my boyfriend, Jeff, ready to make their way down the line of desks. I remember my red face, but not whether I'd answered my eleventh-grade teacher, whom I'd always adored. "What up, Señor G?!" I'd yell across the crowded corridor as we'd pass each other between classes. But if *he'd* been paying attention, Señor Gomez would have seen that Jeff was far too cute to ignore in the back row and that I was paying plenty of attention. In inglés. *Duh.*

I was a bookworm, not that anyone would have known it. Never once did I hide under my bed covers with a flashlight, like my sister did, reading an assigned title. Instead, while Carol was off studying and writing another A paper for her Honors English class—*show-off*—I was wrung out from giving my all to after-school sports. As Mom cooked dinner to a Mozart concerto, and Dad napped following his 4:30 AM start time and evening commute, I'd lie on the floor of our den library and salivate over volume after volume of the hardcovers lining the walls. That's where Astrology, Near-Death Experiences, Ancient Greece, King Tut's Egypt, Medieval Armor, the Great Painters of the Renaissance, the Lost City of Atlantis, and Cheese Logs from *Bon Appétit* magazine came to life. I'd smell the see-through onion-skinned pages of the leather-bound editions of the 1910 *Encyclopedia Britannica*, with their intricate drawings of Guggenheim's printing press, and imagine the grinding of the gears, the *ooohs* and *ahhhs* of enraptured readers. I prayed that my destiny had something to do with penning books that, like these, stood the test of time.

Despite the fact that I could barely spell, I was proud to be the Cyrano de Bergerac for my girlfriends, begging me to ghostwrite letters to their latest crush. My joy was in the social aspect of school, and athletics. How could I sit still when there were hills to climb on my ten-speed, track meets to run, football games to pom-pom for, tennis matches to win (barefoot on 100-degree courts, thank you very much). Assignments? Who needed them when you could learn the good stuff on your own?

So, how do you go from having every report card since kindergarten declaring, "Linda has a hard time sitting still," and "She talks too much," to fulfilling your dream to enter a world that's as totally sane and respectable and quiet and intellectual as writing? Could committing to school help with that? I wasn't sure it was worth the soul-selling risk. My mother had taken me to a holiday party where she worked at Stanford University. After making small talk with a bunch of gossipy complaining PhDs, I walked away thinking, *Personality much?* Even Stanford couldn't teach joy.

Seth Godin, author of twenty bestsellers, including *This Is Marketing*, *Tribes*, *Purple Cow*, and *Linchpin*, as well as teacher and marketing whiz.

Our culture has a dreaming problem. It was largely created by the current regime in schooling, and it's getting worse. Dreamers in school are dangerous. Dreamers can be impatient, unwilling to become well rounded, and most of all, hard to fit into existing systems.

The dreams we need are self-reliant dreams. We need dreams based not on what is but on what might be. The only way out is going to be mapped by those able to dream.

In the connected age, reading and writing remain the two skills that are most likely to pay off with exponential results. The effective writer in the connected revolution can see her ideas spread to a hundred or a million people. Writing (whether in public, now that everyone has a platform, or in private, within organizations) is the tool we use to spread ideas. Writing activates the most sophisticated part of our brains and forces us to organize our thoughts.

While access to information is becoming ever easier (you'll soon be able to take every single MIT course from home), the cultural connection that college produces can be produced only in a dorm room, at a football stadium, or walking across the quad, hand in hand. The right college is the last, best chance for masses of teenagers to find themselves in a situation where they have no choice but to grow. And fast. That's the reason to spend the time and spend the money and hang out on campus: so you can find yourself in a dark alley with nowhere to go but forward.

Valarie Kaur, civil rights leader and bestselling author of *See No Stranger: A Memoir and Manifesto of Revolutionary Love.*

The heroes in *Harry Potter* were students. They were young and wielded magic when the grown-ups wouldn't or couldn't. Think about education as a place to learn spells—and gain a little protection out in the world.

I remember graduating from Stanford University. A professor called me into her office and said, "I don't say this very often, but you have to go to law school." I said, "No, no, no, no." It was the last thing on my mind. My single most important educational moment was in the streets, protesting the Iraq war and getting arrested for the first time.

The professor said, "You're a woman of color. I see you. You have an activist's heart. You're going to keep ending up out in the streets. If you want people to listen to you, you have to get your degrees."

She was talking about degrees as if they were armor. You don't go into battle without a sword and a shield, without armor. This wise woman in my life was saying, "Get your degrees to be able to fight the good fight in the world—and to be safe." Even then, how safe is it? But as safe as you can possibly be.

Cheryl Strayed, #1 *New York Times* bestselling memoirist (*Wild*, made into a movie starring Reese Witherspoon) and author (*Tiny Beautiful Things*, *Brave Enough*, and *Torch*). 🖋

There are all paths to the mountaintop, as they say. College is important to different people for different reasons. I grew up working class in rural America. I didn't know anyone who had written books, and I didn't know of many people who even read books. So, college was an incredibly important portal for me to pass through.

After *Wild* was a big hit, reporters would always say, "Oh my gosh, your life must have changed so much." I'd say, "Not really." The only way my life changed significantly with the publication of *Wild* was that I could pay my bills with more ease than I had before, which was none. But really, when my life changed is when I went to college, and I saw that there was this whole world of people who painted and wrote and acted and were scientists and mathematicians, all of which suddenly became accessible to me and was an important piece of my becoming a writer.

You write a book one page at a time, one sentence at a time. I didn't know that myself before I wrote my first book. You have to do the work and teach yourself what the work is. There's the education. I learned a lot. But to learn how to be in a new part of society? Everything about that was magic.

I managed to get to college (despite being very distracted by a wickedly cute water-polo-playing frat boy at the USC Beta house), yet somehow didn't visit those counselors enough to realize I was three years in and REEEEALLY should've taken certain courses *right after* those other ones (Algebra 2 follows Algebra 1, Spanish 3 follows Spanish 2), or the info mysteriously falls right out of your brain, and you'll never be able to catch up. And, whoops! The major I'd chosen, Psychology, required Calculus and Statistics, which I'd already dropped twice, each, on account of not remembering any Algebra. When a teacher mentioned I'd need another four years after this to ever make any money with my psych degree, I quit. Yeah, with just three classes to go. I'd become an entrepreneur and a writer. I could *see* it. Why waste another penny of my parents' money?

My ever-supportive mom and dad were game. "I never worry about you," Dad said. "You always land on your feet."

Over the years, my lifelong dream to write grew fierce. I finally admitted to myself that it was *time* and was keyed up about an actual project—but aside from having no training or credentials, there was just one more little problem. I didn't know *how* to write. Raw talent was one thing, but craft was harder than I'd bargained for. Growing up, I'd figured that, unlike my sister, I'd be a kid while I was a kid (*wasn't that the point of childhood?*). Looking at Carol all sleepless and hunched over her desk, I trusted that scripting my real-life experience would one day come as naturally as biking, running, or smashing tennis balls around. *We have time. We're all going to be successful anyway!*

I sure as shit didn't want to have to go back to school to write. I could figure it out. Books were in my DNA. The shelves of my childhood home groaned with them. Mom had been the president of a book club for ten years and a founding member for longer. One of her best friends, Kay Sprinkel Grace (yes, her real name—and yes, she does), was a famous nonprofit fundraiser with many books to her name, one of which was dedicated to my parents. My father's best friend, Charles Sailor, was a big-time *New York Times* bestselling author who sold millions of books and lived in fancy Bel Air and wrote screenplays and hit TV shows. Carol and I had driven around with "Uncle Chuck" in a limousine on his book tour for *The Second Son* and marveled at how the biggest names in Hollywood—Newman, Redford, Stallone—wanted to bring that book to film. I was even more dazzled by the bulging canvas sacks carrying fan letters to his house by the tens of thousands from the post office. *If I could be like him,* I thought, *I'd really have the power to help this world!*

This writing thing couldn't be that hard. *Everyone's doing it!*

But Carol, who got annoyingly good grades, graduated a year early from high school, won a statewide journalism award at eighteen, and got into the USC Journalism school, scoffed at my first try:

"Why do you have *six* commas in every sentence, Linda?"

"I put one in whenever someone pauses," I answered.

"That's not how grammar works," she said. "People have to breathe!"

Meg Wolitzer, *New York Times* bestselling author of many novels, including *The Female Persuasion*, *The Ten-Year Nap*, and *The Wife*, which was made into a critically acclaimed movie starring Glenn Close and Jonathan Pryce.

My college writing courses [at Smith College and Brown University] gave me confidence, but it took a while. You need to hear things again and again—somebody saying, "That line is great," or, "That doesn't work." Then you make a connection: "Oh! Wait a minute! The reason that line doesn't work is that I'm doing that same thing I did last time when they told me that line didn't work." You start to see patterns. Only after doing it a dozen times can you go off and not do it that thirteenth time.

Dr. Jane Goodall, PhD, DBE, is the founder of the Jane Goodall Institute and UN Messenger of Peace. Goodall is best known for the groundbreaking research into the lives of wild chimpanzees in Gombe, Tanzania, now spanning more than sixty years, and has written many books for adults and children, including *The Book of Hope*.

Louis B. Leakey wanted me to attend [college] because I had a mind unclouded by the reductionist theory of the animal behavior people. When I was told that I shouldn't talk about animals with personalities, minds, and emotions, I knew the professors were wrong. But at Cambridge, I was taught to think in a logical and scientific way so I could carry on with what was then rather revolutionary: talking about animals as individuals, which wasn't done in animal behavior at the time, and to apply this logical way of thinking.

I think that's helped my writing. It's helped me to think things through really carefully and realize that, "Well, I've said this paragraph, but actually, it's contradicting something I said earlier, so let me get these two paragraphs together and make sense of it."

Luckily, I'm a Leo, and we're super driven, even grandiose. I was on a mission. I. Would. Figure. This. Out. And I did—although not without having to work through a lot of shame and guilt around leaving school. Thankfully, Dad lived long enough to see the release of my first book, the cover of which he had emblazoned on a T-shirt surrounded by black lettering: "Got my daughter's book yet?" But when he was diagnosed with stage 4 cancer not long afterward, just five years after we'd already lost Mom to the dreaded disease, I was desperate to make good on the promise I'd made to them when I'd enrolled at USC—that I'd graduate. All I had to do was convince my former dean to agree to a trade. Seemed simple enough.

If I could give my father the assurance that I'd walk across that commencement stage after all, he'd *have* to live to celebrate that long-deferred milestone, right? You hear it all the time, people practically rising from the dead to attend some extraordinary event they'd never miss. And, if it were too late for him to witness the ceremony, at the very least he'd go to his grave knowing that his and Mom's sacrifices weren't in vain.

Universities sometimes grant college credits for work experience. Surely the writing I'd published and consulted on would cover the three measly courses I was missing. Arriving at USC, I checked my reflection in my rearview mirror and prayed I was worthy of the special circumstance.

I barely breathed as the dean reviewed my transcripts, examined my first book, and paged through magazine articles I'd laid out for her.

"And I'm halfway finished with my second book, a title I'm co-authoring for a blind cop," I said, breaking the silence. "He was shot in the face at a highway drug checkpoint. He's a PhD, a therapist for police, fire, and military personnel, so I'm using many of the lessons I learned here in my psych courses."

The dean looked down, shook her head. She took her glasses off, closed her eyes.

"I'm so sorry, Linda. Maybe if you'd published a math book in Spanish"— the third class I'd dropped—"or written a psych textbook, perhaps we could count that as course—"

"I just hoped I'd qualify because my writing is so psychological."

"I'm sorry," she repeated and began to gather my magazines into a tidy stack.

She spent the next half hour outlining my options, which mostly amounted to investing years and tens of thousands of dollars on tuition and tutors before I could even think of donning a cap and gown.

Tom Hanks, typewriter-obsessed Renaissance man (and Oscar-winning actor, screenwriter, director, producer, and musician). He's published essays in the *New York Times*, *Vanity Fair*, *The New Yorker*, and his first book of fiction, *Uncommon Type: Some Stories*. ❧

I always feel like I'm still six units shy of getting a degree.* A friend of mine was getting out of high school, and he had an uncle who said to him: "So, you're going to go to college?"

My friend said, "Yeah. I'm going to college."

"Good!" said his uncle. "Here's the deal. I will pay for you to go to college as long as you want to go to college. Because I'm going to tell you right now. The moment you leave college, you've got to work every day, for the rest of your life."

That's why, hey! I'm still six units shy of my degree!

Gabrielle Bernstein, #1 *New York Times* bestselling author of *The Universe Has Your Back*, and many other bestsellers, including

---

* Fun fact: Tom studied theater at Chabot College in Hayward, CA, and transferred to Cal State University, Sacramento. In 2010, *TIME* magazine named Tom one of the "Top 10 College Dropouts."

Super Attractor, May Cause Miracles, Judgement Detox, and *Happy Days.* 🌿

I had a big belief that held me back—a story I told myself that said: "I am not smart enough." When I was in sixth grade, some kid told me I was stupid, which changed the trajectory of my life. It was a really traumatic event for me and ultimately led me on a path of excelling in the arts. I went on to get a BFA in Theater and turned my back on academia. I just did not identify myself as someone that was going to thrive in that way. My literary education ended in the eighth grade. That was it. I could barely string a sentence together, had the worst grammar, and couldn't spell.

I sometimes feel like, "How am I even associated with all these writers?" Even to this day, I catch myself saying things like, "Oh, I'm not really a writer." People say, "Are you kidding me? You've published seven [*now more!*] books." And then I hear my guides. I have a nice little dialogue with my guides who surround me. They're like, "Get over yourself. You are a writer!"

I'm proud to be able to show people that may not identify as literary that they can know they're writers. They can say: "Well, if she could do it with nothing past eighth grade English, I can too."

Walking through the quad in a defeated daze, I felt as old as the very bricks of Doheny Library. I sat down at the feet of the famed Tommy Trojan statue, where many years prior, I'd been photographed for the cover of the 1998 USC Trojans Gift Catalog. Mom and Dad loved that. "Tell me something good," my father would always say when he saw my name on his caller ID, believing I had "God's phone number." I rummaged for my cell and dialed his number.

"Daddy," I said, my voice cracking upon hearing his. "I'm here at 'SC. I'm going to get my degree."

"Are you doing this for me?" he asked, his voice shaky. I pictured him in his kitchen, his past surgeries to his jaw and mouth making it physically hard for him to speak.

"Yes. But I want to," I lied.

A pause. "Linda, no. Not for me. The reason I wanted you to go to college was so that you could be happy and successful. So you could thrive. You are the happiest, most successful, thriving person I know." For once, I was rendered speechless. *Should I remind him that I still sometimes struggle to pay my bills?* "Besides," Dad continued. "It's going to take you years." He was right about that. The dean had said it would take at least three . . .

"And in that time, how many books will you not write that would have helped how many people?" Silent rain fell from my eyes.

"Look around," he said. "How many students do you see on campus right now?" I couldn't count that fast. It seemed like thousands. "How many of them will write books? Most of them will graduate, but how many of them will write books that change people's lives?"

"I don't know, Daddy."

"I free you, sweetheart. Let it go."

Abby Wambach, soccer legend (GOAT), two-time Olympic Gold Medalist, and #1 *New York Times* bestselling author of *Wolfpack, Wolfpack (Young Readers Edition)*, and the memoir *Forward*.

From the perspective of pleasing others, I would want to go back [to college] and honor the promise I made to my mom and get my degree at some point. Do I think going back and completing my college education is going to change me in drastic ways? Probably not. I'm pretty well-baked at this point. I might not ever do it. And that is also okay. My wife [Glennon Doyle] helped me understand that people travel many different roads, and it doesn't mean one route is more successful than others.

If and when I [go back], it'll be because I want to draw myself closer to that self-esteem and that self-worth that, for whatever reason, is tied up in this promise I made to my mom.

The sun dipped into the sea behind me as I drove east on the Pasadena freeway toward home. I'd soon be rejoining my sister, Carol, to be with Dad in his last days, but I felt grateful. Only hours before, I believed I'd squandered my education and my parents' hard-earned money, let them down, let the system down, let myself down. Now, thanks to Dad's benediction, I could remember my college years and once again smile. And, unlike my father, I had time for a fresh rewrite, a new personal narrative about who I was and what I was capable of. Here I'd thought I was going to give Dad a gift, but he gave me one worth so much more.

My father understood that a classroom setting wasn't the only place from which to gain wisdom—or to pursue the dream of writing. As Mark Twain said, "I have never let schooling get in the way of my education." Yet, for many of us, high school or college were sources of shame and discouragement. Some let a lack of credentials stop them from pursuing their writing dreams. Some allowed grades to determine their worth. Others took writing classes or pursued an MFA in hopes that the degree would pave an easier path to talent and publication, and (of course!) it sometimes did. The successful writers in this book span from degreeless to teaching at the university level, yet one thing they all have in common is the universal desire to share what's in their heart.

Martha Beck, *New York Times* bestselling author, life coach, and O magazine columnist. Her books include *Expecting Adam*; *Leaving the Saints*; *Finding Your Way in a Wild New World*; *Diana, Herself*; and her 2022 Oprah's Book Club selection, *The Way of Integrity*.

I feel like the reason I got three Harvard degrees is so that I could say to everybody, "This is bullshit. You do not need it!" I've been to the mountain. Trust me! I checked in all the places they told me things were hiding, but there's really nothing there, so do whatever the hell you want. What I always tell people when they're starting to write or become a coach is that if you told me you went to a Le Cordon Bleu school and became a 5-star or Michelin-starred chef, I would be impressed. But if you gave me something you cooked and it tasted disgusting, I would not care about your degree.

My degrees gave me my ticket to say things because, "Oh, she went to Harvard." There is a ticket to your mission, but it does not have to be a college degree. I think it's an antiquated system that frankly needs to be minimized.

Nobody in any college or institution can give you what you need to contribute to the world, which is a genuine message. What I've observed watching people over the years is that if you have something important to say in the world, the Universe will give you an opportunity and a platform from which to say that.

Tomi Adeyemi, Nigerian-American novelist, and author of the #1 *New York Times* bestsellers *Children of Blood and Bone* and *Children of Virtue and Vengeance*, and named one of *TIME* magazine's 100 Most Influential People of 2020.

I had great teachers [at Harvard], but I applied for a fiction writing class five semesters in a row over two and a half years and got rejected every time. When I finally went to ask the teacher why he was rejecting me, he pointed to a bunch of superficial grammatical, copy edit–level things like commas. I asked, "Okay, but is there any feedback to my content since everything you're saying is surface level?"

He said, "Well, if you're making these mistakes, I can't teach you how to write."

I now tell my writers to live for your Hair Flip moment. Every time someone says something out of pocket and left field—especially if you're marginalized, which is going to happen—expect it. Did I learn to write at school? No. Did I become angry enough to sustain the passion and perseverance and intensity needed to cross the threshold? Definitely.

I love the experience I had at Harvard in many ways. But I get emails from people saying, "Do I have to study English literature at Harvard to write?" I didn't learn to write at Harvard. I learned to write on my own. I was told I was a bad writer at Harvard, that I had no future in writing. Someone in high school once said I'd work the fryer at McDonald's.* People don't know shit. You decide what you're going to learn. You decide what you're going to be. Then do it. And if you have to do it in spite of things, even better.

I hope it goes without saying that if you're currently enrolled in college or plan to go, more power to you! When my son threatened several times to quit film school, despite the debt I was racking up, I was having none of it.

"But, Mom!" he'd whine. "You and Dad didn't finish college!" True. But looking at my kid, I saw a young man who needed structure, a place where people expected him to show up, connections I didn't have, and new philosophies. Hardly a week goes by—eight years later—that he doesn't thank me for forcing him to finish.

Many people, past and present, knock college. In *Between the World and Me*, Ta-Nehisi Coates writes, "I was made for the library, not the classroom. The classroom was a jail of other people's interests, the library was open, unending, free." Ray Bradbury, who read EVERY book in the library over ten years, was also not a fan of colleges and universities, believing that teachers held prejudices, but libraries never did. But no one can deny that, particularly for people in rural areas or developing nations, higher education can be the most reliable ticket out of the poverty that steals time, motivation, opportunity, and creative drive.

---

* Fun fact: At twenty-three, Tomi received one of the biggest young adult publishing deals ever, including preemptive film rights sales to Fox/Disney/Lucasfilm. Paramount Pictures now has the rights to the series and Tomi will write the screenplay and executive produce the adaptation.

Far be it from me to knock MFAs; the do-it-yourself way can take a lot longer! When it comes to college, there's no right answer, only a wrong one. The wrong answer is believing you *must* have a degree to write. Degree or no degree, I believe one truth: We writers long to share our stories because there *is* a path forward for us. Don't worry. As you're about to see, if writing and publishing scare you, you're far from alone. Moreover, you can always borrow some of my father's faith in me. I carry it close, but there's plenty to go around.

2

Paying the Rent

Making a Living Before It Pays to Write

"The best way to appreciate your job is to imagine yourself without one."
~Oscar Wilde

Making a living. We've all gotta do it unless you have a patron/sugar daddy-mama footing the bills while you craft your great American, or (these days) un-American, novel. *Ahh. The easy life.* Could happen. Does happen. But yeah, back to reality.

Your bed office might look like a comfy indulgence to the critical observer, but between forgetting to eat, blink, or breathe while wrestling those story lines, functioning at full capacity in the outside world can feel comical to tragic. If your "real" job (or side hustle) requires an excess of chair-sitting and brain-twisting, your writing practice will suffer. Few paychecks come easy. But many writers choose physical jobs (caretaking, carpentry, cleaning, driving or delivery, gas pumping, barback or waiting tables, personal trainer, plant or outdoor nursery work, dog-walking—to name a few) to avoid adding to the overthinking they're already doing. Some even prefer working nights (security, warehouse or grocery shelving, janitorial, marrying for money) to write at home during the day while the world's busy clocking in.

When a book is calling, it's oh-so-tempting to quit your day job to gamble purely on your words. Not so fast. That seemingly "dead-end" gig that's terribly beneath your skill set might pay off in ways no one, not even you, could foresee.

Winter, 1988

"Get a FUCKING job!" my husband of ten weeks yelled, his eyes like lasers. I couldn't speak or move. Watching his temples throb, I was convinced he no longer loved me. My body caved in on itself as I crouched in the corner, bawling.

"It's like all of nature was celebrating your union," my sister had said about our wedding. Butterflies flew around our heads, frogs croaked in a nearby brook, a cat rubbed our minister's ankles. Jesse and I hadn't known each other long.* But it was insta-love in the health food store's produce section for two raw food—obsessed vegans. At twenty-nine, he was tired of being a playboy. At twenty-three, I was idealistic enough to believe in love at first sight. Having just gone through a traumatic breakup at USC, I needed therapy and a year alone. Instead, I married a six-foot-two, blond-haired, blue-eyed ex-model who ate like me—*no one* ever ate like me—and promised to nourish me.

"I will cover our bills until you know what you want to do with your life," Jesse had said. He was rich, practically—*an actor with $18,000 in the bank and national commercials running!*—affording me plenty of time to not worry about moneymaking while I got to know my new man. I couldn't quit my multilevel marketing scheme "job" fast enough. My inventory of hair restoration serum had been rotting past expiration dates in my apartment anyway. Diane, my best friend and "business" partner, and I couldn't sell a bottle because it was crap. Crap is especially hard to peddle without a work ethic.

---

* Jesse is not his real name, but oh how the Jesse James outlaw sound of it suits him. We're no longer married and bless him; he's given me the freedom to write about him and our relationship as I choose. Sweet—thanks, bud! But rather than continuously stare at my ex-husband's name while working on and publicizing this book, I've decided to roll with this for sanity's sake, if you don't mind.

"All you have to do is keep the cat alive and pay the rent while I'm gone," Jesse said, laying cash out on the counter. I drove him to the airport for his trip to Budapest, Hungary, to shoot *Howling V: The Rebirth*. While Jesse pretend-ran for his life from a werewolf that would rip his prosthetic neck out, I went "window" shopping on Melrose Avenue with Diane. That was when the bluest sky-blue turquoise necklace stole my money.

Jesse came home from the filming, and I can't recall how I justified losing half the cash earmarked for our landlord. But having gone straight from living off my father's bank account to Jesse's and never once balancing a checkbook, I couldn't for the life of me understand why my groom was so enraged by the whole thing. How could a bauble make such a dent in our account?

"Maybe the bank's wrong?"

Jesse wasn't amused. Then I slipped in another teensy issue I'd neglected to tell him about: my $12,000 student loan debt.

Joy Harjo, three-term Poet Laureate of the United States, musician, playwright, author, and member of the Muscogee Nation. Her writing includes nine books of poetry, two award-winning children's books, and memoirs *Crazy Brave* and *Poet Warrior*. ❧

When I was eighteen, I got a job at the Mini Serve Gas Mart filling cars. I loved working there. It was outside. Usually, jobs for women, like the ones I was qualified for, were inside, like waitressing. I enjoyed visiting with people. I made a miniskirt in the Shell Oil gas colors, and cars started lining up. I knew how to fill gas without showing anything. It became a very popular place. When I left there, my boss said, "You're the best worker I've ever had. If you ever need a job, come back."

Dean Koontz, one of the world's most highly paid writers, having sold over half a billion books, has authored numerous suspense thrillers that incorporate horror, fantasy, science fiction, mystery, and humor. Most of his titles have appeared on the *New York Times* Best Seller list, with fourteen hardcover and sixteen paperbacks reaching #1. 🌿

I had sold a couple of paperback novels and a number of short stories, but I wasn't anywhere close to making a living. My wife said, "I'll support us for five years. If you can't make it in five, you'll never make it." I tried to negotiate her up to seven, but she has Sicilian blood, so she wins every negotiation.

It was a generous thing, which is her nature. It took almost the full five years, but at the end of that period, she was able to quit her job and go to work on the investment, business, and foreign rights sides of my writing career. She says in some ways that was a mistake because when she worked for somebody else, it was only forty hours a week.

Get a fucking job.

Job???

Truthfully, I was ashamed of not contributing financially to our togetherness and surprised to access deeply buried feelings I harbored that men were supposed to take care of their women. *Where'd that come from?* Certainly not my mother, a subscriber to *Ms.* magazine, who held a full-time job for years and championed women's rights in the workforce.

I'd lost my patron—a crushing blow—but it's not like I needed or deserved one. I wasn't even yet a writer, although I'd always hoped one day I'd muster the courage to try. In the meantime, the jig was up. Time to earn a living or risk losing my man. But who would hire me?

Desperate not to return to retail, as I'd done in high school and college (which mostly made my wardrobe expand more than my bank account), the Bodhi Tree Bookstore was the only building I could stomach visiting daily. With a staff of a hundred, they weren't hiring. Until the owners, Stan Madson and Phil Thompson, received my ode to the fifty self-help and woo-woo titles I'd read and affirmed I'd peddle from their shelves.

During my shifts, I purchased enough books, crystals, and incense to open my own store and decided to supplement that spiraling income by doing what I always did—praying for guidance. Not in a formal, religious kind of way. More in a God-is-my-best-friend-and-wants-what-I-want way. When a sudden cinematic vision of my life as a dog-walker for the rich and famous stopped me cold while walking through Beverly Hills, I thought I'd just made up the best job on God's green earth: Puppies and exercise for money, not to mention something I was actually qualified for—what could be better?! I ran home to mock up my flyers.

"That's the craziest shit I've ever heard," Jesse said when I showed him my creations. "You think people will pay you ten dollars an hour to walk their dogs?"

"No. I think they'll pay twenty-five," I said—and off I went to broker a deal with the manager at the Pet Department on Melrose, who hired me to work for cruddy pay on my off days at the bookstore for the trade of promoting my new biz on-site. Never mind that I wasn't licensed or bonded to work in people's homes—you should have seen my business cards! Who can resist a tabby kitten sitting atop a collie's head?

Laura Munson, *New York Times* bestselling memoirist, author of the bestselling novel *Willa's Grove*, and writing coach. The flurry of comments on her 2009 essay, "Those Aren't Fighting Words, Dear," published in the *New York Times*'s "Modern Love" column, crashed the *Times*'s website.

The moment I realized that I was a writer, in the eleventh hour of college where I had been studying theater and film, it was nose to the book—no distractions, no excuses. That meant swatting away every shiny brass ring that came into view. *A cush job in advertising with a 401(k) and health benefits?* Nope. *A tony position at a blue-chip art gallery in Manhattan?* Sorry. *You want to give me storefront property in Lincoln Park for me to start my own bookstore to pay my parents back for a favor???* Uh . . . so there is *a free lunch?* Still, thanks anyway. "I'm writing my first novel, and I can't have any sexy distractions. It's gonna take some time."

There were years of writing what I knew were "exercises in learning." I didn't go get my MFA. I wanted to cut my teeth on life. And what does a WASPy twenty-year-old know about life other than the dread coming-of-age rebel story? I needed to bash around on this beautiful and heartbreaking planet for a while, and to write my way through it. And so, there was the first novel. And the second. And on and on for fifteen years, sitting at the intersection of heart and mind and craft that is the writing life.

I vowed to take whatever job I could to make ends meet and stay fully committed to the writing life. It was one thing, really: obsession. And a lot of humor. How else do you justify to yourself, your parents, and everyone you know who is not a writer (pretty much everyone), with a fancy-ass prep school/private liberal arts college education under your belt, this resume: delivery truck driver, cocktail waitress, house cleaner, nanny, barista, dog-walker, birthday party musician, eulogy writer, switchboard operator, apartment manager, flower shop schlepper, and, my favorite of all, morning prep "cook" for a hippie café in Seattle, in the dark at 5:00 AM, elbow-deep in hummus and falafel ball construction? I chopped a lot of veggies that year. I still can chop veggies like no one's business.

I'll never forget the voice. I'd only worked at the pet store slinging kibble eight weeks when he came in, but I'd have recognized Paul Williams anywhere. I'd stayed up many a late night with Mom watching his frequent playful banter with Johnny Carson. She was a giddy fan of the petite, blond actor-songwriter whose seventies hits like "We've Only Just Begun," "Rainy Days and Mondays," and "Evergreen" (for which he won an Oscar with Barbra Streisand for the first remake of *A Star Is Born*) were part of the feel-good soundtrack of our home.

"How are Chewy and Tasha?" Lenny, our most senior sales guy, was chatting up Paul at the checkout.

"Perfect as usual," he answered. I had one puppy-sitting client at that point. Pet Companion was still mostly a figment of my imagination, but the day Kevin had hired me, I gripped my temporary badge with my new schedule and looked up into the heavens with pure faith. "Thank You, God," I had said, smiling into the noonday sun. "For allowing me to meet the most amazing clients here. Magical people who will change my life."

So why was I hiding behind the flea-and-tick shampoos, picking at the ties of my polyester smock as Paul and Lenny talked?

Brushes with fame aren't uncommon in LA, where you might look up to find yourself queuing behind a favorite celeb at the ATM or pickup line at the corner bakery. A friend once stood at a urinal next to Brad Pitt (he swears he didn't peek, but he's hyper-competitive, so I'm not buying it). I loathe the idea of being one more in a multitude of interruptions in a famous person's day. Just because someone's work puts him or her in the public eye doesn't give me permission to get all up in their face with my own personal performance piece. Paul seemed in a hurry anyway.

Two days later, the pet store phone rang.

"Hi. This is Paul Williams. I'm going out of town and need a place to board my huskies. Do you know of a good kennel?"

Silently thanking God for answering my prayer, I relayed the digits of my top pick. "By the way, Paul," I added, "if you ever need a professional dog-walker, I'm one, and I *love* huskies!"

"How soon can you be here?"

Joel Stein, humorist with former columns in *TIME* magazine, the *LA Times*, and *Entertainment Weekly*. Stein's latest book, *In Defense of Elitism*, is his decidedly not-so-snobby attempt to wrestle back honor to the intellectual elites from the populists.

Straight out of college, I was desperate for any job. I sat at a bookstore in California and wrote thirty cover letters and resumes and sent them to every magazine. The only reason I sent one to Martha Stewart was that when I was interning at *Newsweek*, there was a woman named Susan Weyland, who I never talked to but was very attractive. When she quit, I was like, "Where is Susan Weyland going?"

People said she was the new editor of *Martha Stewart Living*, and I was like, "What is a Martha Stewart Living?"

"Martha Stewart is a woman in Connecticut who does crafting and gardening and throws dinner parties."

I remember thinking, *Oh right, so she probably started this magazine in 1820 then?* Growing up with a feminist mom in the seventies, I couldn't imagine that there was a current woman crafting and gardening in Connecticut. It blew my mind. I sent an application there because I thought Susan was attractive, which was not the best reason to apply anywhere.

I was hired as the sole writer for Martha's TV show, which didn't last very long because I didn't know how to keep a cactus alive, wrap a present, or write for a TV show.

The man who opened the door to Jesse and me looked tired, his hair a mess, his mood somber. He hardly resembled the Paul Williams I'd grown up watching on late-night TV, or the Paul Williams who, twenty-five years later, would accept Album of the Year at the 2014 Grammys for Daft Punk's *Random Access Memories* and be interviewed by Oprah on *Super Soul Sunday* about his bestselling book, *Gratitude and Trust*.

But that day in 1989, Paul had just bottomed out because of a long-term drug and alcohol addiction and was about to check himself into rehab.

After running with his sled dogs through the narrow cliff roads of the Hollywood Hills, Jesse and I found ourselves sitting on the tiled kitchen floor with Paul, the pups in our laps, as we swapped stories of miracles and healing. It was quickly decided: Paul wanted us to move into his estate for six weeks to care for his home and the dogs while he sobered up. This was the man who, flanked by Kermit the Frog, sang "The Rainbow Connection" to little kids everywhere; how bizarre to think we'd be helping him wrestle his demons to the ground.

It was thrilling—going overnight from our modest rental to living like rock stars. Our new bedroom had an English garden, a white picket-fenced view overlooking a sea of shimmering city lights. With its own phone line, maid service, and all the organic kiwis and papayas we could eat per his account at a local gourmet grocery, we'd hit the lotto, the kind naive transplants secretly hope for when arriving in the City of Angels. *I know! I'll meet a celebrity and become his BEST FRIEND!*

When Paul returned from rehab and found his house transformed into a home, complete with freshly cut roses in vases and homemade soups simmering on the stove, he asked us to please stay, indefinitely. If my husband had worried that perhaps he'd married a spoiled daddy's girl, imagine his relief that Pet Companion was now blossoming as a result of this stability. During free hours, I distributed my flyers to people's front doors, and within two short months, I had a full roster of canine clientele, rock-hard calves and thighs, and more cash than I could fit into my fanny pack each week. Money issues solved one sweaty hill climb at a time. Adieu, pet store!

"I gotta hand it to you, babe," Jesse said, his eyes bright with admiration as we toweled off Brodie and Peanut, our two rescue Border collies, following a swim in a client's pool. "You smashed this one out of the park!"

Steven Pressfield, author of *The Legend of Bagger Vance*, which Robert Redford turned into a film. He's also the author of *Gates of Fire* (taught at the US Military Academy) and many books on creativity, including *The War of Art*.

I never wanted to be a writer as a kid. My first job in New York was in advertising. I was like a copy-cub. My boss, Ed Hannibal, quit and wrote a novel that was a big hit. I was twenty-two years old, and I thought, "Well, hell. I'll do that too!" Thirty years later, I finally did it.

Every project is like a hero's journey. You have the call. There's the refusal of the call. The crossing of the first threshold—all the way through the hero's journey, as Joseph Campbell would describe it. You're constantly battling enemies. It's always been that way for me.

Dog walking was going surprisingly well. But then Carol, my little sister, had to throw cold water on my whole operation.

"My friends and I are worried you're not using your brain," Carol said as I corralled a Malamute-Rottweiler duo owned by a freakishly flawless Victoria's Secret model and her French singer hubby. The sun was hot overhead; even the backs of my calves were burning.

"What do you mean?" I answered, shocked that she—who by birth order default always looked up to me—had just flipped the balance of the universe.

"I mean, don't get me wrong," Carol said. "It's amazing what you've built. But you're so smart; we think you should be doing more than just hanging out with dogs all day." *We think.* My chest felt tight. I faked a smile, knowing Carol would never out and out try to hurt me. But that she'd been talking behind my back about how my career wasn't measuring up felt like a kick to the head.

Wasn't bringing joy and relief to animals enough? Buddy came to mind—an eight-year-old golden retriever client who stood by the door with his leash in his mouth every morning for hours before I arrived. Would office work at a nearby high-rise make for worthier work? Besides, dogs were in my blood. My clients were icons, yes—Kirk Douglas, Kiefer Sutherland, and Catherine Oxenberg, to name a few—but my love affair was with their four-leggeds. Mom and Dad hadn't allowed pets in our home until I was nearly ten, so I'd silenced that ache by scaling neighbors' fences like a jewelry thief to quiet howling dogs left alone by their overworked and traveling humans. This job I'd created for myself was just an extension of what I'd always done, only now I entered through the front door with keys and alarm codes while making cash money. Heaven.

Was Carol saying I was supposed to give this dream job up? What did her bratty friends expect, anyway, with their coveted degrees that led them to six-figure corporate positions?

But bit by bit—*or was it dog shit by dog shit*—I grew restless. I'd been doing this for five years with hardly a break. Monday-through-Friday regulars packed my days; weekends and holidays were even busier. What I wouldn't give for a Christmas Day where I wasn't covered in saliva and dog hair!

Am I playing small? Ignoring my destiny? Wasting my potential? These questions nagged at me, even while I enjoyed every mile and milestone.

There were worse ways to earn a living—millions of worse ways—than being covered in puppy kisses while exercising in front of homes so coveted that people rode tour buses to catch glimpses of them. Being an animal excrement engineer, as Carol called me, was a small price to pay for all the love. Plus, the mere thought of trying to do something, anything, else, flooded me with the panic of having to prove myself—a clear indicator that any entrepreneurial success I'd realized thus far hadn't bolstered my confidence much in the smarts department.

The only things I'd ever loved as much as dogs were books and writing, yet the idea of being a writer was as pie-in-the-sky as an actual sky filled with pies. I recalled those children's books I'd written and illustrated as a nine-year-old. Dad had fawned all over those, but really, that was kid stuff. Become a legit writer? *Puh-lease*. If God had literary plans for me, they would have to appear as a literal act of God.

Sue Monk Kidd, *New York Times* bestselling author of *The Book of Longings*, *The Invention of Wings*, *The Mermaid Chair*, *The Dance of the Dissident Daughter*, and *The Secret Life of Bees*. 🌾

I didn't start writing until I was thirty years old. I grew up telling people when I was ten that I was going to be a writer. I remember reading *Jane Eyre* and being swept away.

But it was the pre-feminist South in a tiny town of three thousand people in Georgia. There was such an encultured feeling that girls became teachers, librarians, nurses—that kind of thing. So, when it came time to go to college, that's what I did. I followed the more traditional path and became a nurse. I have said many times: I think it was a failure of courage on my part. I had not grown enough at eighteen to step outside of the culture that raised me to find enough strength to do my thing.

It took me another ten years. On my thirtieth birthday, I was so homesick for myself. I wanted to write so badly. I thought I was very old. I remember having two toddlers, and my husband was sitting having cereal. I was in the laundry room washing clothes, and I came in, and I announced it—my big annunciation: "I'm going to be a writer." Of course, I had never studied writing. I didn't know anything about writing. But I started, and I never looked back.

Ann Patchett, bookstore co-owner and author of *The Dutch House*, a finalist for the 2020 Pulitzer Prize for Fiction. Ann is also the winner of the 2002 PEN/Faulkner Award for her novel *Bel Canto*, and has written seven other novels as well as assorted nonfiction and children's books. ✒

Like Sue [Monk Kidd], I grew up in the pre-feminist South. But the advantage I had is that I went to a convent school for twelve years and was raised by nuns—women who were career women who bucked the system. No one is happy when their daughter becomes a nun. They had to walk a hard path; they'd made choices that had to do with their bedrock faith. So, the idea of having a calling—something that was bigger than your own choice—was something I grew up with and believed.

The nuns always told us that "God will tell you." Maybe He'll tell you that you should be a wife. Maybe He'll tell you that you should have a religious vocation. And maybe He'll tell you that you should be a teacher. I thought, "Well, all right. God's told me I'm going to be a writer." In my mind, that lined up perfectly. It gave me early permission to not get married or have children.

Unbeknownst to me, my doggy day job was precisely where my writing career would start. And it continued to be my part-time day job while I wrote at night. Between what I made by walking dogs and what we saved by living with Paul and eating from his fridge, I was contributing to our lives as much as Jesse within three months! *Take that, hubs!* That non-brain-drain doggy job that fed my heart without taxing my frontal lobe allowed me to use the lion's share of my brain power for my eventual book. Years later, I laughed when reading Stephen King's memoir, *On Writing*, in which he suggests writers and wannabe writers take "mindless" jobs to support themselves before their writing does so that all their intellectual mojo can be saved for the page.

The next time you feel cursed—"losing" months or years to a seemingly unrelated gig, or having to punch a time clock working for The Man—remember the examples throughout this chapter, or one of these legendary ones: Harper Lee was an airline reservation attendant. Stephen King taught English to high schoolers and moonlighted as a gas pump attendant (just like Joy Harjo!) and janitor (if you'll recall, his wife fished his *Carrie* manuscript out of the trash!). John Green was a chaplain at a children's hospital. Long before Maya Angelou became an American poet, memoirist, and civil rights activist, she'd been a fry cook and a nightclub dancer. John Steinbeck dropped out of college before becoming a manual laborer—informing his Pulitzer Prize–winning *The Grapes of Wrath*.*

An additional point: Everyone's gotta eat! If, like many a writer, you happen to find yourself working in a restaurant, keep your ears and eyes open for the gold mine of conversation and customers' traits for future dialogue and characters.

Jillian Lauren, novelist and author of the *New York Times* best-selling memoirs *Everything You Ever Wanted* and *Some Girls: My Life in a Harem*. The STARZ TV series *Confronting a Serial Killer* depicts the story told in her latest book, *Behold the Monster*. 🌿

I've never thought of that time [living and working in Brunei in the harem of Prince Jefri—detailed in her memoir *Some Girls*] as a chain of events, but there was a creative impulse underneath all of it. And sometimes, that creative impulse led me to what has

---

* Fun fact: Steinbeck was a dog lover—his *Travels with Charley* was about his poodle, Charley, and their road trip. His setter, Toby, also heavily influenced his work, chewing up the only draft of *On Mice and Men*, forcing Steinbeck to rewrite the entire manuscript.

ultimately been my life's work, writing. And sometimes, it had a certain wildness, or shadow side, that led me to make some more poor decisions. But very entertaining [and profitable] ones. I survived it, so it has been, like Nora Ephron says, "all copy."

I don't have a crystal ball to advise you where to spend your research and writing time or how to earn your money. But heads up! Beyond being in the right place at the right time, with people or puppy-love "chance meetings," your muse may be cooking up all sorts of additional magic.

3

Permission and Prophecy

When Faith—Yours or Another's—Fuels You

"I want to thank my parents for somehow raising me to have
confidence that is disproportionate with my looks and abilities."

~ Tina Fey

*How do I KNOW I can do it? Why do I feel that I'm the one to tell my stories,
share my message? Who the heck do I think I am, anyway?*

These thoughts plague every writer—at least at first, and often even
once they've got a shelf full of titles and awards. As humans, and especially
as creatives, most of us need encouragement from outside of our limited
self-perception. Someone who believed in us at the start of our writing process, maybe even before we did. Someone who could see and declare our talent
aloud—*"You know, you've got something here!"*—and ignite our fire.

"You're going to be switching careers soon to do something really big."

Drew Lawrence, a popular Vedic Astrologer, tapped his pen on the printout
of my chart in his lap. I squirmed uncomfortably in my chair, worried that my
actor husband would think I was trying to hog his celestial spotlight.

I'd dragged Jesse here with the promise that Drew could make superstar prophecies for *him*—foretell a recurring role on TV or even a starring one. Though wildly talented, Jesse hadn't booked a commercial since before our wedding. My attempts to ease the "poverty consciousness" in our home with affirmations and vision boards were often short-lived. Jesse preferred I just stop spending so much money instead. But even he seemed hopeful about this field trip to Drew's, despite the $108 per session price tag. That is until Drew started making declarations about *my* future career success.

"Really? Because I'm a mom, and I have a busy career as a dog-walker," I said.

Drew shook his head. "Dog-walking is not your destiny. You have Jupiter in the sixth house, so you're a healer of animals. But you're here for much more. You'll be dealing with the masses."

I looked sideways at Jesse, one of the most complicated humans I'd ever met. *Clearly, Drew can't see that I love humanity as a concept but find people insufferable.* Jesse and I had gotten married after knowing each other all of two months, so—surprise, surprise—we rarely saw things the same way, only to find out after *hours* of kitchen-table processing that we often did. Despite the love, it's safe to say we fought more in one week than I'd fought my entire life with everyone else combined. With the addition of our rambunctious toddler, Tosh, I could barely handle my little family. To be embraced by the masses sounded like a total shit show.

"Yes, but you're great with people as long as you have downtime." Drew pointed to an icon on the page. "This is Mercury, the planet of communication, and yours is powerful. It's retrograde, so you think differently. See things people don't see. It can make a person lonely at times, hard to feel like you fit in or want to join things, particularly when you're young." He smiled. I smiled. *Wow. Star seer or mind reader?* "The career you have coming has to do with lots of people and writing—a perfect balance of the two. It's big energy. You have one of the most powerful charts I've ever seen."

Wait, whaaaaat? I couldn't fathom what this career could be but felt a sense of giddiness at the prospect.

"Your destiny is guaranteed," Drew continued. "It doesn't matter where you are in the world or what you're doing; this new gig will soon find you."

My head was spinning. "When do you think?" I asked.

"Sometime in the next fifteen months." He turned back to the first page. "Your auspicious window starts this coming August and lasts until next August. You couldn't avoid it if you moved underground."

August?! Wow. That's only twelve weeks away!

Despite my parents' accolades for my typewritten *Groople the Banana*'s crime-fighting escapades in elementary school, grown-up me had no one rooting for my dimly lit dreams of writing. It mighta helped if I'd actually *told* someone when those childhood goals refused to budge. Nope! I'd need a nudge from a higher authority.

Van Jones, CNN commentator, lawyer, activist, founder of the Dreams Corps, and *New York Times* bestselling author of *The Green Collar Economy*, *Rebuild the Dream*, and *Beyond the Messy Truth*. ✦

My mother encouraged me to write from the very beginning. I wasn't very athletic. I was a nerd. I didn't have that many friends. I didn't have much going for me, but I liked to read, and I liked to write, and I liked to draw. My mother encouraged that. She taught typing and office management at the public high school, and whenever she would bring home the white typing paper, I would just get happy because I could fill it up. I would write stories and illustrate them. So, I had a great deal of confidence in my writing from very early on.

Nell Scovell, TV comedy writer, producer, director, and collaborator on the #1 *New York Times* bestseller *Lean In*. Her memoir, *Just the Funny Parts*, documents her decades writing for, among others: *The Simpsons*, *Late Night with David Letterman*, and *Sabrina, the Teenage Witch*, which she created and executive produced. ✦

At my third-grade parent-teacher conference, the teacher complained I made too many jokes during class. She wanted my mother to talk to me about toning it down. Mom said she'd pass the message along. And she did . . . *on my fortieth birthday!* My mother waited thirty-two years until I was an established comedy writer to tell me that my third-grade teacher had notes on my personality.

My mother's unconditional love is one of the reasons that I could withstand so much criticism and rejection over the years. It's my Harry Potter scar.

Sabaa Tahir, #1 *New York Times* bestselling author with two titles on *TIME* magazine's 100 Best Fantasy Novels of All Time list: *An Ember in the Ashes* and *A Torch Against the Night*. ❧

When I first thought, *I'm going to try and write a book,* I was twenty-one. *I'm going to write a memoir about growing up in the desert.* But I was twenty-one! I didn't know anything. I was writing this book, or trying to, and I kept calling my mom to complain. Finally, probably sick of me whining, she said, "Why don't you write a fantasy? You love fantasy!"

"I can't write a fantasy," I said. "No one would take me seriously!"

She said, "What are you talking about? No one's going to take you seriously if you never finish your book!"

Immigrant moms. They just tell it to you like it is. There's no coddling.*

Tosca Lee, *New York Times* bestselling author. Included in her eleven historical novels and thrillers are *The Legend of Sheba, The Progeny, The Line Between,* and *A Single Light*. ❧

---

* Fun fact: Sabaa *did* write that book, *All My Rage,* as a novel. Upon release, it hit the *New York Times* Best Seller list, making her the first Pakistani-American to hit the YA NY Times list for both fantasy and contemporary.

During spring break my freshman year, I was talking with my dad about my favorite books, saying that great novels are like roller coasters, with twists and turns and emotional highs and lows. I blurted out, "I think I'd like to write a book!" I wanted to know if I could build a roller coaster like that for someone else to enjoy.

I was supposed to spend that summer working at a bank as a teller. Mind you, I was terrible with numbers and could never balance my drawer. My dad said, "Okay, I will make you a deal. I will pay you what you would have made this summer as a bank teller if you will spend the summer writing your first novel full-time."

I was all over it! I took on a historical novel about the Neolithic people of Stonehenge and had to do all this research. I thought, *Wow, this is really hard!* The following summer, I submitted it to Writers House, a New York literary agency. I made every single mistake writing that book and submitting it, but they sent me a detailed, generous rejection letter.

It wasn't the result I wanted. But what I took away was, *I am so doing this again!* I think that was such a cool thing my father did for me, investing in me like that. I will always be grateful and would do that for my children in a heartbeat.

Jesse's astrological chart was more sobering—accurately predicting the year his father left for Vietnam, details of his parents' divorce, and, worst of all, how he'd never be able to feel my unconditional love, no matter how much I gave. *Fabulous.* Our drive home from Drew's was uncharacteristically quiet, and I decided to do what every emotionally desperate follower of psychics, astrologers, or gurus does upon getting a mixed-bag reading: take what feels good and ignore the cruddy rest.

The next day, to show the Universe I was doing my part in the co-creation of my coming career miracle, I bought Julia Cameron's *The Artist's Way*, the classic guide to wooing creativity. I committed to finishing every exercise within its twelve-week workbook. I picked Jesse up a copy too.

"It'll be fun! We'll do this together," I cooed. "You're already an artist, and Drew thinks I might be too."

Jesse, a lover of adventure, agreed. We opened our books to chapter one, piping hot mugs of chai tea on the coffee table before us, and dug in.

By my calculations, once the twelve weeks were complete and I'd taken myself on every Cameron-ordered weekly "Artist Date" and dutifully scribbled my "Morning Pages" into my journal, it would be August, my magic window. If Drew Lawrence was wrong, no harm, no foul; I loved my pup clients. But if he was right, look out masses, here I come!

Dean Koontz

I was writing stories on tablet paper when I was eight years old and drawing covers for them and stapling them down one side and covering the staples with electrician's tape so nobody would hurt their fingers. I peddled them to relatives for a nickel. I was publisher, writer, editor, and agent. It's strange to me all these years later; that drive was there for this very thing at such a young age.

My English teacher was a woman named Winona Garbrick, and she was a World War II WAC in the Army, a delightful person, about five foot tall. As small as she was, football players were terrified of her. She took a liking to my writing in ninth grade and nurtured it through twelfth grade. She was the first person outside of an uncle who gave me the sense that I might have something, not just in writing, but that I might have some value. I didn't get a sense of value from my family. So, she has a place in my heart forever.

Marianne Williamson, political activist, spiritual thought leader, and author of fourteen books, four of which have been #1 *New York Times* bestsellers, including *A Return to Love* and *Healing the Soul of America.*

I started lecturing in 1983. After I'd been doing that for five years, I had dinner one night in San Francisco with Jerry Jampolsky. He'd written the first popularized book on the principles of the *Course in Miracles*. He said to me that night, "You ought to write a book."

I said, "Well, other people have told me that, but I don't feel pregnant with a book."

"All of the information you would need is in these talks you've been giving, and you have the tapes."

"Yeah, but I don't know how to get what's in a talk onto a page."

"Well," he said, "let's agree in consciousness in this moment that there's someone out there who could help you take your words from a speech to a book."

Two days later, I was in Los Angeles, and somebody came up to me after my talk and said that they were a literary agent. I gave them my phone number, but I never got a call.

Five days after that, I was approached by a different agent who I never heard from again. Then a few days later, in New York City, another literary agent approached me. He said, "Have you ever thought of writing a book?"

I said, "People kept saying that. I don't know. I don't feel pregnant with a book."

"Well, they're in your tapes."

"I don't know how to get it from the tapes to a page."

"Well," he said, "I can help you do that."

And that's how my book became a book.

Carol Allen, relationship coach and Vedic Astrologer, author of *Love is in the Stars: The Wise Woman's Astrological Guide to Men.** Her entertaining newsletter has been read by millions. 🌿

---

* Fun fact: She's also my bossy little sister in this book—and in life.

For years I insisted I'd never write a book in my industry. There were typically two kinds of astrology books: dense and academic, necessary for students of the stars but a form I could never pull off. Or too fluffy and light with mostly "pop astrology" predictions and descriptions that didn't reflect the amazing wisdom true astrology could provide, and I didn't want to write one of those. Not to mention that there were already so many awesome authors and titles and it had all been said before, and I didn't see anything new I could contribute.

So, for fifteen years I insisted I'd never attempt it. But then one day I met one of my mentors, and he said to me over our first lunch, "You should write a book about what you do."

"No way," I said, laying out the same reasons I just gave.

"Why do people come to you, and how does astrology help them?" he asked.

I lit up and explained all the amazing ways astrology illuminates people's relationships, way beyond the normal "sun sign compatibility" fluff we've all heard a million times. I told him about topics such as timing, aka "Seasons of Love" or "Seasons of Loneliness"; relationship "capacity"—how a person's chart easily shows if they are "relationship material" or too good to be true; "astrological affliction"—the sad truth that many people have deep inborn defects of character that get in the way of them being a good partner to anyone, no matter how compatible, and on and on.

My mentor said, "Is there a book on all of that?"

And it hit me. There wasn't. He hired me on the spot to write it for his online company—to sell the book digitally.* I couldn't believe it. For fifteen years I was just *sure* I'd never so much as start, but in a one-hour conversation we laid out the whole book.

---

* Most impressively, that "little" digital download book has earned Carol hundreds of thousands of dollars over the years.

Six weeks later.

"Linda! You're going to *love* this magic guy I just went to!" Carol said, breathless. "Trust me! You've got to book a session!"

She explained that Guru Singh, a Sikh leader, healer, and master yoga teacher, had given her just the right spiritual prescription in one session to put a stop to her wailing over her recent breakup with Bad Boyfriend. Thank God for that; nothing else had worked. Several of the world's biggest movie stars, in fact—who I imagined could afford the best and probably had A+ level bullshit detectors—also credited this nondenominational, all-religions-welcome Guru character with their emotional and financial freedom.

Hmm. Did I need healing? What if he could confirm Drew's astrological prediction? What ultimately cinched it for me was that Guru had just been named "Best Guru in LA" by *Los Angeles* magazine. Uh-huh. So very La La Land.

I arrived for my session to find Guru's West Hollywood compound abloom in sweet-smelling jasmine. Wind chimes crashed, an unseasonable warning of a relentless Santa Ana wind season to come. Guru greeted me outside, a tall smiling man with a long, dark beard and bright blue eyes, clad in pure white from turbaned head to sandaled toes. His fingers were adorned with citrine and moonstone rings, and silver bangles climbed up one arm. "I've been waiting for you," he hummed as if we'd had a divine appointment planned long ago.

Or maybe it was the fact that I was five minutes late.

We took our shoes off at the door to his office, a white room that smelled of incense and earth, with large flat pillows on the floor. Guru and his healing center were exactly as you'd imagine. Crystals as big as softballs were strewn about. A floor-to-ceiling mirror covered one wall, festooned with hundreds of stickers straight out of a label maker:

"Do not try to fit in; you fit perfectly in you."
"Accept the other as yourself."
"Eternity is not at all logical."
"Time is always here forever, and it's always right now."

Unlike in his yoga classes, where *Los Angeles* magazine wrote that you had to "levitate for space," we sat comfortably cross-legged facing one another on a large area rug. Suddenly, Guru stopped smiling or blinking and looked into my eyes as if evaluating my very existence. Almost a minute passed. I nodded nervously. *Will he see how blessed my future's supposed to be too? Will my aura or vibes reveal the destiny Drew saw?*

"What the *hell* are you doing hiding behind all those dogs?!" Guru scolded.

Well, that was unexpected. *Whoa, how does he know about my dog-walking business? Did Carol talk with him about me?* His penetrating eyes stayed locked onto mine; the ferocity of his stare unnerved me. *Um, am I in trouble? What does he mean, hiding behind all those dogs?*

"You're supposed to be a writer, remembered for at least a hundred and fifty years after your death," he boomed, as if reading my heart. "When are you going to stop avoiding your destiny?"

Destiny?! Writer?! Wait! How does he know about my secret literary dreams? I hadn't told him anything; Carol must have. *But hold up! Not even Carol knows!* I felt enormously uncomfortable and profoundly relieved all at the same time.

"But what am I supposed to write?" I asked. I hoped Guru didn't give the same prophecy to everyone and that he'd have the answer to this too. The only topic that motivated me was educating people on things Mom had taught me about the environment. But that wasn't popular, and in any case, I was no expert. How could I, a diploma-less laywoman, hope to make such topics entertaining to a populace that didn't seem to give a shit?

"Words to heal humanity," Guru pronounced. "You will write words to heal humanity."

Oh, is that all? No biggie, although that was precisely what I yearned to do. But this all sounded ridiculously grandiose, particularly for someone who hadn't written anything longer than a grocery list for ages. Guru kept on, each word speaking to my greatest wish—the one held close by my kid self, where I hoped dearly that one day I'd pen books that, like the aforementioned rows of gilt-edged encyclopedias that graced my childhood home, would stand the test of time.

I shielded my eyes with a groan-squeal and shook my head. "I'm scared, Guru. I don't know if I can do it!"

"Stop! That's horseshit, and you know it!" Guru was glaring at me, or through me, I couldn't tell which. He seemed genuinely irritated. I wasn't used to men scolding me—well, not before marrying Jesse. *Jeez. Carol said he was so compassionate; when does that kick in? And are gurus allowed to swear like this? Can't he see I still have six weeks before my auspicious window opens? Don't these shaman types ever compare notes?*

Guru motioned for me to sit in what looked like a tilted massage chair in a womb of a second room no larger than a walk-in closet. As I lay back, he covered my body in a weighty white blanket and slid cool egg-shaped crystals into my palms and another larger one over my heart that was connected to some kind of electrode or something because it was pulsing and lit from within. As the scent of sandalwood focused my senses, Guru placed bulky black headphones over my ears and shielded my eyes with a soft cloth. My cocooning was complete.

My headset came alive with tinkling bells, birdsong, waterfalls, and what could only be described as space vibrations. Guru held a microphone in his hand and began to speak powerful affirmations that seemed to merge with the mysterious symphony. I tried to memorize the various commandments he was imbuing into my consciousness, but I lost his words as soon as I heard them. *Just relax and trust,* I told myself. My breathing deepened.

An hour later, the faint pinging of a gong woke me up, but I had no idea how long I'd been out. "Keep your eyes closed and wiggle your toes," Guru said as he put a Kleenex laced with lavender oil into my palm and raised it to my nose. The effect was immediate, like fragrant smelling salts. I was suddenly fully in my body.

"Good work!" Guru said, his voice now mellow, sweet. He uncovered my eyes and handed me a glass of Emergen-C vitamin drink before sitting down next to me. "You're ready to step into your bigger life now, aren't you?"

"Yeah!" I answered, careful not to break his gaze. *Am I out of trouble yet?*

"The wheels are already in motion," he said with a wink. Goose bumps raced across my arms.

Anita Moorjani, international speaker, and author of the *New York Times* bestseller, *Dying to Be Me*, which chronicles her spontaneous total cancer healing following a near-death experience, plus *Sensitive Is the New Strong*, and *What If* This *Is Heaven?*

I was a part-time consultant with various corporations, speaking to their employees on culture. I'd had a spontaneous cancer healing following a near-death experience in the hospital. I was spending much of my time writing about it on a medical blog under the name "Anita M" because I didn't want the people I was doing consulting work for to know I had cancer. I didn't dare get out there and speak publicly as myself because I wasn't a doctor.

My friend has a healing center in Dubai, and she invited me to come to speak. I was resistant, but something changed in me in Dubai. This was the first time I was physically and energetically feeling and seeing the impact my story had on people. People were crying. People who had stage 4 cancer and who said the medical world had taken away their hope.

I thought, *Oh my God. This is my purpose.* When I went to bed that night, I was thinking, *I have no idea how this is going to happen. I'm going to leave it to the Universe. I'm going to leave it to my soul to figure it out.*

The next morning happened to be my birthday. I woke up, checked my email, and there was one from Hay House, saying that Dr. Wayne Dyer had discovered my story and asked them to reach out to me to see if I was interested in writing a book—which they'd be happy to publish. I started crying.

"Do you know how hard you are to track down?" said Wayne, who would write the book's foreword. "From the time I read your story to the time Hay House found you was five months! You said you were living in Hong Kong, and that's all we had to go on."

My friend with the center had given me permission. Wayne and Hay House gave me permission. But this is also about becoming ready ourselves. I call this the inside-out view. We think we have to go out there and hammer at the marketing and hammer other people. But no, it's inside. Get yourself ready, and it'll come.

Tom Hanks

My book [*Uncommon Type*] is dedicated to the wife and kids. But it also says: "Because of Nora." When I first met Nora Ephron to talk about *Sleepless in Seattle*, I had a really big head. I thought I was important. Nora had only made one movie I'd seen; Rita took me to see it. I was meeting her under the auspices of: "This is a power meeting and I have clout right now." Nora was beginning to write and direct movies and I was like, "Well, I *really* like your script, Nora. I got some problems with it, but I like your script." It was a snooty-assed relationship that took a while to evolve. When we were actually going to make the movie, she and her sister, Delia, wrote the screenplay. It was originally a draft by a guy named Jeffrey Arch, but what always happens is the filmmaker who makes the film does the rewrite.

We were sitting around talking, and it was probably a three-hour meeting about my character and the story line. I got pushed out of shape because they wrote about a father-and-son relationship, and I had issues. I said, "You guys don't know anything about fathers and sons. You don't know anything! You're women. You're moms!"

Nora said, "Well, what would fathers do?"

"Fathers would look at their son and say, 'You don't want me to go off with a woman this weekend? Too bad! I'm gonna go get laid! What do you think of that?' That's the way fathers talk to sons."

A version of that ended up in the movie. When the movie came out, Nora said to me, "You wrote that scene."

I said, "No, I didn't. I complained in a meeting; that's a totally different thing."

"No, you wrote it," she said. "We didn't have it. You came in and said this, and it's more or less verbatim," which happened in a couple of other places.

To be highfalutin, Nora was the very first person, a member of the same firmament I was in because we were both filmmakers, who said, "Not only are you a filmmaker, but you're also a writer."

When I started wanting to really write, she was there. The first thing I did was an article for the *New York Times* ["The Man Who Aged Me"] about my makeup man of nineteen years, Danny Striepeke, when he retired. I sent her a version of the piece, and she said, "This isn't quite there yet, but it is a thing. Here's what you have to do . . ." Her guidance is something I remember every single day and put to the test in every one of the stories for *Uncommon Type*. It's voice! Voice, voice, voice. Theme is one thing; plot is something else. Character, dialogue—these are all key. But if you don't have a voice, you don't have a perspective; you don't have a POV. Nora is the one who said, "If you want to be a writer, which I think you are, you have to develop voice. This one single thing will lead to everything else."

That said, there are people out there who are wicked talented and creative, but they're waiting for permission, waiting to be invited into the process. They're waiting to be asked or discovered, but that's rarely the way it works. You have to pursue your art twenty-four hours a day. You've always got to be thinking of a story and creating your own outlet for the stuff that's inside you.

We humans are tribal. We crave support and cheerleading. Turns out, we can't all depend on ourselves to take the plunge on a project directed by our own initiative. The majority of us get things done best when someone is on our tail, awaiting results.

To me, that's welcome news! We don't have to feel bad if we're not taking steps to get 'er done. There's no shame in needing to enroll people, true believers, to grant us permission and help bolster our belief. Remember, I *hired* Drew Lawrence, the astrologer, and Guru Singh. They didn't stop me on a street corner and anoint me. I called their phone numbers, made appointments, and drove my ass across town in heavy traffic, looking for a miracle worthy of my Benjamins.

Of course, the reason their words were so meaningful was that they predicted the very thing I already wanted. If Drew or Guru had declared that my destiny was to be an astrophysicist, I would've laughed and walked out, never to return. But they were envisioning my heart's desire.

The good news for you is that you don't have to have a guru. If you want permission, let me give it to you right now. Ready? *Trust your ache.* You have the ache because you have what it takes. Let the very fact that you want something be enough of a reason.

Your desire is the only WHY you'll ever need.

And, in most of the stories throughout this chapter, there was one person, one sacred relationship, that made a significant difference. Twenty-six-year-old me believed I needed permission from spiritual leaders because the stakes were too high and my experience too little. I didn't yet have the confidence. If that's hitting home, identify someone you can reach out to who really *sees* you—right now, before you turn the page. One sacred relationship you can connect with. If you don't have that person, how can you go about finding them as you support yourself? Your people—coaches, mentors, groups, and uplifting friends—are out there, *everywhere.* When you do find them—those who get you, believe in you, and hold the vision if or when you can't—*stay* close.

Every book, every character, every story has a champion. Sometimes, that champion spots the potential within you; sometimes, that champion *is* you.

Elizabeth Gilbert, *New York Times* bestselling author whose works include *Eat Pray Love* (which became a movie starring Julia Roberts), *Committed, Big Magic, The Signature of All Things,* and *City of Girls.*

When I was ten, I wrote a play called *Mona's Proof,* a one-act play. 'Cause I was ten. That was as much juice as I had. It starred all my friends. I also directed and produced it. And it was a musical.

I wrote a song for it that went to the tune of "Fifteen Miles on the Erie Canal" because it was the only song I knew. It's about a girl who goes back in time, and nobody believes her. We produced that fucker. We worked it for months and put that play up onstage in the afternoon in the gym. We had costumes and posters that we hung all over the school. My parents both took off the day from work and came and saw it. And it was . . . it was really good. I stand by that play.

That was the first sense I ever had of, "I made a thing. Look! I made a thing!" There didn't used to be this play called *Mona's Proof*, but now there was. Everyone had to bear witness to it because we dragged them all there and made them watch all ten minutes of it. But it was great. It was a heist. We pulled it off.

A few years later, I was an understudy in the play *Anything Goes*. We got to write our bios in the mimeographed playbill for our tiny high school. Mine said, "Elizabeth Gilbert will travel the world and write for the *New Yorker*." The cute thing is *The New Yorker* still hasn't published any of my articles. They've had to write about me, but they won't let me write *for* them.

There was a sense from a very early age that these two things—writing and traveling—are really important to me. *This is who I'm going to be.* I believed that about myself long before anybody else did. It wasn't like I had a bunch of naysayers in my life. It's just that I knew. There's a point of believing in yourself before you have evidence and before anybody else can see it. The first person who has to believe in you is you, or you wouldn't even bother. What would be even the point?

I feel like I was my first publicist, scripting my write-up in the local school playbill. Like, "Watch this young up-and-coming talent!" No lesser a writer than Walt Whitman did that when he published his first book of poetry. He wrote reviews of it under an assumed name and sent them to newspapers all over New England, saying, "This person is the greatest poet of his age." It happened that he was correct. But there wasn't anybody else who knew that yet. He was the only one who knew. He had to do his own press.

I'm very patient with people who have grandiose visions for their lives because I have grandiose visions for my life. And, who knows? I was never all that comfortable being a teacher of writing. It's just not my nature to tell someone they don't have what it takes. We all have stories of people telling us that. The last thing you want to do is show up in somebody's memoir thirty years later as the asshole who didn't see that the genius was a genius.

Taylor Dayne, singer, songwriter, memoirist (*Tell It to My Heart*), and one of Billboard's Top 60 Female Artists of All Time, with eighteen top-ten hits and over seventy-five million albums sold.

I gave myself permission. I grew up in an apartment building, so I was constantly staring out a second-story window and dreaming. At four or five, I had this moment of listening to the radio and being able to sing along with it. Right there I said, "I know what I'm going to be. I don't know what the rest of y'all are gonna do, but I'm gonna sing like Stevie Wonder or Karen Carpenter on that radio." I knew I'd be heard by millions.

Robert McKee, legendary lecturer of *STORY*. Award-winning author of *STORY*, *DIALOGUE*, and *CHARACTER*. USC professor, whose students have earned over seventy Academy Awards and three hundred nominations.*

Who believed in me? Me! I believed in me. I knew from the time I was eight years old that this was my life. And I never doubted it.

---

* The number rises every year. Don't even try and keep track!

Gabrielle Bernstein

I remember trying to sell my first book in 2008, right at the [stock market] crash. My stepfather said to me, "Gabby, this is a terrible time. It's a really hard time to sell a book."

I was like, "I'm a Lovetarian. In the same way that if you were a vegetarian I wouldn't put meat on your plate, don't put your fear on my plate. I'm not going there."

It was truly the law of attraction. I just believed. My mantra is the Joan of Arc quote: "I am not afraid. I was born to do this." I know this is the work I'm here to do. I am unstoppable when it comes to my career because I chose this path, and this is what I'm meant to do, and I am taking good orderly direction. I'm not in that alignment in every corner of my life, but in my career, I am. In that alignment, anything's possible, so it worked.

Abby Wambach

I needed Glennon [Doyle] in my life as my mirror because there are things I do on a daily basis that she points to and says, "Look! You do it this way! What you just did, most women don't know." Glennon is good at spotting newness and differentness. By unpacking some of the daily interactions I have with my own life, she's allowed me to understand myself more, to show me a newer, more beautiful, better version of myself. That's given me more access to create art. I didn't realize that as an athlete I was also an artist out on the field.

I think a lot of women understand the idea of impostor syndrome, of feeling like a fraud, especially for the few of us that get offered a seat at the table. There's a feeling of, "How did I break through?" When I retired from playing, there were a lot of conversations in our house about how I had a total identity as a soccer player. I achieved everything I possibly could as an athlete, as a soccer player. [Glennon] made me aware that soccer didn't make me special. What I am, in my soul and my being, everything I brought to soccer, is what made soccer special. Everybody has access to that, no matter what you do. You have access to make whatever you're doing special. You only need the invitation and the language to understand yourself as special. I didn't just take off this costume of "soccer player." I, Abby, am still the same person. Whatever I do, whatever I get to be a part of, I'm bringing my full self. That's what makes it special, not the other way around.

At the end of the day, beautiful writing happens because you trust yourself as a writer. You start and keep going. You aren't necessarily "qualified" through a string of credentials, but your dreams come true because you went looking for permission (within and/or without), made it your own, and ran like hell with it.

4

Dream Weaver

Inspiration's First Spark

"Trust in dreams, for in them is hidden the gate to eternity."
~ Khalil Gibran

You want to write, but your creative well is powder dry. Or it spouts off like Old Faithful, leaving you gulping from a fire hose, drowning in words. What do prolific authors know about how to coax and nurture new ideas, and breathe life into them without losing focus for all else?

Lightning bolts. Spontaneous knowing. Dream downloading. You've heard the tales told by the "lucky" few for whom this creative stuff appears easy. They're walking down the street and, boom! A cinematic story line (soon to be a movie near you!) flashes across the screen of their mind. Publishers and Hollywood producers beat a path to their door. But what if you're one of the 99.9999 percent of writers for whom this does not happen? What tips and tricks can you use to inspire your best book brainstorms?

I'm no stranger to magical thinking. While publishers and Hollywood producers wouldn't be calling me anytime soon, what happened next was so surreal that it still feels impossible. Like a miraculous scene unfolding in a Spielberg film.

I bolted awake. Glowing in the reflection of the full moon, the walls, the floor, the hanging philodendron across the room were all perfectly still. This was earthquake country. I knew her signs, San Andreas. But the quaking was all mine.

The clock on the bedside table read 3:01 AM. *What in God's name?!* SIX books—*how is that even possible*—flashed one after the other in my mind's eye as I leaned against our headboard, blinking in the dim. Titles. Covers. Text. Format. Paragraphs slid left to right like a news ticker tape, some stopping to focus, even magnify. I rarely remembered my dreams, much less held onto them, but these words were *alive*.

OHMYGOD!!!! I just finished my last *Artist's Way* exercise yesterday! My twelfth week! And wasn't it August 1—the start of the "auspicious window" the astrologer told me about?! I sat dumbfounded. It had been a mere six weeks since Guru Singh admonished me to stop "hiding" behind my dogs and wrapped me like a burrito inside his woo-woo incantations. And, oh yeah, insisted I was supposed to step into my destiny as a writer. Is this what he'd seen coming?

Careful not to wake Jesse and Tosh, two comforter lumps atop our California king, I grabbed a flashlight and a yellow legal pad from my bedside drawer and tiptoed inside our closet to start downloading.

There, at eye level with my boots and running shoes, with my pulse racing, I took furious dictation—the blue pen in my hand flowing as if powered by magic ink. Soon, the carpet was covered with sixty-plus sheets of animated scrawl.

"Which book will make me happiest?" I whispered aloud, fearing the words would never slow, and I'd be overwhelmed by them. I needed specific instructions. Where to begin? I already felt bonded to each title; panic was imminent.

A voice in my head gave direction: "Start with *Lives Charmed*. A celebrity tell-all meets *Seat of the Soul*. A self-help bible with an environmental twist."

Alrighty then . . .

I'm almost embarrassed to admit this, dear reader, but there it was, all laid out. Step. By. Step. Have you ever felt jealous hearing a novelist speak of stories "given" to them and playing out like movies in their heads—characters dropping in deeply developed, story lines nearly complete? I certainly had. I'd think, *Come again? How does that happen?!* And yet, this was precisely my experience. Only the lead character was *me*!

There I was, walking into the homes of my most "charmed" clients as usual, but I wasn't there to exercise their pups. Instead, unbelievably, I was interviewing them for reality show (before there was such a thing) behind-the-scenes details—the never-before-told tales of what I witnessed every day in their homes. Fame, wealth, love, addiction, epic fails, lessons learned, and most importantly: environmental activism. This was KEY. The whole point of the book—*the exciting and genius part I could never have made up on my own*—was that we'd make eco-issues hip, cool, and profitable!

Could this really be? These were the early days of the internet when the world wasn't yet fully connected by information and urgency. Yet I could see that by weaving in interviews with green celebs about our most pressing environmental issues and the innovative things they were doing to heal our world, we'd give a voice to the plants, animals, and indigenous and marginalized people gasping for air and airtime.

Holy tree-hugging! This was it! My dream life revealed. Eyes wide, I could see my readers en masse—*ohmygod, readers!*—engaged in the drama and success tips, while being educated through the back door about how to save our natural world.

Tom Bergeron, funny man, and Emmy-winning host of three of the most popular TV shows of all time: *Dancing with the Stars*, *America's Funniest Home Videos*, and *Hollywood Squares*. His memoir, *I'm Hosting as Fast as I Can!* is about being Zen and staying sane in Hollywood. 🪶

I wrote my book a long time ago, and it's currently holding up some of the finest windows in America. As a TM, Transcendental Meditator for years, I was writing a book about meditation, really. About being present and in the moment. The [personal stories and] anecdotes I told in the book were the way I lured you in.

Gretchen Rubin, author of several books, including the *New York Times* bestsellers *Outer Order, Inner Calm*; *Better Than Before*; *The Happiness Project*; *Happier at Home*; and *The Four Tendencies*.

I literally get hit by a "lightning bolt" when I get an idea for a book, to the point where I can tell you exactly where I was and what the light was like. I just have to wait for that and trust that it will happen again.

Ann Patchett

There are no ideas knocking on my door. Ideas don't come to me fully formed in visions. I go out and find them. I go looking for them.

I think I have an ability to follow a chain and to not grab on too hard. I'll have an idea, but then I sit with it for a long time because then it will turn into another idea, and it will turn into another idea. And inevitably, by the time I write something, it has absolutely no connection to what I had originally started out with.

Rob Bell, *New York Times* bestselling author of many books—including *What We Talk About When We Talk About God*, *Love Wins*, *What Is the Bible?*, and *Everything Is Spiritual*—and award-winning podcaster of *The RobCast*.

There's this Latin phrase, *Ex nihilo*, [the idea] that there's this nature of creativity that comes out of nothing. Jerry Seinfeld was asked where his jokes come from, [and] there's this great line where he says, "I have no idea. I literally have no idea."

I wrote a kid's story called *A Goat for a Boat* and read it to my daughter's class and then read it on an episode of my podcast. Ron and Don; one has a goat, and one has a boat. And this girl named Eileen Vee shows up with a vat full of chili that was made by her brother Willie, so it's Willie's Chili. What in the world? That is just completely ridiculous and absurd, and I have no explanation other than for some reason I came up with a story about a guy named Ron who has a boat and [a] guy named Don who has a goat.

There are straightforward answers to why you made what you made and wrote what you wrote and were feeling what you're feeling. But I don't know. I pursued a line of inquiry. I wrote the next sentence and then the next sentence came. And I studied and I worked hard, and I was disciplined, and I did research . . . You're putting in your hours but you're also aware that you are opening yourself to great mysteries.

Danielle LaPorte, Oprah Super Soul 100 Leader, cofounder of the *Beautiful Writers Podcast*, and author of *The Desire Map*, *White Hot Truth*, and *The Fire Starter Sessions*.* 🌿

For some people, if you wait for inspiration, you're never going to write. And then, there are those of us—myself, personally—if I'm not inspired, it's no deal. I just don't write. I have to wait. I've got to hear angels in my studio.

Don't ask me how I trusted this would work. It didn't even occur to me that going from my clients' kibble dispenser to translator of their innermost secrets might be a stretch. I just knew this vision had legs and providence. My body was buzzing as if propped on a beehive. Yet, deep inside, I felt a profound sense of calm. I knew I had what it took. As surely as I'd ever known anything, I was certain writing was my Willy Wonka golden ticket.

I thought of my beautiful mother, working so hard behind the scenes as a secretary and editor for her boss at Stanford University. She'd be especially proud that I was writing to try and help our precious planet; it was thanks to her that I had

---

* Fun fact: Danielle is also my co-author on *Your Big Beautiful Book Plan*.

a lifelong preoccupation with falling water tables and rising temperatures. After wasting $65,000 of my parents' money on the college degree I never quite earned, I figured I'd be able to pay them back quickly when my bestseller was released.

Candles sparkle on the table at the Chart House, where I've taken my folks for a celebratory meal. With trembling hands, Mom opens up the ivory linen envelope I've handed her. Inside is a note explaining that I've paid off the mortgage to their home in full.

This is nuts! I'm going to be an author! Tears of gratitude filled my eyes. I leaned down and kissed the carpet. "Thank You, God. Thank You, Mother Earth, for entrusting me with this assignment. I won't let You down. Just show me what to do. I'll study every minute my family doesn't need me. I'm all Yours." My heart was so full it felt like it would pound right out of my chest. I hadn't been wasting my brain all those years being distracted in school. Spirit was just waiting for the right time to put my skills, passions, and connections to work!

I peeked back at our bed, moonbeams streaming down through our skylight. Jesse and Tosh, still fast asleep, had no idea that *everything* had just changed for us. I couldn't stop smiling. The gates of heaven had just swung open.

But you've never written a book before. You've never even taken a single writing class. I waved that pesky voice away. How hard could it be when you're basically taking dictation from God? Besides, I could *see* it, feel the book's life force, and my role as midwife. When Jesse woke up, a miracle—he got it, 100 percent.

"Everywhere we go, people tell you their life stories," he said. "You'll be great at this!"

It was clear. I'd grab low-hanging fruit, start with two of my favorite dog-walking clients for my inaugural interviews—Paul Williams, and model and *Dynasty* star Catherine Oxenberg. Surely, I'd get more eco-minded stars from there.

Paul Williams, Songwriting Hall-of-Famer, actor, Oscar-winning composer, president of ASCAP, *New York Times* bestseller of *Gratitude and Trust*, co-authored with Tracey Jackson, and recovery advocate—sober now for thirty-two years.

When I was twenty-two, a friend invited me to lug equipment for a new band called the Chancellors. The night before, I wrote two songs—my first ones. It never crossed my mind I couldn't do it. I sat down, wrote the songs, and then went out and played them for the band. I didn't know how to play the piano, so I wrote the words and sang them to the melody in my head.

One day, Roger Nichols and I were asked to write a song for a Crocker Bank commercial. We called it "We've Only Just Begun." Roger wrote the melody, and I scripted the lyrics about a young couple starting out with white lace and promises.

A young singing group—the Carpenters—saw our commercial and wanted a whole song. I was floored when it shot up to number one and became one of the highest-grossing songs of all time. Imagine. It had all the romantic beginnings of a bank commercial! I'd desperately wanted to be an actor but ended up backing into the right career by not getting work. It's then that I discovered my real gifts.

Catherine Oxenberg, actress, screenwriter, royal, and first-time author of *Captive: A Mother's Crusade to Save Her Daughter from a Terrifying Cult.* 🌿

I'd always wanted to write a book. But I never would have anticipated that *Captive* would have been my first. I wrote it to save my eldest daughter's life and to protect mine. I was up against a powerful, dangerous, and vindictive cult—and they would have no qualms about taking me down. I had found out that my daughter India was in extreme jeopardy in a cult called NXIVM, and so far, all my attempts to free her had failed. When left with no other recourse, I made the excruciating decision to expose her in the press. I had uncovered what looked like evidence of tax evasion, racketeering, money laundering, identity theft, and sex trafficking within the group. I was afraid that not only was India's life at risk but that she could be coerced to break the law unknowingly.

Early on, I was able to get some other young women out by warning them they were going to be physically branded and spooking them with news of a government raid, which I had used as a scare tactic, but in actuality did happen a few months later. I appeared in a blitz of talk shows, on the news, in magazines. I helped the *New York Times* break a cover story. Shortly after, the government moved in and told me that I didn't have to carry the burden all by myself anymore. The leader, Keith Raniere, fled to Mexico, and I was saying to myself, "If this investigation fizzles out, which it had in the past when other people had tried to bring evidence against the group, how am I going to expose the truth about this cult? How will I ever reach my daughter?" I had never been so scared in my life.

I signed with a literary agent, Yfat Reiss-Gendel, who had me write a book proposal. Simon & Schuster gave me a book deal for a book with no ending, which took a lot of faith. My agent is a miracle-worker.

I was writing in real time as events unfolded, not knowing what would be on the next page. It was harrowing because India refused to communicate with me and considered me enemy number one. I started writing in January and, simultaneously, NXIVM started to fall apart. Keith was arrested in March. The book came out in August of 2018, and other high-ranking members of the cult were still getting arrested on July 26. As the plot kept unfolding, I kept calling my publisher, saying, "Can we add this one more thing? One more thing!"

In the end, law enforcement did not drop the ball, and the criminals were brought to justice. At sentencing, a member of the FBI came up to me and gave me a giant bear hug. "Thank you, mama, you called it! You knew what was happening before anyone else!" My family's nightmare became a story of hope and perseverance and of love triumphing.*

Everything was easy-breezy . . . at first. No matter how late I went to bed, I continued to awaken at 3:00 AM for months, seeing pages of scrolling text. My brain and body were afire. As Vladimir Nabokov defined it: "Ink, a drug," and I was heavily under the influence. Thankfully, my husband and Tosh were nearly inseparable, which gave me plenty of time to start pitching agents and celebs for interviews. Each small writerly step created its own momentum, and we celebrated every win.

At the eleven-month mark—*so much for that "six to nine months" window!*—I'd quit my dog-walking business to study and write constantly. Although I was ecstatic to have found my calling, it was painful not making my own money.

"Most divorces result from two issues—disagreements over finances and childrearing," Carol said, sounding like an issue of *Psychology Today*. *That's just great.* Jesse and I were two for two. He practically had an aneurysm every time I "wasted" thirty dollars on organic juice oranges, which sucked because I was never not going to waste thirty dollars on organic juice oranges. *This California mama was gonna buy the kid 100 percent organic, come hell or high prices!* As a soldier in Mother Earth's army, She'd meet me halfway—of that, I was convinced, and so I pressed on.

Despite being a total beginner, I experienced miraculous synchronicity, doors opening, and vastly improved punctuation weekly, if not daily. That said, the path would be nowhere near as simple as I'd wagered—not the writing, schmoozing, promotion, or the marriage. But I was on a track I'd never leave.

Being gifted a book in a dream is rare; I've yet to interview another author with that same experience. Yet, there are endless ways to get ideas and begin

---

* India was freed, healed, became an author, and got engaged. Keith Raniere was sentenced to 120 years in prison. And Catherine's book became the subject of multiple TV shows—*Seduced* and *The Vow,* among them. Talk about scripting your success!

your writing journey. For some, inspiration whispers softly, or comes in fits and starts, or takes its own sweet time. Everyone's path is unique. Don't stress if you don't hear a thunderclap. Again, all you ever need to get started is the *desire*.

Charles Sailor, *New York Times* bestselling novelist of *The Second Son*, and Hollywood screenwriter for TV shows like *Kojak*, *The Rockford Files*, *CHiPs*, and the debut of *Charlie's Angels*.

I had just finished producing and writing a movie of the week for MGM and CBS. Back then, movies of the week were hot. The first three minutes was called "the hook." You had to hook the audience with that first three minutes so that they came back after that first block of commercials. I decided that my next hook would be an ironworker that falls off a building and lives. I spent two weeks trying to figure out how this guy could survive through the fall.

I was out walking my dog at about eleven o'clock at night when a voice in my mind said, "Chuck, nobody's going to live through a fall like that off of a high-rise building unless God wants them to."

I stopped mid-step and said to myself, "Well, who would God save?" Of course, the first thing that came to my mind was Jesus.

"You can't write a movie of the week about Jesus, an ironworker!" the voice says.

"Well, why couldn't it be another son of God with a whole new message for humanity?" I went back in the house and told the actress I was living with, and she said, "Chuck. You've been smoking too much of that shit."

NBC offered me a ten-hour miniseries off the story pitch. CBS offered me an eight-hour miniseries. And this producer said, "You've got to write this as a book. This is a bestselling story." But I didn't know how.

Nathaniel Branden, who was Ayn Rand's close friend and a psychologist, said, "You can do this. I've got an editor who has edited my psych books for me, and I'll loan her to you." So, I hired this editor, Cheri Adrian, and my ex-wife, Barbara George, and I set about writing the great American novel.

Joy Harjo

I just recently wrote the best song I've ever written, a full-fledged storytelling song with a bridge and a chorus. How did it come? With an instinct, almost a heartache. There was something there. I knew that the only way I was going to be able to deal with it was if I wrote.

When I started, I thought, *Oh, this is a drag*—and it was. Drafts can be that way. You have to have faith. But after I was done, I realized, *Wow! That's the song that I needed for such and such.*

I didn't go in there with that intent, but this is how the creative, intuitive process works. In the civilized world, they teach you that you go after something and pin it down and wrestle it down. And, yes, there's the work of casting it. You have to do your work, to practice, to gain knowledge so that you have other possibilities and modalities open to you. But when it comes down to it, if you ask for help and you're working in the field where inspirations come to you, it's mysterious.

Steven Pressfield

When a book idea comes, it always takes me by surprise. I think, *Am I even interested in that? Where did that come from?* The second thing I always think of is: *Well, nobody in the world is going to be interested in this. This is the dumbest idea I've ever heard. It's totally not commercial, I can't pitch it, and I can't sell it.* Like on the hero's journey, where you get the call and hang up on it, I am in the "refusal of the call" stage.

Then a couple of months later, I'll stumble on the file and think, Gee, *that's a pretty good idea*. That's when I'll plot it out. These ideas come out of left field for me. That's why I believe in the Muse and that we're all being led as artists by some force we can't understand.

The book that just seized me and happened incredibly fast was *The Legend of Bagger Vance*. I wrote the whole thing in about four months and totally on instinct. I'd been trying to do that—write a novel—for thirty years and failing constantly. I don't even remember writing it. But I did eventually steal the structure of it from the *Bhagavad Gita*, the Hindu scripture—one of those books that, in different translations, somehow feeds me. At some point, I had the idea: "Gee, this is a great structure for a story. Let me steal it and transpose it to another arena."

I'm a big believer in stealing. If you can steal a structure from *Hamlet* or *Moby Dick* or something, great. I'm being facetious. I don't mean to steal in the sense of ripping off somebody else's stuff. But there are only so many plots. When the structure of *Romeo and Juliet* or another classic story speaks to you, you might as well use it. Use it as a model, and then do your own thing upon it.*

---

* Steve's onto something. Shakespeare's *Romeo and Juliet* was written between 1594 and 1596 as a remake, "inspired" by earlier poems and plays by other authors—specifically Masuccio Salernitano (1410–1475), Matteo Bandello (1480–1562), William Painter (1540–1595), and French author Pierre Boaistuau (1517–1566)—whose *The Traagicall Historye of Romeus and Juliet* was translated into English by Arthur Brooke in 1562. One could make the case that this was Shakespeare not just stealing the form but essentially crafting the then modern-day master 2.0 version of the same plot and story!

Interestingly, when I told this to one of my besties—my mentor, Betsy Rapoport—a longtime editor in New York, she said: "Yes! I did know that Shakespeare 'cribbed' many of his plots. I remember when we were studying Latin, we translated the story of Pyramus and Thisbe from Ovid's *Metamorphoses*, which is pretty Romeo and Juliet-y: Star-crossed lovers. Families that hate each other, thus a decision to elope. A misunderstanding leads him to believe she's been killed, so he stabs himself. When she sees him dead, she then stabs herself. And this was from *freaking Babylonia!*"

Terry McMillan, #1 *New York Times* bestselling author of *Waiting to Exhale* and *How Stella Got Her Groove Back* (both made into hit films starring Whitney Houston and Angela Bassett, respectively), and eight other bestsellers.

I'd gone to Jamaica because I was numb. I was grieving the loss of my mother, followed by my best girlfriend. And I fell in love with a young man on the trip. He started flirting with me, and I said, "This is a joke. What is he doing?" Then I said, "Oh, what the hell, I'll fuck him. I never fuck anybody."

When I got home, it was as if I'd been resurrected. I'd felt dead, and now I felt alive. That was what made me start writing. It started out as a poem. Then it was a short story. I told him what I wanted to do. He didn't know my writing—he'd never heard of me, thank God. But he said, "Terry, you said that when you write a novel, you just lie. So just lie." And I said to myself, *Well, I guess this young man has given me permission.*

And I wrote a chapter a day, for thirty-one chapters, for what became *Stella Got Her Groove Back*. It was like I was on cruise control. I mean, talk about lying like it was coming out of my nose! There are people that, and I don't knock them, but they outline their novels. I'll put it this way: I'm like a conduit. I'm just here to write what my character is telling me—what they see, what they feel, and what they think. I just write it down. I have to jump out of my own skin in order to do it.

Over the years, several aspiring writers with knowledge of my self-funded artist dates and trips to Drew Lawrence and Guru Singh asked if I'd done anything else to conjure my "magical book dream" that didn't cost money. We'll cover the topic of coaxing creativity via divine support specifically in chapter eight. But there was one mental component that may be worth sharing now . . .

. . . *With a desire to raise a happy child, I was contemplating my positivity and good fortune. A lot.*

Stumble into any self-help event, and you'll probably hear something about the importance of asking high-quality questions. I didn't realize it then, but by asking these things over and over—*What does it mean when people call me charmed? Why* am *I so happy? What do I do to attract blessings?*—perhaps I was setting up my unconscious and the Universe to deliver high-quality answers. Training myself to look for, expect, and attract magic. When I told Deepak Chopra about my book dream on his episode of the podcast, he confirmed my experience, saying, "Reflective inquiry is the only way to access creativity." Then he added this brain teaser: "The question is the answer. So, if you live the questions, you move into the answers."

Robert McKee
Wanting to write in a specific mode is quite often the spark of inspiration. I can't remember much of my first idea. I know I wanted to write a thriller, something psychologically interesting. And a character came to mind. Step by step, I put him in trouble and kept him in trouble until the very end. But I think the inspiration was simply, "I want to write a screenplay, and I'm going to write in my favorite genre." After that, the steps are kind of logical.

People decide they're going to write. They sit down. They make choices like genre and character. And then they begin to put things on paper. There's a theory of writing that I believe in—that the story is already written. The writer's job is to get out of their own way.

There's something in the subconscious mind of a writer that already knows what they want to accomplish. It's not a mystical experience. It's a kind of hunger, a kind of need. It's a desire—a thing you want. Then you start doing it.

Samantha Bennett, popular speaker, creativity/productivity expert, founder of the Organized Artist Company, and author of *Get It Done* and *Start Right Where You Are.*

I stalled out almost immediately after getting the idea for *Get It Done*, because I couldn't figure out what kind of book I wanted it to be. A workbook? Client success stories? Linear or nonlinear? And, of course, I felt like I had to have it perfect inside of my mind before I could start writing.

Then I had the thought, *Why don't I let the book tell me what it wants to be?*

So, I started carrying around index cards, and any time I had an idea for something I thought should be in the book, I wrote it down and stashed it in a manila envelope on my desk labeled "Genius." After a month, I poured all the cards out onto my dining room table and sorted them by topic. Sure enough—a rough structure started to emerge. Whenever I didn't know what I wanted to write, I would reach into that envelope and write about whatever card I drew. It gave a nice "magical fortune-telling" feeling to the writing process.

For what it's worth, I believe that as we live our questions, we can be natural optimists and sky-is-falling doomsdayers at the same time. A typical hour in my head, for example, might reveal any of these polar-opposite scenarios:

1. Doomsday Linda: The world's burning up. Mother Earth's pissed and the big quake's coming. Are we all gonna die any minute now?
   Trusting Linda: We'll see. But right here, right now, you're safe. Look around. Name five things that are working.
2. DL: I'm never going to finish another book, at least not until the crooks are out of Washington. My time and brain have been highjacked by politics. How can I look away?
   TL: Politics have always been a train wreck. For the next hour, turn

off your alerts. What's *one* paragraph you can play with before you do anything else?

3. DL: I'll never finish chapter four. It's a total disaster. Is it even fixable?
   TL: What if you *did* know? Grab a pen and paper, sit somewhere quiet, and ask your book what it has to say.

4. DL: I'm drowning in too many ideas. Have I developed ADD? Is that ever a good thing?
   TL: Doesn't matter. You're abundant. What's the one idea that makes you smile right now? Go there.

5. DL: What if publishers don't want me? Can I still be happy?
   TL: Write what you love. Love what you write. The right people will love it too. What do you love today?

Whether you believe your creative inspiration comes from a higher place or is being fed by your subconscious mind, you've got this. Creating that *relationship*, however you describe it, opens the creative floodgates. Why not give it a try? Seed your daydreams and sleep hours with quality questions and watch the answers percolate in. Before I go to sleep, I will often still pray for specific dreamtime instructions. "Something I will remember, understand, and be able to implement," I say when putting in my cosmic order. And guess what? Every so often, I still bolt awake at 3:00 AM, quaking with insight.

5

Scared Much?

Silencing the Bullies, Inner and Outer

"If you're horrible to me, I'm going to write a
song about it, and you won't like it."
~Taylor Swift

You're talented. Amazingly strong. You've overcome more in the past ten days than some people do in a lifetime. You know what you know, and you're great at what you're great at. You're on a mission! So, why the high-stakes fear? Have haters from the past taken up space in your head? *I'm a newbie. A fraud. Ill prepared.* Or perhaps you've published before, but worry you're not meant for more . . .

It's time to silence the lies—your own or those from ignorant people who once declared your ineptitude. Everyone starts off a beginner, right? Get ready to hush the negative voices by seeing how the pros overcome imposter syndrome. Also, studying the right books will magically bolster your confidence. Take it from me. Those voices were loud, and I needed help!

"Whatcha get on your SATs, Linda?" *Uh-oh.*

When it came to sitting down and writing my book, thrilling dreams and early enthusiasm weren't enough. Several naysayers in my head—the ghosts of high school Mean Girls—loomed large.

Place: Los Altos High School, the quad.

Time: Senior year.

Mood: Fucked.

Our lunch break almost over, my classmates and I milled around, waiting to enter the main auditorium to vote for Senior Superlatives. Four smarty-pants girls from a wealthier part of town sat in front of me, pompous smugness coloring their faces. They knew full well I hadn't excelled on my SATs. Surely, they'd seen the class rankings just printed and posted, with my name recorded for posterity in the bottom third.

It didn't help that one of them got all giggly around Jeff, my boyfriend. How was I to know he'd said no to her invitation to attend last year's Sadie Hawkins dance to go with me—a girl from the low-life flats, who was shallow enough to be a pom-pom girl and whose biggest career plan was to enroll in Foothill Junior College in the fall?

My SAT numbers? The nerve! Crap. Think fast, Linda. You can't tell them you got a 980! Don't they give you something like 400 points just for getting your name right?

"Umm. I got 1253," I replied casually before sauntering off to join a clique of lovable misfits. *My* people. I could hear laughter behind me and turned to see the girls shaking their heads. One jumped up and ran to Jeff's group; fun-loving jokesters clumped together like partridges in the grass. When their covey all turned my way and busted a gut in unison, I thought, *Oh, this isn't good.*

What had I done wrong? I slow-motion replayed the last two minutes, reliving every word and facial expression. I'd answered their SAT question quickly enough, with an air of nonchalance . . . hadn't I?

Joel Stein 🌿

You don't become a successful humor columnist without having gotten teased. It drives you to take on the powerful and famous with jokes about their haircuts from the safety of your computer screen. Without it, I'd be a contract lawyer.

Lee Child, creator of the Jack Reacher book series. With over 100 million copies sold, Jack Reacher—which has also been adapted for both the big screen (starring Tom Cruise) and streaming television—is the "strongest brand in publishing," according to *Forbes* magazine. 🦋

I grew up in a city [Birmingham] that was rough and tough—this was a long time ago. Society was totally different and emotionally, very inarticulate. Nobody could express themselves. We resolved things by fighting. It was just like breathing. On top of that, my folks were very ambitious for us. They wanted us to have what they did not have, a good education and to do well. When you're in a city like that in a school like I was in, that's like having a target on your back. You are too big for your boots. You're above yourself. There is no worse sin in Britain than being above yourself. So, I was constantly fighting.

Deepak Chopra, author of ninety-two books, including *Quantum Healing*, *The Seven Spiritual Laws of Success*, and *Metahuman*, and Fellow of the American College of Physicians. 🦋

I used to debate the haters, but I've let that go. If you have the voice of the bully or mean reviewers in your head and you want to be independent of their criticism, you also have to be independent of flattery because they're equally dangerous. You become totally dependent for validation, and then you're either instantly flattered or perennially offended for the rest of your life. And that's not a good way to live.

Leeza Gibbons, Emmy Award–winning talk show host, celebrated radio host, Hollywood correspondent on *Entertainment Tonight* and *Extra*, and author of two *New York Times* bestsellers, *Take 2* and *Fierce Optimism*. ❧

You really do have to love your haters. You just do. There will always be people who don't get you or who go out of their way to try and make you feel bad. I would get tripped up along the way, but I always came back to this: "I believe in me." My parents told me to believe in me because they believed in me. I'm sure you've experienced people who don't believe in what you're doing, who don't see the vision. And maybe you haven't taught them how to receive you because you haven't yet stepped into your authenticity.

It didn't occur to me that my authenticity as an intellectual genius was so easy to question, dressed as I was in dolphin shorts and tank tops on cold foggy mornings. (How's a sixteen-year-old supposed to know that she's unconsciously trying to keep people's eyes away from her frizzy hair and crooked teeth? I mean, I didn't get braces or start reading self-help until college.) Although my natural-high self was as unlikely to be voted "heartiest partier" as "most likely to succeed," I should have suspected I wouldn't be excluded from the ballot. After being voted "Biggest BSer" of our class twenty minutes later, it hit me that SAT scores must not use odd numbers and probably end in tens. *Why did I say 1253 and not 1260?!*

By far, the deeper disappointment about being labeled our school's Biggest Bullshitter—on card-stock keepsake posters, no less—was that I felt I'd disrespected my father, who'd taken an oath in his twenties never to tell a lie, and which inspired him to say, "My, that *is* a baby!" or "Quite a haircut you've got there!" when pushed beyond silence.

I felt sick I'd dishonored Dad's commitment to honesty to save face, only to have it blow up spectacularly in my face. As a full-out daddy's girl, I never wanted to take his unconditional love for granted, especially when I did crap like read *Linda Goodman's Sun Signs* until two the night before a math test and then bring home a D on my report card. I suppose the fact that I woke up smiling every morning at six gave him hope; we could barely drag Carol and her straight-A's out of bed after her fourth push of the snooze button. If Dad could believe in me so unflinchingly, then damn it, I would too.

Valarie Kaur

Ever since I was a kid and heard my first racial slurs, I have noticed this voice in me I call "The Little Critic." So many of us, especially people of color, hear this voice. *You are not smart enough. Not good enough. Not strong enough. Not white enough. Not American enough.* I feel like my life has been this power struggle between the critic that wants to make me small (who's just trying to protect me because it *is* unsafe), and this wise woman, the warrior in me, who says, "Oh, my love. You are brave enough."

Poet Audre Lorde said, "We can learn how to mother ourselves," so I say to myself, "Breathe, my love. Push to show up one more time, one more day."

In my first meetings with my publisher, Chris Jackson, I felt like I had impostor syndrome. Like, "I can't be worthy." I'm ashamed to say that it lasted a long time. Anytime I missed a deadline, or I didn't feel like the pages I sent over to him were good enough, I'd think, "Is this worthy of him?" He never gave me any reason to feel that way, and instead, at almost every turn, Chris was holding up a mirror to superpowers I couldn't see.

There's a line from an old Hindi film that keeps coming back to me: "When my faith falters, I will have faith in your faith in me."

Nell Scovell

The only way to move forward creatively is to allow yourself to be judged. I think that trips up women more than men. In general, people don't love being criticized. And when people ask me for advice, I always say, "Try to see feedback as constructive, not critical. Use feedback to make yourself a better writer, or to make yourself more confident that what you did evoked the response you wanted."

Fearing the blank page is like fearing an empty dog dish. It's just something you fill every day. I'll be honest, being a professional writer since 1981, the year I started getting paid, I still marvel at how bad my first drafts are. You would think by now I'd be over that. And yet, I finally figured out that's the process. I can't tell you how many notebooks I have filled with ideas for stories and plays and screenplays and pilots and articles that never panned out. But if you enjoy the process, you're ahead of the game.

Buoyed by parental and mystical support, it felt as if my writing destiny was reasonably goof-proof. But how to beef up my intellectual confidence to nullify any internal bullies that might remain? Dad said that the world's most successful people had one thing in common: They were big readers. Perhaps everything I needed to know was just a page away? With the help of a brainiac clerk at Bookstar on Ventura Boulevard, three titles made my Linda University Reading List.

Strunk and White's *The Elements of Style*, a slender prescriptive guide, gifted me pearls like the difference between hyphens and dashes and avoiding the rookie error of weighing down text with filler words ("so," "just," "like," "that," "really," "very," and "pretty"). I mined that baby night and day and must've read this passage twenty times: "A sentence should contain no unnecessary words, a paragraph no unnecessary sentences, for the same reason that a drawing should have no unnecessary lines and a machine no unnecessary parts." Yikes! Will it surprise you to learn that I still struggle with this?

The Chicago Manual of Style, one of the most widely respected manuals for usage and grammar, stressed the importance of brevity (*double yikes!*), where ellipses go, and how to punctuate abbreviations and quotations. Use numerals or spell out numbers? According to *CMS*, you spell out numbers from zero to one hundred; starting with 101, you use the numeral. What happens when you write a paragraph with "mixed numbers"—some above 101 and some below 100? In that case, you should express all the numbers in that paragraph as numerals. (Sheesh. Pull that one out at parties; it's a real crowd-pleaser.)

Julia Cameron's aforementioned *The Artist's Way* sent me on regular Wednesday Artist Dates to French cafés, bookstores, and parks, where I performed confidence rituals under redwood trees (you shoulda been there). Armed for hours with a journal, my favorite blue ballpoint, and an open itinerary, I followed Julia's instruction to spark whimsy and create a sense of playfulness. Hump Day couldn't come fast enough. I was becoming an artist!

To ensure I never missed an inspiration, I stashed paper and pens *everywhere*—my car, bathroom drawer, by the bed, in my dog-walking pouch. The world was my canvas, and words, my constant companion. With each hour of self-study and time spent living "as if," my self-esteem as a writer blossomed, and those Mean Girl voices of yore grew fainter.

Maybe this was how they did it—*all those bestselling authors?* Using their fear, pain, or shame as fuel, they improved their art and odds. I loved the idea of learning how to write a book by turning to books, the hunt of it, and could feel myself getting smarter, braver, every day. I knew that as long as I stayed motivated, my future success was largely up to me.

Cheryl Strayed

One of my few rituals is that almost always before I start writing, I'll peruse my shelf and pick up a book, usually poetry, and read a little something. A snippet, a page, a few poems, just to shift my brain into that other place where we make language on the page. It's really helpful. I think we need each other. We stand on the backs of those writers who came before us. I always feel that I couldn't write without that reading, without that place that's made when you read language you love.

Tim Grahl, managing partner and publisher at Story Grid Universe and author of *Your First 1000 Copies*, *Book Launch*

Blueprint, Running Down a Dream, and the young adult novel, *The Threshing.*

I told all of my friends to buy and read a copy of Steven Pressfield's *The War of Art* because it was the first time somebody put into words what we were struggling with. I've been in therapy for years now, and I've learned that you can't solve a problem that doesn't have a name. Until you can take something and set it out on the table and talk about it and not feel like it's just this mess inside of yourself, you're never going fix anything. Steven's book gave me the name "Resistance." The stories he tells made me think: *This is the thing that's been destroying me!* That did the dual thing of 1) giving me a problem to solve, and 2) making me feel less crazy and less alone because I am the king of the mental bullies. I can out-bully anyone in my head.

Gabrielle Bernstein

The only book I ever specifically read for writing was *How to Write a Book Proposal.* I purposefully avoided being told how to write because what was most important to me was to write as I speak and to write in my voice. As soon as I started to try to be anything but that, I lost what made my books good. So, my books are not literary masterpieces, but they're a transmission of what I know to be true and what I hear coming through me.

Jane Goodall

I *love* Shakespeare—one of two books I took with me to Gombe. I didn't have much time to read because I was up at 5:30 AM and coming back at dark, writing up my field notes by a lantern late into the night. But I took Shakespeare with me because I didn't want to be without him.

Steven Pressfield

I read the same things over and over. The great books are like a wonderful healthy vegetable juice, whereas some of the bad stuff is like junk food. I go back to the same movies, the same books. I don't know why. I think it's a deficiency of imagination on my part. A lot of my work is based on the ancient Greeks. Go back and just name any of them—Thucydides, Herodotus, Plato, Euripides, Xenophon, Herodotus—they were so clear-minded. There's no neurosis or modern poisons in there.

The two writers who have most influenced me in the book world are Ernest Hemingway and Henry Miller. There's a compilation of Hemingway's wisdom called *Ernest Hemingway on Writing* by Larry W. Phillips, who culled nuggets from *A Moveable Feast* and a number of other books by the master. As for Henry Miller, he's one of my heroes. He struggled for so long and was so true to his own star and such an original. I used to sit at the typewriter and literally copy pages from Miller and Hemingway—I mean pages and pages—just to try and understand what they were doing and how they did it, and to get the feeling of a writer who really had a voice.

As I write this, over three hundred thousand books are published every year in the United States by traditional publishers, with another one million self-published, leading me to believe that at least as many mental bullies are being silenced. Let's jump ahead for a full-circle moment at my twenty-year high school reunion, where the meanest of the smarty-pants girls came unglued.

In a surprise twist, our senior high school class president, John (who got a perfect 1600 on *his* SATs and was there on the quad's grassy knoll the day of my cruddy score fib), sent our graduating class a mass email labeled: "Top 18 Reasons to Attend" our Los Altos High twenty-year reunion. Before the final bullet on the list ("If you are there, you, too, will be popular") was mention of *me*! In a move Daddy cheered from his deathbed, John declared that I was now a "noted speaker and bestselling author of *Lives Charmed*," with my website address included, proof for any naysayers.

Jesse and I walked into the reunion hotel ballroom, and I couldn't sit down without being interrupted. I couldn't dance. Or eat. It was like I was a bride or a visiting dignitary. At one point, my classmates stood three-deep to shake my hand or hug me. Was it possible I now lived in a world where *I* was the smart girl, worthy of intellectual discourse? Up was down, day was night, dogs were sleeping with cats! Even the smarty-pants girls came over to congratulate me. Well, all but one of them.

"Um, Linda," she hedged when I walked up to say hello. "So, when you write a book for a publisher, do they hire somebody to clean up your work after you're done with it?" Her eyes were darting about like pinballs. Clearly code for: *But I thought you were too ignorant to write a term paper, much less a book!*

"Well, every book goes through a copy-editing phase," I said. "Mine included. But I've done that, too—cleaned up other people's work for a publisher." SPG's mouth gaped open, her forehead crinkling. Clearly I, a Bear of Little Brain, had failed to comprehend her. She tried again.

"No, what I mean is—" she continued, certain I'd misunderstood, "when you write a book for a publisher, there are other people present to clean up your stuff when you're done, right?"

Good Lord, after all these years, she was *still* going out of her way to try to prove me ignorant! Then it hit me: It was in part *because* of her criticism that I'd worked so hard to rewrite my history, leapfrog over my limitations, and believe in myself when others wouldn't or couldn't. I wanted to thank her for being so blatantly transparent. *I see your disbelief, and I raise you my hard-earned self-esteem, girlfriend.* Any residual shame I carried about my low SAT scores evaporated as if hit by a master delete key.

Go to those reunions, you guys. Ya never know. *(Although, after writing this, I'm now a little nervous to go to any future ones!)*

And know this: Every bestselling author, whether voted "Best Smile" or "Most Likely to End Up on *America's Most Wanted*," succeeded because they overrode their hesitancy.

Jillian Lauren ❧

I have doubts weekly—a feeling that I can't do this, I can't go on, or this isn't the right project. For me, self-doubt has always been part of the noise of my process. I think that's very common for writers and artists. I've learned to say, "Thank you very much for your input, oh lovely brain of mine. I'm going to shove that right now and do my work for the day."

Anne Lamott, author of one of the most successful writing books ever, *Bird by Bird*. Her other bestsellers include *Operating Instructions*, *Almost Everything*, *Help Thanks Wow*, *Grace (Eventually)*, *Dusk Night Dawn*, and *Traveling Mercies*, as well as several novels. ❧

E. L. Doctorow put it so beautifully. He said, "Writing is like driving at night with the headlights on. You can only see a little ways in front of you, but you can make the whole journey that way." And I don't believe that for a second because I have a raging anxiety disorder. I like to know where I'm going to end up, what I'll see along the way, how I'll feel at each stage, and when the hell I can get home, which is secretly the only place I ever want to be.

I got sober thirty-plus years ago, and for the first four or five years, I thought of it as practicing having feelings without thinking about killing myself, or suppressing them, or rewriting them. I was a victim of extreme bullying because of this crazy, frizzy hair. I was way too smart and way too sensitive. It was all about trying to cover that up, armor it, or burnish the surface. Those were the only operating instructions I had. Little by little, I started to realize that we're all in the same boat. You hear when you first get sober, "Don't compare your insides to other people's outsides." But that took me years to believe because I'd see people with silky, long, smooth hair or beautiful teeth, and I'd think, *What kind of problems could you have if your hair looked like that?* But I realized that we had all become clenched in terror of falling and landing on our butts or having people see our deepest, truest, inside self.

I always tried to emulate people I thought had the secret launch codes. When I was first becoming a writer, I wanted to write like Isabel Allende, or Ann Beattie, or John Updike, because they had the codes. My fourth book, *All New People*, was my first sober book. About that time, I realized I didn't have to squinch and clench and burnish the surface and pretend to be smarter and more evolved than I am. That I just needed to, bird by bird, tell the truth in my own voice.

Lee Child 🌿

I feel terribly insecure because I've got to deliver a book a year and it's got to be good, even if I have no clue what to do. The way I feel when I'm doing it—it's like I'm a movie stuntman, and I just jumped off a high building. And I'm hoping like hell that the stage crew gets the airbag in position just in time.

Marie Forleo, author of the #1 *New York Times* bestseller *Everything is Figureoutable*, based on her concept from Oprah's Super-Soul Sessions. Founder of the online business program B-School, MarieTV, and *The Marie Forleo Podcast.* 🌿

I am a creative machine. If you remove one part of me, it's not going to stop me. It's going to take a lot more than a [recent] hysterectomy to slow me down. That said, I felt really insecure about my writing. One thing that helped me while writing *Everything Is Figureoutable* was to continue the practice of not editing as I went. I had to keep reminding myself, "Marie, it's okay. Get it all down. It doesn't have to be even remotely 'perfect' at this point. Even if this paragraph doesn't connect with the last one, or we don't know if this will wind up in the book." The more I gave myself permission to get everything down on the page, the better.

My greatest confidence boost ironically came from a minimum-wage job. At the Bodhi Tree, one of the most popular spiritual bookstores in the world, we were always hosting some marquee author for a party or signing. Intimidating—or so you'd think. Yet, I couldn't believe the disconnects I witnessed—the self-help divas who behaved appallingly because they could; the wealth gurus who drove up in shitty cars; and the always bizarre relationship "experts" going through yet another nasty, public divorce. It was comical and hard to know whose currency to trust.

I didn't yet know what I'd write, but my desire to become an author was growing, as was my fascination with those already living the dream while truly walking their talk.

"After shelving thousands of books for you, Stan," I said one day to the co-owner, "and meeting many celeb writers here, I've realized something."

"What's that?" he asked.

"I didn't think I was smart enough to write a book. But now I see that there's no way *every* one of these thirty thousand titles on your shelves is written by someone smarter, funnier, or more deserving than me. Statistically, that's not even possible!"

Stan laughed. "You're 100 percent right about that," he said.

To this day, Stan says that my signing for *Lives Charmed*, the book I was struggling to birth here, remains "one of the biggest selling events" of the Bodhi Tree's forty-year history.

Remember that the next time you feel unqualified!

Tomi Adeyemi ❧

There was a period when *Children of Blood and Bone* was out to different publishers. Choosing a publisher is as stressful and important as choosing the right person to adapt a project. If you're strong-willed, your hands are still on the steering wheel, but then twelve other people jump into a four-seat car, and everyone wants to play a different song.

But Sabaa [Tahir] told me something crucial when I asked if I could pick her brain and use her as a mentor. That moment unlocked the beast within me. At the end of a two-hour call, Sabaa said, "And, Tomi?"

"Yeah?"

"MAKE THEM PAY!"

I remember it viscerally, the unlock button going off. The permission to value my worth and believe in my story. Now that I have a career, I still find myself repeatedly activating those buttons, turning those switches because, as creatives, we come from a beggar's mentality. As a woman, a marginalized woman, it's easy to feel lucky just to be able to breathe this air. But no. I had to adopt the mentality that, "No. I don't think I'm lucky to make you a *lot* of money!"

You have to get aggressive, even if only internally. Because otherwise, things don't go well. You can't create something like Beyoncé if you're not willing to ROAR when you need to roar. You can't create if you're not going to say, "And where is my equity?" You have to be ferocious. You have to believe that all of it is yours. That you're worthy of it.

I listen to a lot of Beyoncé, and a lot of Cardi B. I know I'm fucking worth it. I pump their words into my veins because the entire world, our entire society, is screaming the opposite.

Sabaa Tahir

The worth issue is a challenge you see a lot in immigrant communities. At least in my immigrant community, there's the feeling of, "Oh, I don't deserve it. And, if I get it, it's because of the will of God," which I'm not arguing with. But I have two older brothers. I feel like a lot of men walk in this world differently than women do. My brothers, and also my husband—who are men of color and have dealt with their own situations and issues of being marginalized—were like, "Why wouldn't you get a lot of money for your book?" To them, it's like, how could you not expect to get paid well for producing something that you tore out of the bedrock of your soul?

I'd pitched *Ember* as a series. I'd even laid out for the publisher what the other three books were going to be. But because we were asking for a lot of compensation, they said they could only do one book. I remember asking my agent, "Do you think they'll buy the other ones?"

"It doesn't matter what I think. What do *you* think? Do *you* believe?"

I had to ask myself, "Do I believe in this story? Do I believe in what I've written? Do I believe in this thing I've poured my soul into for six years? Do I believe in the stories of these people who are going through the worst things possible and that deserves to be told in a way that's accessible to young readers?" I had to dig deep. "Wait. I would not have spent six years on this thing if I didn't believe. I absolutely believe." And that was that.

Rosie Walsh, British documentary producer and author of six novels, including the international bestsellers *The Love of My Life*, *The Man Who Didn't Call* (in the UK), and *Ghosted* (in the US). 🍃

Writing is a very difficult job. We spend a lot of time sitting in a room, not talking to people. Crucially, we don't get feedback often. Even if you clean toilets for a living, people say thank you, or they give you a tip. Whereas as a writer, you could go months, if not years, without getting feedback from anyone. I think that's quite crazymaking.

I'm like a car. I have to get serviced. I have a coach who I speak to who really helps. Just a couple of days ago, we came up with a new approach, specific hours I work each day because I've struggled as a new mum to make myself sit and write. And not just that, but we came up with affirmations, mostly to do with confidence and trusting myself. I think that's a problem for most writers. Deep down, we don't trust ourselves. For example, when you chop out a bit of text, I often paste that prose into a separate Word document. It's as if I don't trust myself to come up with another great phrase or metaphor. But I'm never going to go into that document again. So, I'm trying to use affirmations of trust because, most of the time, my default is to believe that I can't.

In my eyes, our level of confidence comes down to what we're prioritizing—our dreams and projects or what other people think of our dreams and projects. Despite how the smarty-pants Mean Girls immortalized me in the time capsule of our high school superlatives (*bullshitters rule!*), I survived. Was it painful? Eh, a little more than pushing out my son during natural childbirth. But their reasons for why I couldn't succeed helped me zero in on why I would. Their smallness gave me a bigger WHY. Have you given any thought lately to *your* why? Now might be a good time to revisit what moves you to write in the first place.

Fact: You have no say in what people say. But you sure as hell have something to say about to whom, and what, you give your energy. Whenever you're feeling blocked, keep turning to your studies; wisdom from your favorite writers will help ease your fear. And ask yourself the following questions:

"Where am I putting my focus?"
"What's going on with my beliefs around my writing?"
"Do I still love this project?"

If your pages no longer please you, consider what it will take to get back to the love.

With each phase of writing and publishing my first book, I never forgot my why—being a champion for Mama Earth. My commitment to and faith in Her overrode anyone else's doubt. *Easy for you to say,* you might think. *You had that magical dream of six books.* True. Seeing them together gave me a world of faith. I mean, who cares about Mean Girls when God's giving you direct marching orders? But you have marching orders too. Just ask your desire where it comes from.

So, how can you rustle up your belief? Focus on your magic? Supercharge your self-confidence? I strengthened mine with Guru Singh's spiritual B12 shots; meditating until my ass went numb; studying eco-warriors and marveling at their courage; reading so many books on craft I was left practically cross-eyed (plus, hiring an editing coach—more on that coming up); and rewriting chapters constantly. I shared my work with only those who felt safe. The more I kept at it, the surer my footing.

Once you've zeroed in on your why and reconnected with your excitement, your words will more easily flow. The bullying voices, past or present, will become as teeny as a tsetse fly. You won't even hear them. *Are you done yet? Because I'm busy.*

By putting your fabulous focus on yourself and your dreams, countless others will be inspired by the confidence and preparation it took for you to believe in yourself and your writing.

6

Schedules and Sneaking Around

Finding the Time to Write

"The greatest thief this world ever produced is
procrastination, and he is still at large."
~ Henry Wheeler Shaw

What if you're too busy to write? Or your focus looks like trying to meditate while snowboarding? You wake up before the sun, filled with grand intentions. But by 6:00 PM you're shaking your head. *Not again. The day flew by with a thousand distractions and nothing to show for it! Will I ever break this cycle? Will my book ever get the attention it deserves?*

Time's a bitch. None of us comes out alive. Every writer I know and that you're about to hear from is in a daily battle to wrangle this sucker—their schedule—to get to the Promised Land, affixing "The End" to their tale, preferably without blowing up their life. Some writers are better at it than others. While the healthiest authors I know can rally 24/7 when nearing a deadline, they mostly choose not to. They've learned to write fast in any location or situation and miss few dinners with the fam. They've achieved a measure of "life balance" without sacrificing health or happiness, at least not for long. (Their kids,

89

incidentally, are less likely to grow up and pen a tell-all.) And, then there are the Time Debtors—those teeth-grinding, hair-thinning, eyes-burning-as-if-in-a-sandstorm writers who forever push the limits of their schedule, energy, and relationships.

Some, like me, fall somewhere in the middle of these two camps.

It must've been our kid's nose, an inch from mine, that woke me up.

"Morning, little buddy," I whispered, praying that if I didn't make any sudden movements, our towheaded two-year-old would fall back to sleep. No such luck. Seemed like I'd just gone to bed, having closed my laptop at the first streaks of daylight. Through slits, I found Tosh already dressed—proudly filling out his new Baby Gap sweatshirt and stone-washed jeans. They'd just arrived in a big FedEx box, a gift from one of Carol's sorority sisters whose corporate gig at the Gap in San Francisco meant she could help the financially and fashionably challenged for pennies on the dollar.

God, he looks cute, I thought, running my fingers through his baby-fine curls.

"Hurry, Mama! Park!" T commanded, jumping off the bed. "You, me, and Daddy!" Just then, Jesse appeared, carrying a mini hot pink baseball bat my folks had given us. Our son was quite the attraction, swinging for the fences and often clearing them. Neighbors called him "Bamm-Bamm."

I tackled Tosh back into our pillows. "You two sluggers go and have fun and come back and tell me all about it. Mama's gonna study." I kissed them good-bye in a group hug and tried not to shut the door behind them with too much enthusiasm. Once out of sight, I beelined to my computer. Are you kidding me? Ninety whole minutes of quiet, all mine!

Sue Monk Kidd 🌿

I'm hearing from so many women who are talking about the need to have time for themselves. They struggle with that, particularly younger women. It's a theme among writers who have a longing to write. I remember that when I had two toddlers, it's very hard.

I think there is some kind of innate conflict if you go the mothering route. If you're with the child, you want to be writing. If you're writing, you need to be with the child. It's hard. Fortunately, it's relatively temporary. Although, at the time, it feels like forever. My daughter likes to tell the story of the time I forgot to pick her up at school. She was the last child out there because I was in my writing room. She said, "I'm going to be on a therapist's couch because you never thought to come get me!"

Maria Shriver, mother and grandmother, award-winning journalist, writer, former First Lady of California, Alzheimer's advocate and activist, and author of numerous *New York Times* bestselling books, including *I've Been Thinking*, *Ten Things*, and *And One More Thing Before You Go.*

I usually try to write early in the morning. After my meditation, I'll think of something, or somebody will send me something, or I'll watch the news, and it'll jog my memory or motivate me.

For [*I've Been Thinking*, a compilation of essays]—and I do the same with speeches—I blocked out time on my schedule to compile and write other pieces because I noticed that unless I treated it as an appointment with myself, I couldn't get it done. I wrote out on my schedule—9:00 AM to 12:00 PM—so nobody could interrupt me. Then I hoped nobody bothered me.

Joel Stein

It's clearly a huge mistake to write in your house. It's just stupid. If you have kids, if you have anyone—*if you have a refrigerator*—it's just a bad idea to write in your house. I don't abide by that. I built a home office, which now I feel committed to, although my wife's turned it into a pottery area. I think just getting dressed and showering and going somewhere else is a big help.

Jenny Lawson, author of the *New York Times* bestsellers *Let's Pretend This Never Happened*, *Furiously Happy*, *You Are Here*, and *Broken*. Proprietress of the Nowhere Bookshop. Jenny's popular blog, *The Bloggess*, "is mainly dark humor mixed with brutally honest periods of mental illness."

I will have an idea of what I want to write about, with some small little notes. Until I come up with exactly how I'm going to make it into the chapter, it will just live in my head. It may be months before it finally hits that I need to do it chronologically or in a list form. *Oh! I know how I'm going to do it!* When I have that inspiration, and it rarely happens, I'm usually out walking when it comes. I will run into the house and scream, "No one talk to me!" If anything interrupts me, it's gone. Completely gone. If I'm lucky, I will get fifteen minutes' worth of writing in. That's enough to at least give me an idea that this is how this is going to look.

Jillian Lauren

I'm very disciplined to the extent being a mom will allow me to have a regular schedule. I have an office, so I leave the house. I sometimes work in my yoga pants in the house, but I go to an office because it helps me stay clear of the minutiae of daily life.

Then I work in a very timed way. I say, "I'll write for an hour and a half, and then I get to have some almonds, give myself a little treat." I dangle a little carrot in front of myself. I try to write six days a week. I'm a big believer that you get a book written by putting one word down and then following it with another word and following that with another word. There isn't too much magic involved.

By putting a strong framework around my day, that gives me freedom in the actual work itself. To be messy and creative and wild and stuck. I also turn off my social media. The internet will not break without you.

Sabaa Tahir

I have a hard time separating work and family, partially because I'm at home with my kids a lot, so I have to write when they're around. It's very much like, "Oh my God, did you finish your homework? And can you please set the table?" while I'm also writing a battle scene.

My kids can always tell when I'm not there. They'll walk up to me and say, "Mama, Mama, Mama, Mama!" I might not even be at the keyboard. I might just be staring off into space, but my oldest son says, "You have that look on your face like you're about to kill someone in your book!"

"Come to the gym with us!" said Jesse the next morning, picking up his Adidas bag and leaning over to lace up his high-tops. Tosh climbed onto Daddy's back and up onto his shoulders.

"Thanks, you two Muscle Men," I said, "but Mama needs to stay here and wrestle chapter three." Jesse scrunched up his face. "It's all good!" I sang. "We'll do popcorn and *Mary Poppins* tonight!"

Later, my friend Kelly called, wanting to meet for lunch at a spot she knew I loved on Ventura Boulevard. "What's it called? I feel like I haven't seen you in a thousand years!" she whined.

"I know! Marmalades. I miss you too! But next time."

And on it went. I refused to shirk my duties as Domestic Goddess and cooked every breakfast, lunch, and dinner; walked our dogs each morning and evening; vacuumed daily and ditto on the laundry; grew organic squash and basil; blended my own pesto and breastfed my kid until he was old enough to drive. (Okay, that's a slight exaggeration.) Something had to give—some*things*. I missed countless requests: Birthday celebrations. Dinner parties. Double dates. Even a family reunion. But *Lives Charmed* was barely readable, and if I ever hoped to finish it (and make up for the income I'd lost by no longer working while I wrote it), I had rules of punctuation to master. Story arcs to figure out. Interviews to secure. Tapes to transcribe. Have I made it clear we couldn't bank indefinitely on my husband's acting income?

And can we talk about typing for a sec? Despite taking it in high school, I was an absolute slowpoke. A two-hour interview took weeks to transcribe. My paranoia didn't help any. I was tortured by thoughts that someone would steal my ideas and get to market first. Visions of word robbers climbing through our windows to run off with my computer haunted me. So obsessed was I about loss from fire, theft, or asteroid that I snail-mailed myself self-addressed envelopes containing titles and chapter ideas just in case I ever had to prove ownership through a stamped date on a postmark. When a computer crash wiped out twenty especially hard-earned pages (this was before I'd mastered floppy disks—kids, look it up!—or there was such a thing called cloud storage), I wept like I'd run over our Border collies. Every afternoon my HP printer churned out recycled laser copies of whatever chapter I was on to stash for safekeeping under the couch, behind the stereo, and in the trunk of my car. *Obsess much?*

The way I saw it, stealing time for my art before some lucky bastard stole my thunder was paramount. *Stealing.* That's what it felt like: ripping hours off from people, hobbies, and pastimes I treasured but could no longer make room for because I was driven. Pangs of guilt would hit when saying no so often, but my book beckoned like a sexy suitor in a clandestine affair. It didn't seem to matter that I was writing in the middle of the night until my family got up for the day; as long as I had guaranteed hours to myself followed by quality time with them, my goofy smile was visible morning 'til night. But I would have to safeguard my sanity from those who judged me for all the time my writing was taking.

"Writers are selfish," a friend's husband remarked at one of the few barbecues I'd attended that summer. "The very act turns people into assholes."

I wasn't an asshole for all the hours I spent writing, was I? I didn't feel like it, but I was highly attuned to how fast time was moving in my quest for blocks to concentrate, and I worried about being seen as inconsiderate or self-involved. People, like the muse, are noisy, not to mention needy, and more often than not, adorable. I adored my people, but was it selfish to always want to get back to the page? Was it wrong to eye the door, plotting my next disappearing act, which, come to think of it, rarely fooled anybody? Anyone with eyes at Tosh's eventual Little League practices could see me in the stands glancing down at the pile of papers and red pen in my lap.

It seemed to me that the sooner I made peace with how often I'd rather be writing than doing most anything else—even being with those I cherished—and get some structure around the insanity of it, the more present I could be with loved ones when I wasn't writing.

Martha Beck 🌿

I think it's an oxymoron to say we're "stealing time" to have healthy boundaries. It's not stealing to be healthy. It's stealing from our health to do anything that harms us. I'd say everything except our true nature is stealing our time. I'm stealing time when I show up at some appointment that no one really needs. The only time I'm *not* stealing time is when I'm absolutely in accord with my true nature. Everything else is stealing.

I remember thinking the night before my fourth birthday, *Oh my God, I haven't gotten enough done! I'm almost four! I have to get going!* I have a weird sort of clock inside me. I'm very distractible, but in school, when it was time to get started on something, that internal clock would turn on, and I'd know: I have to do that *now.*

I had never thought of being a writer. I only wanted to write a memoir about my experience with my son, who was prenatally diagnosed with Down syndrome. One day the clock turned on inside me and said, "Write that book now!" At the time, I had three children under five. I was finishing my doctorate at Harvard while teaching as an assistant professor. And I had severe fibromyalgia that made it impossible for me to use my hands most of the time. It was incredibly slow and laborious. I think I probably lost literal decades of sleep because I pulled all-nighters constantly. I wouldn't advise that, by the way.

It was very strange. My hands would freeze when I tried to work on my dissertation. But when the clock went on, my pain would clear, and I'd work compulsively. I wrote the last hundred pages of that book [*Expecting Adam*] in one sitting, in seventy-two hours.

Jennifer Rudolph Walsh, editor of *Hungry Hearts: Essays on Courage, Desire, and Belonging*; founder of Together Live, former board member and global head of Literary, Lectures, and Conferences at William Morris Endeavor (WME), representing luminaries like Oprah, Brené Brown, and Dani Shapiro.

The truth of the matter is that when you actually uncover your purpose and shift your life to prioritize the things that serve that purpose, everything changes. Time almost magically opens up and slows down. You will find doing things "on purpose" gives you energy rather than depleting you.

Lee Child

Nothing of value is ever achieved in the morning. I get up leisurely and mess around drinking coffee. Maybe I do a couple of emails and read the news. Then I take a shower, get dressed, and it's usually around one o'clock before I start writing. Obviously, I could work late. We've all worked twelve, even twenty-four hours, when we need to. But I find that there's a quality threshold you hit, some kind of fatigue in your mind.

When it comes to balancing my writing life with my love life, it's hard. I don't want to be pretentious, but to a certain extent, we writers belong to the world. We belong to our readers. I think that's an awkward situation for a spouse. You're sharing the person in certain ways with the amount of stuff you have to do, quite apart from the time commitments, which are huge. So, it's a pretty difficult thing to manage, to be completely frank.

The lucky thing for Jane and me is that we've been together forty-five years, but it's like we've been together for five years, nine times. Life changes, obviously. I think where people run into trouble is that your partner's life changes, and you diverge. We've been very lucky that we've had these five-year segments where we're both into what we're doing.

We're strong individuals. She doesn't live through me.

Tom Bergeron

My wife, Lois, and I are also very strong individuals. We're perfectly comfortable on our own. We're just, and this is a bit of a cliche, I suppose, but it's true: We're better together.

To the point of belonging to the public, I was thinking when Lee [Child] was talking, about my daughter Jessica, who's now thirty. When she was a little kid, we were coming out of a restaurant outside of Boston where a number of people had come up and said hello because of a TV talk show I did in Boston in those years. And Jessie, who was probably four, said, "Daddy. Does everybody have to watch your show?" And I said, "Honey, that's why we can afford to eat in a restaurant."

Marie Forleo

My secret to getting it all done is that I don't. I'm extremely good at saying no. I love disappointing people, not from a harsh place, but I'm the queen of disappointment on my team to people that might want me to do X, Y, or Z. They'd say, "This is a really great opportunity." No.

I think it's useful and important not to tell ourselves the lie that we don't have the time. What I've seen in my life and for other people is that if it's important enough to you, you make the time, and if not, you make an excuse.

Right now, I'm in recovery from surgery. I'm not waking up at 5:00 AM, and I'm not writing, and I am not working. This is a season and a stage for me to heal. Creating something from nothing takes an enormous amount of energy. Right now, my physical body needs the focus. So, I'm not advocating for people punishing themselves or forcing themselves to be a productivity machine on autopilot. But for most of us, at some point in the game, you're like, "Oh, I would really love to do that, but I just don't have the time." Nine times out of ten, that's not the truth.

Elizabeth Gilbert ❧

My creative rhythm goes by seasons. There are seasons for writing. It's almost an agricultural clock. I think part of the reason I used to have trouble writing when I was younger was because I didn't recognize the seasonal aspect. The fact that you must have whole seasons of preparation before you can begin working. I would just sit down one afternoon and be like, "I want to be a writer." Open up a notebook. "Hmm. Got empty page, got nothing, right?" I would never do that to myself now.

I'm working on a novel about New York City showgirls in the 1940s [*City of Girls*], and I've been researching it for a year. I'm going to research it for another year or two before I begin writing. I'm collecting everything I can: Language, reading books from the 1940s, interviewing former showgirls, reading memoirs, watching old movies from the forties to figure out how people spoke and dressed. Laying the foundation. I'm not writing, except notes on index cards. I can go for two years without writing because I'm in the season of preparation. And then, when it comes time to write, there's another level of preparation, which is: Clear off the calendar, make space, and set aside time by saying no to everything. I'll have big chunks of months where I don't have anything planned. And that takes months to lay out too.

I would never sit down on a random afternoon and begin something without years of work building up for it. I clean the hell out of my house because I love to sit down in a clean space and write. I also know that once I get going, it's not gonna get cleaned for like another year. And then, when the house is clean, and the note cards are all in their boxes, and I've got my research done, and I've got my time set down, then it's farmer's hours. When I wake up at 5:30 AM that first day to begin, I'm in the best possible place. I have so much of my work already done, ready to go, so that I'm not alone with an empty notebook and nothing to say and knowing nothing about what I'm talking about.

And then it goes fast. People will say to me, "I can't believe you wrote *The Signature of All Things* in a couple of months." I was like, "I wrote that book in four years." It's just that I did the writing in a couple of months. But only because I did years of work to get ready. When it came time to do it, it was basically fill-in-the-blanks, count-by-numbers kind of stuff.

Terry McMillan

The bottom line is that I have rules, even for myself. I had an office, and my bedroom was right next to my office. My [then] husband, he knew, don't mess with me when that door is closed. My son knew it should be an emergency. When my door's closed, I am off-limits. When I open the door, just look at me. If I don't look back at you, that means I'm still writing. I'm thinking about something, so don't say anything. Even my dog knew, don't mess with Mommy; she might not pet me. My cat, Dilbert, knew too. Everyone knew: "If she walks by us and doesn't acknowledge us, don't fuck with her."

I learned not to feel guilty. Because when I gave my time to my husband or my son, I gave all of it. They just had to respect what I was doing. I'm sitting here lying my ass off [as a novelist], and I've got to keep these characters straight. Sometimes, your interruptions complicate that, and I don't want to be derailed.

Not only that, but people should have something else to do to keep them busy. I don't want to be your source of entertainment and undiluted joy. There's a time and place for everybody and everything. Some people go to work in an office. I love the fact that I can write in my pajamas, in my flip-flops with a mask on my face, and nobody is judging me. When I need to take a nap, I take a nap, which I'm going to do as soon as we're done here.

One afternoon Tosh and I walked into Barnes & Noble, and there it was: the relationship book I'd seen in my original book dream, with the same title and everything! It was pimped out on the front table with surrounding red construction-paper hearts for Valentine's Day. Of course, I understood I lacked the credentials to dispense relationship advice. But still. What the actual what? *I'm not even done with book one! What does this mean for* Lives Charmed? *Is someone about to publish her next?*

Some days found me panicked—stalking and stealing time like an addict pursuing her next fix. On others, though, I moved through my days as if I had all the time in the world, knowing God had the situation under control and that things would get even easier once our kid was grown. (Wink.)

I also experienced the opposite problem: difficulty setting myself up to write. Anne Lamott calls this "aerobic mole checking"—where we jump in and out of our chair to attend to something, anything, rather than write. This happens to me around national elections, where I'm far more likely to watch the news and prepare comfort food and feel guilty because I'm *not* writing than feel guilty because I'd rather be writing.

Point being, time has been around a reeeeeallly long time—almost forever—and yet despite sundials, DayRunners, and iCalendars, most of us still wrestle with how to spend it. I even gave a TEDWomen talk about "Time Debt"—how we often mismanage time, overspending it attending to others while underspending it on our own goals and dreams—and still struggle to manage it!

Robert McKee

Part of the digital phenomenon is that it's human nature to jump from thing to thing. The internet has offered us an opportunity to be what we used to be when we were primitive and walking across a landscape noticing this, noticing that, noticing, noticing. You never knew where food was, and you didn't know where danger was, and so people were extremely alert. The mind was trained to jump from this to that to this to that and not get fascinated because if you're standing there fascinated, something terrible could jump you from behind.

So, it's human to allow yourself to be distracted. It's in our genes. A writer has to have discipline. A writer has to be like Steven Pressfield, right? If you call Steve, you'll get a message that says, "Sorry. I'm writing. Don't bother to leave a message because I won't pick this up for another two months. But in two months, call me. I hope I'm done by then."

Steven Pressfield

I have very consciously tried to simplify my life. Especially as far as social media goes. If I'm going out to breakfast with guys from the gym, everybody will have their iPhones out except me. I refuse to do it.

As I'm getting older, I can do more in less time. I probably get twice as much done now than I used to. Two hours lately might equate to four hours. But I certainly don't need any more than that. In fact, any more than two hours and I'm totally exhausted. To clarify, there's the busy work of returning emails and ordering books to give away and all the stuff you "have" to do. And then there's *work*. I file the former under "bullshit." But I think that's probably true for most people, like athletes, for example. They're stretching and going to the gym to work out, but when they get to the field where they have to perform, it's a couple of hours, at most.

And when I'm done, I'm a big believer that the office is closed. I turn off my brain completely. I don't worry about anything I'm working on. I consider that I've paid my rent of being here on the planet, and I take the rest of the day to enjoy myself.

Cheryl Strayed 🌿

Growing up, we were told that somehow, we're supposed to be able to force ourselves to do the things in life that are difficult instead of doing the things that are easy. But it's a challenge for everybody. The ways we've all come up managing that are wide and varied. But, for me, they're wide and varied on a day-to-day basis. Some days I succeed at saying, "I'm not going to let anything interfere [with my writing]. I'm just going to get this work done." And other days, the entire day goes, and I have to go to bed feeling ashamed because I never did turn to the work that I was mostly meaningfully supposed to be doing. A big process for me is learning to balance forgiving myself for that, for letting myself down, and also being the kind of captain of my own personal boot camp and saying, "Today, you aren't going to [turn on that TV]."

Sadly, nothing works for me better than a deadline. That's been my saving grace many times—when somebody's about to start harassing me because they expect something in their hands. That's usually when I best get to work.

Seth Godin

People do not like this [answer] because it's extremely simple. Here we go. I don't go to any meetings, and I don't watch television. So, I save seven to eight hours a day over most people. In those hours, I do a couple of things. One: I write like I talk. If you write like you talk, you never have to deal with writer's block because you never have talker's block.

Number two: I don't use Twitter. I don't use Facebook. I'm not willing to get sucked into the maelstrom of social media just so somebody else can make a profit. Instead, I have made a decision about what I want to accomplish and have picked the channels to do it in [i.e., teaching, books, the blog]. I have stuck with them, even when they were hard. Trying a lot of little things doesn't pay off nearly as much as sticking with a few big things.

Meg Wolitzer

My husband, Richard Panek, is also a writer. It depends on the project, but we sort of tag team each other, which is helpful in terms of having a clean apartment. If one of us is finishing something, the other knows to take up the domestic slack.

I sometimes feel that we're kind of like two people who work in a law firm: "Hello, Jim. Hello, Sue." Actually, we pass each other without talking. We don't even say, "Hello, Jim. Hello, Sue." We just sort of ignore each other during the day. We like to come together at night. Not to show each other work, necessarily; I usually show my editor my work first, because it's so intense, so incestuous to be married to a writer and have it all be about work all the time. At night we often like to watch British television and not think about our work. Although we do talk about writing problems we're having, and certainly have a lot of advice we can give each other.

My life is set up to write. When people tell me they don't have time, I say, "What's the book you want to write, and what's holding you back?" A friend of mine, with her first book, made a vow to herself. She was going to write one page a day, and at the end of a year, she was going to have a book. And she did!

Danielle LaPorte

One phone call can ruin your whole day. I need space. Mondays are my for-sure free-flow writing days. I look at my day planner, and I'm like, "Oh! Nothing. I don't even have to put on mascara." I know that if there's no mascara involved, I'm gonna write the best stuff I've written all week.

I need home time. I need to not be traveling that much. For the last three months while writing *White Hot Truth*, it was nothing, zero. I missed birthdays, apologized to friends, I'm not coming up for air. There was a lot of yoga pant wearing and not a lot of yoga classes.

Abby Wambach

When you have kids, at the end of the day, when they go to sleep, it's never in my consciousness to think, *Oh, I wonder what happened in the sports world?* I rarely watch live sports anymore. Children—their lifestyle and schedules—don't allow for it.

I'm going on [a] book tour next week, and I'll be on the road for three weeks. After big periods of work, where we have to concentrate a lot of energy into one thing, Glennon and I will go on a trip a few times a year. That allows us to rejuvenate, to reconnect, to hit the spa, and get obscene amounts of massages. It's important for us as individuals and for our marriage. We find ourselves out in the world, giving of ourselves a lot. You can only do that so much before you lose steam or give too much. We're not perfect by any means; we're still trying to find the right balance between how much we give and how much we have to replenish.

We're constantly working. Glennon's always creating. So, getting those periods away, where we can unplug from our phones and off of social media, are lifesaving, life force–filling times for us to reenergize and refuel for the next six months. We also want to make sure we aren't at the mercy of this cell phone, this device that takes our attention, where I'm saying yes to this phone, and I'm saying no to Glennon, the human being sitting next to me. I think I've spent more of the last twenty years of my life on the phone than I did in actual communication and interaction with real-life people.

Van Jones

I'm very lucky that my [ex-]wife, Jana, is full-time committed to our boys. She's an attorney and was completely capable of going out and building a career for herself in law but decided that she wanted to be a full-time mom, and also a full-time help to me.

Everybody doesn't have that, doesn't have that person in their life who's capable and willing to make those kinds of commitments and sacrifices. I'm deeply appreciative of her for that. So, before I start bragging about how great I am at time management, I'd like to point out that I'm cheating. I've got massive help.

Tim Grahl

I always joke that I would be the easiest person to murder because there is very little variance to my schedule. I do the same things at the same time every week, so I don't have to think about it.

I keep my keys in the same place and have only two pairs of jeans and twelve colors of the same T-shirt I roll through. Since I don't care about how I dress, just give me something that makes me not look like an idiot. Since I don't care about my schedule as long as I can get my work done, let me set that. Same with eating or exercising.

Here's something I don't care about: cleaning my house. I do care about having a clean house, though, so by hiring somebody, I don't have to worry about it. They've got a key to my house and come in and clean every two weeks. Done. Of course, you do those things as you can afford to invest in them. Anytime a thing is not helping you get where you want to go but still has to be done, systematize it. Get it off your plate, or just stop doing it in order to have the time for the things that matter.

Gretchen Rubin

I get up at 6:00 AM and go against the conventional wisdom, especially for a morning person like me, that your morning is your most creative and energetic time. I cannot settle down to do anything until I've gone through my email and my social media. I spend an hour before my family wakes up answering emails and going through my social media, of which I have a lot.

Then I get my family up, make breakfast, walk my daughter to school, and I'll either go to the gym, or if I'm doing original writing, try to figure three hours sometime in the day where I can write. When I'm in my home office, I have three monitors, and I'm totally connected. When I'm trying to do original writing, I will often go to this little library that's just a block from my apartment and work there, where I never connect to the internet.

When it comes to scheduling deadlines, there are marathoners and sprinters. A lot of people deny their nature. I'm a marathoner—somebody who likes to start well in advance and have plenty of time. I work steadily, and I work often. Marathoners don't like to be up against the deadline and like to have a margin at the end. That's what ignites our creativity. That's how we get ideas—ruminating over and over in time.

Sprinters, by contrast, are people who prefer to work up against a deadline. They like the adrenaline of the deadline and feel that's when their ideas come, and they're most productive. (This is not the same as procrastination.) If they start too early, they can burn out, lose interest, or feel really inefficient. They think, *Wow, it's not due for two weeks!* so they kind of mess around, fitfully, but then they only start truly working on it right up against the deadline.

It's important to know yourself. Then you can foresee what kind of issues might arise. If you're a procrastinator, you have to work on your procrastination. And that's a whole other subject.

Dean Koontz

The character Jane Hawk, in this new series, is so real to me that I can't wait to get to my desk in the morning, and I'm reluctant to stop working at the end of the day. But throughout my career, I've always clocked ten-hour days. Sitting for an extended period of time, I fall more completely into the fictional world than if I'm working two or three hours in the morning and an hour or two in the afternoon.

I get up in the morning, walk the dog, and I'm at my desk by six thirty, seven o'clock. Then I work straight until dinner. I usually do that six days a week. It's one of the ways the fictional world becomes real to me. For me, a character's almost everything in fiction. If you're not swept away by the character, even the cleverest story won't work. I want characters who, in the first few pages, come alive, to the point of where you're saying, "Where is this person coming from?" That's Jane. Her attitude, her fortitude, and the way she looks at the world were so different that I became absolutely fascinated with her in three or four chapters. I'm finishing the fourth book with her now, and she's gaining a depth I never saw coming. That is one of the greatest gifts a writer can get.

Dani Shapiro, bestselling novelist, author of *Still Writing,* and the memoirs *Devotion, Slow Motion,* and the *New York Times* bestseller *Inheritance.* Shapiro's also a writing teacher and the creator/host of the wildly popular *Family Secrets* podcast.

Don't compare your life as it is today with somebody who's been doing this for twenty years or longer. I have students who, one I'm thinking of in particular, was a psychologist and an AIDS researcher and had two young children, and she wrote both of her first novels, which have been published, in the hours between five and six thirty every morning before her household woke up. She created this absolutely sacred disciplined space where that was going to be her time to get her writing done.

There's never a good time to get married, have a baby, or get a puppy. But you do those things, and your life expands. Same with writing a book. The underlying takeaway here, as I see it, is about *focus.* It's clear, there's no "right" way to schedule your writing—first thing in the morning, late at night, all day long.

Not all inner clocks tick alike. Every writer has to find their rhythm. Ray Bradbury said, "Anyone who wants to be a writer should write at least one thousand words a day. Every day." On the contrary, ask Alice Waters if she writes daily and she'll likely say, "Oh, God, no," as if that's the most horrific idea she's ever heard. It's a brain thing and a personality thing and a time-of-life-thing and a what-else-is-going-on-in-the-world thing.* (In Alice's case, it's also a food thing. As founder of one of the world's best restaurants, Chez Panisse, in Berkeley, California, and the Edible Schoolyard movement, she's known to rarely sit down, unless it's to eat.)

I have author friends who shut everything down while on deadline, sequestering themselves in a hermetic bubble. Whereas I've written 100 percent–focused in my best friend's noisy kitchen, her kids and dogs running around the table, her hunky husband serving me soup, as Coldplay blared through my headphones. Hyper-focus is easy for me. Although, when reliving painful memories for my divorce memoir in process (material that requires me to, as my sister puts it, "pull my spleen out through my nose"), there's no music or merriment happening. For those bits, I prefer the dark stillness of pre-dawn, cozily mummified in the blankets of my bed-office. It's cheaper than therapy and feels just about as healing.

Figure out how, when, and where you're in peak flow. Then ask: "How can I best protect this sacred space?" Obviously, turn off your phone and alerts and consider using a timer. And never underestimate the power of headphones and/ or a "Do Not Disturb" sign on your door. But your options are many: Should you put a ritual around your focused writing time? Will lighting incense help you stay on track? How about putting your writing sessions in black ink on your calendar? Do you need to hire help or trade kid duty with a neighbor? Would getting up an hour earlier or staying up later do the trick? If partnered, have you tried asking them to feed the dogs and little ones more often?

---

* Fun fact: Beethoven wrote for only four hours a day! In fact, lots of composers and writers had super sane schedules. They'd sit a spell at their desk and then break for lunch, followed by a walk and game-playing in the parlor. Maybe they'd write for another hour or two. Their days seemed quite lovely and mostly drama-free.

And then there was Mozart. Oh, beloved Amadeus. You could say he was one of the lucky ones, attaining rock-star popularity during his lifetime. But Mozart also spent money like a rock star and soon found himself up early tutoring students, only to have to race off to perform for the king and kiss his ring, and then dash back to create a concerto for some rich patron before he could steal time for his own art.

A client of mine was surprised how easy it was to slip out for half days on Saturdays to the library while her husband watched their two babes. "I get more done on my book on those weekends than I have in years," she said. (And bonus: Her kids became college football experts!) That's not to say her house didn't look like a laundry/breakfast bomb had hit in her absence. "There were socks on the toaster and crumbs in their shoes! How does that happen?" she cried-laughed to me. But once she stopped expecting her man to parent as she does (or practically any other responsible adult), her word count and happiness soared.

Reminder: You're not selfish! You've got skills! Stories to tell! A POV that heals! Your voice is unique only to you and your God/Muse and has put you in situations you've triumphed over and given you a dream to help others triumph too.

Your job is to figure out your best working style. Then set your life up accordingly. And be flexible. One schedule might work well for two months or even two years, and then it might not work at all. If you'd like step-by-step instructions for creating your own half day, weekend, or month-long writing getaways, please check out my "Going Dark to Write" blog post on BookMama .com/BWBookLinks.

Okay! You're doing this! You've given yourself permission; silenced the meanies; located and loved on your why. You're committed to studying and practicing your craft, all supported by your book-tactic schedule. Your focus is for real. This is where things start to get *really* fun.

7

The Honeymoon Phase

Excitement, Execution, and Gaining Momentum

"Beauty begins the moment you decide to be yourself."

~ Coco Chanel

This is just beginner's luck, your brain argues. *It can't continue to be this easy.* You've been on fire, waking up hours early or going to bed far later than usual—sometimes both!—and yet you still feel like you could scale the Himalayas without supplemental oxygen.

Inside your own little writing bubble, you can scarcely even remember that blabby inner critic: *But remember those other projects you started and never finished? How do you know this isn't just another hobby, draining your time and cash?*

Critic, schmritic! Enjoy the honeymoon phase when it shows up—the sweet spot where you're finding your rhythm and being carried by early momentum. The work seems sacred, even blessed. You can't wait to sit down and pour yourself into the art of stringing letters, words, and sentences together to tell your stories. Make no mistake, mastery is daunting, and resistance takes many forms. But, man, did I ever feel like I was living the dream.

"It's happening! My book's really happening!"

I placed the tape recorder on the coffee table between Paul Williams and me, my hands shaking ever so slightly. Even though I'd been walking his dogs for years, I'd never formally interviewed him. *I'd never interviewed anyone!* The Oscar statue in the corner and the gold and platinum records surrounding us from their wood-paneled perches reminded me I was mind-melding with a creative legend. I couldn't wait to ask Paul about his writing process!

On a clear day like this, you could see all the way from his hillside Tudor mansion in Hollywood to Santa Monica. As the rays of the sun reflected off the ocean beyond like a bowl of cut sapphires, I was struck by the contrasts. Paul's home faced the edge of a continent, butting up against an ancient sea formed hundreds of millions of years ago. And yet, he and the others I'd be interviewing in Tinseltown, despite their considerable wisdom and accomplishments, would be forgotten relatively soon. Earlier owners of his home—movie actor Peter Lorre (*The Maltese Falcon* and *Casablanca*) and director Orson Welles (*Citizen Kane*)—were little known to today's young moviegoers.

All the more reason I hoped to bring out the best in us both. Uncover timeless truths that would be as relevant and valuable in 50 years or those 150 years Guru talked about. Learn how Paul kept up (or reenergized) his momentum—turning flashes of inspiration into a decades-long reign of *Billboard* hits, Grammy Awards, and other plaudits. I pressed RECORD and double-checked to make sure the red light was on. Exhaling for what felt like the first time all day, I lowered my shoulders and sank into the overstuffed chair.

"Was there anything about your mindset as a kid that contributed to your later success?" I asked.

Paul smiled sweetly, recalling his youthful courage in the face of his father's alcoholism. "Unable to handle the fear in my family," he said, "I remember consciously replacing my anxiety with thoughts of grandiosity. I came to believe that I was so special that one day I'd be able to do things nobody else could do. You know, because we manifest destiny for ourselves, I managed to do that in some ways. I had two choices: Either I could continue to be this little guy who was afraid of everybody, or I could be a force that would not be deterred from whatever it wanted."

Goose bumps. *I* wanted to be a force that would not be deterred from whatever I wanted! I snuck a peek at my recorder, making sure every word was being captured.

When Paul, who stands at just five-foot-two, admitted on tape that cocaine had once made him want to "shoot basketballs for money," we couldn't stop laughing. I thought I knew him so well. We'd talked for hours on his carpeted stairs—him crying about a lost love he'd never recovered from and me reliving similar pains—but that afternoon a world of stories and philosophies opened up. It hit me: We're all so busy, we rarely take the time to ask—*really ask*—our friends and loved ones the deeper questions.

It seemed like every query I had elicited lightning-fast brilliance. Why couldn't my everyday conversations crackle like this?

"I hope you don't take this the wrong way, babe," I said to Jesse that evening, "but I think that was the most rewarding conversation of my life." My husband, who saw the glow on my face and my new sense of adventurousness, encouraged me on.

Taylor Dayne

An audience will never reward an artist for holding back. You create momentum by showing up and going for it—as if you're opening up for Michael Jackson or singing with Prince in every show.* I don't see how someone can fake it to make it, honestly. When you get onstage and you get in the pocket, emotional honesty means you're expressing all your vulnerability. That's second nature to me now. A muscle I've developed. When you're an actress, you must live truthfully in imaginary circumstances. When I'm onstage as Taylor Dayne, it's as truthful as it gets. I'm counting how many people are in the seats. I'm wondering if I'm touching the last row. It's my name on the marquee. It's like getting on a bull and riding in a rodeo.

---

* Both of which Taylor has done.

Joel Stein 🌿

There was a group at Yale called "Porn and Chicken" that was watching porn and eating fried chicken once a week. They wouldn't reveal their names; they wouldn't let any press write about them. I called them and said, "Will you let me write about you guys if I bring a porn star?" They said yes. Then I just had to find a porn star and some fried chicken, and I had a scoop. That's how you do it in journalism. That's how you create your own momentum.

The next few interviews flowed just as naturally. I'd never felt more at home doing anything. Prepping for interviews wasn't studying—it was PLAY! The kicker: My interviewees seemed as happy about our chats as I was. Why was this so easy?

"You're throwing yourself into a great love," Carol pointed out, just as I'd done with Pet Companion. For no reason other than fun, I'd always watched every episode made by Dick Cavett, Merv Griffin, Johnny Carson, Joan Rivers, Phil Donahue, Oprah Winfrey, Leeza Gibbons, Barbara Walters, Larry King, and David Letterman—and read their books, unintentionally studying the craft of interviewing much of my life. Perhaps some of that "boob tube" hero-worship focus had rubbed off?

Success creates its own momentum. It all starts with movement—putting an idea down on paper, into your laptop, onto the voice memo app of your phone. Visiting a museum or traveling to a specific location can open up a new world. As can making an appointment to interview someone for a chapter or for character development. According to the laws of physics, objects in motion tend to stay in motion. Cultivate momentum, and your progress and ideas will spring to life and carry you forward.

Terry McMillan 🌿

It's the process of this craft that I love. It's one act of discovery after another. I try to tell these young writers that if I already know how the story ends, why bother? If I get married and know we're going to get divorced, why bother?

I love when I throw a pen or a pencil across the room because my characters told me what to write and I did it. I wrote what they wanted me to see, and sometimes I jump up from the chair and walk across the room and jump up and down. I'm like, "Thank you, thank you!" My feeling has always been that it's the journey, not the end, that counts. How I get from here to there—it's all the stuff that happens in between. I can make some shit up, just to put a ribbon on it. But that's not what I'm interested in doing, even though it might appear that because of my "so-called voice" people think, "Oh, she's so down." They don't understand. I'm listening to what these people are telling me and what they want me to say.

Charles Sailor

To build momentum in a piece (which, in turn, helps everything else flow in a life-imitating-art kind of way), I want my reader to see, feel, taste, and smell every scene. To make my descriptions come alive, I try to get all the senses into every scene. I wrote for *The Rockford Files*, *Kojak*, and *Charlie's Angels* in the seventies. There are really good writers out there who do it all the time, but I couldn't get the visual in there as well as I would have liked. With a book, there's so much more space to build momentum.

In writing a novel, even your smallest character can have something special about them. Even if they're only on one page, you want the reader to think, "Oh! That reminds me of somebody!" Or, "Gosh, you know I've seen that before." Paying tribute to your characters is imperative. They all have to be able to stand as individuals. Your reader has to be able to see them and understand them.

Patricia Cornwell, one of the world's most prolific authors, selling over one hundred million copies in her Scarpetta thriller series alone. She's been described as a real-life female James Bond, and penned the first forensic thriller (*Postmortem*), paving the way for an explosion of entertainment featuring all things forensic across film, TV, and literature. 🍃

What you're really doing as a storyteller is taking people to places they can't go. Whether it's a castle or a morgue or some beautiful place, that's what we're supposed to do—transport them. Descriptions are the most fun, and the worst things, especially when you're not sure what something's going to look like and you're in the damn car! It's like, "Damn it. They're in the car again and I have to describe what they're seeing out their damn window."

Writing is a pane of glass and people should pass through it without being aware of your words. If you don't transport people, if they're too aware of your words, they get in the way. It's not so much about what you describe but how you do it. The cadence, the rhythm of the sentence.

Two things I would tell anybody who wants to be a writer, particularly of novels, is to write poetry, write poetry, write poetry. It teaches you to think in terms of images and it's the music of prose. The other thing is to read a good screenplay because it's so visual. Man, if you can make people walk through a room the way Jonathan Demme does in *Silence of the Lambs*, you can do something.

Dean Koontz 🍃

I don't outline. I don't do character profiles. When the character comes onstage and starts to form, I do what Robert [McKee] said and get out of the character's way. This sounds odd to some beginning writers who say: "You're creating the character. You can't be surprised by the character." Oh yes, you can. This character does things that floor me. And sometimes when I'm writing a book that has comic dialogue, I'm laughing out loud as if I hear it, not as if I'm writing it. Those are the moments when you know the characters because they're speaking like real people. The way they sound and come off, and what they're doing—it's not wooden or planned. That's when you know the fiction is working.

My contemporary, Mark Helprin [author of *Winter's Tale*] who has been around as long as I have, says something I totally agree with—that a lot of modern fiction leaves him cold because it doesn't deal with descriptives of the world we live in, both the natural world and the world we've made. The English language is so rich that when you allow yourself only flat discussion of action and character and you don't use all the tools in the toolbox, you're leaving something crucial out.

I don't go on for six pages describing a room, but I love to use a moment of description. When I describe the sky, or a landscape of snow, it needs to serve certain functions. One of them is the mood of the scene. And it needs to be saying something—no matter how subtle—about character or the character's state of mind because every scene is written from the point of view of one character.

Steven Pressfield

To foster early momentum, I'm a big believer in The Foolscap Method. Foolscap meaning a single sheet of yellow legal pad. One of my mentors, Norm Stahl, said, "Steve, God made a single sheet of foolscap to be exactly the right length to hold the entire outline of a novel." That was a great breakthrough for me. If you can put something down on one page, it eliminates all the preciousness, research, resistance, and avoidance that comes up. And it also makes you answer the question, "How does this damn thing end?"

> So many of us will start at the beginning and we don't know where the hell we're going. Once I know the end of the story, I work backwards. If you have the climax when the Terminator comes after Sarah Connor, then you know you have to lay in the beats that have to happen to lead up to that.

While spending my days writing felt like living a dream, weird shit happens in dreams. You're walking and out of nowhere you're flying over Paris with an eighteen-foot wingspan about to crash into the Eiffel Tower. A few interviews under my belt and—forget walking!—I was ready to fly to the top of my wish list.

Leeza Gibbons, the object of my fixation, embodied the charmed ideal. Beautiful, naturally happy, proclaimed a "great mom" on magazine covers worldwide. With two shows on TV (her daytime talk show, *Leeza,* plus a long-time co-hosting gig at *Entertainment Tonight*), it seemed unbelievable that she had an even bigger radio presence, ultimately logging more on-air hours than Dick Clark or Casey Kasem. I *had* to have her in my book! I even fantasized that I'd make my television debut on her talk show. This wasn't entirely far-fetched. Jesse had acted with Leeza's husband on a nighttime soap opera in the Caribbean, and we'd shared a meal the previous year. Plus, we still had their phone number.

Somehow, God love it, Leeza and her husband agreed to come to dinner, perhaps lured by the bribe of Paul Williams and his then-wife, Hildi, joining the guest list.* Jesse and I had saved enough money while living with Paul to now rent a sweet two-bedroom home in the Valley. I had no plans of hitting Leeza up with an interview request that night but hoped to establish a solid sisterhood connection so that when I did ask, she'd be delighted to say yes.

Like a bad dream, a trance came over me the morning of our meal. I became obsessed with cleaning. I had *no* idea why I was suddenly scrubbing every inch of our rental house, including all window tracts with a toothbrush. By 6:00 PM

---

* Fun fact: Paul's now happily married to writer Mariana Williams for seventeen years.

on the appointed day, the place was gleaming like a new set of false teeth—a plus since we'd be eating on Indian blankets on the floor. *Oh, did I forget to say we didn't yet have a dining room table? Not to worry. My homemade pizzas were so mouthwatering it wouldn't matter.*

Except, by the time everyone arrived, I was so spent from my janitorial frenzy that after a quick hello, I went to the kitchen and flung my homemade pesto pizzas into the oven as if they were Frisbees. Hildi, a major gourmet who owned all of Martha Stewart's cookbooks and actually used them, saw me tossing mushrooms and peppers into the hot oven and gut-laughed before shrieking, "Linda! What are you doing?! You can't throw veggies in the oven like that. You're barely looking at your food prep!"

"Who cares, Hildi?" I said. "I'm too tired to care." She looked at me as if I'd lost my marbles, which of course I had.

Jesse rang the dinner bell and we sat down to eat on our blanket table. Exhausted from orchestrating this magic moment, I was equally drained of sparkling conversation. But we were just in time to watch *Entertainment Tonight*. There she was, Leeza, opening the show on the television, which was also on the floor. Paul, bless him, acted like nothing was amiss, as I watched Leeza watch herself, no longer the slightest bit concerned whether she liked me or not.

In a blink, dinner was over. Imagine that. Something about Leeza having an early call at the studio. My attempts at seducing her for best-friendship and a future interview had fallen flat. Hmph. How had I so royally blown my chance? You'd think I'd be heartbroken. Any clearheaded person would have been. But remember my mission. It seems that one of the benefits of believing you're doing God's work is a sense that anything is salvageable. You can mess up a million ways, but the universe will rearrange itself in your favor.

Caught up in a whirlwind of "inspiration," I stayed up half the night to write Leeza a pitch letter, sending off a single-spaced screed spilling over with misspelled words and long-winded babbling. Leeza graciously called to thank me but said she needed to keep her stories for her books.

A more realistic person might think, *Okay. I had a nice book dream. But you don't set your sights on Major League Baseball when you never played Little League.* A Greek chorus might also add: "And remember, all of your participles dangle." But still flying high on momentum from all the prior ease I'd experienced, I didn't question the outcome. I would continue focusing on what I loved, keep going where the juice was, and trust things would work out. Besides, no matter how odd I might have seemed at dinner, I had been at least partially successful. Does Leeza Gibbons know where *you* live?

Turbulence comes and goes, but momentum is more constant than we think. It carries us inevitably toward our dreams, even when everything looks like a crash-and-burn.

Samantha Bennett 🦋

When I get stuck, I have a trick I use to keep up my momentum. This kind of cracks me up, but I put in "placeholders." So, if I can't think of a good teaching story, I'll just put in "Insert Fabulous Teaching Story Here" and keep writing. Or if I know I haven't phrased something properly, but I can't seem to fix it in the moment, I'll write, "Something Like This, But Better." I find that it lightens me up, which is pleasant, and it reminds me that not every sentence has to be perfect right away. I'm just trying to get something on the page, so I can see what's going on, and then I can circle back and make it better.

The best advice I ever read was this: "Everything is Entertainment." Even if you're writing a chemistry textbook, make it entertaining. Now, entertaining does not necessarily mean funny, of course. But it does mean that your writing should be emotionally engaging. It should have a good tempo and pace. And remember to use all those delicious storytelling tricks like open loops, suspense, and buttons. My definitions: Open loops are unanswered questions that keep your curiosity piqued as the story unfolds. Suspense is using a bit of mystery and surprise to keep you in the present moment. Buttons are the satisfying close to the story that usually calls back some element from the beginning. In comedy, the button is the punch line that ends the scene or story.

Martha Beck

Even though it's mesmerizing and addictive to be in the writing process, once something feels "finished," I find it hard to get into the flow again. I try never to finish a day's work at the end of the chapter because then I'll wander off for six days and not get back to it. I have to play all these psychological tricks in my head to stay consistent. If I write at least into the second page of the new chapter, then I feel as if I'm still in the process.

Tosca Lee

You have to put in the time. You've got to sit there like a squirmy two-year-old for a while until you start to lock in and engage. We all love the flow state, no matter what we're doing, that sense of losing track of time. Things happen naturally and it's like you're channeling. But it's not always like that. Sometimes writing is a grind. You have to push through the times that don't feel ecstatic. It comes down to sitting in the chair and putting in the hours until it clicks along.

I can usually write a novel in three or four months, not counting the research. I like to write pretty fast, otherwise, I start losing my train of thought. If I take a day or two off in the middle of a project, it's hard to pick up those strings again. I used to be a ballerina in my earlier life, and I liken it to ballet because one or two days away from the barre, and other people may not know it, looking at you. But you know it because everything's harder.

At the beginning of a novel, I don't get a lot of words. Stephen King famously writes two thousand words every day. When I start a novel, I'm not getting anything close to two thousand words. More like a paragraph or two as I sink into the story. If I can get in a solid four hours, and six the next day, that's pretty good. Closer to deadline, I start pulling longer and longer days. Eight hours. Ten hours. Then twelve, fourteen, and sixteen. I hit two thousand words a day, then four thousand. Maybe six thousand or more. I wake up with red eyes and put on the clothes I wore the day before, excited to get back to it because I've got so much momentum.

Anita Moorjani

I check in with myself about how I'm feeling. If something is not feeling good, I'll check in again the next day, and the next day. If it doesn't feel good continuously, it means it's not for me. Then I have to figure out a way to let it go. I realize, "Okay, this project, whatever it is, I'm not aligned with it. It's draining me." I'll have to reevaluate it or figure out a different way of doing it.

Did you see how loving these folks are with themselves? How beautifully they set themselves up to succeed?

It's been a sweet process for me to go back in time and relive how very kind I was to myself. In taking large swaths of time to practice writing without telling hardly anyone and studying to my heart's content, I created my own honeymoon phase. There was none of the pressure I'd felt in school. My growing creative self was nurtured in an atmosphere of promise from the day I first learned how to use a laptop to the three friends I chose for my first interviews. They all made me feel safe. If I'd started with Leeza Gibbons, a virtual stranger at the time, the stakes would have been too high. Her "no" could have devastated and embarrassed me, possibly causing me to give up altogether. Instead, it rolled off my back.

Nia Vardalos, actress, Academy Award–nominated screenwriter (*My Big Fat Greek Wedding*), and author of the *New York Times* bestseller *Instant Mom*—with all proceeds going to adoption groups.

Writers don't really talk about, "I'm going to write a book." Writers write. That's the thing that I try to tell people. Talk less, write more.

I also didn't start off writing the hard stuff—the parts I didn't want to write. Clients will often say to me, "I know I have to begin by getting down the pieces I'm avoiding."

"Who says?" I answer. "No wonder you're running from your desk!"

Many projects include painful bits—dredging up sad memories or talking to recalcitrant interview subjects or doing research that feels like it's bruising your brain. Why in God's name would you start there? Go where the juice is! Where your joy is. Build up happy feelings. Learn to trust yourself. Enjoy a little momentum. Then, later in your journey, you'll be more ready to face the tougher climbs.

When Pulitzer Prize–winning Lin-Manuel Miranda started writing *Hamilton* (a Broadway show with forty-six songs!), I heard he reached out to composer Stephen Sondheim and said something along the lines of, "I just want to write the songs that I want to write first—is that allowed? Is it okay if it's not in chronological order?"

Sondheim supposedly confirmed that was the *only* way to do it—to work on the stuff that made his friend the happiest. I love imagining these two greats having this conversation, and I will absolutely ask Miranda for confirmation and details when I have him on the podcast. (Did you catch that, dear reader? Pretty slick affirmation/intention setting, yes?)

When *Hamilton* was nominated for sixteen Tony awards, I bet the Tony voters that year felt the elation Lin-Manuel had coursing through his veins while scripting his masterpiece.

What part of your work are you happiest about and like the most? What one small action can you take to get the ball rolling? Are you juiced by research? If so, get your giddy up to the nearest library. Or to your grandfather's hometown. Or to a cabin by that shoreline in Maine where your lead character falls in love. Immerse yourself in the world you're building. If listening to your inner narrator in meditation gives you clarity and a natural high, schedule that sitting time as if it were as sacred as a meeting with a top literary agent. If you're the type that needs structure and geeks out on outlining or writing on note cards, fill up your cart. May I suggest recycled or FSC® (Forest Stewardship Council®) certified paper?

Again, know who you are and what you need based on your style. For most of us, writing a book is a lengthy journey. Let early momentum keep you airborne.

8

Dancing with the Muse

Coaxing and Cultivating Creativity

"I'm not in control of my muse. My muse does all the work."

~ Ray Bradbury

Okay, God. What gives? I've been patiently awaiting my writing miracle, and You're surprisingly quiet. Is there something I'm missing? Some ritual or mantra or prayer that unlocks the muse?

Liz Gilbert, a two-time guest on my *Beautiful Writers Podcast*, brilliantly explained in her TED Talk "Your Elusive Creative Genius" that artists since the dawn of time have ascribed their creative mastery to a power greater than themselves. If you're struggling to come up with something awe-inspiring, is it solely up to you? Surely a person can't be penalized if their snoozy muse is asleep on the job! And if divine inspiration is real, it begs the question: How can we mere mortals gain favor from the gods?

Libraries are filled with books written by authors who beseeched the heavens and their muse to give them inspiration, protection, and compensation. There isn't a writer alive who doesn't want their creative endeavors to carry on when the honeymoon phase inevitably ends. That's when many of us call in the big guns: God, Allah, Oneness, Source, Fruity Skittles, the Universe, you name it.

Why not take the lead and kick your own butt into gear? Set up a writing schedule that works for you, and maybe use my coming example to take risks when networking with others who can fast-track your journey *while* you perform your rituals and say your prayers, if you choose. That way, if no One appears to deliver the secret codes, you're still writing and taking action—which, remember, creates momentum.

Regardless of where beautiful writing originates (a force outside of us or an inside job), I believe in the magic without *and* within, between my ears and inside my God-given heart (and, uh, um, caffeine). Then I hug a few trees and beg Mother Nature too. You know, just in case.

Jesse, on the other hand, being an actor, took a more dramatic approach.

Tosh was playing at a friend's house when the phone rang. It was the call we'd been waiting for: Jesse's manager had news about a screen test he'd done at NBC for a new love interest on *The Young and the Restless*. I ran to Jesse's side. He leaned down so my ear was close to the receiver.

"They adore you," his manager said. "You killed it in there. But they've given the part to a bigger name. I'm so sorry."

Jesse hung his head and began to weep. I sat by quietly, knowing this would take time. They'd already negotiated the money for this starring role. We were days from living on Easy Street, at least for a contractually guaranteed three years. Soon Jesse's face grew crimson with anger.

"Okay, God. What the hell's going on? Do I have a target on my chest that says, 'Fuck me'? Nothing, and I mean *nothing*, has worked out for me lately, and I don't deserve this!" Jesse was yelling now. "I've been a good man. A good father. A good husband. I provide for my family, or so I try, but You keep fucking with me!"

"Jesse! Stop," I said. "You can't scream at God like that! You're going to get hit by a downed power line or crushed by falling bricks."

"Fucking town! Fucking Hollywood! Fucking God!" Jesse screamed.

"Babe!" I yelled back, bordering on hysteria. We'd been slammed hard recently—Jesse had barely lived through a bout of peritonitis, a result of a burst appendix. He died on the operating table before coming back to life and hadn't worked in months. "Do you want things to get worse?"

Jesse shook his fist at the ceiling. "I don't deserve this! I don't deserve to lose my career! I didn't deserve to nearly lose my life. And, what the fuck has Linda done? She *really* doesn't deserve this crap!" *Okay, that's better.* I made the sign of the cross over my chest as Jesse's tirade slammed on.

"Never mind. I don't give a fuck what You think, God. Enough! I have dominion over my life, and I want it to change now. I want fun. Give me fun! I want some FUCKING FUN this goddamned minute!"

"Are you done yet?" I asked, scanning the skies for lightning bolts.

"Yeah, I'm done. Fuck it." He walked into our bedroom, flopped onto our mattress, and fell into a fitful sleep. Two hours later, just as Jesse was beginning to stir, my cell phone rang.

"Lin? It's Randi!" I could hear static, telling me she was overseas. We'd met the dark-eyed, long-legged beauty in St. Martin when she and Jesse and Leeza's husband acted together for the soap opera.

"How the heck are you?" I asked. "Where are you?"

"I'm in Milan. Just finished a modeling shoot. On a yacht." She laughed. "Girrrl, you'd flip if you could see my life. That's why I'm calling."

"So, life's still beautiful?" It had been nothing but since the Philadelphia native, Randi Ingerman, had moved to Italy. With her buxom bosom and waistline the circumference of my wrist, Randi had learned Italian and become a pinup model and movie and TV star. I called her The Rome Madonna.

"Yes! Ridiculously beautiful. And it's about to get more so for the two of you as well. Pack your bags. I'm flying you to Miami. We're going on an all-expenses-paid, nine-day Caribbean cruise. I'm christening a new luxury liner. You'll act as my assistant for an hour. Carry a clipboard; take one page of notes. That's it. I've already reserved your stateroom. It's about time you guys had that honeymoon you never got. You deserve some fucking fun, am I right?"

So, yeah. That was mind-blowing. An Italian pastry cruise, if you can believe that. Between the bomboloni for breakfast and the tiramisu, cannoli, and brioche buffet at midnight on the upper deck—*gotta love those Italians*—Jesse and I both gained eleven pounds.

Patricia Cornwell 🌿

When I had the idea for the twenty-fifth *Scarpetta* novel, it had been five years since *Chaos*, number twenty-four in the series. I imagined Dr. Scarpetta sitting in her garden.

I said, "We haven't seen each other in a while. Would you like to work a case?"

"Well, maybe," she said. "It depends on what it is."

Anita Moorjani 🌿

After my near-death experience, I realized that our soul is made purely of energy, and that we're predominantly souls more than physical bodies. We act like we're physical beings, but our physical self is only the tip of an iceberg. Our real self, our soul, is our energy being. When you believe that you are just this physical being, you bend yourself out of shape, like a pretzel, to try and fit in to please other people.

But when I crossed over, I realized we all are huge spiritual beings. Our soul is powerful and has a purpose. "Wow! This is much bigger than anything I could ever imagine!" I wished everybody knew this about themselves.

When you're living from this place, you become guided. When you think you're a little physical being, you think you have to run around physically worrying about this and that and changing this and changing that. We put all this burden on the shoulders of this little physical body that is scared and running around trying to change the world. This physical body starts to get worn down because this little physical person is afraid. But when you live from the soul, you have a very different perspective. You stay guided.

Paul Williams

The first job I got when I was newly sober was to write the words and music for *The Muppet Christmas Carol*. It was the perfect job for me. It's about a man's spiritual awakening. In some ways, I was Scrooge.

Disney wanted the first number to be Scrooge's "I Am" song. The doors open. We see Michael Caine's feet as Scrooge, walking through mud and splashing water and snow. Little creatures get colder as he passes.

I went out, took my tape recorder and a piece of paper and a pencil. I'd read Dickens's original and the script. I sat in the park and said, "Big Amigo, you know what this song needs to be about. All these amazing forces up there somewhere are in and out and around me and within me. Let me know when you have an idea."

I picked up a bloody mystery and started reading. About three pages in, I set it down, not thinking about what I was supposed to do. I went, "Okay. You see his feet. He's walking . . ."

Then the lyrics *poured out* of me: *When a cold wind blows, it chills you, chills you to the bone. But there's nothing in nature that freezes your heart like years of being alone.* I couldn't write it fast enough. I had no conscious connection to the process beyond the fact that my subconscious was on it. Just as you try to remember a name—everybody can relate to this—you're trying to remember a name. You can't think of his name. He's been your favorite actor for your entire goddamned life. *Why can't I remember his name?* All of a sudden, you're in the shower, you're in bed in the middle of the night, and *boom!* It pops to the surface. Who did that work? Who went through all those filing cabinets up there looking for the name? And you go, "Oh my God! Arthur Hunnicutt!"

That magical, mystical power my wonderful composer friend Richard Bellis says we mistake for procrastination is "percolation." It's not procrastinating! You get a job to do, you avoid it, you avoid it, you avoid it, and you've got four hours until you have to turn it in. You sit down, and it pours out of you. Why? What's been happening? It's been percolating. Those guys upstairs have been doing the work!

Anne Lamott ❧

Thirty years ago, I used to wake up and go, "Oh, God, it's so hopeless, I'm so sick." And now I wake up, and I say to God, "Hi!" And then I offer myself to God to use me and do with me as He or She chooses.

And I pray not to be such a big whiny baby. I know a few people who are in dire medical emergencies. I lift them up for perfect healing—whatever their destiny is. And then usually around that time, my grandson has crawled into bed with me. And he starts shaking me because he doesn't know I'm praying. He thinks I'm sleeping and that I should get up and start discussing his plans for the day and what he would like for breakfast.

So, I have kind of "life on life's terms" prayers. I pray all day, every day. I mostly pray, "Help. Thanks! Wow!" And I pray to stop being such a whiny baby.

Despite how well that worked, telling God to go fuck Himself, I never saw Jesse tempt fate in that way again. My friend Rhonda Britten later said he'd indeed summoned the power of the Universe by finally committing 100 percent to himself at that moment, but future prayers needn't be so heretical. As for me, I stuck to sage lighting and dream seeding.

Just as I was about to overturn couch cushions in search of coins, Jess was hired as the face of a major American car company in six states. *Oh my God! We can pay our bills!* I leaped into Jesse's arms, and we both cried. This wouldn't be Richie Rich money, but it would afford us time—maybe a year, possibly more—for me to write without getting another job and space for him to continue to be a guilt-free, mostly stay-at-home dad and *SportsCenter* aficionado. Of course, I'd be a wealthy author one day, able to step in and repay the favor by taking care of us when his car gig ended. Because even in the Land of Make-Believe, *every* good gig comes to a close.

That night I had my first interviewee dream. I was sitting across from Robert Wyland, the environmentalist and whale muralist listed in the *Guinness Book of World Records* for creating the largest mural in history. Jesse and I had stumbled into Wyland's Laguna Beach gallery the previous summer on an uncommon day trip to the ocean and had stood in awe of his creations.

"That guy's dope, but is he famous enough to help you get a book deal?" Jesse asked, seeing the letter I'd just typed up to Wyland's publicist.

Ahh. *The* question I'd been dreading: *Would my interviewees be hot enough?* God forbid I pick anyone in the B-, C-, or dreaded D-list category, despite their wisdom and experience. I'd already imagined this concern echoed in future publishing conversations and could feel my defenses rising.

"True, Wyland's not a household name," I said. "But that only makes him more deserving of being highlighted!" I'd just learned of his audacious goal to paint a hundred life-size marine murals on skyscrapers, sports arenas, and massive structures across the globe. "With his Whaling Walls, he's spreading awareness of the fragility that lies beneath our waters," I continued. "He should get all the press possible!"

Jesse got it, but I knew others wouldn't, and we were short on time. Back at USC in 1984, my environmental engineering textbook warned of the "50 reasons the oceans would be dead in 50 years." That was ten years ago already! We desperately needed to throw a little light on this brush-wielding visionary, who, by the way, rocked some movie-star good looks as well.

I proofed my "Pick me, pick me!" pitch and faxed my request. Planet Earth required whale-sized warriors, and Wyland's mission was galactic. But they turned me down. Was it because I was a nobody? Probably, but there was no getting around that fact just yet. I knew what *I* wanted—hot whale guy in the pages of my book, healing vibes to the seven seas and beyond. *But what did Wyland want?* Everyone, no matter how high up on the celebrity food chain, has goals. Help them reach theirs, I figured, and we'd feast together.

When in doubt, research! I discovered that Wyland had a foundation, one that educated schoolkids to be better stewards of the oceans. I went to bed awed with a prayer on my lips: "If there's something I can do to get Wyland to do the interview, please tell me what it is." When I woke up, the introduction for Wyland's future chapter in my book—all three pages of it—was parked in the white space of my mind. I just had to bring it into physical form.

I raced to get it down before saying a quick prayer to Mama Earth and Tosh's latest crush, Ariel (*who's to say little mermaids don't have big pull?*). I pushed REDIAL on the fax machine, and *bam*! My ode to Wyland's environmental heroics was the lure that, once cast, landed my big fish. He said YES! Our lunch interview in Laguna was set for the following week. Once again, my brain or guardian angels—*something seemingly tapped in*—was telling me what to do. When I followed those instructions, I found myself floating in flow.

"It's the craziest thing, but many times when I'm painting a mural," Wyland said, looking out on the crashing surf from our table, "I turn around and see a whale or dolphin raised up out of the water watching me paint." The crack in his voice and the faraway look in his aqua sky-blue eyes made me see it too. I put my fork down, speechless.

"I know there's nothing I can ever do with my life that would make me feel more connected," he continued.*

Yeah. I know the feeling. Nothing made me feel as alive as having these chats. I felt as if I was deeply connected to my life's mission, and I prayed that with time I would be as courageous as my interviewees. How was it that when Wyland and others got "the call" to do their work in the world, they answered with their whole being? Where did they get their belief? Their stamina? The sheer daily commitment to keep showing up? Would I have similar staying power? *Please, God.*

---

* Fun fact: In 2008, twenty-seven years after he started, Wyland finalized his epic one-hundredth Whaling Wall. Spanning over twenty-two acres—*Google them!*—in fourteen countries on four continents, these murals are viewed by an estimated one billion people a year.

Van Jones

It's a mystery. We could all just be trapped in some virtual reality game, and we might be some totally other alien species. Who knows?

It seems that humans tend to have some awareness of something beyond our immediate five senses and can find meaning and comfort and even direction. Whether it's called faith or intuition or the muse, I find the more space I give that in my life, the better my life gets. And I find the less space I give that in my life, the worse my life gets.

For me, without being a fundamentalist or anything like that, I can just say what works for me. When I open my heart and myself up to a deeper purpose, better words come out, and those words are of more use.

I think the other side of that is having something to say. That took longer because it's a crowded field of young African Americans whose parents came through civil rights and who want to make the world a better place. Putting in ten or fifteen years of work and coming out with some novel ideas about the workforce, about green energy, that kind of gave me something to say. And then leaving the White House and working at CNN and with Newt Gingrich and with Prince and President Obama—that has all given me something else to say.

Steven Pressfield

Early in my career, I went through a really rough time. I came out of it by saying to the Muse: "Okay. I'll follow you. Tell me what to do, and I'll do it." I believe completely that if you pay attention to her, the Muse, she keeps coming around. And if you don't, she's pissed off. Like most women, it's about attention.

I always say that the Muse is the only female in my life that I've always been faithful to and the only one who's always been faithful to me.

A writer, or any artist, serves the Muse. That's why you can't command the Muse; you can only invoke her. Do you know what kite surfing is, where you have a kind of parasail above you, and you surf along the water with lines going up to this parachute above? I feel like we, as writers, we're on the surfboard down on the surface of the water. But there are lines extending above us, and the power is coming down from that. When the wind hits that sail, hits that kite, it pulls us. If we look at this from the inside out of a writer's career, or a singer's career . . . you're going to have a body of work. One album is going to follow another and another. I see those as Muse-driven projects. When I finish one, I ask partly what it is that I want to do next, but also what do you, the Muse, want me to do next?

I believe we're all born with a destiny. There are the works we're put on this earth to write as writers. I think that if the Muse is flying overhead looking down and sees somebody with that attitude, she's very happy because that's what she wants. She's asking: Is this person a true servant of mine? I think the way you best court the Muse is by being willing to do whatever it takes to do your work. To not be distracted. Keep going no matter what.

Thankfully, the Universe continued gifting me pearls. I was still hush-hush about my writing, though. Mainly to safeguard my growing but still delicate belief I could pull this off. Except, one day, a friend of a friend came over and without knowing a thing about her other than that her jeans were organic, and that we each made homemade almond milk for our kids, my gut kept saying, *Tell her about your book!* So, I did. A week later, at her insistence, she introduced me to Pierce Brosnan and his soon-to-be wife, Keely Shaye Smith.

At the Brosnan beach house in Malibu, the crashing surf and cawing seagulls were nearly as distracting as the actual movie star in the house—*James Bond*! I was swept up into devastating, 007-worthy firsthand stories of real-life ocean activism on a scale I'd only imagined might exist. I nearly threw up when Pierce and Keely played film footage for me taken by their friend from a hidden camera on a fishing vessel documenting the massacre of dolphins en masse. (Schools of tuna often swim under pods of dolphins, leading to all sorts of excruciating, high-stakes tragedy.)

Pierce and Keely worked tirelessly—and successfully—to get Congress to establish dolphin-safe fishing laws, resulting in the 1990 Dolphin Protection Consumer Information Act. They also helped halt the construction of a salt factory on the banks of the San Ignacio Lagoon, one of the last gray whale breeding and calving spots on Earth. (And in 2016, the Brosnans produced *Poisoning Paradise,* an award-winning documentary that exposed the experimental toxic test sites where dangerous pesticides are sprayed unchecked and upwind of vulnerable neighborhoods in Hawaii.)

Keely's smarts and courage energized me. With each new interview, my love for champions in the environmental trenches grew, further fueling my why and my mission to keep scripting stories affecting the flora and fauna that couldn't speak for themselves.

Marianne Williamson

I dedicate what I'm writing to God, which means to love—that it might be of service, that it might be of use. I think we heal in life one a-ha at a time. That's every writer's hope—that there's going to be an a-ha in something you wrote.

Whenever I hear all that stuff we're "supposed to do" to be successful, my advice is to ignore it. Go into the peace of your heart, meditate, pray, and ask for guidance. Then, yes, listen to experts. But they will be your consultants. The deepest decision-making will be from that still, small voice within that you will hear in the silence of your heart.

That is the creative process! The same place you go to find the right word to say, or the right word to write, or the right color to paint. It's the same place to go to when deciding to promote your book or whatever. It's all sacred. As Einstein said, "Either everything is a miracle, or nothing is a miracle."

Leeza Gibbons 🍂

I repeat my mother's advice to me, which is to show up, do your best, and let go of the rest—with faith that God is working with you and through you.

I always used to have music playing when I walked out to meet the audience on my talk show. It made it easy for me to do the same little jump and clap every time, which was just an anchor to ground me in the moment of, "Okay! We're here! Do it!" And then, I'd have to show up. In a neurolinguistic programming kind of way, that put me in performance mode, where I let everything else go—the nails I didn't get done, the dry-cleaning I didn't pick up, and that we were having pasta again for dinner. Ritual helps me put the focus where it needs to be and let God in.

Every few weeks, I'd visit Guru Singh in his office for a session and give him the lowdown.

"I'm all for calendars and to-do lists and networking, Gu," I said. "But without being given pages of text in my dreams or following hunches like coming to you or revealing my innermost secret writing desires to a virtual stranger in my kitchen, I'd be nowhere." Guru's crow's feet crinkled. "Is that God, my muse, intuition, or just plain old luck?" I asked.

"Of course, it's God!" he exclaimed. "But labels don't matter."

"I'm just grateful my GodMuse isn't fickle," I said. It wasn't easy being dependent upon celebrity involvement, but their words afforded me endless material. With a muse that felt more like a doting mum, ever ready with a helping hand or cookie sheet of freshly baked story lines, I was willing—make that *happy*—to do the grunt work to earn my muse's respect.

Please, tell me what to do, I'd beg, my arms wrapped around the trunk of a tree or extended outward toward the horizon, my toes in the earth. I started each day on reverential hands and knees, ready for duty, thanking God for the privilege of doing this work. Each night found my forehead pressed to the ground before hitting the sheets.

Who do You want me to pitch this week? Who will be open to this mission? How do You want me to open the next chapter? Thank You for giving me clarity when I wake up.

Following my on-and-off-again Guru-inspired morning meditations, I gratefully took the answers, guidance, and visions I'd been given and grounded them in my daily to-do lists. My actual writing prayer was simple: "Thank you for writing through me today. Use me to help the trees." To that end, I figured my muse and Mother Earth and I were in a relationship—one in which she could count on me as I logged the hours in front of my screen; pitched VIPs far more often than was comfortable or logical; sequestered myself with only my family and my writing to keep me company for weeks at a time; and ended each day bleary-eyed from the strain of endless studying.

Elizabeth Gilbert

I don't pray before I write. And I wish I did. I wish I prayed more. I don't have a prayer practice, to be very honest with you. I have a very sketchy meditation practice, but it's nothing I would teach or advise somebody to imitate because I think there are a lot of other people who engage at that level a lot better than I do. Not that it's a competition, but there are people who have really deep, really rich meditation and prayer practices, and sometimes I look at them with envy, and then I think, *Why don't I do it?*

And the thing is, I forget. I forget, and it's very hard for me to pray. This is terrible. I've never said this before, but we're speaking the truth here. It doesn't serve anybody not to. It's hard for me to pray when I'm not desperate. Prayer to me is still tied up in some sort of idea of desperate pleading that I go to when I've reached the end of myself, and I can't handle things, and I don't know what to do next, and I feel lost, that's when I'll turn to prayer. And I don't think it should really be that way. That might be something I need to look at and explore.

It's weird. I don't even do a joyful prayer. It's usually too caught up in joy and excitement for me to pause and do that. While I do not pray before I begin writing, when I am writing, I am my most authentic, most actualized, most in-tune, and most devout self. So, it could be that my prayer is that.

I have a very mystical relationship with my books. I believe that each one of them has its own soul, something it wants to be. My job is to work with it, to steward it into being what it wants to be. Not what the market wants it to be, or even necessarily always what I want it to be. A lot of the times, when I'm stuck with a book, I'll just talk to it and ask it, "What is it that you would like to be?" Once it's done, we can see whether anybody wants it or whether it's marketable in that form.

Mary Karr, award-winning poet and author of the critically acclaimed and *New York Times* bestselling memoirs *The Liars' Club*, *Cherry*, and *Lit*, as well as *The Art of Memoir* and five poetry collections. 🌿

I do a sort of centering prayer exercise before I write, which is fifteen to thirty minutes of just following my breath. And I get on my knees a lot in the middle of the day. I might say the old Hemingway line: "Just say the next true thing." Or I hit my knees, and I say a lot of swear words and shoot the finger at the light bulb and say, "Why do you want me to do this if it's this damn hard?"

I figure even if I'm ranting and raving at God, at least we're having a conversation. I also do something called the Examine of

Conscience every night, where you kind of replay your day and look for evidence of God in the day. But also, when I'm really in a bind, I'll pray the Litany of the Saints, which is, I don't know, maybe a forty-five-minute event. It's a good way of clearing my head.

Danielle LaPorte

When writing and collecting my stories, I just say, "May I be of service. I hope these are useful." Yeah, that's always the prayer, "Make me useful."

Elizabeth Lesser, cofounder of Omega Institute and *New York Times* bestselling author of *Broken Open* (and several other bestsellers, *Cassandra Speaks* and *Marrow*).

We call it "Spiritual Practice" for a reason. In the same way, if you played the piano and practiced the scales over and over, it's boring because you're not practicing to become a great scale player. When my boys used to play basketball, they'd go outside and bounce the ball over and over. You're practicing those monotonous things it takes to become an artist or an athlete. When you have a spiritual practice, you're practicing the art of living—living with potency and kindness, and purpose. You're practicing to actually get somewhere.

Does prayer coax the muse? Does a relationship with your higher power grease the door to creativity? Those who believe wisdom doesn't just come from you but *through* you say yes. You're never alone. The whole endeavor's not all on your shoulders.

The two founders of Alcoholics Anonymous, Bob and Bill, were very different, but together they published one of the bestselling books of all time, referred to as *The Big Book*. Bill was super mystical, referring to his recovery like a "hot flash," a sudden white light and sense of well-being while in treatment that freed him from addiction. Bob was ultra-pragmatic and practical. Bill said a higher power saved him. Bob said it was the fellowship and principles of the program that saved him.

I don't believe it matters if you think your story is dictated by Mother Nature or your dead grandmother, fairy beings from the sixth dimension, or your years of training, research, and blood, sweat, and tears. What matters is having enough faith to keep showing up.

I can't say for sure why I was given the dream of my first book or the total blind belief to pull it off, but the Bible says to ask, so I asked. And I still ask. Then I make it easy to receive, my writing tools at the ready. I'm all about grunt work. But I also love sacred rituals. Ideally, I start with a clean writing space and then light a candle or sage and thank God for working through me to help save forests. (If you haven't noticed, this book is printed on Forest Stewardship Council® paper, meaning that it's certified to have come from responsible sources that support forest conservation. #DreamInProcess)

Whether you're bowing your head in solitude, pirouetting through your office to loud music, humming a mantra or a spiritual hymn, or tap-tapping away at your keyboard with cats snoring on your desk, do whatever makes your space feel sanctified, popping with possibility. You're going for that sense of being plugged into your source—the bat signal to the Universe and your unconscious mind that it's time to take this sacred shit seriously.

PART TWO

Toolkits and Dream Teams

The Nitty-Gritty of Delving Deeper

Let's dig into accountability buddies and whether it's time to join or create a genuinely supportive support group while you design a solid practice that outwits bad habits and time sucks. We'll cover organizing strategies that will increase your sanity and productivity. Next, we'll clarify your overall vision and see to it that you embarrass yourself less with lessons from outrageous networking tales. Then, we'll focus on shortening your learning curve so that when it comes time to sell your work, you're ready to deliver the goods agents and publishers want most. Finally, we'll share tips for staying focused and continuing to progress no matter what life throws your way.

We'll start with getting support for your writing. Creative alliances don't just happen. And giving and getting high-quality feedback isn't always intuitive. There's an art to creating art together.

9

The Power of Shared Belief

Writing Groups and Accountability Buddies

"It takes two flints to make a fire."

~ Louisa May Alcott

Do you prefer being alone, finding people thoroughly exhausting? Or do you recharge at your writing circle or book club dinners, basking in the company of great storytellers and curious readers? Or are you somewhere in between?

I'm a homebody who prefers to write for days on end without interruption. All that to say, I live by the mottos: "Writing is better when shared" and "Friends don't let their friends write alone." With the right support systems, writing gets stronger—whether your feedback's coming from one, two, or twelve. Validation. Refinement. Permission. No matter if you're a loner or the belle of the ball, who doesn't want an answer to this question: *Was it good for you too?*

We think of reading and writing as solitary endeavors. But they sure don't start off that way.

With my head on my mother's shoulder and footie pajamas barely hanging over the end of the couch, my eyes were glued on the colored drawings of *Dorrie the Little Witch,* an enchanted girl with a black cat named Gink and a powerful and wise, if not intimidating, mother they called Big Witch. As Mom read from the series during our nightly ritual, I ached to *be* Dorrie. Never mind that, despite her grand intentions and pure heart, she was always landing Gink and herself into trouble—casting misshapen spells, befriending dangerous wizards, accidentally turning Cook into a blue horse. "Her hat was always on crooked, and her socks never matched." I could relate. But no matter how hairy the situation author Patricia Coombs set up for our protagonist, Dorrie's inherent goodness would win out. Every mess she'd instigated or had been thrust upon her would magically right itself, just in the nick of time.

Sharing Dorrie's harrowing escapades with my mom, a witness to the magic, helped me believe in my own magic. When Dorrie's story line made me laugh or cheer, Mom laughed and cheered too. When my pulse would race, my mother's comforting presence let me know things would be okay. We were IN it together.

Books were my parents' greatest shared joy. When not reading to Carol and me, they'd look up from their novels or *New Yorker* or *San Francisco Examiner* articles to read to each other from their leather recliner chairs, a Bach concerto tinkling over the hi-fi. "Honey! Listen to this!" they'd call out. I never could figure out how they'd keep finding their places with so many interruptions, but I secretly loved the chaotic camaraderie of it.

I also loved Mondays (*still do!*), which were Library Days. Sis and I would tumble out of Mom's Buick Riviera and race to the front door of the most magical building in town. We'd carry teetering stacks back home, buzzing with excitement as we scanned the spines, eager to start traveling through time, space, and place, craving both bookish solitude and a longing to share our adventures aloud and compare notes, like Mom and Dad.

Sue Monk Kidd 🌿

My first reader is my daughter.* She's an excellent reader and gives me great feedback. It surprised me how great she was. I thought maybe it would be good for her as a writer, but it turned out it was best for me. I give her every chapter of my work, and she reads it, and she will respond to it and tell me what she thinks. And she has some good suggestions. For *The Book of Longings*, I said to her, "It's very important that I portray the character of Jesus as having some playfulness about Him, some humor, some ordinariness too."

She said, "Why don't you have Ana give Him a haircut?"

I thought, *That's brilliant. I'm going to do that.* And I did.

Laura Munson 🌿

My writing life has been my refuge since I was a little girl. But there was a time in my early twenties when I started living the writing life with the express intention of making a *career* out of it and knew I needed to be around people who understood this longing. That's when I joined a writing group that met every Monday for five years in Seattle. We had rules: no socializing until afterward. Tea. Kindness. Some of the best feedback I've ever gotten was from those women! We are still very close and take annual retreats together, even though we all live far from each other. I think that's because we were young together, helping each other dream big. I love thinking that their support helped me make my dream come true.

Valarie Kaur 🌿

No one gives birth alone. And the role of the midwife is perhaps just as essential as the body doing the creating.

---

* Ann Kidd Taylor, co-author of Sue's *Traveling with Pomegranates*.

Jenny Lawson

It's hard to listen to criticism. You're not going to get better if you don't. But it's also hard not to get steamrolled by it. My husband no longer gets to read my books. He does have the opportunity to. I say, "You can read it, and if there's something that you see and you're like, 'Oh, don't put that in there.'" But he knows enough to know that the way that he gives criticism is actually harmful to me. It makes me feel like I never want to write again, and that everything I write is terrible.

Instead, I have three friends who are my beta readers. I will call them and read to one of them. I'll listen for, are they laughing at the right place? Do they stop me and go, "Wait, what is this?" I know that they're going to encourage me and be very honest. Then I can fix it and call the next person a week later and be like, "Okay, let me read this," and they'll be like, "Am I the first one hearing it?" and I'm like, "Oh yeah, totally, totally. You're the first one." Because I am a liar.

After that, it goes to my agent and she's so kind and so good about saying, "I love this. I wish it was a little bit more . . ." She's found the "Jenny language." Then it goes to the copy editor. You don't realize until you write a book how many people are going to see it and go, "I don't like this, I don't like this, I don't like this." If you have a personality where you already sort of hate yourself, and they say, "You've got a lot of run-on sentences," then you're like, "I'll never write again!"

It had been a full year since my book dream, and yet I was still nowhere near publication. With Mom 350 miles away; Carol, a whirling dervish of busy; and my best friend, Diane, now married to an NFL quarterback and living in Arizona, I was in need of a little chaotic camaraderie. And magic. Enter, Big Witch.

Meredith, my new friend, was stunning, with long, jet-black hair, bright green eyes, and ivory skin taut around her high cheekbones. She felt instantly familiar when Jesse and I bumped into her in a store, and Jesse, who'd already met her, introduced us.

"You have to come to my house Wednesday night!" Meredith declared. A dozen or so female fellow creatives (a Hollywood script supervisor, a producer, a painter, a few actresses, some entrepreneurs) met weekly for moral support and manifestation mojo. A way to unburden themselves so they wouldn't need to endure their lows alone while also bringing positive vibes and healthy structure to their lives and goals.

Uncharacteristically shy, I hesitated.

"Come on!" said Meredith, herself a singer-songwriter. I loved her certainty. She felt powerful and wise, mothering even, despite our close ages. I had a sense she knew things I didn't and would up my game.

Did she ever! From our first meeting, I thought SHE was the one who should write a book.* In a town that breeds some of the fiercest competition in the world, I was embraced as if I'd been a founding member all along.

Wednesdays were my favorite day—a chance to get dressed up and surround myself with femininity for a change. The women had years of mastery beneath them but didn't mind that I was a breastfeeding, sleep-deprived mom at the very start of learning my craft.

With organized precision, Meredith ran the group with a timer and bylaws, and like real adults, we went sanely around the circle, sharing our triumphs and setbacks, and garnering feedback and encouragement. I tried not to be too obvious about my obsession with the bowl of Thin Mints at the center of the table. *Do the others not see what I see? Those evil little Girl Scouts!*

Meredith had been in several high-profile bands but was looking for the right match. "You're going to be huge!" I told her. I could *feel* it. I felt similarly about Janet, a budding actress who'd moved to LA from Texas, where she'd been a homecoming queen, a Dallas Cowboys cheerleader, and a flight attendant. She and her Crest-white smile had been in the Hollywood game for a while. Unlike so many golden children who swiftly hightail it back home when pitted

---

* I'm working on Mer; stand by.

against so many other goldens, Janet wasn't going anywhere. She wore success like an aura around her head. It was merely a matter of time.

And then there was Carrie-Anne, an actress whose face I'd seen on TV but couldn't recall where. *She's so sweet and pretty,* I thought upon meeting her. Her sense of calm was hypnotic.

Sabaa Tahir 🌿

Find writing friends like Tomi [Adeyemi].* It's life-altering to have these people in your life who remind you of why you write and who help you focus on good when things seem really difficult. A writer or writers whose work you admire, whose work you can learn from. It's a gift.

Bronwyn Saglimbeni, communications coach, blogger, podcaster, and speaker, who has written, directed, and produced more than 175 TEDx, TEDGlobal, and TED talks. 🌿

When it comes to community, so much of it depends on where you are in the journey. For me, it's got to be about the work and the quality of the output, not the deeper relationship dynamics that come with a group of people who are intimately connected. Of course, the group needs to be compassionate and fair, but I'm *definitely* not there for friendship.

A writing retreat was powerful for me, because it was like I received a Sacrament of Writer's Confirmation: *Yes, I can write. YES, I am a writer.* The power came from the intimacy and connection I felt with the brilliant women in the group.

But once I was confirmed and convicted in my desires and plans, the handwringing was over. It was time to place ass firmly

---

* Fun fact: Tomi says on their episode of the podcast that she "gently stalked" Sabaa after reading *An Ember in the Ashes*. Before that book, Tomi didn't know it was possible to write a young adult fantasy book—like the bestselling ones she'd then write—where the hero wasn't white.

in the chair and *write*. I then used the "Write-In" Wednesdays in a private Facebook Group (shout-out to my Beautiful Writers peeps, whom I adored!). I've since quit Facebook, but I would show up at a certain time, and we would hold each other accountable for a few hours, checking in at the beginning and at the end. It was heavenly.

I don't look to writing groups for friendship or even connection. I go to be reminded that *I am a writer* and that I get to take that role seriously. I go to be reminded that when the timer goes off and it's time to write, I write. Being with others who take that seriously helps me get going and stay going when I want to run screaming from the chair.

I've never gone skydiving, but I'm guessing that the last five minutes of the flight are silent, as everyone goes into a deep place to find their courage. The people on the airplane are together, but mostly in silence . . . their proximity and presence in that moment of risk is the gift. There's no talking, bleeding, weeping, or bitching. It's just surrender, the girding of loins, and then the jump. That's how I like my writing groups—just enough connection and accountability, so I feel supported and able to get down to business.

One day, after a meeting, following on her heels like a puppy to her office studio, I asked Meredith about a manifestation technique I'd heard about—where I was told to imagine just a snippet of what I was hoping to create.

"Do you think that could work?" I asked. "I have a hard time quieting my mind and worry I'll see and then manifest the opposite of what I want."

Meredith laughed. While she wasn't one for quick fixes or "spells," as it were—preferring to do the real emotional and physical work most people tried to circumvent—she was open-minded, curious.

As she talked, Meredith's masterful guitar-strumming hands punctuated the air.

"It might be helpful for you to try and slow that racing mind of yours down to a slow crawl, Linda," she said, her eyes smiling. Was my nervous energy that obvious? People had told me that when Jesse and I walked into a room the way we fed off one another was a little like standing next to a tornado (Mer would say more like "two transformers touching: buzzy"), but I thought that was really all about *him*.

"It's so common to hear pro athletes these days talking about visualizing," Meredith said, considering the topic further. "So, it makes sense that it's safer to see just a fraction of what you want than trying to control the whole scene by telling God how to do His job. Don't give your mind too much time to wander."

As I drove home that night, full of gratitude, I vowed to regularly slow my brain down to imagine just a few seconds of landing dream interviews for my book. I would hold an image on the screen of my mind for a short but concentrated time, and then let it out into the Universe.

Not unlike Dorrie, who flung herself into things broom first, I was unaware how misshapen the results of my "spell" could be in the hands of a new initiate.

Rosie Walsh

When I realized that the solitude of writing (and lack of feedback) was impacting my emotional health, I decided to find a writing partner. I asked a few trusted friends, and they all said they were too busy writing. I was beginning to give up when I went to a friend's party and saw a woman who said, "I know you don't really know me, but is there any way you'd be willing to take a look at what I'm writing to put me in the right direction?" This is the crazy bit. She said, "I don't know what I can offer you in return, but I have a coaching and teaching background [English], and I'd happily look at any of your words, although I'm sure you wouldn't want my opinion."

She offered me more than I could possibly imagine. We began sending each other material and we'd meet for two hours, occasionally longer on a Wednesday morning, spending roughly an hour on each manuscript. It was transformative. No matter how much I'm struggling with my work, I can always give helpful feedback on hers, which reminds me that I am a storyteller. And likewise, no matter how much I'm struggling with my novel, she's always got helpful feedback. She's gotten me out of so many holes. So many great bits of *Ghosted* are courtesy of her.

Terry McMillan ✎

Many years ago, I was accepted into the Harlem Writers Guild. I was working on a short story called "Mama, Take Another Step." I had to read it in front of these writers, some of whom had already been published. I remember I had two shots of tequila first because I was so nervous. I had never read in front of anyone.

As soon as I read the piece, a woman who would become my best friend raised her hand and said, "Honey, that is not a short story. That is the beginning of a novel. You might as well finish it." There were fourteen people in that room, and I'll never forget it. Some of them were saying, "She's right."

I said, "I don't know how to write a novel," and they said, "You'll learn. This story is not finished."

Sometimes the group sees what you can't.

The gals of our support group were *really* there for each other—which felt comforting, seeing as how some of us were living hand to mouth with all those big dreams yet to come true. There was a lot to be said for being in the trenches together. My crooked hat and mismatched socks couldn't compare to the style and glam of most of our support group members, yet I reveled in feeling a part of such a select few, grateful to have been chosen. Like the Marines, only without the threat of combat. With the *right* group, good Lord, magic happens when women come together.

Elizabeth Gilbert

I was lucky enough to be able to read a draft of Marie [Forleo]'s *Everything Is Figureoutable* at the beginning. That's always such a vulnerable thing for people to share their work when it's at that stage, when it's not lacquered and polished. To be trusted with that—I take that very seriously. I know what it feels like to hand an unbound manuscript to somebody.

You always have to ask the person, "How can I be of service? What can I help you do with this?" There are so many different ways to read an unbound manuscript, and sometimes people just need you to say, "You're doing great. I'm so proud of you, little bunny." Pat, pat, little head. Sometimes that's what I need. I'll tell my friends, "I don't want your criticism. I just want your encouragement right now because I'm not ready to be criticized yet." And then other times it can be very laser, where you say, "Tell me how to get out of chapter five. I'm stuck." If you really trust somebody, you can ask, "What is your broad sweeps opinion?"

Jesse and I would move out of state before I could witness firsthand the phenomenal results of their discipline and support. But years later, I would carry my favorite parts of our support group dynamics into an actual writing group that, after twenty-three years, is still rock-solid supportive. When we began our bi-monthly lunches at Marmalades on Ventura Boulevard, I was the only one of the five of us with a published book. Over a few years, we'd support each other through the birth of more than twenty books, countless courses, and an Emmy. I'd also bring forth the best of *both* groups in the creation of my writing retreats, where countless dreams have been realized.

These days, when I think of support groups, I envision trees in a forest, the roots a jumble of interconnections deep beneath the surface of the soil. In his bestselling book *The Hidden Life of Trees,* author Peter Wohlleben writes that trees and human communities are alike in their advantages of working together.

A tree is not a forest. On its own, it can't establish a consistent local climate and finds itself at the mercy of wind and weather.

"But together," writes Wohlleben, "many trees create an ecosystem that moderates extremes of heat and cold, stores a great deal of water, and generates a great deal of humidity. And in this protected environment, trees can live to be very old." Support groups can likewise form a protected climate that nurtures their members to create art that may live well beyond them.

Writers are an introverted bunch, so we can miss out on the benefits of being in a class or group. We're also sensitive; our muses can wither from a single unkind word. Like trees, we need to develop thick skin. We do this by learning to ask for the support we desire while tuning out the feedback that isn't helpful or constructive, primarily if it's delivered by someone with a different sensibility, writing in an unrelated genre, or who would never in a billion years read a book like ours.

Carol Allen

I have several friends who quit writing altogether after getting horrible feedback from teachers and/or other "writers." I was blessed to have the most wonderful writing coach, who I credit with finding my voice and being one of my most meaningful cheerleaders who helped me fall in love with writing and believe I could do it. But what was tricky was that everything I worked on were projects he'd *never* want to read. He'd always want me add elements to the work that, for me, were completely off tone—like adding sex scenes to my heartwarming essays about my love of cats. (And yes, I realize there's a pussy joke in there somewhere.) "Go darker," he was constantly encouraging.

At one point, with his insightful help, I wrote a screenplay. It was the most fun I ever had, and again, it was something he'd never purposely read, and if made into an actual movie, I knew he'd rather stick needles into his eyeballs than ever go see. But I was in love with it, which was always my litmus test. So, I kept all the silly, whimsical "chick lit" elements that had clearly made him exasperated every time I read aloud in our small writing group. I submitted it to a Los Angeles film festival, one that he happened to enter a screenplay to, as well. Guess which script won best screenplay? Yup, the goofy "girlie" one without a single dark character, or sex scene. (To his credit, he seemed genuinely happy for me. Whew.)

Van Jones

It's okay if you need a check-in partner beyond your editor. It's okay to be a part of a group. Don't move at the slow pace of the group; go as fast as you can. But I put that out there because I think when people imagine someone like Toni Morrison, they see her sequestered in a basement somewhere for twenty years. She's a social person. She knows a lot of people. She gets out a lot, and it helps her work.

There's a mythology out there that you, yourself somehow, are supposed to solely and individually go into a basement and create all this stuff on your own. And if you can't, it's because you suck, and you just need to suck less. That's really destructive because even writing a book is a team sport. You need support. I've sometimes employed ghostwriters on different parts of things because I know what I want to say, but I don't have the time to do the research. Because I'm a person that's in the community, I have people step up and try and help me do different things. You want to think about the community effort you're leading, the one you have the main responsibility for. But you're also trying to consolidate community wisdom. When the book is published, to get the book bought and read by anybody, you're going to have to engage your friends and allies anyway. It's not just you by yourself. I want writers to give themselves permission to build a support team for themselves.

Feeling isolated wherever you are? Does the idea of trying to envision your book and write it as a one-person show sound lonely (not to mention slightly crazy pants)? Well, this fun factoid won't help (at least not now; you'll thank me later—everyone does):

Your friends and even family members won't read your book. Probably not ever. This often includes your nearest and dearest.

Don't worry. You're not special. It happens to all of us. Maybe because they can't stomach the possibility of not loving it. Or they're sick to death of hearing you talk about it and resent how it steals your time. Perhaps *they're* short on time. Or they love you for you and don't need further convincing of your worth. Maybe they just suck. *All the more reason to find your book people.*

Remember, reading and writing—where your first teachers gave you feedback, perhaps even gold stars—started as *collaboration.* Think about who you can bring with you on this journey that wants to be there. You may have outgrown those footie pajamas, but that doesn't mean you don't still need a shoulder to read on. Writing and world-changing are better with a bud, or a group—as in, richer creativity, flatter learning curve, stronger results. More sanity. And laughter. Fellow word-lovers can help you blow past apathy, excuses, overwhelm, and writer's block.

I recently read that while penning *Little Women* in the 1860s, Louisa May Alcott sent the first dozen or so chapters off to her publisher, but both parties thought them dull. Thankfully, she enlisted the opinion of several young female readers, who called the manuscript "splendid," giving them the confidence to publish the book. Its immediate success was a surprise to both author and publisher, but not to those "little" women who saved the day.

Go find your support, your writing confidant, your group! There are factors to consider—such as the size of your gatherings, how often you'll convene, and where (in person, on video, via email). Will you focus on one person's work or several? How many pages/words should everyone contribute? Will you read work aloud or come to the meeting with notes, having already read the allotment? Have fun figuring out what will best support you. (This is your creation, after all!) Some people thrive in an environment with a healthy dose of competition and lots of voices. They don't want to show up without having done their homework while other members are on their A-game. But if that leaves you wanting to hide in the bathroom, how's about finding a great coach? Or perhaps an intimate retreat would be ideal.

Aditi Khorana, former news journalist, and film marketing executive for Hollywood studios. *Mirror in the Sky* was Aditi's first novel, followed by *The Library of Fates*—a feminist historical fantasy, set in ancient India.

While working on my first book (*Mirror in the Sky*), I, along with a group of eight of my close writer friends, rented a house in Palm Springs for a week. We were all fledgling creatives, barely getting by, juggling various freelance assignments, trying to make it in the world. Renting that house was a commitment to ourselves, our writing, and each other. I remember it being a week of solidarity and endless, loving, determined labor. We cooked together, workshopped together, brainstormed in the pool, sat around the kitchen table reading each other snippets of our work. In the evening, we mixed cocktails while we edited and read each other's pages. It was glorious. Now I do this at least once or twice a year with writer friends. It's generative, inspiring, and so much fun.

It's important to create goals within your support group that provide sturdy, healthy boundaries. I use a timer at my retreats, so everyone knows how long they have to read and share, and no one hijacks the space. Say a prayer or set an intention at the start of each meeting, and watch breathing slow and shoulders relax as you declare it a sacred space where everyone gives their best and receives exactly what they need. Have each member state what kind of feedback they prefer before they read. Some like nothin' but the brutal truth. Others will be utterly devastated by any hint of a negative comment.

A technique that works for many is a so-called "feedback sandwich." Begin with what you like about someone's work. Offer negative criticism in a constructive way: "When you wrote this, it lost me because . . ." or "I didn't understand what you meant by . . ." Then finish up with positive remarks. In her classic *Bird by Bird: Some Instructions on Writing and Life,* Anne Lamott warns about people who take an "almost orgasmic pleasure" in tearing down others' work, probably because they're not solid enough to create their own. Some tough love can be too tough. But feedback that lacks specificity and constructive criticism won't grow you as a writer. And when you're on the receiving end, give yourself permission to sit with feedback; don't feel you need to respond in the moment. Take what resonates and leave the rest.

Sometimes you've got the right writing with the wrong folks. Ask yourself: *Are these my people? Do they stretch me? Do I respect them enough to show up every week or once a month?* If you're woo-woo and they're not, you might feel judged; you'll need the strength, vision, and confidence to say, "No thanks, that's not what this piece is."

Feelings are contagious. Science has proven that we feel the emotions of those around us. The "right" people make us believe that all things are possible. Your writing buddy or group will help you have faith in your grand intentions and see options you didn't know existed. They will motivate you to keep going because you want to show up for others the way they show up for you. Teamwork = dreamwork.

10

Seduction of Seclusion

Where Writers Find Their Peace

> "Solitary trees, if they grow at all, grow strong."
> ~ Winston Churchill

Solitude. *Noun.* "The state of being or living alone, seclusion. Remoteness from habitations, as of a place; absence of human activity. A lonely, unfrequented place."

Lonely? Unfrequented? I respectfully disagree, Dictionary.com. Most writers I know feel anything but lonely inside their busy, populated stories. When I look at the word *solitude*, I see *sol*, or "light of the sun." Seclusion is the power source on which my writing depends. Solitude connects us to the light within where our stories reside. *PS. Dogs asleep at your feet, even better.*

As we saw in the previous chapter, writing communities matter, but there's a time for connection and a time for seclusion. Storytellers need to hear themselves think and thus require plenty of peace and quiet. Even extroverts, party people, who get their best ideas and do the bulk of their research out in the world, must go within at some point to tap into their inner light.

It's a challenge, chasing solitude.

Godforsaken peace and quiet. That's what we were going for when we'd moved from Paul's estate to our rental home in Studio City.

It took years to shake off the residue of having lived in Hollywood. The morning the Sunset Strip turned hellish as shotgun-wielding citizens surrounded our car at the start of the LA Riots. The grief following the tragic accidental death of Brandon Lee on the set of *The Crow* while I was taking care of his Siamese cats. * Fighting with loved ones over the Nicole Brown Simpson murder, a woman Jesse and I were just getting to know, in a town suddenly hotly divided in the glaring spotlight of the world's largest media circus.

Amid all the noise and craziness, the protective mother in me longed for a more peaceful place to raise our boy—and my book baby, too.

Steven Pressfield 🪶

The artist's journey is a dangerous one. That's why we avoid it. Like the mystic and the renunciant, the artist does her work in an altered state of consciousness. She's seeking herself, her voice, her source, and she has to enter that dark forest alone. It's in this forest where the rules are different, the hatters are mad, and the principles inverted. But not going in will make her totally crazy. It's hard. I mean, Hemingway blew his brains out, right? You can go in too deep.

But the great thing about being a writer or an artist, as opposed to, say, a football player with bad knees who's out at forty, is that you can do it for your whole life. Even failure is just another step on the way to success. You can keep going, dust yourself off, and write another one.

I purposely ignore my [Malibu] ocean view and turn my writing chair toward the wall. We're all working inside our heads. If we're

---

* Brandon was, incidentally, best friends with Carol's then-boyfriend, now-husband, Bill Allen. A longtime actor and author, Bill's written about Brandon in his fabulously irreverent and mystical memoir, *My RAD Career*, and is helping to make a documentary about his life.

writing *War and Peace*, we're seeing Napoleonic battles in our mind's eye, so we don't need a view.

Rob Bell 🌿

[As a writer] your mind is elsewhere. You have to surrender the obsession with metrics and data. Because for many people their work is directly tied to tangible outcomes. They work this many hours, this many clients were served, and this many deals were transacted. When you enter into this kind of territory, all you know is you spend eight hours figuring out how the blue shoes related to the stepdad and the Toyota. You're trying to figure out that theme or that chapter. It's just a totally different kind of work.

Sometimes, I'll be trying to come up with language to describe something and it'll turn over and over and over and I will realize, "Oh! Other people get done with work and go home and don't even think about it." This is just what I do. It exists in some other category. It doesn't make a lot of sense. If I keep looking around, trying to figure out why my work happens to be this way and why this tires me and this energizes me—I think I just died to the need to make sense of it. At some point, it got too tiring. I'm going to let it be whatever it is. But yes, I like [the word] obsession. I think I've made peace with it. It feels a lot less obsessive because this is the work. This is what it takes.

Patricia Cornwell 🌿

We all know what it's like when you're at the end of that first real draft. My rule is: I do not allow myself to operate dangerous machinery. I'm not kidding! Like a helicopter or a fast car, or any car. You're not yourself! I always say that you're kind of Alice going through the looking glass when you write a book or do any art. You're channeling something. You're transporting, going somewhere else. And then you come back. It's kind of like the astronauts. They're not used to gravity for a while.

Sue Monk Kidd ❧

I need a writing cave all the time. I have a room upstairs that I converted into what I call my "study." My husband says, "What are you studying up there?" It's a real sanctuary for me. I love my solitude.

Sandy and I have been married for fifty-one years. We have a wonderful rhythm too. He lets me have my solitude and my time, which I think is beautiful.

Tosh was finally napping as I sat at my desk, a blanket mummifying my middle. Jesse was at his SAG-AFTRA softball practice. A paragraph I'd edited nine times clicked into place. *Deep breath.*

Just then, our neighbor's ear-splitting leaf blowers fired up and a cacophony of dogs—ours and everyone else's—barked in unison. As I raced to shut our windows, Tosh popped awake, eye rubbing.

I had no sooner quieted Little Man after the tornado of dust and decibels—*where did I save that file again?*—when a UPS truck pulled up across the street, catapulting the dogs once more into a high-alert bark-fest. Add to that the seemingly daily sirens, car chases, and police helicopters chopping over nearby Ventura Boulevard, and I was stressed. Writing sessions aborted. Again. But this was Studio City, an enclave of the Valley, known for its grassy parks and outdoor cafés! How could our picturesque residential street be so disruptive? If I couldn't write here, what hope did I have for any semblance of a healthy sleep schedule?

Sabaa Tahir 🌿

With things like the UPS driver ringing the bell, I kind of love those interruptions because it's this beautiful reminder that I ain't shit. Makes me work harder. When I'm really in my feels, and I'm deep in the story, and then my son calls and he's like, "Is there any pizza left, or did you finish it all?" with that accusatory note in his voice, or my mom is calling to yell at me about something, I'm reminded that I'm just a person.

Ultimately, it connects me deeper to the humanity of my characters. One of the things I think about writing these books is that you forget that it's not all bad. You can be writing through awful things, and your characters are still going to laugh and have crushes and fall in love and be annoyed with the person they love. I feel like those life interruptions, for me anyway, are a great reminder of the rhythms of life.

Tim Grahl 🌿

I actually do the opposite of what Steven [Pressfield] does in turning towards the wall. I have a business to run. If I come into my office and I sit at my desk, I want to run the business. So, I tend to write at coffee shops. Having people there helps me.

I have tried to come into my office to work, but I start to feel lonely like the walls are closing in. In coffee shops, I put on head-phones and block out the world. Something about being out while I'm writing allows it to flow for me in a way sitting at my desk doesn't. I usually only spend about half the day at my office. I'll find a coffee shop, or I'll sit outside somewhere—anywhere, where there's action that allows me to focus.

Every once in a while, I'll be at Starbucks, and a friend will come in, and I'll say hi, and then, "All right, I'll talk to you later." Like, I'm not here to talk. I'm here to get my work done. We can talk later. Of course, this is in [Steven Pressfield's] *Turning Pro*, this decision of, "If I'm going to do this, there are no half measures."

Following Guru's directive, I was now meditating daily. And a regular visitor had been showing up: a Native American man with long black braids, tanned leather skin, charcoal eyes, and a red bandana. Every time I closed my eyes, there he was. *I'm not going anywhere, just so you know.*

I hadn't the foggiest idea who he was. But when my sister's boyfriend, Bill, told us about a medicine man by the name of Thomas One Wolf, I got chills. He'd met Thomas when actor Lou Diamond Phillips brought him to authenticate depictions of Native Indians for the film *Sioux City*.

"Tell Linda he's the real deal," Lou said. "If she can get to him, he'll give her the interview of a lifetime for her book." Only problem was, getting to him. For starters, Thomas didn't have a phone, and he lived in a forest somewhere in northern New Mexico off a maze of unmarked dirt roads. Plus, he was "really private."

I was getting used to forgoing sleep to write in the middle of the night. But what felt oddly urgent was that I finally understood Jesse's desire to move out of town, to start over somewhere simpler. It broke my heart watching his dehumanizing auditions. In rooms of forty men who looked just like him, my husband waited anxiously to hear his name called to go before the Hollywood firing squad: casting directors and producers sitting stone-faced, daring him to do something fantastic or just hurry up and die already. After Jesse yelled at an old lady for glaring at our dog, who was crapping on her lawn, by the way, it was clear. All that memorizing and schmoozing and driving only to sit by the phone (literally, before cell phones), to hear that, yet again, someone else got the part, was breaking him.

What scared me even more, however, was that I'd started feeling disconnected from Jesse in flashes at home. Our everyday togetherness felt increasingly worlds apart, as I entered the addictive and bustling realm of my book—an unknowable and unreachable place for Jesse, no matter how much I tried to involve him.

So, when the Northridge Earthquake threw us out of bed at 4:00 AM, killing people in a nearby apartment complex, I packed up our car and the pups for a visit to New Mexico. Lou said that Thomas One Wolf had land for sale. His property, where he lived "close to the earth" in a cabin on raw land at the base of the Rocky Mountains, sounded exactly like what my hubby and son, with their Cherokee roots on Jesse's mother's side, needed. At the very least, I hoped our road trip could be a reset for our family. And, if Thomas happened to grant me an interview for the book while we were there, my accountant said we could use the trip as a write off!

When I told Diane about how Thomas had cobbled together a community of like-minded sweet city transplants on three thousand acres of raw land, with residents only too happy to relinquish their garage door openers and swimming pools for a kind of solitude they'd never dreamed existed, she was horrified.

"You're kidding, right?" Di said. "You're writing a book based on celebrity interviews and thinking of leaving Los Angeles for the middle of nowhere? You're out of your mind!"

"Maybe so. But Jesse's Chevy spots are paying the bills. We've got to try, Di. He's going to lose it here. I can feel it. And I need trees."

Martha Beck ❧

I wrote an allegory [*Diana, Herself*] about a brown baby found on a trash heap. She ends up going to a forest and gets lost there because she has to be outside of culture to find out who she is. That retreat to the forest is something I've done. I started only doing seminars in the African bush or in the mountains in California. It came to me at a certain point that if I was around people, I couldn't know who I truly was. I've spent the last three years in the woods. And it's been incredible. I want every woman to find a forest where she's away from people, away from even the vibrations of people, because there's that little telepathic thing happening—we all need a forest inside our mind, our house, our heart—a forest where we can go to be away from culture and find out who we are.

Charles Sailor ❧

For your work to be as pure as possible—whether you find yourself in a secluded mountain cabin or a busy restaurant—I always recommend you listen to classical music, whether you're a fan or not. The pieces are so emotionally driven that classical music will help drive your story. Find pieces that you enjoy—with no lyrics, for background music. You don't want to listen to anything with lyrics because it will get into your head and keep you from composing. I like to think of writing as if I'm scripting a symphony. The words should sing to your reader; they should crescendo. I have a group of about thirty classical CDs I'll alternate through, depending on the type of scene I'm writing.

Arielle Ford, bestselling author of many books, including *The Soulmate Secret* and *Wabi Sabi Love*. Former book publicist to Deepak Chopra, Marianne Williamson, Wayne Dyer, and Neale Donald Walsch. ❧

I get my best ideas while taking early morning walks on the beach in La Jolla. Brian, my husband, jogs and talks with homeless people and feeds the birds while I dream up blog posts or story lines in whatever book I'm working on. I have to live near the ocean. The sound of the waves and the smell of the sea clears my head.

"I can't wait to get out of here!" Jesse exclaimed as we headed east on the I-10 in our eco-tin can with Brodie and Peanut curled up in balls asleep next to Tosh. The farther we got from the city, the happier we became. Driving through the sprawling deserts of New Mexico with the windows down, we felt like wild horses cut loose from ground ties. As we wound through the mountains outside of Santa Fe, with its blue skies and white puffy clouds and red mesas rolling on for miles, we sang along to Bad Company at the top of our lungs, our spirits renewed.

"Pull over!" I squealed, three miles from the Tres Piedras diner where we were scheduled to meet Thomas One Wolf. I bounded up a hill overlooking the valley, the tail end of the majestic Rocky Mountains in the distance. An ocean of sage rippled before us like waves on what was once a seafloor. Hundreds of thousands of acres of forest surrounded us.

I took in a deep breath of pine, outstretched my arms with palms to the sky, and yelled: "This is it, Jesse! We *have* to live here! This is our place!" Jesse and the dogs beamed beside me.

When we pulled up to the diner, Thomas One Wolf stepped out to meet us. *Oh my God.* Long black braids, tanned skin, charcoal eyes, and a red bandana. Exactly as I'd seen in my meditations.

"Welcome home, Brother! Welcome home, Sister," Thomas said, hugging us. Then he turned to Tosh. "Well, Little Dude, you and I are gonna have some big fun while you're here!" Tosh swelled like a balloon.

We followed Thomas One Wolf's truck through miles of dirt roads, past abandoned stone cabins from centuries past, across dry creek beds up into a thick swath of pinyon, traversing the land he'd secured to save from future "unconscious development." After a lunch of beans and tortillas prepared by his wife, Sheri, in their simple cabin amid tens of thousands more acres of protected Bureau of Land Management trees, Jesse and I were already making plans to build a modest cabin before the first snowfall.

That night on the land, a trillion stars twinkled down on us through the skylight of a borrowed trailer. We slept like hibernating bears. We'd come home. The next day, leaning against an ancient cedar, I made more progress on my book than I had in the previous twenty.

Laura Munson 🌿

I live in Whitefish, Montana, near Glacier National Park. Thirty years ago, if you had told me I'd raise two kids here, I would have said, "Are you kidding? I'm a city girl!" But it keeps me on my knees in humility. We're on the food chain here. There are grizzly bears wandering around in my backyard! Montana feeds my muse, and it won't let go.

You know how a grove of aspen trees is one organism? That's how I feel taking a walk in the woods. Something always happens in the form of inspiration, awareness, and connection. You can look out the window, sure, and still feel connected. But I try to take walks in the woods every day. It makes me (and my muse) feel new and inspired to go back home to write.

Danielle LaPorte

I feel closer to everything on an airplane, and I also feel like I'm getting away with something. You cannot find me. I'm inaccessible to everyone. I feel hermetically sealed.

Our frontier life at an altitude of 8,600 feet in New Mexico was our *Little House on the Prairie*. Stunning campfires under the Milky Way. Outdoor cookouts and sing-alongs. Nature walks. Vision quests. Sweat lodges. Our community went to bed with the sun and woke up with the sun. With virtually no human-made lights visible anywhere at night, our star-scape was more entertaining than anything on TV. We went our first year without ever plugging ours into the wall.

Peaceful? You bet. Not a leaf blower, UPS truck, ambulance, or helicopter in sight or within earshot. Tosh and his five-year-old little face with missing front "toothisus" would call out to me in the mornings, even though Mommy was always in the same spot: sitting at the kitchen table, outlined by the picture-window view of another stunning desert-sky morning, blissfully immersed in her writing. I loved stealing the last moments of quiet time before my family would bound out of bed for another day of chopping wood, building forts, cooking, cleaning, reading, drawing, and playing with my growing blue-eyed snuggle bug.

Townsfolk called us "Hollywood." As in, "Hey, Hollywood!" because to them we could seem like a pretty big deal when they saw Jesse on TV. But they had no idea how not-Hollywood we really were, or how much we appreciated how *chill* they were and that we could now raise our boy in a place where he didn't have to dress a certain way or keep up with the rich kids. Heck, in these parts, he was the rich kid!

Playing frontier woman filled a gal's days. We had a cabin to finish. Locals to meet. Groceries to fetch (Taos was a two-hour round trip). Abandoned puppies to raise. Meals to rustle up (notice my country drawl)—on a wood stove, no less. Jesse became a volunteer fireman, and each morning, I helped out at Tosh's two-room schoolhouse, where kindergartners shared a room with eighth graders. Writing time was mostly relegated to the middle of the night and pre-dawn hours when my family was asleep. What else was new?

Surprisingly, Diane was wrong; moving out to the boonies was the best thing I'd done to woo interviews for my book. Thomas One Wolf, with his wise ways and sweat lodge ceremonies, was quite the attraction for those who had everything but still felt a nagging sense of emptiness. A steady stream of Angelinos braved our backwoods dirt roads to sit at his feet, my family and I front-row attractions in the exact right circus.

People who paid others to do their chores respected me for my wood chopping, water carrying, and outhouse-ing. As I served them my chai tea at one of our "Feast Ways" (Thomas's version of a good old-fashioned potluck), they seemed to take me more seriously. "Hey, check out this chick who chops her own wood. She really walks her talk!"

I looked up to Native Americans, even as a young girl, and fantasized I was one. Dad said that perhaps I had been, in my "last life." I'd been a church-loving kid, even going by myself, but I'd never felt more connected to God and my creativity than in an ancient sweat lodge ceremony. This being the early nineties, the term *cultural appropriation* wouldn't mean anything to me for many years. But I did worry from the start about going where I wasn't welcomed, stepping into sacred places that weren't mine to step in. I didn't want to anger or offend anyone, especially not native ancestors.

But Thomas One Wolf and Grampa Pete Concha (Thomas's adopted father and the Consique, or spiritual leader, of the nearby Taos Pueblo) would have none of it. They were in a growing camp of Native Americans who believed that their sacred traditions were precisely the thing that could help bring healing to the plighted land and "all two-leggeds."

"No weaving is strong with too many dropped stitches," Thomas would say. "All beings are equally vital to the Universal blanket." As the times were dire, Mother Earth's healing demanded that the entire human family rise to a level of unity and cooperation we had never before seen. "Besides," Thomas declared, "Ceremony does not need me to protect it. Its Truth will pass through time unchanged by man."

I just thanked my lucky stars for being included. The community they'd built allowed me a greater sense of peace than I'd ever known. With the right amount of neighborly support and family interaction, with loads of seclusion, where no one knocked on our door for days at a time, my heart was happy, and my writing was thriving.

Dani Shapiro ❧

In the years since *Devotion* came out and I was on Oprah, the pace of things has picked up. It becomes up to me to say, "I need to go back into the cave. The writing has to happen inside the cave." It's easy to come out of the cave. You blink. It's bright out and a lot of fun—all sorts of things to see and do! It's harder to go back in the cave. The longer you're out, at least for me, the harder it is to go back in.

The last time I was in LA, I was staying at a friend's guest house, where the conditions are ideal. I got a ton done. No one to bother me. The phone, if it rang, was not for me. Finding ways to make time sacred is hard. Lack of interruption is essential, but uninterrupted concentration is harder and harder to come by. Coming up, I know I have most of the months of April and May off. If I don't schedule anything—if I don't accept invitations and just say no—no matter how enticing—and create quiet around myself, I will be able to accomplish an awful lot. The work has to be the central thing, and then everything else can arise out of it.

Ann Patchett 🌿

My husband, God love him, is a doctor who gets up in the morning, puts on a suit, leaves the house at seven o'clock, and comes home at seven o'clock. When I am working every day and deeply engaged, I'm a terrific wife. I'm so glad to see him. I do not wish to travel or sequester myself. I'm done by four o'clock, I don't ever write at night, and I am thrilled to go downstairs and make dinner and share it and be with him. I'm so grateful he takes me out of my head and grounds me, loves me, and all of that.

When I hate him, and when I am a crummy wife, is when I'm not writing. Because when I'm not writing, and I want to be writing, I blame him. *If it wasn't for the fact that I had to make you dinner, if it wasn't for the fact that I'm doing laundry, and getting the gutters fixed, and making your life so easy, I would be writing a brilliant novel.* That's when I'm a bitch.

So, this my friends, is the universal lesson: When I am happy with myself, I am happy with others. The older I get, the more I realize that it's the journey inward that counts. It's Dorothy at the end of *The Wizard of Oz*. If it was never in my own backyard, I'd never really lost it, to begin with. If I never get on another plane, if I never drive more than five miles from my house, it is fine because I'm on the journey inward.

Life in nature was grounding us, reconnecting Jesse and me. I did worry, though, about discontinuing my sessions with Guru Singh. Guru's influence on my confidence had been profound, and, convinced he'd be a game-changer, I was so glad to have been able to connect the gals from my support group with him before we left town.

Fortunately, moving didn't mean Guru and I would lose our friendship. Quite the opposite. Instead, he and his beautiful wife, Guruperkarma Kaur, began camping on our land and even bought their own eighty acres!

New Mexico was a sanctuary. Without TV, I was free to see my goals rather than the endless stream of media images that once distracted me. And just as I'd hoped, it *was* infinitely easier to hear my book in the woods. After each nightly writing session, before getting into bed, I'd look at my list of chapters to edit upon waking and know precisely where to go next. I would finish my manuscript in this peaceful spot, with a more singular focus than any I'd ever had or would again.

Terry McMillan ✔

I'll tell you how I find seclusion. I close the bathroom door.

I lived in Wyoming, for a year, and wrote a book. The snow helped me a lot. I liked the sound of snow.

I now live in Pasadena. It's pretty quiet. But I don't care where you are; there are people who live in New York City and write. You can block out the outside world if you're inside the world you're writing about. I've been doing it for years. I did it when I had a baby. With one ear, you're listening for him to cry, but for the most part, when you're in the zone, you're in the zone.

I lived in Brooklyn, and let me tell you, the trash guy could be going by, dogs barking, but when you're in your world, you're lost in it.

But I'll look for reasons to get interrupted. *Am I thirsty? I think so!* Especially if I've written something that's perplexing or a little painful, or I don't understand what's happening, and psychologically, spiritually, and emotionally I don't know if I want to go there. I can think of a reason to walk to the refrigerator! By the time I come back, I'm poised again. I can go back and pick up where I left off. I love stopping in the middle because I can tell if I'm bull-shitting myself. If it's lost, it means I *was* bullshitting myself. Sort of like sex.

Not everyone requires actual seclusion in nature. Some writers simply cannot create in total quiet; they find it deafening. They need the chaos of the coffee shop, the thrum of music playing, the laughter of children nearby.

We all have to find what works for us, our way of tuning out the world to tune into our inner light. Never in a million years would I have guessed that in living as far from the LA lifestyle as I could imagine, we'd be introduced to incredible creatives to interview. Or that by leaving town, we'd suddenly find ourselves on Hollywood party circuit guest lists (not that we attended many), cementing for me the fact that we don't have to have everything in life "figured out." We just have to keep following the good-feeling gumdrops through the forest. It's like that idea from *Frozen II,* or recovery, that Glennon Doyle talked about on one of our podcast episodes: the idea that you just have to do the Next Right Thing. For me, that next right thing was taking my man to a place where he could breathe and where I could hear.

11

Cookin' with Gas

Productivity, Mindset, and Energy Hacks

"There is no sunrise so beautiful that it is worth waking me up to see it."
~ Mindy Kaling

It takes ENERGY to create beauty from nothing. But what if doing Life takes all you've got? Toni Morrison famously wrote at the "edges of the day." *Edges? What edges?* David Sedaris says you must sacrifice one area of life (work, family, friends, or health) to be successful. Two, if you want to be *super* successful. *Seriously?*

The annals of literature are full of speed freaks and alcoholics who delivered their literary masterpieces in drug-induced altered states. Stephen King says he wrote his bestseller *Cujo* intoxicated on cocaine and blackout drunk. Ayn Rand admitted to taking massive doses of amphetamines while writing *Atlas Shrugged*, working for days without sleeping. Paul Williams told me he penned "some of the most famous codependent anthems of the 1970s" higher than the Hollywood sign just a few hills over from his house.

Wouldn't it be nice if us mere mortals could do that—forgo rest and recovery and live like immortals while churning out global hit after hit? But is that the best idea?

There's no one way to eat, drink, rest, or live. Each of us writers needs to find our balance of nutrition, sleep, exercise, and even meditation and personal boundaries to best fuel up to fill up the blank page. Getting intentional with self-care with these time, health, and sanity-saving life hacks makes for a sweeter song.

BEEP! BEEP! BEEP! BEEP!

"Linda! Turn that shit off! It's three in the morning, for God's sake!" Jesse moaned. "If you're going to set the alarm this early, you know the rule: Get it on the second fucking beep!"

"Sorry!" I cried, leaping out of bed with such force I tweaked my lower back. "Ouch! No worries. I'm good!" I sang as I pushed the OFF button. "I had that nightmare again, babe. But this time, Seal was *nice*!" I kissed the cheek of my already sleeping husband and lay back for a minute, trying to hold onto the last wisps for clues. This was a breakthrough—the possibility of an interview with the singer Seal. Enough to get me a literary agent. I'd been dreaming about my favorite rock star for months. But instead of the usual horror, where I'd feverishly chase him through a Hollywood party only to have him disappear like cigarette smoke in the night sky, this time Dream Seal had met my eyes and said a simple and glorious, "Oh! Hello, Linda." Dream Seal knew my name!

I'd been obsessed with the British singer-songwriter since "Crazy," from Seal's debut album, became my anthem three years prior. I'd never met the man, but his voice, his lyrics, his shoot-for-the-stars commitment to total mastery made me feel invincible.

As Seal sang about miracles happening and how we'd never survive without getting "a little crazy," my own crazy goals—specifically the one about saving forests of trees—felt doable. At least while awake. It was nighttime where my story lines got all jacked up, and I became a groupie stalker, and Seal my frustrating fugitive.

Except, the chase had ended! My dream progress had to be a sign, right? Careful not to stir Jesse as I slunk out of bed, I tiptoed downstairs to my desk, a harvest moon pouring through the picture window like an MTV music video.

Seal is going to be in my book! I lit a candle and said a prayer of thanks before starting my pitch letter to Seal's representation.

You'd think I would have been a walking zombie with all this middle-of-the-night theater, but on the contrary, I was buzzed. Friends marveled at my lack of sleep and output of daily woodchopping. But outside of being fueled by my mission, there was nothing mysterious about it. In my mind, my endless energy was thanks to keepin' it raw.

Elizabeth Gilbert ❧

When working on a book, you make the decision to write the night before, so you make the decision to not drink a bottle of wine, to not stay up watching *Breaking Bad* until two in the morning. You decide that you're going to write the next morning and all of the next mornings to come.

Lee Child ❧

I've noticed over the years that I do my best work when I'm hungry. When I'm physically hungry, to the point of being able to feel it. I thought it was just me, and then I happened to read a scientific paper with new research that said that when we're hungry, the creativity center in our brain lights up. It's an evolutionary inheritance.

A million years ago, when we were hungry, we came up with a better plan to catch the next woolly mammoth. We're trained to do it subliminally and atavistically in our brains. When we're hungry, we become more creative. If I were eating, for instance, I would be happy. I wouldn't need to hunt something down.

"Here comes the watermelon killer!" Thomas One Wolf teased as I entered his yard for a Feast Way potluck. Neighbors were setting up, their red faces glistening from having just exited the sweat lodge. As they grazed on the usual fare—mac 'n cheese, Fritos and bean dip, coleslaw, barbecued meat, baby carrots with ranch dressing, and Jell-O, cornbread, and Oreos for dessert—I knew my fruit salad was safe. Despite the tropical colors glowing from the glass bowl in my arms, no one ever made a move to feast on my dinners.

"You have the weirdest diet I've ever seen," Thomas said as I spooned pineapple and mango into my mouth.

"You're just jealous," I said. "All of your coffee guzzling can't compete with the natural high I get from grapes."

"Sour grapes!" he shot back, dunking a cookie in his mug of black coffee—his second pot of the day—and waving it in my face before broadcasting, "Never trust a tea teetotaler!"

It's not that I didn't have a conventional sweet tooth. I was the granddaughter of German bakery owners and could inhale a plate of snickerdoodles faster than you could say, well, "snickerdoodle." (Ever pound on a neighbor's door in search of old Halloween candy? No? Yeah. Me, either.) But our rural life and big-city dreams required reserves of energy I wasn't willing to piss away.

Mostly vegan, my primary source of fuel came from whole, unprocessed foods like raw fruits and vegetables. It helped that Jesse's diet was as strict as mine. When you don't let meat, dairy, alcohol, sugar, sodas, coffee, chemicals, smoking, or drugs of any kind—not even an aspirin—pass your lips, you're pretty much a freak or a bore, at least back in the nineties, before our weird ways became hip. Luckily for me, our marriage was based on a mania for smoothies and salad—a near-total compulsion for crisp greens drenched in extra-virgin olive oil and lemon. Soy cheese, too, during those hog-wild special occasions.

Nell Scovell 🌿

To get in flow, I use sugar. And coffee. Yeah, like a morning bun, something with sugar and cinnamon. I wrote my book [*Just the Funny Parts*] right after the 2016 election. I was so grateful for the times I was able to get into flow and not think about politics. Not to ignore them, but to continue my work.

Raised on organic meals made from scratch, once I'd moved away from Mom's healthy table into the Delta Gamma sorority house at USC, every meal was a smorgasbord of fat-and-sugary delights, and I promptly gained the dreaded freshman fifteen. Did they really expect us to learn portion control around unlimited quantities of Cap'n Crunch, waffles, and eggs Benedict—all before noon? I was so exhausted I missed half of my first classes! Until I started eating 90 percent raw. Feeling once again shot out of a cannon in the mornings, nothing short of a fruit famine could lure me back to the dark side of pancake brunches and late-night pepperoni pizza runs.

But every magic potion comes with a price. How could I date normally with my purse full of raw veggies and a list of dos and don'ts as long as a line of celery sticks to the moon? I was no picnic to take out to eat. And God forbid anyone took me on a picnic! I hated being so high fucking maintenance (except at my vegan Thanksgivings, my time to shine!); no boys ever matched up to the "health-o-meter" in my head. Which is why, when Jesse and I met at the health food store and discovered a mutual passion for produce, it was love at first bite.

In New Mexico, our strict diet seemed to pay off. Even while chopping wood, carrying water, and building our cabin amidst monsoon rains and relentless spring winds, Tosh, Jesse, and I never experienced a hint of the common yearly cold or flu. I simply didn't need as much sleep and felt more nourished by the sleep I did get. So, when our alarm sounded at 3:00 AM, I could pop downstairs, sit down to my book, and turn on the soothing sounds of Seal—grateful for another chance to speak my miracles and get a little crazy.

Geneen Roth, the first to link compulsive eating and dieting with deeply personal and spiritual issues, has authored ten books, including the *New York Times* bestsellers *When Food Is Love*, *Lost and Found*, and *Women Food and God*. ☙

I have gone through many different kinds of diets: vegetarian, pescatarian, vegan, macrobiotic. Most people don't realize that it's possible to feel better because they've been eating what they're intolerant of or allergic to and never come into balance, where they realize, "Oh! This is what it feels like to be me when I'm not craving, craving, craving something because I don't feel good."

Recently, I have been focusing on Life Force. Aliveness. What increases your life force, your presence, your energy, your vitality, your radiance? And what depresses it? That's when what to eat becomes a much easier decision. In the process, you learn so much about yourself because you're really paying attention. You're honoring and cherishing your truth, the being you are.

Maria Shriver 🌿

I eat very differently than I used to. I eat blueberries. I put BrainON or MCT oil in my coffee and in my shakes. I take supplements that I never used to take. I'm stricter with my sleep. I go to bed earlier. I meditate every morning. I try to eat more protein and fats. I try to cut back on sugar, although it's really hard for me. I have a real sweet tooth. People say, "Do you actually do everything you say religiously?" I'm like, "No!" You can find me walking through an airport, and if I smell those Bretzels, I'm in the line.

Martha Beck 🌿

Sugar has a heroin-like effect on the brain. I was addicted to food the way heroin addicts are addicted to heroin. I identified with drug addicts so deeply. I used to coach at a methadone clinic in Phoenix because if life coaching works, it should work for a homeless heroin addict, right? I'd say, "I think you're supposed to feel the way you feel when you're on heroin. You just have to find what makes you feel that way." Reward yourself with something *other* than food. Find something that gives you that feeling. For me, it's painting or writing. But when a nutritionist adjusted my food away from a vegan diet to one with more protein and fat, it was weird. I was obsessed with food, with sugar, for decades. And suddenly, the cravings were gone.

I once went into a complete physical crisis because of a lack of sleep. When I was doing my dissertation, what I found was that women could have everything but sleep. We're massively sleep-deprived. I did all-nighters at least twice a week, with babies and everything. I read studies that said women today talk about sleep the way junkies talk about drugs. Now I think one of the great powers of the feminine is the power of rest.

Rest? Quite the concept, Martha! I looked up the definition on Dictionary .com: "the act of ceasing work or movement in order to relax, refresh oneself, or recover strength." *Hmm.*

"I don't understand how you can sleep on the floor!" Jesse said, seeing me grab a blanket off the couch mid-conversation and snuggle up to Brodie on the carpet. "Don't you want to go to bed?" Nah. When Mama was done and had to snooze, there was no time to lose.

Never wanting to miss a thing, I'd always tried to squeeze too many things into a day. Naps? Even as a kid I was a morning person *and* a night owl, so who needed them?! But with the added demands of parenting—*making almond milk takes a good two hours, and the cleanup, omg!*—I accepted that when my lids got heavy and my brain shut down, nothing could be gained from faking it or pushing through. By default, I was starting to *respect* sleep. Even daydream about it. Not so much the nighttime kind—*don't mess with my writing hours*! But I'd started collecting stories about famous nappers like Einstein, who was rumored to nap on top of getting ten hours (!) a night, and Thomas Edison, whose schedule of three to four hours nightly I could relate to more. (How fascinating that his invention of the light bulb was the one thing that more than anything else has interrupted all our sleep.)

Not everyone has the luxury or ability to fall out in the middle of the afternoon, but because I wrote from home and had time off between Tosh's school drop-off and pickup time, I learned to feel good about catching an hour's shut-eye after lunch. My family then got the best of me. For my book to have what was left, fruit fuel alone wasn't enough.

Arianna Huffington, founder and CEO of Thrive, founder of the *Huffington Post*, and author of fifteen books, including instant international bestsellers *Thrive* and *The Sleep Revolution*. ☙

I'm totally committed to my sleep. Ninety-five percent of the time I get my eight hours. I wake up feeling fully present and recharged.

The idea that we need to power through even when we're exhausted is a myth. We can see this most especially in sports, where sleep has become a competitive edge for top athletes. I see so many people suffering unnecessarily from lack of sleep.

We also see it, of course, in our political leaders, with candidates bragging about being sleep-deprived. I think we need to get to the point where parading your exhaustion like a badge of honor is no longer celebrated.

Danielle LaPorte ☙

Something happens to me after 9:30 PM where I'm like, "I can still do more. I can fit more in." I've been noticing it a lot lately. I'd like to say, "I'm good this week," but it's not true. It affects my capacity to write. I have to trick myself into saying, "If you go to sleep, you're going to be a better writer tomorrow." It's not a trick because it's actually how it works.

I can vouch for the curative fueling effect getting the right amount of sleep has on my writing. When I get my solid seven hours, my ideas are clear. This is how precise I've noticed it to be. I know what to cut. And I can write longer. There's that bewitching time at 3:00 PM where you get that natural dip. If I'm not well rested, I'm done at that dip. If I'm well rested, I just need some water and a piece of fruit. And I can write clear-mindedly until about five thirty to six.

Guru Singh, revered teacher and third-generation yogi, spiritual leader, and author of many books, including his memoir, *Buried Treasures: The Journey from Where You Are to Who You Are.* ❧

My wife and I go to bed early, between nine and ten. I bring through my best writing during the ambrosial hours, which is from 3:00 to 5:00 AM. There are several things available during that time and a couple of things that are unavailable, like the distractions present throughout the rest of our day. Anybody that has ever gotten up early to do something finds they can get multiples done during that time.

In the ambrosial hours, since there's nothing else going on, and the visible rays of the sun are not stirring up all of the things you think about, the things you see, the things you relate to, the people you know, your mind is more of a blank slate. Many writers, musicians, artists, and the greatest scientific minds get up early in the morning to utilize those sweet hours of the morning in order to achieve that which they couldn't otherwise.

To be really practical, it's easy to get up early if you drink a lot of water before bed. You're going to have to get up early in order to pee.

Another trick is that I don't eat anything sweet after sundown. If you do, your brain's going to be super active before going to sleep. It won't have enough rest by the time the ambrosial hours come around to be able to get up. You want to stay away from foods that turn into sugars and carbohydrates. If you eat anything after sundown, it should be green leafy vegetables or a green drink.

Diet is very important, as is drinking lots of water and movement, like yoga. But what's equally important is to set an intention before you go to sleep. Give yourself an assignment—a dreamtime command. Tell yourself you're going to wake up early, and you're going to have these ideas that you'll immediately write down. That's why *The Artist's Way* talks about "morning pages." Early morning hours coordinate the universal mind with your mind so that you have access—like connecting to the internet—to the vast reaches of universal concepts and ideas and answers to questions and solutions to problems.

If you're a caretaker or parent and already exhausted, go to bed earlier. Work up to it, starting ten or fifteen minutes earlier. Then the next week, ten minutes earlier still, and so on. In three weeks, you'll be in bed a half hour earlier. That half hour is going to give you a lot more rest because the sun's energy as the earth rotates is coming towards you after midnight. But it's going away from you before midnight. So, the kind of sleep you get before midnight is worth multiples of the amount of the kind of sleep you get after midnight.

Fake lights are also a problem. For a million-and-a-half years, early humans went to bed with the sun and worked with firelight or candlelight. Fire casts shadows. But when you have a room filled with incandescent lights, there are no shadows. Everything is lit, backlit, front-lit, top-lit, bottom-lit. The brain, used to functioning in a world of shadows, is suddenly confused because it's only been out of the world of shadows for the last, say, 120 years. When you get up in the morning early, and you start to use the infrared light of the sun, which is invisible light, you have access to those deep recesses of your genetic history, of your cosmic history. This is where true creativity comes from.

Napping notwithstanding, the downside of having a lot of natural energy was that it was easy to push it. Overdo, over-give, over-commit. I still said yes to too many people and invitations until I saw it hurt my writing, at which point I wised up quickly. When people-pleasing stops feeling like a payoff, boundaries become easier to embrace—even, I dare say, occasionally fun!

Elizabeth Gilbert ❧

I said yes to everything until I had a nervous breakdown. I so wish I could've learned to protect my time differently. But I had to get sick, strung out, and broke, and then realize I was of no service to anybody, including myself. It's hard for me. I'm a pleaser. I go through life wanting everyone to be made satisfied by my presence in their life. I spent years never saying no to anybody because I have this terrible fear that they would be terribly disappointed. That they wouldn't like me as much.

You know what I found out? My worst fear was absolutely fucking true. There's a reason I didn't do it for thirty years. People hate it. There may be some level at which they respect you a little bit more, but mostly they're just mad in a way I am when people say no to me: "Wow, she's changed. She's kind of a bitch. Oh, she thinks she's better than us."

The trick is you have to let that be. You have to sit with the discomfort that comes with the no without trying to rescue them from their disappointment: "I see your disappointment, and I'm going to let you have your disappointment. My no stands because I'm aware of the limits of my human energies, and the limits of my capacity, and the limits of my mortal life. And I can't do everything. I'm sorry."

It's a muscle. You have to get in shape for it because it's really hard. I still don't find it easy. But I absolutely find it necessary.

Samantha Bennett ❧

As long as your work remains unwritten in your head, it has no effect on anyone. Except you. And not in a good way. Don't you have time? Are people clogging up your schedule? Even fifteen minutes a day can move mountains. Set your timer and prove to yourself that the world has space in it for your work.

Dani Shapiro

When you have an hour, make it a sacred hour. Do anything that will keep you plugged in to the work. If you can do that every day at the same time, it's amazing what can happen. When I wrote my first novel, I did this for my first couple of books—three pages a day, five days a week, fifteen pages a week, sixty pages a month. If you adhere to that discipline, you could have a draft of a novel in half a year, which is nothing in terms of writing a novel.

I always tell my students to touch their projects every day. It doesn't mean you're going to have the whole day to do your work—sometimes those are the worst days, actually, where you have the whole day, and suddenly it's gone.

I didn't have any problem "touching my project every day," as Dani says. Writing had become a passionate force of habit, one of life's non-negotiables. Another thing that was second nature to me was getting out in nature.

"You're always so high when you come home from your morning walks!" Diane said, her bedhead of a blowout cascading around the coffee mug in her hands. We were visiting her place in La Quinta in the desert, and while everyone was still asleep, I'd left for ninety minutes to watch the sunrise while walking the golf course at the base of the purple mountains.

"Huh? I am?" I answered, aware that my morning exercise habit, where I walked outside wherever I was and marveled at the beauty around me and thanked God for my blessings, always filled me up on the inside. Still, I was unaware it was so obvious on the outside. What mother doesn't need time away from her family? I loved my people hard, but Jesse and Tosh were live wires themselves, and I couldn't wait to run out that door every morning to be alone and soak up some stillness before the mayhem commenced. It also gave me the chance to contemplate the chapters I'd been nurturing for hours already.

"Yeah. You've always been like that," Di said. "Coming home blissed out. It's just your thing."

Endorphins, it turns out, are pretty much everyone's thing—including Di's, who, despite being an Olympic sleeper, is a hardcore lifelong competitive athlete. Getting your heart rate up does a world of good, increasing blood circulation and metabolism as a flood of neurotransmitters like serotonin or norepinephrine leads to lower levels of depression, fatigue, and stress. (*See, kids, that runner's high from track practice really can beat out a drug high—without tearing through your lunch money!*)

> **Kelly Noonan Gores**, writer, producer, director, and star of the award-winning *Heal* documentary, host of *The HEAL Podcast*, and author of the book *Heal: Discover Your Unlimited Potential and Awaken the Powerful Healer Within.* 🌾
>
> Nature is always my go-to. Anytime I feel the slightest illness, stress, or spinning in my head, I step outside and put my feet in the earth, barefoot on the ground or in the sand. "Earthing" [the title of another book and documentary] is so important, especially when I'm in the overstimulating environment of a big city. The negative charge of the earth lowers your blood pressure and inflammatory markers. After twenty minutes or so, it does all these amazing things for your health, taking you out of stress mode and into rest and repair mode, opening you right up to that space where creativity happens.

God love him, forever the optimist, Guru kept prescribing meditations for me as my practice ebbed and flowed. But more and more I argued that my writing *felt* like meditation, which Guru concurred. Thus, moving my body outside where the only things talking to me were my story lines and songbirds was my preferred writing break.

Deepak Chopra

Meditation increases our connection to creativity because, done properly, it takes you beyond thought. Meditation allows you to go to the source of thought, which in Eastern wisdom traditions is called consciousness. Consciousness is that which makes any experience possible, including the experience we call thinking, and of course, perception and everything else associated with the mind. And yet, meditation decreases mental activity and ultimately transcends mental activity, where all creativity lies.

Our choice to protect our art may be the most meaningful decision we make. But we can have the most enviable eating, sleeping, and self-care habits, and our books still won't get finished if we're not vigilant with time management. Sorry to be a downer. I know we covered time in its own chapter. But our habits and relationship to time are forever intertwined, so let's briefly revisit this topic.

Over the past fifteen years, I've hosted over four hundred driven, brilliant, healthy, savvy, and abundant writers at my writing retreats. As disciplined as they are, time issues are the number one challenge that trips them up, stalling their momentum and putting the brakes on their flow. And I'm right there with them.

If I'm not careful, I'll get pulled into the Time Suck to End All Time Sucks of entertainment consumption. My son, who lives nearby and knows all the best movies, can turn nearly every night into an excuse to watch some must-see something, which inevitably leads to me staying up too late, eating too heavily, and impeding my own creative productivity.

But it inspires my writing! Fills my creativity well! I need to know what's out there! It's family bonding time! Check yourself, is all I'm saying.

Get a load of these stats: The average American—who we've already assessed is chronically sleep-deprived—takes less vacation time than a medieval peasant while watching an average of *five* hours of TV every day! I was nearly in that camp years ago, as a "Time Debtor," one who robs tomorrow's energy for today, not unlike those speed freaks and alcoholics at the start of this chapter.

A friend who'd been attending meetings at Debtors Anonymous told me I was living with something called "terminal vagueness": the inability to see yourself and your situation clearly, which can result in bad habits and denial that can shorten your life. Two of my biggest productivity killers at that time, checking online news every hour on the hour and watching both *The View* and *Oprah* every day, wouldn't kill me, though they weren't likely to take me to Bestsellerville, either.

I was lucky; my now-hubs (who clears four hundred emails before I get up and has never been late for an appointment in his entire life, I shit you not) lovingly shamed me into tracking my time on a graph, breaking up my day into fifteen-minute increments. Truthfully, he was super cute and took three hours on a Saturday to build me time-tracking spreadsheets while painstakingly teaching me how to use them—*nearly effing impossible*. Thankfully, there are apps for that now. The sixty all-nighters I'd pulled the year before I met him to save my home, my kid, and my career after Jesse and I divorced (a story for *Beautiful Writers II*) was not something he thought I'd live through again.

The result of my tracking? *Whoa.* A hefty chunk of my life had been passing me by while my already tired eyes watched other people living their lives on screens.

Ann Patchett 🌿

My time "secret" is no television, no social media.* In the spirit of honesty, we do have a TV in the house, but I don't know how to use it. I've always hated television. People tell me about all of these amazing series and how the best writing is on Netflix, and I read the serious reviews in the *Times*. But I just think, where would I find the time to binge-watch a TV show? And, if I wanted to pick up a hobby, I don't want it to be based around my eyeballs. My

---

* Ann doesn't have her own social media accounts, but Parnassus, the bookstore she co-owns, does.

eyeballs are exhausted. I don't want to stop reading so I can watch a series!

My son, husband, and I now have a standing movie-night date at our house (Sundays following dinner—yay!). Even Tosh, who helps run a thriving business he co-founded, now sees the benefit of scheduling our fun. Pilots and surgeons follow checklists to save lives. Professional athletes never stop studying the fundamentals to keep their play at its peak and their careers vibrant. Getting back to the basics of taking care of ourselves, our time, and our art makes our "off-time" one of the most creative acts of all.

12

The Blues, Boredom, and Brick Walls

*Persisting Through the Messy Middle—
In Life and in Your Manuscript*

"The roughest roads often lead to the top."

~Christina Aguilera

Ever feel like you'll never finish? Like you're on mile 13 of a marathon, but you can't find the water stand and your friend, who was supposed to show up with PowerBars, is AWOL?

People cheered you on at the start. They'll celebrate you at the end—whenever that is. But here in the middle? It's just your bored dog, your mountain of bills, and your waning faith in that crazy idea you had . . . *how long ago now?*

Steven Pressfield calls art a war for a reason. An enthusiast might see a beginning of big send-offs and USO girls in flirty dresses boosting morale. The ending is all ticker-tape parades, kisses in Times Square, and giddy family reunions. But my mind goes to the long, painful, messy middle—all foxholes, land mines, and bread lines. Comparing one's writing to combat may seem hysterical. But for anyone toiling away, who might be experiencing loss after loss while struggling to maintain their energy, I'd never tell them they're not in a battle.

If you find yourself trudging through the Messy Middle, where the honeymoon phase is long gone and the finish line nowhere in sight, I feel you. I've been you. Practically every author has been. This, too, shall pass. In the meantime, may this chapter's culmination be your own aid station.

My mother was dead. We didn't even know she'd been sick. One morning Mom woke up yellow—her eyes and skin colored with a banana-peel filter. "There's nothing we can do," her doctors swore. Mom's pancreas and liver were in retreat, and their invisible fight would be over in ten short weeks. Carol and I moved in and closed ranks alongside our father, waiting for the inevitable.

"Are you happy? I mean, *really* happy?" Mom had asked me the previous Mother's Day, with the kind of urgency that only makes sense in hindsight. Her gaze looked odd, cloudy somehow, as if behind old glass. I chalked up the longing in her voice to a rift with her dear friend and resentment at work. Mom was fifty-nine. Watching her daughters start businesses and go full throttle toward their creative dreams forced clarity. "I should have been a librarian, a journalist, a writer," she said, picking at her shirtsleeve. "But I was too scared."

It was precisely Mom's sacrifices that gave Carol and me our courage. I desperately wanted her to feel the kind of fulfillment I was experiencing, playing with exciting story lines, not the dry scientific ones she edited for her boss at Stanford. And I needed help! Finding time for library research on potential interviewees was a struggle. If anything was making me unhappy, it was how fast time was disappearing and how hard it was to accomplish my self-imposed writing goals. So, I hired Mom on the spot as my part-time research assistant! To ensure that my pitch letters sparkled, she combed the university library for little-known details of the celebs I hoped to entice.

The girl who'd spent her lonely, motherless childhood with her nose in a book and her body in Palo Alto movie theaters for weekend double features was a Dewey decimal system of endless trivia about those glamorous few who make

make-believe believable. *I must find the money to keep Mom on payroll.* How could I ever have imagined getting this done without her?

"This is the best job I've ever had!" Mom said, handing me a packet of all things eco-warrior Woody Harrelson, taking my hundred-dollar check but never cashing it.

Cheryl Strayed

The greatest thing in my life is humility when I'm trying to write. I've learned when I say that "the way it feels to be writing a book is that you can't write a book" is that it's a very common experience for writing to feel impossible. It's just part of the making. I think it's very hard to make something out of nothing, which is what we're doing when we're writing. Where there was no short story or script or book, we're making it, bringing it into the world. And it just requires a lot from us.

Right now, I am trying to land the ending of a short story I'm writing for an anthology. I've spent the last week or two trying to land that ending, and the whole time I'm thinking, *I give up; I can't write a short story. I just can't.* And I know that that's one sign that, in fact, I am writing a short story.

Yesterday, I thought about one of the things I wrote in *Tiny Beautiful Things*, in the column, "Write like a motherfucker," where I said, "Well, basically, listen. Writing's hard, but coal mining's harder." Yesterday I realized, "Nope. I was wrong about that!"

Nia Vardalos

I have a voice in my head, constantly, with every stroke of the keyboard keeping in time or rhythm saying, "You're a fraud."

I'm currently writing something right now. I'm in the last two scenes of the third act and I am lost. So, I'm going to print it today. I'm going to read it old school, out loud. Walk around, pace, and then, hopefully, find it. I don't know. If I don't, I have to just give myself that space of failing today, going to bed with that feeling of being lost. It's okay. I've been here before. I must trust that I'll get out of it. I say that with bravery in my voice, but I don't feel it.

Anne Lamott

Bird by Bird was a story from my childhood. My older brother, who was not a good student and didn't care, had this fourth-grade report on birds due. And he hadn't started. He had the whole semester to do it; it was due the next day.

We were at this tiny little cabin and my brother, who's a tough guy, started crying. My dad put his arm around his shoulders and said, "Just take it bird by bird, buddy. You've read a little bit about birds. Write what you've just learned about birds in your own voice and then either draw or cut out a picture." Then he said, "We'll start with chickadees. Then we'll move on to pelicans. Little by little, bird by bird, something will use you to get itself written."

After Mom's memorial, Carol and I made sure Dad knew how to use the ATM, cook himself dinner, and operate the washer. But once back in New Mexico, I was a weepy mess. I called my father at his office in San Jose. He picked up on the first ring.

"Tell me something good!" Dad sang. As much as I hated to give him evidence to the contrary, I couldn't fake it today.

"I'm not feeling so charmed right now, Daddy. Jesse and I have been fighting about money, and I miss you and Mom and Carol and Di, and my support group friends. *Lives Charmed* is taking way longer than I thought. I've got so much content, but I'm worried that if I don't get some bigger names, I'll never get an agent."

"Oh, sweetheart, it's just a numbers game. Concentrate on the yeses! You're so close."

Numbers. I hoped he was right. I'd initially thought my book would be in stores within a year. I'd been writing around the clock for several years already. You can only check typos so many times. I worried that the lesser-known names I'd already interviewed—whose stories I adored—would end up cut by my future publisher, and I didn't want to keep adding people that weren't a lock. Other superstars would likely follow a celeb as big as Seal or Sting (or Jennifer Lopez or Michael Jordan), and I could get this waiting game over. To live the life I was supposed to be living so I wouldn't end up like Mom, feeling I'd wasted so much time.

I hadn't heard from Seal's people, so instead, clearly crushing on singers with one name, I wrote again to the singer Sting via his Rainforest Foundation. His publicist and the director of his charity had both assured me they loved the idea of my book and would make sure Sting and Trudie knew about it, but months had gone by. Short of going down the Amazon in a canoe to find him as his foundation negotiated a treaty between Big Oil and indigenous tribal elders, I didn't know what else to do. Like my husband, I was powerless, waiting for the phone to ring. I'd rather have heard, "It's not gonna happen" than the answer that never died—the everlasting gobstopper of, "Maybe," or "We'll get back to you."

Glancing out my dusty window toward the bleak horizon, it seemed that nature couldn't decide if she should laugh or cry either. *Is there something I'm not seeing?* Wait! What I did see was . . . *Crap!* . . . *Are those mouse turds on my bookshelf?! What next? Hantavirus?* Attacking them with a wet sponge, I spied a framed photo of Meredith and me. *I should call her. Carrie-Anne too.* While I hadn't bonded as closely with Janet, I wondered how she was doing as well—no doubt all still struggling like me. *Soon! I'll make time for a reach out soon!* But even as I said that on the inside, on the outside, I was shaking my head.

Who was I kidding? I'd been a total disaster staying in touch with people since moving out to the sticks. I'd already canceled day trips with Meredith: once when Peanut had a litter of puppies, and we rescheduled our ski trip. Jesse was offered tentative work on a documentary soon afterward; again, we canceled. I could hear Mer's disappointment, but being an off-the-grid wife and a mother while building a cabin was a full-time job. Driving into town to call Carol and Diane every few days and my folks once a week was all the keep-up I had in me. With every free second, I tended to my book and the many people in its pages. *There will be time for everyone and everything once it's done!* When my mother-in-law cried to me for not making enough time for her, tears ran down my face too. But other than sending a few more cards a year, it would be a long while before I'd change course.*

"Discipline equals excellence, and excellence brings freedom," I remember ex-Olympian gymnast turned author Dan Millman saying. It became my mantra. At thirty-three, I could no longer fall into the splits, but I had an athlete's focus. Maybe the BBQ guy back in Studio City was right. Perhaps the act of writing was selfish and turned people into assholes?

Don't go there, Linda. Your heart is good. But could everyone please give me a little space?

I pushed my support group friends from my mind. Guru Singh would be visiting soon. He'd give me the sense of California connection I craved.†

Cheryl Strayed

I wish somebody would tell me how you're a writer and also a mother and a member of a domestic unit, a family. I've been grappling with this so hard lately. I just have no idea. It's such a struggle. All I can say is I'm trying lately to take the advice I've occasionally given as Sugar,‡ and that is to remember to take the long view.

I have a book due. I have all these projects in the works that I'm trying to finish, and I'm in the slow lane because I also have to do things like figure out what's for dinner and how to get so-and-so to basketball and the other one to their guitar lesson. And I'm like,

---

* This was before I'd learn the hard truth, following my parents' deaths, that time isn't always our friend.

† In Brooke Baldwin's incredible book, *Huddle*, she writes: "A huddle is a place where women can become energized by the mere fact of their coexistence. A huddle is where we can lift each other to succeed, thrive, and if I may—get amazing shit done." Dang. I had amazing shit I wanted to accomplish! If I'd only known then that more quality women in my life, not less, likely held the keys to my dreams.

‡ For Cheryl's popular advice column, Dear Sugar.

"Okay, well, this, too, shall pass." With the long view, I realize this is just an era of my life. In five or six years, my kids will be off at college, hopefully not in prison. No, college. And, in that same way when they were toddlers, those days felt endless—where it was just trying to get people to nap and eat their vegetables, and I thought they'd never end—they did end. What I have to remember is that I'll look back on these days and smile. I won't feel the sense of panic and despair that I sometimes feel when it comes to making time for my work.

Nia Vardalos

What Cheryl [Strayed] described when she said that she was feeling ashamed for not doing the work, I think these emotions are important. Trying to create an idyllic situation to write within doesn't inspire art. Mood inspires art. That's why maybe it's better to write in New York or Oregon, than in vapid LA.

I think it's okay to have those days. Definitely. Because how we feel is going to come through our fingertips. I say, embrace the shame spiral. Something great is going to come out of it.*

Jesse and I drove down to Santa Fe to sell some of Mom's things in their seasonal flea market near the Opera Center to bring in a little extra cash. In the slot next to us was June, a forty-something woman with tanned, ruddy skin and bleached blonde hair held atop her head with a rusted clip.

"Whacha doing here, missy? Haven't seen you before!" she said, her smile revealing a few missing front teeth.

"Oh, I'm selling some clothes that don't fit me to try and fund a writing project that's getting expensive."

---

* Fun fact: Nia adapted and starred in the critically acclaimed and hugely successful stage production of Cheryl Strayed's book *Tiny Beautiful Things*.

"Yeah? That's cool. What ya writin' 'bout? A mystery or a romance or somethin'?"

"Nah. An interview book. About the environment, mostly."

"No shit!"

"Yep. To encourage people to stop clear-cutting old-growth forests for junk mail catalogs and toilet paper and stuff." Jesse shot me a look that said, *Why waste your breath?*

June looked away for a second, twisted her brow, picked at a scab on her arm with blackened fingernails. "Not while I'm alive, they won't!" she hollered. "Not on my watch. I will NEVER allow them to do that shit to the trees even one more day. Those assholes are *toast!*" She grabbed the cigarette from her boyfriend's hand, took a long drag, and blew out a plume of smoke as she rearranged the trinkets on her folding table.

Is she for real, convinced that she alone could police the world? I was struck speechless, trying to reconcile the mad ravings of a woman seemingly incapable of curbing her destructive tendencies, much less those of a global industry.

On the drive home, I prayed people didn't likewise scoff at my environmental "lectures," as Diane called them. Once again, my mind drifted to my support group friends. If anyone understood the drive behind my mission, it was Meredith, Carrie-Anne, and Janet. How had I been so busy as to let those friendships flag? Grandma had warned me as a kid not to get too full of myself or burn bridges. "Old people live with the scars of being burned," she'd said. (She also said to eat lots of fiber, never use credit, and those ripped jeans make you look like no one loves you.)

"I gotta call the girls," I said to Jesse. "Meredith will get it. I feel so stuck. Like I'm in constant motion, but also in creative no-man's-land."

"Welcome to my world," he answered. "At least you're writing your own material. Imagine if you had to say someone else's bad lines—and you hardly ever got the chance!"

Before I could call any of my former support group friends, I woke up to find one of Peanut's now-grown puppies lifeless, cold to the touch. Just the day before on a routine visit to our veterinarian, he'd been given a clean bill of health. Now, as grief overtook our family, I forgot about the big world outside of our little one and failed for a while to make *any* calls, be it for business or friendship.

Sarah Manguso, Guggenheim Fellow, writing professor, and author of eight books including the novel *Very Cold People* and nonfiction books *The Two Kinds of Decay*, *The Guardians*, *Ongoingness*, and *300 Arguments*.

I have a piece of advice about creativity I think about constantly.

I was in the first year of my poetry MFA, the first day of a workshop class with a new instructor. I was intimidated because I was the youngest in the class and the only first-year student. I had stuff to prove. I composed a poem; I believe I was attempting to rework something of Wittgenstein's, which I hadn't read. If I armed myself with this great thinker's authority, I would be okay. I would fool everybody into thinking that I knew what I was doing, or maybe even that I knew things that they didn't.

My teacher, the brilliant poet Dean Young, read my poem. After a sort of cursory treatment of it, I asked him a question about Wittgenstein. It was one of those questions that were half legitimate but half my needing to prove that I could be there. Instead of answering, he took a breath, let my question breathe, and then said, "Sarah, the important thing to remember is that I only have like forty or forty-five more years left to live."

That was his way of teaching me that I'm writing for a mortal reader who has some time to read but not that much. Most of my readers would not give three hours trying to suss out exactly what I was trying to do in this ridiculous attempt at a poem. And it burned all of that pseudo-intellectual pretension right out of me.

Sabaa Tahir

Every book is a new mountain. I know nothing about mountains, but I'm weirdly obsessed with mountain climbing documentaries and novels. Every mountain is different. You'll face unique problems on each one. If you get to the top, it's going to be because you managed to adapt and evolve to that particular mountain.

Books are similar. You have to evolve and adapt to the book you're writing. If you start thinking, *Oh, I got this*, there might be a flatness to what you're writing because you're not pushing yourself to do something different, something better. To try harder. To solve a problem in a different way. To approach a plot issue more creatively. To approach *yourself* in a different way because how much of it is digging into ourselves and those darker places in ourselves and excavating them.

Steven Pressfield

An analogy I use for the creative impulse with regard to your novel (or whatever you're writing) is that, like a tree, resistance is the shadow that immediately appears of that tree. The resistance always comes second, following the growth. There would be no resistance if you didn't have a great idea percolating. To me, the writing process on a specific day is like diving into a cold pool of water. Your resistance is to the act of diving, but once you're in and swimming, if you're lucky, the grace appears, and you're over your initial resistance. The two of them, resistance and grace, go hand in hand. I think they're equal and opposite in some crazy, Newtonian way.

Guru's white Plymouth rounded the corner of our long driveway, a dust cloud whirling behind him. Who would believe that a guru who meditates from three until five every morning, wouldn't eat animal products to save his life, and wears all white because of its purity would drive like a bat out of hell? I wondered how his children had made it into their teens—maybe on account of all that prayer.

"He's here!" I squealed. Jesse, Tosh, and I bounded down the front steps with the dogs.

"Hey, Super Gu! You look great!" I yelled before throwing myself at him. He hated it when I called him that, or "Gu Zilla"—my favorite because of how tall he looked walking amongst the gnarled cedars around our house. "Linda!" he would scold me. "'Gu' without the 'ru' means darkness, for God's sake."

"Did you hear the fantastic news about Meredith?" Guru asked, a mischievous glint in his eye. Of course, she'd become one of his most beloved clients and protégés. Before dropping out of civilization in the 1960s to study with an indigenous tribe in the desert of remote Mexico, he himself had been a singer and guitarist with Warner Bros. Records on his way to superstardom with hits on the radio and jam buddies in Janis Joplin and Jimi Hendrix.

"What news?" I asked.

"She just got her dream record deal with Capitol Records. It's going to be really big, Linda. Their biggest signing since the Beatles. You should call her." He was watching me without blinking, the proud patriarch. Meredith and I were from the same spirit family, he'd always said.

I could feel tears forming in my eyes. Happy tears. Jealous tears. She deserved this more than anyone. But what about me? I'd waited too long! Damn. I couldn't contact her now, not her or any of the women; I'd just look like an opportunist, a fair-weather friend. I'd lived in Hollywood long enough to have seen it: When people go from obscurity to fame, everyone comes out of the woodwork expecting a seat at the party.

Do NOT let Guru see you cry! Do not let Guru see you cry! As I struggled to catch my breath, the thing that hurt the most was that she'd never know how proud I was.

"Sounds like there won't be any more five-dollar concerts in dive bars for her," I said, awash in nostalgia remembering the time Carrie-Anne and Janet and I had held Tosh's fingers at one of Meredith's concerts as he danced on the table in nothing but his cloth diaper.

"No, the days of her playing small venues are long gone," Guru concurred.

Kelly Noonan Gores 🌿

When you're stressed out, you're in fight or flight. Your higher brain centers and your creativity are turned off because your body needs the energy to fight for your life (real or imagined) or to flee. The antidote is FUN.

Sometimes you need to walk away from your book for a day, a week, a month, and completely let your mind clear and let fun bring you back to your creative process. If you're letting the process deplete you, you need to do things that generate joy. Wakesurfing is one of my joy generators. But do anything that makes you smile and takes you out of your mind.

Guru Singh 🌿

We identify more profoundly with what we're struggling to achieve than what is easy to achieve. The path of creativity is so fulfilling because we put more energy into what we're creating than the struggle it takes to create it.

A writer has to believe that their work is the best that's ever been written. That opens up the inspiration channel. You cannot write if you're in desperation, right? Desperation means "without spirit." Inspiration means "in spirit."

Of course, we have a long history of brilliant writers—some of our bestselling writers of all time—who were miserable during the writing process but sold millions of books. That's because theirs was the best misery that has ever been experienced. Think of it. They were usually drunkards. Their misery was so intense that it allowed people to think, *Well, my shit's not that bad.* When you build a house, you have to have a kitchen and a bathroom. Your bathroom is where all of the waste goes, and your kitchen is where all the nutrients are. Everything has to have balance. There has to be agony and misery to have ecstasy and inspiration.

Tosca Lee 🍃

You have to be in love with your story. For me, if it's that much of a grind, maybe I don't love the story enough. Or maybe there's something that's not intoxicating enough about it, and you have to go back and examine and say, "Where is this dry? How can I spice things up and make it more exciting?"

And sometimes, you have a love-hate relationship with it because the way you wanted the story to work, or the way you thought it needed to be written, isn't how it wants to be written. Or you just realize you feel way in over your head. Sometimes you have to upend everything and pull all the wires out, doubting yourself and questioning your every move the entire time. At that point, you have no choice but to trust something beyond yourself and your own capabilities. It's not comfortable, and I've always hated it when this has happened. But it's always produced my best work.

As Guru and his dust cloud hurtled out of sight, I couldn't stop obsessing. *The largest recording contract with Capitol Records since the Beatles?* Could that be right? A twang of nerves gripped my stomach. *If Mer's going to be that big, there's no way I won't see it, even from out here.* How could I hope to "rise above," as Thomas One Wolf would surely advise, if Meredith were everywhere?

Maybe I *could* handle it. Diane was sporting a five-carat sparkler on her ring finger and could withdraw up to $50,000 before her quarterback husband even noticed (not that she did, but still). She lived with many of the trappings of fame, and it didn't mess me up. But I could call Di whenever I wanted. It was odd sometimes, going from being broke together in college and more recently losing our shirts in that hair restoration scheme to now seeing one of Princess Diana's coffee tables in her entryway. But we were sisters.

I needed to put this in context. I'd lost my sisterhood with Meredith, yes. I could meditate endlessly on how I could have been a better friend. But nothing could take away from the fact that she was amazing—a fucking genius. She'd worked her whole life for this. Given concerts as a kid. Mastered songwriting, multiple instruments, and a level of inner emotional work that felt so advanced to me that she might as well have been talking in a foreign language. She'd formed several bands and lost record deals, but Meredith woke up every day ready to get up on any stage. She'd always had "it." For it to have taken this long defied reason. And while I'd originally thought my book would be out in a year, my few years had nothing on her many! I had to get out of my small self and use Meredith's success as inspiration, fuel!

Stay focused, Linda. On your dreams. Your mastery. You can't be a great writer and steward for Mother Earth if you're wallowing in jealousy.

The following dawn at my desk, my breath visible from the light of the candle flame, I felt grateful for these quiet hours: just my words and me. The writing was going well in the sense that I had no writer's block. And I loved poring over chapters to ensure no typos clunked up my text. But I continued to feel perpetually fucked getting those last A-list names. What if I never got any others? Would my book be good enough without them? I'd have to trust in all I'd done to get this far.

Samantha Bennett 🌿

Expect the voice in your head to say, "This is terrible. This is crap. No one will ever want to read this. Quit now before you embarrass yourself." It's incredibly loud and persuasive, this voice, and as far as I know, it never really goes away. That's the bad news. The good news is that everyone has that voice; it's not unique to you, and it's like the voice of an overprotective parent trying to keep their kid safe by not letting them have any fun.

I find these phrases helpful when I'm in the gap and responding to that voice. I've even been known to say them aloud as I work:

"Yes, this may be crap, and that's why God made editors."

"Yes, this may be crap, and I can't make it better until I get it out on paper."

"Yes, this may be crap, and I have given myself permission to write and then delete the whole thing if I want."

"Yes, this may be crap, and I am in no position to judge. I am a terrible judge of my own work."

"Yes, this may be crap, and I'm just going to keep going here for a few more minutes anyway."

Whether your Messy Middle comes in the form of a stall in your life, or your manuscript, delays and setbacks are just part of the deal. No one's immune. As you might guess, Steven Pressfield's "resistance" is the same as Rhonda Britten's "fear," and as my astrologer sister's "It's just not your 'celestial season of success'—yet." Your therapist could argue it's all an opportunity to go inward and bolster your self-esteem. But what most writing and creativity coaches would tell you is that this is just the process. Welcome to the creative life. Making great art is hard work. It can feel never-ending. Mastery takes time and effort, and everyone's path is different, so keep going. Use whatever label feels true for you to hang onto when you're in the thick of it so you don't create more work or drama for yourself.

Although drama puts you in good company . . .

Steven Pressfield 🖋

For my first book a million years ago, I got 99.9 percent of the way through, and I blew up my marriage. I blew up my entire life, really. It took me years to recover. In looking back, I had no idea there was such a thing as resistance, but that's exactly what it was.

I think the hero's journey in our life is when we're thrashing and scratching around trying to find our destiny, why we were put here on this planet. We go through all kinds of adventures, and at some point, we completely crash like an alcoholic that finally wakes up in the gutter and says, "Oh my God, I *do* have a problem with alcohol." At that point, we say, "I can't live this way anymore. I've got to get it together." That, to me, is the turning-pro moment. We switch from our hero's journey to our artist's journey and commit. The issue is no longer how much we're drinking or how many drugs we're doing, or how many affairs we're having. The issue becomes: "What's my gift? What was I put on this planet to do?" You're ready to get your shit together, carve out two or four hours a day to do your work, support yourself, and take care of your family.

Once we've made that turn and boarded that train, we're on it till the end of the line. There's no other journey left, except maybe passage to the next life.

Robert McKee 🌱

I wrote the foreword to [Steven Pressfield's] *The War of Art*, where I talked about how I'm the ultimate procrastinator and was once as blocked as a Calcutta sewer. I tried every single piece of clothing I owned on and then categorized everything.

Resistance still plagues me the same way. You just have to fight your way through it. I'm working on the book for *Storynomics* right now, and this past week, I spent three days on one paragraph. It's really a good paragraph now, but yeah. And the only thing you can do is not get out of the chair. If you stay in the chair, sooner or later, it will get written.

Mary Karr 🌱

When I'm stuck, I just work. Hours and hours and hours. I can outwork people who are naturally more talented. I'm a pretty good editor. When I have a flamethrower on my butt, I can write for a long time. I work at the walking desk for a few hours, then I'll go to my other desk, and then I'll go to the table, and then I'll get in bed and work on my laptop. Then it's like fourteen hours later. I sort of kid myself that I'm starting over every time.

I also keep a commonplace book where I write down better people's work, and it gets my hand moving across the page. When I'm *really* stuck, I give myself a page and an hour deadline. I'll say, "You have to do one page a day or five hours, whichever comes first." If you're writing bad stuff, one page is a boatload. It can take you a long time. And sometimes, you come in, and you are cutting the ten pages, so you wind up doing negative ten pages. It's not about getting more pages. It's about logging the hours, even if it's writing and discarding the less good work.

I started trying spiritual stuff during a nervous breakthrough after I quit drinking. It was the place I surrendered, the whole process of which I wrote about in *Lit*. I'd tried intellectual, chemical, pharmacological, penis-related solutions. I'd tried to solve my misery a million different ways. And I thought, "What if my problems are spiritual?" That overhauled my life in the most luminous way.

Lee Child

I have two mottos. One is: "I'm not afraid of stress. Stress is afraid of me." The other is: "I can't grow any more talent, but I can certainly outwork anybody else."

I wasn't in a war, but resistance was building. What helped me at this Messy Middle stage and at later stages—and I've heard this from lots of writers—again, was to tap into my *why*. To stay focused on where I wanted to go. Not *how* I was going to get there—that's not all under our jurisdiction—but to see and feel the gift of realizing my goals.

When memoirist and novelist Laura Munson was on my podcast, she talked about struggling to keep her hope after writing fourteen unpublished novels. One afternoon, in total frustration, Laura wrote an "author's mission statement" to remind her of the point. She tacked it up over her computer, where it still sits.

"I write to shine a light on a dim or otherwise pitch-black corner to provide relief for myself and others." Those words from Laura's hand to herself affirmed for her that writing was not only "my practice, my prayer, my meditation, my way of life, but sometimes my way to life." I've never written a definitive mission statement—more like a thousand iterations. But they always include two themes: writing about the natural world in a way that engages readers, authors, and publishers to embrace more sustainable practices, while reminding people they're magical.

That hasn't always precluded me from stressing about results and timelines. When all I could see was the loss of my mother and my support group friends, against the backdrop of my unrealized career goals, I forgot that I was on a journey. One in which my mission, my *why*, was a long game. But you know what they say about patience—it's often rewarded. On the other side of all that stalled energy? Breakthroughs and book deals! By trudging through our stories, they're eventually ready for market. And, if you're lucky, all those friends you didn't have time for might forgive you.

If you were to write yourself a mission statement, what would it say? Put it down in black and white (or color!) and tack it up somewhere for reminders when you get stalled. Hell, get the word *Remember* tattooed on your wrist—as in, *Remember, you're a writer, so write!* I eventually did. (Momentarily painful, yes. But easier than crafting my mission statement!) By scripting the results you're looking for, your dream feelings of connection, abundance, love, ease, and freedom will become a visual GPS to carry you through the messiest of middles.

13

Bagging the Big One

Catching and Keeping Your Literary Agent

"Hell hath no fury like a hustler with a literary agent."
~Frank Sinatra

L iterary agents, the ultimate gatekeepers. They hold the keys to the king-dom. Get you across the moat, past the dragons, and before royalty—the editors and publishers who can knight you with a career.

Your relationship with your agent is a kind of marriage. They birth the baby with you! And just like partners in a marriage, they won't always text you back, pick up their socks, or help with those 3:00 AM feedings. At the end of the day, hopefully, you'll get custody. *I kid. I kid.*

You may have heard the jokes, like a version of this one: A struggling writer returned home one night to find his cul-de-sac roped off, his street teeming with police, fire, and emergency vehicles. His house was burned to the ground. When he got to his driveway, a uniformed officer pulled him aside.

"I'm sorry to inform you that your literary agent went berserk, came to your house, killed your family, and torched the place."

"Are you kidding me?" the writer replied. "*My agent came to my house?*"

This hits home because agents, especially the good ones, are busy. Which means they can be less communicative than we'd like—except perhaps for the authors here (who've sold millions, even tens of millions of books). Plus, of course, the few agents I've interviewed for these pages. But many a dream has been dashed by putting too much faith in one human. When it works, though—oh, happy day! Your agent will take your ass to the party and then cover it, so your pockets aren't fleeced on your way to the dance floor.

Doing it alone without an agent requires building your own castle. In the 2019 film version of *Little Women*, Jo was her own agent and negotiated to keep her copyright, which ensured that she and her family would reap the benefits for years to come—smart! (Fun fact: Director Greta Gerwig based this movie-only scene on Louisa May Alcott's own publishing negotiations.)

That's not me. And it's probably not you, either. If not, buckle up, buttercup. You need a fucking agent! With over a thousand literary agents in the United States and another thousand outside of the US, there are plenty of places to send your work (the "how" of which we'll focus on more specifically in the next chapter). With hundreds of thousands of mainstream books published every year, there's simply too much competition out there. Agents have access. A great agent helps cut through the clutter to match writers with the right editors and publishers. Most publishers don't read unsolicited manuscripts, so agents are your way in.

Where do you find these agents, and how can you make it a win-win? For me, it was as easy as a summer day. Until I let him see me sweat . . .

Finally! I was ready to gamble that my book had enough content to be agent-worthy! My interviews with thirty or so fascinating people (initially half well-known, half unknown folks with extraordinary stories) made me confident in the book's merits. I didn't yet have a Seal or a Cher or an Oprah, but I was especially proud of the latest big name I'd snagged.

I'd wanted to profile a champion in the gay community. But who? One evening by candlelight in our uninsulated cabin, I opened *Vanity Fair* magazine to a ten-page article entitled "Sandy's Castle." In it, I learned about the legendary talent manager Sandy Gallin, who'd discovered just about everyone. He'd helped book the Beatles on *The Ed Sullivan Show*; made Dolly Parton a household name; produced *The Sonny & Cher Comedy Hour*; managed Richard Pryor, Barbra Streisand, Michael Jackson, and Nicole Kidman; and won an Oscar for an AIDS documentary. I imagined vaulting over Sandy's moat straight into his kingdom.

Instead, drawbridge up! No surprise: the man who'd only given four interviews in his career didn't answer my letters. But I couldn't get his face out of my mind, so I hunkered down, read three memoirs and biographies by Sandy's buddies—Dolly Parton, David Geffen, and Barry Diller—and *knew* my next step.

Sandy had an odd saying he repeated whenever he wanted to connect with someone. "They can kill me, but they can't eat me." By the third time I read that line, I had chills. *Bingo*. It only takes one connection to change the course of your life. I booked a trip to Los Angeles where I'd stay with Carol and borrow her car.

Dani Shapiro ❧

I was determined when I started at Sarah Lawrence that I was going to finish and sell my first novel before I got my graduate degree, which is a completely unreasonable goal.

A friend of mine saw a photograph in a magazine of two very powerful agents in New York, who were the co-heads of one of the biggest agencies. My friend looked at the picture and said, "This woman looks like she's been in psychoanalysis; she will understand your work."

I did everything wrong. Based on my friend's astute publishing advice, I picked up the phone and called the agent.*

She got on the phone, and said, "What's it about?" I stuttered something. She said, "I'll take a look at it." I walked down to her office and hand-delivered a box of my manuscript with a cover

---

* Dani's former agent, Esther Newberg at ICM, is a legend in the industry. What Dani did was akin to an unknown actress cold-calling Steven Spielberg.

note. The next day, my phone rang, and it was the agent, saying, "Can you come in tomorrow at three o'clock?"

She hasn't been my agent for the last twenty years, but our first meeting was very intimidating. She said, "I think I can sell your book." And she did, within days. I went from feeling totally washed up and having ruined my life—a completely messed-up kid who did not have any kind of bright future—to in a short period having my first novel come out at twenty-seven and being described as precocious with all these achievements. Then I suddenly had a graduate degree and started teaching. There's no one path.

With Jennifer Rudolph Walsh [Dani's agent at the time of this interview], there's a kind of beautiful mirroring that goes on. This is what good parents do for their children, good friends do for each other, and what spouses and partners do over the course of a life—cheerleading you in the biggest way in terms of energy and reflecting at you that you can do this.

Jennifer Rudolph Walsh

It's an extraordinary journey to be on with somebody who's unfolding and having the unfolding of their life, as a seeker, reflected in the work. I'm a perfect match for somebody like Dani [Shapiro], who writes from what's inside of her heart and what's happening to her in the moment. Sometimes it's like a magical salve over what's often happening for me as well.

I want to say to Dani, my beloved, that it's mutual. People feel that a relationship between an agent and writer is very much that the agent gives, and the writer is served by that relationship. And the agent is paid for that relationship. Those things are true. But in addition to that, in the relationships that are most nurturing and thriving, it's a two-way street. The magic is in the reciprocity. In all the ways that Dani has changed during the twenty-some-odd years we've been in relationship, I've changed as much too. I'm an agent, and I'm also producing and curating a tour [Together Rising]. That doesn't happen overnight. It happens when people like Dani are holding my hand, reflecting truths back to me, bearing witness to my life over decades, dancing at my children's bar and bat mitzvahs. And really, not only just holding my hand but seeing me in a certain way and holding up that possibility to me.

Once in Los Angeles, I was standing in front of the rack at the card store, weighing my odds.

Doomsday Linda: Should I do it?

Trusting Linda: It's funny as hell.

DL: They've got prettier, more appropriate cards.

TL: Nah. Sandy will either think it's a dud or he'll laugh, but he's not going to hate me over it. At least I'll get a reaction. There's nothing to lose.

I took the postcard to the cashier: a drawing of Jesus knocking on a large wooden door with the words "Let me in." Underneath, I wrote: "Because you can't kill me or eat me, you might as well meet me."

Next, I went to my favorite LA bakery, Mani's on 6th Street, whose fruit-juiced-sweetened "faux nut" donuts had a line down the street ever since Michael Jackson sang their praises to the media. Mani was gay and much loved in the newly named LGBT community. There was no way Sandy Gallin wouldn't know this bakery.

Believing Sandy's assistants would appreciate being included, I filled several gift bags with Mani's pricey nondairy chocolate cream heart cookies. Sure enough, after buzzing me in, they oohed and aahed over my care packages. Thirty minutes later, Sandy's lead assistant called.

"He laughed his ass off at your postcard," she said. *Yes!* He'd actually read my previous letters, and with this final act, I'd finally motivated him to lower the drawbridge. Within the hour, I had Sandy's cell number, home phone, and beach house lines.

Apparently, Jesus is a book savior too.

"You know more about me than I know myself!" Sandy said when our interviews were complete. "You should be a reporter!" This meant the world to me, seeing as how he'd spent his career shying away from reporters when it came to his personal life. As he signed off on his final chapter, thanking me, I felt an enormous wave of gratitude for the instances when the odds and/or the heavens seemed to sway in my favor.

Four and a half dedicated years I'd been at this already, reading about other newbie writers getting big book deals in the pages of *People* and *Vanity Fair*. I wanted my literary champion!

Ann Patchett 🌿

Maybe you send your work to twenty different agents, but you want to find the person who loves your work and feels passionately about it. It's not a club where the door is locked, and you can't get in because you don't know the right person.

I used to live in Montana, and I absolutely loved it. But there were people who believed that to get published, you had to be a New Yorker, to know somebody on the inside. You had to have the secret handshake. Nobody in Montana had the secret handshake. That's just not true.

There is no more slush pile; no more sending your manuscript to Random House. You must get an agent. It is the only way the system works anymore. One of my neighbors is a novelist, and we dog-walk together. Her agent retired, and she sent her new book to three or four different agents, who rejected it. This is a woman in her sixties who has published a lot of books that have not done spectacularly well but have sold. She was worried. Then she sent it to an agent who said, "Oh my God, I've been waiting for you my whole life. I love this book so much. I can hardly wait to work with you!" How fantastic that somebody didn't take her because she was a friend of a friend, as a favor, but not really connect to the work. She held out for true love, and she found it.

It didn't even occur to me to query multiple lit agents. I had my heart set on only one—let's call him Dan. I'd read all about him in an industry magazine. He'd sold a ton of titles and written books about the business of publishing, too, so he knew the game. He'd be my MVP. I guessed he'd tell me I still needed a few marquee-name interviews before I had the star power to land a book deal. But couldn't he help with that too?*

I hummed as I packaged up four hundred pages of interviews in a FedEx box (so it appeared more important) and triple-checked the Table of Contents to be sure every page was where it should be. I'd crafted an intro letter about our eighty-five-year-old neighbor, Stye, who dug septic holes, his frail frame and toothless grin atop our tractor. I was always afraid I'd look out the window and see Stye flying off the yellow iron in a windstorm. This felt like it could be a good hook—Dan had written a funny ditty about tractors in one of his books, about how if he weren't an agent, he'd be driving one.

I placed my letter over the title page of *Lives Charmed*, having no idea you're not supposed to send work out without first being invited to after sending a respectful one-page query letter. Who knew that four hundred pages of interviews were *way* too much material, especially for a manuscript in progress? *Kids, don't try this at home!* I hadn't heard of a query letter (the one-pager that gets your boot in the door) or a book proposal (the necessary business plan summarizing your book—the topic of our next chapter). Anyway, I never much liked doing things the way you're "supposed" to. I sealed up the box and drove forty miles to Taos to the nearest FedEx drop-off.

Three days later, our shoebox-sized cell phone rang.

"Linda, it's Dan. I just read your book, and I'd love to represent you," he said. Horns honked in the background. *Manhattan! He's in honest-to-goodness NYC!* My insides were ready for liftoff.

"That was fast! I only sent it on Monday," I said.

"Yeah, well, that was the funniest letter I've ever received. I'll overnight you a contract tomorrow, and we'll get this book sold." With my heart racing,

---

* Newbie-move alert! Your agent *may* be able to help you network, but it's not likely. Especially not in the beginning of your relationship. Don't bank on your agent making you more saleable. Make yourself attractive to agents and publishers by tackling the hard stuff and becoming "agent ready" before you shop for representation.

I hung up and spilled down into the kitchen into Jesse's arms. Getting an agent is nearly as hard as getting a publisher and I loved that my husband was excited too.

Gretchen Rubin 🌿

I've had the same agent the whole time. I'd gone in to talk to another agent through a friend of a friend. We sort of ended up together. She was early in her career, and I was just starting out. A total love connection. She's had a huge influence on everything I've done. I feel fortunate to have somebody who has a lot of insight, not only for the books I'm writing and editing but in a larger sense of social media and blogging. She was the one who said, "I think you'd like to have a blog." She was clearly right.*

I'd barely blinked and my literary agent was coming to our house! Dan had a wedding to go to in Santa Fe and said he'd enjoy the drive up north.

"You'll have to make it through a few miles on unmarked dirt roads," I warned him. "Friends say it's like going on safari, only with roaming dogs instead of big cats. But we do have a Native American sweat lodge ceremony in it for you if you'd like."

"I've wanted to do a ceremony for years!" he exclaimed.

So, this was the answer. You follow your spirit and let go of everything that makes "sense," and then you get it all back in spades. I wanted to jump up and down in front of Dan but kept outwardly calm.

Pine needles crunched underfoot on the big day as we made our way through the forest. "There should be an auction for your book," Dan said. "I think it could garner around $50,000." My God, our bills were only $2,000 a month; $50,000 would be life-changing!

---

* Fun fact: Gretchen's *New York Times* bestseller, *The Happiness Project*, led to a successful blog by the same name. The success of one fed the other. A win-win!

And did he just say that publishers are going to fight to bid on my book?

We walked past Thomas One Wolf's teepee to his Inepi, a round igloo-like structure he'd made from bent tree limbs and covered with blankets. Thomas was waiting for us, tending the bonfire that heated the lava rocks he'd soon have brought into the lodge one at a time on a shovel.

I tried not to stare at Dan's pale white legs in his shorts as he peeled off his sweatpants before stepping into the dark, small space and the door to the lodge was closed. *Oh my God . . . I'm doing a sweat lodge with my New York agent!* Thomas One Wolf respected the fact that we had a publishing powerhouse in our midst and didn't crank up the heat as he did for veteran lodgers. Still, the coals were hot, and I hoped Dan was doing okay over there. Thomas sang his native prayers and drummed, and occasionally I could see Dan through the blackness when Thomas sprinkled sage, lavender, and sweetgrass over the rocks, and sparks lit up the dark. But with the first ladles of water poured over the stones, and the intense steam coming off them, Dan had covered his head with a towel, and there was no way to get a read.

"That was great," Dan said dully afterward.

"Really? How do you feel?"

"A little dizzy, but I'm sure I'll be fine." He wobbled on his heels. Back at the house, we sat down to dinner. Jesse and I loaded up our salad plates as we always did.

"I'll just have a bit of soup," Dan said, looking pale, feebly accepting a bowl of potato leek.

"Are you sure you're okay?" I asked, watching lines of sweat run down his cheeks.

"Not . . . really." He was wiping his face with his sleeve. "I think I may be getting the flu." Instinctively, I put my hand up to his clammy forehead.

"Oh, I'm so sorry. Would you like to lie down?"

"No. I think I'll take off before it gets dark." Minutes later, Dan hugged me goodbye, strapped on his seat belt, and burned rubber in the dirt (can you burn rubber in dirt?), hightailing it to the freeway as if fleeing flaming spears.

"Too bad about your agent!" Jesse said.

"Yeah. That was a bummer." But inwardly, I was smiling. *Dan used the word* auction! *That means a bidding war! Maybe it'd sell for even more than he thought?*

Shit was getting real. We weren't just playing *Little House on the Prairie* anymore. My writing and publishing dreams were starting to come together, and I questioned briefly who we'd have to become to live a bigger life. Did Jesse and I have what it took? Would we grow together through the inevitable changes? Was my skin thick enough?

Was I really *ready?* I wished that Dan was a bit chattier. I had sooo many questions.

Laura Yorke, avid horsewoman and literary agent (and ex-veteran book editor and publisher at three Simon & Schuster imprints before moving to Putnam, co-founding the Golden Books Adult Trade division, and acting as editor at large of ReganBooks/HarperCollins).

A dream client is somebody aware of the industry, who knows what it's like today, not how it used to be, because it's changed. They're aware of the time limits on a relationship because both agents and editors have so much material thrown at them all the time. If they don't understand what that kind of overload is like, they listen to you when you explain it, and they accept it. For instance, it can take months for an agent to give you an answer to whether they're going to represent you. And then, it can take months for editors at publishing houses to come back to you with a response.

A nightmare client is bitching about that. When you get rejections, a nightmare client refuses to think that maybe it has something to do with their writing or with other books in the market. An angel client says, "You know what, thank you so much for trying. I know that it doesn't always fly." Having a dialogue with a dream client is a back-and-forth. It doesn't have to all be pleasant, just one that's open and honest. They can hear what you have to say about what you're trying to do for them and what you are telling them about the industry, whether good or disheartening.

It sounds like such a yenta thing, but I feel that I'm a match-maker. I put authors with good writers (if they need one), and I do the same with authors and editors. You just figure it out. I think that's a critical part of the job on both sides, matching people correctly.

Without a word about our aborted dinner, Dan recovered, and we were all systems go. He called to invite me to lunch the following month when he and his wife were coming to Los Angeles for meetings at the Four Seasons. Could I make the trip? Heck yes, I could! I'd never had lunch at the Four Seasons. I'd give my country duds a wash and be right the hell over.

"You've got a few things to do before we can get this book sold," Dan said before hanging up. "But we'll get you ready!"

I didn't know what he meant by "a few things," but with my chapters nearly done and him at the helm, whatever he had in mind was just fine by me.

A client once called me the "keeper of her dreams," which I took as the highest compliment. What could be better than holding someone's greatest wishes in your hands? That's what I wanted with Dan—for him to carry the near-impossible bigness of my mission and never put it down. That's a tall order for any relationship.

Despite sharing sacred sweat in Thomas's lodge that day, and Dan eventually selling my book, we never had more than a sweet, surface-y connection in my eyes. I adored him then and still do (I continue to connect him with clients, whom he often gets published). But at that time in my career, I ached for more handholding and mentorship. A sucker for a soulful, soulmate-type relationship between writer and agent (which I believe I have now), learning to stop looking for more from Dan didn't come naturally.

While finding your agent person can sometimes be remarkably easy and fast, Thomas One Wolf's frequent saying that "things take time, and big things take big time" applies here. A good rule of thumb is that big agents take even longer. But in my experience, if you've crafted a solid query letter/pitch and emailed it to agents interested in your genre, you *will* receive requests to see your proposal and sample chapters. And, for heaven's sake, learn about the world you're inhabiting—hopefully this book is helping! A few of my favorite go-to guides when you're looking for just the right literary love match include publishersmarketplace.com, writersmarket.com, and *Jeff Herman's Guide to Book Publishers, Editors & Literary Agents* (a classic, which tells you who they are, what they want, and how to win them over).

Keep the faith. Your team is out there, praying for you to show up as much as you're praying for them.

14

Beautiful Book Proposals

Enchanting Publishers with THE Book About Your Book

"It takes as much energy to wish as it does to plan."

~ Eleanor Roosevelt

"What do you mean, I have to write a book about my book?!"—says nearly every wannabe author when first hearing about book proposals. I know what you're thinking: *Aren't business plans for businesspeople? I'm a creative, a tired one at that. I started writing so I wouldn't have to do crap like this! Can't publishers just read my manuscript? Are you really saying I have to crank out boring, garish marketing copy? I hate having to sell myself. And what if I decide to self-publish?*

I get the dread. The idea of another thousand-mile journey sounds exhausting. Trust me, you need to stay the course. Yes, your proposal can be as riveting as the rest of your prose; in fact, that's the key to a proposal that sells. And if you decide to publish your story on your own, you'll have every stage mapped out, making finishing and marketing your book infinitely easier.*

---

* Full disclosure: I'm no expert on self-publishing. Outside of self-publishing *Your Big Beautiful Book Plan* with Danielle LaPorte, and depending on her massive platform for marketing, I've preferred to publish my titles with traditional publishers. Depending on platform size, time, and resources, self-publishing could be a painful learning curve or a beautiful thing. In most cases,

It didn't take me long to go from hating book proposals to being their #1 fangirl. Just as you wouldn't build a house without a plan, publishers don't often publish books without them either. A book proposal is your chance to script your book's success. When you start with the end in mind and sketch the landscape of the intricate world your book will inhabit, you not only enrich your story's content but give agents and publishers a vision in which to invest. A well-written proposal (even for fiction, as you'll see) compels a publisher to fall in love and commit to a long-term partnership.

Translation: Proposals get you PAID and PUBLISHED!

There are approximately three quantum leaps and five leaps of faith, ten giant steps, and a thousand baby steps to getting your book on the shelf. Enter your book proposal. Hatch your plan. Plan for amazing.

***

"Do you have my mommy's book?" Tosh asked the clerk at the Brodsky Bookshop in downtown Taos.

"I don't know, sweetie," the woman answered, a pile of titles resting against her hip. "What's the name of Mommy's book?"

"Charmed Lives!" Tosh said, tall on tippy toes. I put my hand on his shoulder and explained that right now Mommy's book, *Lives Charmed*, lived only on my computer, but that as my biggest fan and future publicist, I'd put Little Man here in charge of letting this nice lady know as soon as it was out. She laughed and gave me her business card and Tosh a packet of dinosaur stickers that he proceeded to paste all over his arms.

On our drive back to Wind Mountain, I reminded T-man that he and his pops would be roughin' it alone for a few days while I went to LA.

With my book still on his brain, Tosh said, "Is that guy you're going to see on the big airplane going to put your book in that store?"

"He sure is, Bug. He sure is."

---

you can get to market faster and have total creative control. But it's all on you to run the business of printing, distribution, and marketing. With hybrid publishing options, new publishing models spring up all the time. So far, I choose to spend my limited time putting my focus on becoming a better writer while aligning with a time-tested publisher. But you have options!

Vibrating with excitement, I arrived at the Four Seasons ten minutes early to see Dan, a feat since my relationship to time could be described as on the "casual" side. Unlike my father, who'd had a lifelong love affair with checking his watch, I rarely wore one or worried about a few minutes on either side of an appointment. But this was different. This was Lunch with My Agent Day!

I walked past oversized windows looking out on a lush patio, my eyes drinking in the scene of this beloved second home to out-of-towners and in-towners alike. How lovely to be in my old dog-walking stomping grounds, with clients like Kirk Douglas and Catherine Oxenberg living just up the street. Instead of a fanny pack bursting with poop bags, I was decked out in Diane's hand-me-downs: fancy Seven jeans and a fitted cashmere sweater.

The hostess took me to Dan's booth.

"Linda!" Dan said, getting up to give me a hug. He introduced me to his wife, Janet, also a lit agent. Before I could unfold my linen napkin, Dan got down to business.

"I can't shop *Lives Charmed* until you write a book proposal," Dan said. "But it shouldn't be too hard. You've seen one before, right?" Wondering why he hadn't mentioned this earlier, I glanced at Janet, who was quietly buttering her bread. I had not, in fact, seen or heard of a book proposal. Dan pulled out a manila folder with a sample proposal he'd brought for me to study. I hoped my face didn't register the horror I felt.

The waiter came to take our orders. Then Dan said, "You'll need to have an Overview section, summarizing the book and why you're the best person to write it. And an About the Author section, which gets into even more detail about who you are. There's a Competition section that outlines the top sellers in your genre." This sounded hard. Couldn't we all agree that I'd just done enough hard, writing four hundred pages of a manuscript? Dan's wife must have seen my glazed look and jumped in.

"For that section, you just need to read the top books like yours and outline briefly how your work is similar and why it's different. And—"

"How long will this take?" I interrupted, feeling dizzy.

"A few weeks or months," Dan said. *Months?* "Maybe longer. But it's worth taking the time to make it professional."

Janet nodded. "There's no rush," she said. *Says who?* Jesse was good for about three more months of fairy tales, tops.

"And I'll need one more thing before I can take your proposal to publishers," Dan said, pausing to look around.

". . . Yeah?" I asked. *Good God, now what?*

"Who else do you know?" Dan said, coming back to focus and searching my face. "Can you get access to any more celebrities? Because publishers are going to want a few bigger names."

Seth Godin 🌿

It's really hard to have empathy for the acquiring book editor [at a publishing house], but you need to try. And that means, understand that she has to read twenty of these proposals today, she only gets to pick one book this week, or one book this month, and that there's a lot of social capital on the line, not just money. The purpose of the book proposal is not to prove that you have written a great book. The purpose of the book proposal is to make it unbelievably obvious that if she doesn't buy this book, she will regret it.

Most people can't write a book good enough to deserve a book proposal like that. But when a book proposal like that truthfully makes it clear that someone else is going to publish this book and you will regret it, those book proposals sell in two days. It always works. But the hard work is making that part true. And the way you make that part true is writing a book that people can't forget, writing a book that changes people, that they can't not talk about. We try to avoid that and instead write a better book proposal. But I don't think that's the way to do it. I think the way to do it is to write freely and often, to share it and share it and share it for free [blogging], until one day, you discover that strangers are asking you for that thing you wrote.

I still recommend that some people publish traditionally. There's no question about it. What book publishing does has nothing to do with paper. Nothing to do with printing. Book publishing is the act of bringing someone else's idea to people who don't know about it but will be glad to have heard about it after they've encountered it. That's really difficult, expensive, and time-consuming. If you can find someone talented and passionate, who will pay you money in advance for the privilege of doing that for you, I strongly suggest you explore the idea.

Laura Yorke

If I get forty projects a day as an agent, think how much one editor gets.

"Linda, don't panic!" Diane said when I walked out onto Burton Way, blinking back tears.

"But I've interviewed everyone I know, Di! I'm sure the hotel's filled with celebs, but what can I do—pretend I'm room service and start going door-to-door?"

My greatest fear was staring me in the face, that I'd fall short of the fame needed to wow anyone, and thus never get my writing or green dreams off the parched ground.

"If only I was a novelist and the only stories I needed came from my own head!" I whined. I could barely hear Di's attempts to calm my fears as images flashed through my racing brain. Jesse and Tosh disappointed in me and ceasing to believe. Me letting my mother and Mother Earth down by not fulfilling my eco-promises. The dramatically lessening snowpack and frequent lightning-sparked wildfires in our forest back home. The sight of deer and rabbits racing en masse to the highway to save themselves during each blaze. Snowdrifts as high as chimneys as recently as five years ago, and now a dusting of inches. But it wasn't just our forest. The same was happening in forests everywhere. I had to hurry!

"Linny, you haven't come this far not to succeed," Di said. "Come bunk with me and Chris at Caesars Tahoe for the July Fourth weekend. The Isuzu celebrity golf tournament's then. We'll get you an A-list athlete."

Chris Chandler was nearly as good at hitting little white balls around on grass as he was at throwing big brown ones on artificial turf. Coming from the LA Rams to the Houston Oilers and now Atlanta, he'd recently been named the starting quarterback for the Falcons and would ultimately take them to the Super Bowl. By being their third wheel for the tournament, I'd have access to any superstar NFL, NBA, PGA, or NHL name on the roster and get to snuggle with my new goddaughter, Ryann Mae, who was just four months old.

"You can schmooze to your little heart's delight," Di said. "But there's one rule. Don't get too stalkery and embarrass Chris."

"Oh hell, Di. I can't promise that!"

Mary Karr 🍃

I always write a book proposal because I take a week or two to think about the book and what I want to do, and what's going to be in it, to map it out, though what I map out is almost never what gets written. Plus they give you money with a proposal, and I'm a big fan of shoes.

I'll tell you the biggest secret—the real secret to this whole game: Learn how to write. If you write the best book you can write, you'll sell it. And if it's not that good, then write it again. When people ask me the secret, I spent twenty years getting ready to write *The Liars' Club*. And I wrote it a bunch of different ways, and I rewrote it, and spent nine months on the first chapter. So, if you spend a lot of time on every piece, you'll make it better. It's an art, a made thing. You don't just vomit onto the page.

Publishers don't read, but agents read. If you turn in a book like Vladimir Nabokov's *Speak, Memory*, if you turn in a book like *The*

Bluest Eye, trust me, they'll notice from the first sentence. If they're only looking for you to have fifty thousand followers on Facebook, then you're dealing with stupid publishers. Write something good. It'll find its audience.

My lucky stars, wouldn't you know who was sitting not twenty feet away from us at the blackjack table at Caesars Tahoe, on our first foray into the casino?! Air Jordan . . . His Airness . . . *the* greatest basketball player of all time, Michael Jordan! *How do you like me now, Dan?* MJ wasn't just a superstar. He was the whole galaxy. I couldn't have written this scene any better. Except the part where I didn't have a snowball's chance.

"Di, get a load of that," I said, nodding toward the table where Michael sat with his close friend, Charles Barkley. "Can you believe those women?"

Di smirked, accustomed to the gold diggers who hang around alpha males with big bank accounts. MJ was surrounded by at least forty, maybe fifty, women who were just standing there, watching his every move. Their hair perfectly coiffed, nails recently painted, bodies swathed in slinky outfits and high heels, these women were hot as hell and on a mission from there too.

"Oh, that's nothing," said a man eavesdropping next to us. "They'll be here all day. Yesterday they stood here for seven hours straight."

"But he's married!" I said. "With kids! It's not like he's going to ride off into the sunset with any of them. He's not even smiling. He doesn't know they exist!" My next thought terrified me. *Do I look that desperate?*

I could forget asking him for an interview. MJ was too famous, the price too high. But Charles Barkley, whose star shone only slightly less dimly, seemed plausible. I'd read his autobiography, *Outrageous!*, in which he said that he might want to get into politics one day, so maybe "Sir Charles," as sportscasters called him, would be more amenable?

That afternoon, Di stayed behind to watch John Elway and Chris in the final few holes of the tournament while I lined up for the PGA shuttle. I noticed a tall Black man standing in front of me holding court in front of a large group. It was Sir Charles Barkley!

"Yeah, and I told them where they could stick it!" Charles bellowed. The crowd roared. The bus started loading, and I sat three rows behind Charles, within perfect earshot.

"My mother can't believe I'm a Republican now," he yelled over the hum of the shuttle's engine. "'But honey, you used to be a Democrat. What happened?'" he mimicked his beloved mama. "Well, Mom, I got rich!" The people around him laughed again. Here was my opening. I knew it was risky—Di would die three times over—but I couldn't not try.

"She'd rather you be a Republican and her personal ATM than a poor Democrat!" I yelled, borrowing a line from his book, as best as I could remember. Charles let out a gut laugh and whipped his head around.

"You got that right! Who said that?" His eyes found me grinning, and he gave me an air high five. Phew. That was risky. But I had his attention.

"That was hilarious," Charles said, waiting as I exited the bus. "Great delivery."

"Thanks. Guess you can tell I've read your book. You're a hell of a writer. *Speaking of which . . .*"

"Girl!" Di squealed when I showed her his cell phone number. "You nailed a three-pointer!"

Elizabeth Gilbert

A proposal for me now doesn't look like a proposal for me twenty years ago. I'm able to say, "Hey, you guys. I want to write this book. Do you want to be part of it?" It's a lot simpler, obviously, because I'm already inside the system. Hopefully, no one will lose money on me. I don't think I'll ever lose the tap-dancing instinct, though. Once a tap dancer, always a tap dancer.

I wrote a book proposal for *City of Girls*; I'm trying to remember now if I had *Big Magic* finished. I don't think I wrote a proposal for *Big Magic*. I think I just sat down and wrote it, and then I offered it along with this book proposal for *City of Girls*. So, it was kind of a bundled package, probably ten or twelve pages long. It wasn't enormously long because I didn't yet have a huge amount of research done. But I had written what is still the first few pages of the book, where Vivian says, "When I was nineteen years old and an idiot, I came to New York to live with my Aunt Peg who owns a theater in New York City." I wrote that whole beginning piece about her getting kicked out of Vassar and her parents not knowing what to do with her and then putting her on the train. So, I actually began the book and said, "This is where it's going to start, and then from there, these are the main characters, and this is essentially what's going to happen."

As often happens, I had the whole story mapped out, but it didn't turn out that way. When I sat down to write, it wasn't exactly what I had knocked out because the story had its own ideas. But the general idea was pretty close. At that point, if you were a first-time novelist, I know that a great deal more would be expected and demanded of you.

Dressed up for dinner that evening, I exited our room and stepped onto the elevator. As it began its descent, I looked at my reflection in the mirrored elevator doors. I'd never be mistaken for a supermodel, like Di, who resembled a cross between Carol Alt and Cindy Crawford. Still, my wavy brown hair was halfway behaving tonight, and my skin was surprisingly unblemished for a change, even glowing. The elevator stopped on the twenty-ninth floor. The doors opened, and standing alone before me was the tallest, best-looking man I'd ever seen—Michael Jordan.

"Hi, how ya doin?" Michael said as he stepped inside, holding my gaze. He flashed that same toothy, pearly-white smile from the Hanes commercials, and my stomach flipped.

"Great, thanks," I answered. No need to ask how *he* was doing. Everyone knew he'd just won the NBA world championship for the fifth time. He was here on vacation, playing with his buddies. He was great! One more sexy and genuine smile from this superstar, and I was a goofy fan, like everyone else.

Wow. This is it—my chance to make a name for myself and a difference. How hard could it be? Michael was a captive audience to my world-saving mission, and I, clearly in God's pocket, was in the right place at the very right time. I had twenty-eight floors to make a connection. Twenty-seven. Twenty-six . . . Twenty-three. Twenty-two. Twenty-one . . . I looked down, giggled awkwardly, and out came the single most brilliant words any interviewer or salesperson has ever uttered:

"Um. You wouldn't want to be interviewed for a book I'm writing, would you?" Eleven. Ten. Nine . . .

"Nope. Don't think so." Seven. Six. Five . . . "But thanks anyway," Michael said as we touched down in the lobby. Not exactly the type of "elevator speech" all aspiring artists know to be ready for. *Who knew that was literal?!*

Just like that, and on perfect cue, the elevator doors opened. *Oh, God. He's leaving.* In desperation, I added, "Your best friend Charles is doing it."

"I can see why," he said with a wink and then stepped out into the crowd. My glowing cheeks now flamed with failure.

Total air ball.

At the end of the longest evening of my life, I called Jesse with the update. He'd been cautiously optimistic about me making yet another trip for my book. Things were taking far longer than I'd promised, and he'd been dropping all sorts of hints lately that I'd need to start looking for a job in our one-horse town. But he was stoked about Charles and laughed at my Jordan encounter, even as I bitched about the female zombies surrounding him.

"Honey," Jesse said, a professor giving a lecture. "You can't knock 'em. They're just holding out hope that he's not happily married and that he's in the mood to share the wealth. He can't spend all that money by himself! And besides, it works both ways, babe. Maybe Charles said yes to you because he wants to sleep with you."

Well, apparently not badly enough. Charles and I played phone tag for a month before the energy totally fizzled out.

Maria Shriver

I'm trying to think if I were in the elevator with Michael Jordan, what would I actually ask him? I think one of the things that well-known people really miss or don't get enough of is normal questions, an occasion to be themselves. When I'm on an elevator, what has meant something to me is usually like, "Thank you for your work on Alzheimer's," or "My mom has Alzheimer's, and I know your dad did too. How are you doing?" In my journalism [career] when I did that, and then followed up later with an interview, I always got an interview. Start with the human connection.

I licked my wounds back in New Mexico as Thomas's gentle teachings continued to infuse our way of life. When we gathered wood, we gave thanks to all our relations, mindful that our walk needed to be in every way in love, honor, and respect. Interestingly, my writing hours were the same as Thomas's "vision hours" and Guru's "ambrosial hours"—3:00 to 5:00 or 6:00 AM when both men believed the earth was freest from thought forms and when access to God or the Great Spirit was easiest.

Di convinced Chris to purchase eighty acres of raw land to our left, and they flew out to have Ryann ceremonially baptized by Thomas and Grampa in the Inepi lodge. As Thomas held the perfectly peaceful baby Ry in the dark sweat lodge, singing to and praying for the littlest angel in our midst, five-year-old Tosh tended to the sacred fire outside as he'd been trained by Thomas.

Every chance I got, I studied the recent addition to my Linda University Reading List: Jeff Herman and Deborah Levine Herman's *Write the Perfect Book Proposal*. That's where I learned I needed to create a one- or two-sentence description of my book, the so-called "hook" or "elevator pitch." *You don't say.* Book sales representatives only have about thirty seconds to describe your book to potential bookselling accounts. Wouldn't it have been nice to have mastered that *before* my MJ elevator fail!

Trying to come up with a snappy book summary hurt my brain. I couldn't! Jesse had the idea to look up some of the most successful movies for their loglines to use as inspiration—a one- or two-sentence descriptor of a story.

"A weatherman finds himself inexplicably living the same day over and over again." —*Groundhog Day*

"A small-time boxer gets a supremely rare chance to fight a heavy-weight champion in a bout in which he strives to go the distance for his self-respect." —*Rocky*

"When a killer shark unleashes chaos on a beach community, it's up to a local sheriff, a marine biologist, and an old seafarer to hunt the beast down." —*Jaws*

"A heartwarming, how-I-made-it-tale from a working writer you've never heard of, and inspiration and advice from the legends you love." —Psych! That's from THIS book! (Books have loglines too!)

Tosca Lee 🦋

I have fun creating my loglines. They're really hard to write, even though they're so short—*because* they're so short. But you know what? It's a great exercise because you need to summarize your story in a line or two. Break it down to the essentials. I always think of the *TV Guide*. When you go through the guide channel on your TV, there's a short little explanation. Or go to the *New York Times* list and look at the books on the top of the list. There's a very short one-line summary of each book. For *The Line Between*, I wrote: "A young woman gets ousted from a doomsday cult just in time for the apocalypse."

After the logline I like to add a sales handle, which in this case reads: "Inspired by actual headlines, *The Line Between* is a frighteningly realistic apocalyptic tale featuring the multi-faceted characters and breakneck pacing Lee's thrillers are known for." Lastly, I add a hook: "An extinct disease has re-emerged from the melting

Alaskan permafrost to cause madness in its victims. For recent apocalyptic cult escapee, Wynter Roth, it's the end she'd always been told was coming."

Ta-dah! That's what the hook is supposed to do, hook your reader. The sales handle is how you're going to hook the sales team because when this proposal goes to a publisher, it must not only get by the editorial committee but also the marketing and sales committees. The sales handle says why the book is relevant. It explains my strengths as the author—the "why me?"—that I'm bringing to this tale. The hook is the part that says, "You know you want to read this."

I always include a section in my proposals called "The Appeal." That's important because it talks about why this story now. It could be anything from the fact that witches are really in right now, which is true—it used to be vampires. Or it could be because of something in the news that's timely. It could be because this really appeals to a certain demographic. This is your chance to say why this book, and why now?

Patricia Cornwell

The book [Autopsy] starts with a woman's body down in [Scarpetta's cooler]. You're going to find out soon enough that this serial killing case is connected to something that's going on in low-Earth orbit, in an orbiting commercial laboratory that's top secret. And [Scarpetta] ends up having to remotely deal with the death scene that happens in outer space.

The official logline for Autopsy is: "Scarpetta returns to Virginia in a post-pandemic world and must hunt a cunning serial killer terrorizing Scarpetta's own city while politicians cover up the truth." That's the blurb the publisher wants out there everywhere.

> But if I were going to try to write something clever, that you might see on the side of a bus going by in Los Angeles, I would write: "From space to ground, to six feet under."

I never did come up with an elevator pitch for *Lives Charmed*. The subtitle came close—as subtitles often do: *Intimate Conversations with Extraordinary People*.

But the book proposal Dan gave me to study had a detailed marketing plan that got my imagination fired up. For instance, I called the Brodsky Bookstore and asked if they'd give me a letter for publishers, stating that I'd be invited to do a signing in their store—that they'd promote. Affirmative! Encouraged by that yes, I asked the same of the Bodhi Tree Bookstore. Again, the answer was all green lights. The owners, Stan and Phil, did me a huge solid by putting in writing that they'd give *Lives Charmed* its own window display in their store, throw me a book party, and promote the book and signing in their monthly catalog to forty thousand subscribers.

Next, Catherine Oxenberg approved her chapter, which was a win! Not even counting her career as an actress, her status as European royalty—second cousin to Prince Charles, granddaughter of Princess Olga of Greece, granddaughter of Prince Paul of Yugoslavia, and named after her great-to-the-seventh-power grandmother, Catherine the Great of Russia—had left her exhausted by paparazzi and tabloid lies. It had taken me a long time to get her to trust me with her powerful story of the healing she'd done recovering from incest, bulimia, *and* Hollywood.

"I've been trying to write my story myself for years," she'd finally said, "but it's just too damn painful." I'd been holding my breath she wouldn't pull out, so Catherine's enthusiasm excited me to no end.

Sure, I was back to crafting more what's-in-it-for-them letters to try and land celeb interviews, but the more I studied Dan's sample proposal and the Hermans' proposal book, the more creative I felt. I could do this—I *was* doing this! I was back in the flow. Momentum was my ally. I had an agent. A mission. Helpful friends. And a plan. Soon, I'd be publisher worthy!

Marie Forleo 🪶

I gave myself a challenge for *Everything Is Figureoutable*. I kept saying, "I want to get this proposal done!" But in running my business, I was not making the time.

One day I told my agent and one of the women on my team, "You know how they do these hackathons in tech companies where they'll take twenty-four or forty-eight hours and produce the product, and everybody stays up all night, and they're kind of cracked out on caffeine or whatever, and they get it done?" I said, "I want to do a version of that for this goddamn book proposal because I'm so tired of hearing myself talk about it. I know it's in there, but I can't seem to get it done."

I set up two days where I told everybody to leave me alone, and I worked with the woman on my team and my agent. I said, "I want to get this to the 80 to 90 percent mark over these two days." And I did it. We spent another few weeks getting it from 80 to 100 percent. That can be the most difficult—getting over the finish line. But I had so much created in these two days because I forced myself to do it. It was one of the most effective ways to get that thing done.

I had seven or eight different Tables of Contents—*maybe this one, perhaps this one, maybe this one*, until I figured out the one that felt like it served the book best. And then here's the truth. I'd spent so much time stressing over that damn Table of Contents, and it frigging changed the moment I started writing!

Proposal, DONE. Sample chapters, ready. Next stop—Book Deal Express! Dan was taking *Lives Charmed* to auction, where publishers would fight for my book baby. I hadn't asked many questions and Dan was a man of few words, so I didn't know much about the process. But what I did know was that this day couldn't come fast enough!

Remember, it only feels like you can't write a book or a book proposal. All the greats feel this way. But by taking your book proposal one section at a time, it gets done. As you've heard me say, if you have the ache, you have what it takes.

Danielle LaPorte and I noted in *Your Big Beautiful Book Plan*: A book is more than just a book. Much more. Writing a book could direct the course of your career for the rest of your life. It could lead to infinitely important connections, multiple revenue streams, spin-off products, breakthrough ideas, and international relations. It could send more business your way. It could change another person's life for the better. It could start a revolution.

Excited? Terrified? A little bit of both? Understandable! Book proposals are beasts. But they're easily tamed with time and TLC. Fortunately, planning for success makes you more creative. Again, here's what I tell writers who are scripting their books and don't yet feel ready to tackle their proposals: Go where the juice is. Diving deep into a story line that's intense or highly detailed in your book requires all your focus. Let's say you're currently pulling your spleen out through your nose, as I referenced in chapter six. Maybe, as I was doing, you're reliving painful memories from your divorce. That's going to require you to work from a very different part of your brain than writing sales copy! If you're in it, inside your story, stay there. When proposal ideas bubble up, get them up and out as quickly as possible on a voice memo, a piece of paper you throw into a file, or as a note on your computer. Honor the creativity coming through and then dive back into your book.

When it's time to write your proposal, I recommend giving yourself self-imposed, scheduled deadlines and sticking to them. It's easy to live in "terminal vagueness," where time keeps evaporating. In developing your book plan, you'll scrap parts you spent hours toiling on, get stuck on ideas, pray for breakthroughs, and stretch and grow—just like writing your book! And I trust you'll come to love the process. Or at least not be a total hater.

For a free PDF of my favorite sections of a winning book proposal, go to BookMama.com/BWBookLinks. Just like good clothes open all doors (especially if they're from Diane), a good proposal will open publishing doors.

PART THREE

Losing Your Religion

*Handling Disbelievers and Haters (Even
When That Hater Is You)*

In this era where uncertainty and frustration abound, it's easy for you to get discouraged and feel like the world is mad and others are seeing results far faster than you are. Many writers ditch their laptops at the first sign of rejection or even when they're thisclose to the finish line. Let's ensure you're not one of them!

In this section, you'll find stellar guidance on keeping the faith alive when dealing with "noes" and the green-eyed monsters of envy, jealousy, and doubt. (Ever feel like the last kernel in the popcorn bag to get any heat? Been there. #ThisTooShallPass #LookForMagic.) We'll also cover: mining your life for the best stories, the importance of editing to distill your message, tips on surrendering to the process, and advice on learning to listen to nature when surrender ain't so easy.

15

Rejection Only *Feels* Like Death

You'll Laugh About This One Day

"My first movie, *Private Benjamin*, got turned down by every studio
until the very last one, but I just kept thinking, *Why are you people
not seeing that this is a hit movie? What is wrong with you?*"*

~ Nancy Meyers

You've heard the saying, right? "Rejection is God's protection"? My sister
was the first one to soothe my soul with this mantra. I don't recall the context; I'm guessing following yet another book rejection. But my relief was
so immediate that she's whipped it out many times since. Basically, anytime her
big sister felt forsaken—a not uncommon experience for someone who plays
full out in love and life, "in the arena," as Brené Brown reminds us.

Alas, rejection isn't always a spiritual experience. It takes time to get our
ego out of the woodchipper, to rebuild our self-esteem from sawdust. One of
the jobs of a creative is to make our belief in our goals bigger than our belief in
those who doubt them.

---

* Fun fact: *Private Benjamin* was one of the biggest box office hits of 1980.

Many authors talk about how, if they could, they'd go back in time and not publish their first book. They'd wait until they and it were better, readier—details not obvious at the time. I shopped a book once that didn't get a deal. Crushed, I called Carol, Diane, and Danielle LaPorte in soppy tears. Was I being protected? My goodness, yes! I look back on that book and *cringe*. No part of me now would like to see her traipsing her story lines unsupervised throughout the world.

Oh, how I wish I'd known then what I know now about patience, trust, and right timing. Alas, lessons take as long as they take . . .

Judy, our postmistress, handed me the mail. "It's a letter from New York!" she said. I noted the familiar green and black emblem of my literary agent's office.

"Oh no," I answered, exhaling.

"No negativity!" Judy squealed. "This is it! Go ahead and open it. You've sold your book this time; I just know it!"

"Dan would've called if it were good news." I sighed.

"Oh." Judy, herself a closeted novelist, looked as if she might cry. "Well, I feel in my bones that your big break's right around the corner. You hang in there, sweetheart."

God love her for caring. Judy saw it as part of her job to keep track of all two hundred of us within the town limits of Tres Piedras, including stragglers who couldn't afford post office boxes. The whole town seemed to be pulling for me. Not much action happened around these parts, other than eighty-five-year-old Bunny once accidentally letting her horses out near the freeway and wielding a lariat like a rodeo clown in her nightgown in broad daylight. Suffice it to say, when I went to the big city—any city—for meetings, a whole heap of folks lived vicariously.

Back in the car, I ripped open the envelope, my heart pounding. Maybe Dan *had* forgotten to call? As soon as I saw that he'd included *two* letters, I knew to steel myself. I read the first page aloud in monotone:

Dear Dan, thank you so much for the chance to see *LIVES CHARMED*.
While I think this is an intriguing idea, I'm afraid the names in this
anthology just aren't a big enough draw. Without bigger names, I just don't
see it working. The author seems fabulous, though, and I'd love to see
other things from her. But in the meantime, I'll have to pass on this one.

_____, Executive Editor, St. Martin's Press

"Other things from her?" *Which* other things, exactly? Of the six original
books I'd envisioned in my first book dream—*no biggie, just over eighteen hundred
days ago*—three of them had already come out by other writers. If I didn't get a
publisher fast, who knew what kind of delays or dangers might befall this book?

Without bigger names. My eyes welled up as I tallied the countless trips to
FedEx in Taos for copies and mailings; how many times I'd queried each celeb
before they said yes; the rounds of edits I'd submitted for their approval once I
did finally get them on tape and written up; how many hours of study and practice and phone calls and back-and-forth I'd done; and the travel to Los Angeles
when I could get a meeting. Then I thought of Jesse. How hands-on he was with
Tosh; how much he was counting on this; how he'd backed me as much as he
could emotionally and financially but no longer seemed as amenable. I'd been
living on affirmations and feng shui-ing my abundance corners, but my vision
wasn't happening, and Jesse and I were getting run ragged from living so close
to the bone.

Wet snow covered my windshield. I turned my focus to the second letter.

Dear Dan, thank you for giving me the chance to consider *LIVES
CHARMED* by Linda Sivertsen. We feel that readers will want to know
about the lives of ordinary people who do extraordinary things—not these
already famous and rich individuals. As a result, we've decided to pass on
this project. Best of luck placing it elsewhere.

_____, Executive Editor, Penguin, USA

Wait, what? Did I have too many big names—or too few? And I'd *had* those
ordinary people doing extraordinary things in the book! I'd spent over two years
interviewing them and highlighting their deserving tales in the very pages Dan

had initially loved. I'd begrudgingly red-lined most of those painstakingly writ-
ten sections when publishers kept asking for more fame. Was this Penguin lady
saying she might have actually liked the book had those stories been included?
Was I wrong to have ditched them? Should I put them back? I felt light-headed.
I sensed someone outside my window and looked up. Thomas and Sheri One
Wolf were standing there, shivering. I rolled down my window.

"What's so important that you gotta read in the car?" Thomas asked. "Come
join us for breakfast!"

"Oh, no thanks. Got more rejection notices from New York."

"Hmm, thought so. What's that make it—number twelve or thirteen?"

"Thirteen, but who's counting?" My lower lip began to quiver. "Most want
bigger names. Pretty sure Julia Roberts and Tom Hanks would do it." Thomas
grimaced. He did that every time I talked about my "ego-filled" celebrity book,
even though as a natural-born storyteller and movie freak, he was as giddy as a
kid at Disneyland whenever anyone famous visited.

"At any point, Sister, you can let Great Spirit pull the wagon," Thomas said.

"Oh, cool! Can you set that up for me?" I lobbed back, which made him
laugh.

"You know, getting what you want won't make you happy," he said, with a
shrug. "What will make you happy is becoming who you need to be."

What did that mean anyway? I was trying to become who I needed to be,
which seemed connected, at least to me, to Native American prophecy concern-
ing the destruction of our Mother. Wasn't becoming a "better" person part and
parcel of my mission to help the ecosystems of those four directions Thomas
was always bowing to? I wished I could be as free of desire as Thomas. He never
much asked for anything. Didn't believe in telling the great "Grandfather" how
to do His job. His only prayer, ever, was "Thank You."

Van Jones

It's so funny, nobody wanted to publish my first book [*Green
Collar Economy*]. It was 2007, and I was working in Oakland, trying to get low-income urban youth jobs putting up solar panels. It

was very simple, a project called Oakland Green Jobs Corps. At the time, though, that was a new idea and a radical one. We had some success. We got Nancy Pelosi to push for legislation. We got George W. Bush to sign a bill called the Green Jobs Act. It spread versions of my program across the country.

I wanted to write a book about it, but in the publishing industry, there was no model for this book. The universal conclusion was, "Black people don't read green books. White people don't read Black books. We've got a Black environmentalist and nobody is going to read this guy's book!" I'd gone to every major publisher. All of them had turned me down.

But luckily, Gideon Weil was a new, young editor at Harper-SanFrancisco, which is now called HarperOne. He'd heard me speak and thought well of my potential. He thought everyone was crazy, that I'd have a huge audience. Sure enough, we got the book done. It debuted on the *New York Times* Best Seller list and is in six languages and over one hundred US universities last year.

If you're a writer and you're trying to say something truly new, you've got to find in yourself that extra strength, that extra lap or two or three. Somebody will find that connection with you. But it takes an extra kind of belief and commitment in what you have to say.

Jillian Lauren ❧

I have a novel that I wrote that didn't sell. It was my first book. I call it, *The Practice Book*.

I said, "If I don't sell this book, I don't know what I'm going to do. I'm going to kill myself. I'm never going to write again. This is it."

And then I didn't sell it. I didn't kill myself, obviously. And I didn't stop writing. I sat down to write another book. I think I was about forty pages into that new book when somebody asked me at a party what I did.

I said, "I am a writer." That was the first time those words ever came out of my mouth. "Okay, I'm a writer. I'm going to keep writing."

Patricia Cornwell ✍

When I first went to the morgue, I was a reporter. The reason I went there was to do research, never thinking that it would take me so long. I ended up working there for six years.

By the time I started my first book, *Postmortem*, I'd been down working in the morgue for four years. I'd written three books nobody wanted and thought I'd totally ruined my life because I couldn't even go back to journalism. By that point, I'd been in the morgue longer than I'd been a reporter. The *Washington Post* told me, "We don't have a morgue beat."

So, I have four practice books. I'm a big believer in leaving some things as practice books. I'm grateful. They deserve not to have gotten published, with twenty pages showing an autopsy. I'm a slow learner, but I hang in there.

"Whaaaat? I thought your agent was going to hold an auction," Diane boomed over the phone. "Doesn't sound like an auction to me!" I appreciated how quickly my best friend championed me. But our realities couldn't have been farther apart.

"When I called him on the day he'd said he'd hold the auction, he never called me back," I sniffled. "I don't want to bother him because everyone says there's nothing agents hate more than being nagged."

"That's such a crock, Linda! Chris can call his agent anytime he has a question. That's the guy's job. That's how he makes his money! Hold on, Lin . . . *BRIDGET!*" Diane hollered. "Don't forget when you're packing that it can get cold at night in Kauai. The girls will need more than just swimsuits! Sorry, Linny. Where were we?"

"I was saying that I'm not a quarterback in the NFL, and my agent doesn't make millions off me, so it's a little different."

"Still, what a chump. Hey, that's my other line, and my masseuse just arrived, so I gotta go. Love you!"

Chris was on a winning streak with the Falcons. While Diane sat snugly in her 18,000-square-foot mansion in Atlanta, I was freezing in a double-wide metal trailer I now shared with Sheri a few days a week. This "office" of sorts by the freeway and parked behind the diner gave me access to the finer things, like occasional hot showers, a phone line from which to conduct interviews, and a fax machine. Our heater was on the fritz for the second time that month, so I wrapped my jacket around my waist a little tighter, remembering the pampering I received when I last visited Di, where their masseuse gave me the mother of all massages, my hands and feet cradled in velvety-soft warming mittens and booties.

Laura Yorke

I'll tell you a little bit about the auction situation. When you have meetings with editors, the book often goes to auction, which is what you want. You don't have meetings with publishers unless it's going to be a big book, probably six figures.

My client Steph Jagger's book [*Unbound: A Story of Snow and Self-Discovery*] was very much a six-figure book. In fact, publishers scrambled and responded to it so quickly after I sent it that we initially had nine meetings. When I sent out an email saying, "I've got serious interest in this, do you want a meeting?" a lot of people said, "Oh my God, yes!" before editors had a chance to bring the book to their editorial board, which consists of their publisher, director of sales, director of publicity, and other editors. All those people weigh in on whether or not the imprint should make an offer.

Once the editors went to their editorial boards, that number came down to five meetings. I said to Steph, "I am going to look at you with a certain look, saying, 'Okay, I'm going to talk to [this editor] about a preempt,' but I'm going to look at you and you look at me back if you agree." Steph did.

> It's a relationship business, and I loved [that editor]. I said, "Karen, just preempt." And she was like, "Yeah, I'm going to go talk to Jonathan," who is the publisher of HarperCollins. She called me back later that day with the exact number I was thinking of, and we closed the deal. It was a nice number. A rare and a nice number.

Shake it off, Linda! Di has three little kids to your one. She needs those massages more than you do! And maybe you misunderstood Dan? Did he say "auction" or "sub-mission"? Feeling crazy, I got up and blasted Seal's silky-smooth voice from Dad's old stereo, my morning anthem. My creative, grown-up Pledge of Allegiance. *Miracles would happen. I'd survive. But only if I got a little crazy . . . (er, crazier?!)*

I looked at Tosh's photo on my desk and felt a flood of gratitude for the chance to be his mother with actual time to write. Not all moms were so blessed. I'd been reward-focused, for sure. But my journey was pretty damn lucky.

Listening to Seal got me pumped yet again to make the litany of calls to Hollywood agents and managers and to write my pitch letters to anyone who could get me closer to the names on my wish list. If they refused to take my calls or read my notes, well, at least I'd done my part. Seal's words sang through the air. *In a sky full of people, only some want to fly,* the song went. Let no one ever say I wasn't trying.

Tim Grahl 🦅

If you practice getting rejected, the pain you experience with each subsequent rejection lessens. It's a lot easier to work through the criticism of a five-hundred-word article than it is on a book that took you two years to write. By releasing my work in small batches to a small audience, I inoculated myself against the criticism that would come by releasing bigger, bolder projects. If you put out a blog post and people think it's stupid, your life changes zero. A few people that you don't know don't like you anymore, which is okay.

Steven Pressfield 🌿

Before agents are even involved, that's when it's just between you and the work itself. After that, then you're into the insanity of the commercial world, where half the people who reject it didn't even read it, or probably 99 percent of them didn't even read it. And the other 1 percent are idiots.

Or maybe it's just no good. You never know. But the books I've sold have almost always had only one bidder. Everybody else rejects them. That's just my experience. Rejection seems to be the rule and not the exception.

The book that sort of got me going in the world was my second book called *Gates of Fire*. It was turned down by everybody except my now-business partner, Shawn Coyne. He was at Doubleday at the time. So, without him, I'd be making this speech to you from the front seat of a New York taxicab, as Alan Alda once said about his wife, Arlene.

Carol Allen 🌿

The publishing world can be *brutal*. Years ago, I had an agent who thought I'd for sure get a deal within two weeks, with an advance of five figures or more! She signed me to her tony NYC boutique agency and submitted me to fifteen publishers right away—and then I never heard from her again. A writer friend finally forced me to reach out to the agency who informed me she'd suddenly gotten a divorce and quit, leaving me and who-knows-who else hanging. Later, my sister introduced me to the head editor in charge of acquisitions at my dream publishing house. She read my book and invited me to lunch, only to tell me she "didn't get it." As I stared into my quinoa salad, wondering what we were doing there, she added, "You have nothing." Good times!

But guess what? It's the twenty-first century and there are many ways to get our work into the world. That same book found a long digital life as a self-published ebook that's made me hundreds of thousands of dollars, helped me land major media appearances, and has sold year after year after year, without my ever even putting it on Amazon.com (which, of course, is another viable option, where many thousands of authors and their projects find their audiences).

Dan finally called, after weeks of what felt like dodging my calls. "No, there wasn't an auction," he said. "You have to have more than one publisher interested to have an auction." *Oh.*

After all the research I'd done, I was still a beginner.*

"Mommy!" Tosh squealed when I walked through the door.

"Well, hello, Little Man," I said, leaning down for a hug. "What kind of trouble are you and Daddy getting into?"

"We're making you French toasties!" Blue eyes sparkling, Tosh had egg, literally, on his face. Our son thought the Sivertsen family tradition of serving breakfast for dinner was the biggest kind of fun—and I agreed. "Are you *starving*, Mama?"

"Do dinosaurs poop in the woods?" I asked.

Tosh paused. Licked his lips. Then came the gut laugh. "Daddy! Did you hear that? Mommy made a funny!"

I realized I'd made a big mistake, leaving my latest rejection letter on the table, when Jesse saw it and panicked. After sending Tosh outside with the dogs, we had one of our biggest fights, ever. I *needed* to fire "that deadbeat agent," get a "real job" in faraway Taos, and despite our Indian blanket "curtains" tacked up with nails, it was time for us to cut "waaay back."

---

* I wish I could remember how many messages I left for Dan. I can't say if it was two or five (please, no). But now knowing how busy agents are, I shake my head at my little sweet naïve self. Sorry, Dan!

Fortunately, Jesse soon booked a role as a cop whose head gets ripped off by a bloodsucking vampire (à la *Howling V* after our wedding) in John Carpenter's film *Vampires*, starring James Woods, which paid us enough to stop the hemorrhaging of our finances for a few months until Chevy called with more commercial spots. I continued showing up—crafting those what's-in-it-for-them celeb interview letters, reworking my proposal, fine-tuning my existing chapters, and holding my breath for a book deal.

As I saw it, Jesse and I were cobbling our dreams together and making progress, no matter how stressful or haphazard. Wasn't losing just part of winning? Rejection was valuable intel. If I kept improving, the only thing that could stop me was me, and that was never going to happen.

Seth Godin

I got nearly eight hundred rejections in a row (twenty-five each from thirty or so publishers). That's eight hundred letters with stamps, one at a time, saying, "This is terrible, you are never going to amount to anything. Go away." I wasn't spamming the world with my eight hundred submissions. These rejections were from real publishers in New York, whose job was to buy real books from people who wanted to make them.

But you learn. You don't keep doing the same thing again and again. You say, "Well, that didn't work. Let me try something else." And if you are enough, you'll keep showing up.

Marianne Williamson

[With] a professional failure, like my having run for Congress— as you know, I lost—afterward, I had a lot of painful things to look at. When you have a public humiliation, you have a public failure. I lost so much of my own money, so much of other people's money, people who had donated. I felt I had let down our community; so many people had been so nice.

Not all suffering creates growth. If you don't face the lessons to be learned, then you don't grow. The *Course in Miracles* says, "It is not up to you what you learn, it is merely up to you whether you learn through joy or through pain." The Universe is constantly giving us opportunities to learn through joy. We do not have to learn through suffering.

But if we repudiate love, if we repudiate forgiveness, if we repudiate mercy, if we hold onto the past, if we try to control events, if we try to control other people, then we will suffer. And then, if we do learn the lesson from the suffering we caused, we will go forth and not have to create all suffering anymore because we're going to be different. We're going to do it differently.

I had to forgive other people [after I lost]. I had to forgive myself. I had to go through every single tear. I had to go through every single sleepless night. I wouldn't be able to speak about it now had I not processed all that, and you better believe it was painful. But I had to learn.*

Rhonda Britten, Emmy Award-winning life coach on NBC's *Starting Over*. She is the founder of the Fearless Living Institute and author of four bestselling books: *Fearless Living*, *Change Your Life in 30 Days*, *Fearless Loving*, and *Do I Look Fat in This?*

Here's my #1 mantra against rejection: I can always go back to waiting tables.

Hear me out. One of the reasons we get discombobulated before we try to sell our book or even write our book is the feeling that it must mean something. Maybe it will mean you're special, or

---

* I'm grateful she did! Had it not been for Marianne's congressional campaign, it's not likely she would have run for president in 2020. I was one of many voters who appreciated the deeply intelligent way in which Marianne brought the much-needed topics of love and peace into the national conversation via the biggest news shows and stages in America. Amen to that.

important, or will finally gain the approval of your mother. Whatever it is, writing your book is not the solution to your problems. At least, that's not what it's supposed to be.

Writing a book is a sacred honor that you're called to do because you have something that needs to be said in your voice in only the way you can say it. God doesn't promise you'll be a *New York Times* bestseller. You make up that shit. Sure, your book might sell 150,000 copies as my first book did. But it also may not happen. That's why you must remember WHY you're writing the book and who you are at your core.

Who am I? Love. I want folks to be fearless because then, and only then, may they know they're loved wholly and completely and can give that same love to themselves. To write the book that's yours and yours alone, you've got to be willing to be a waitress (or a server). Or the equivalent in your world. Because if you're okay with that, you'll stay true to the nudge and write the book that will transform anyone who reads it—yourself included.

My promise to myself has always been, I will do what I'm called to do. If that means someday, I'll be called to sling hash again, so be it. If that happens, I know it means there are juicy things to discover about myself while I'm slinging hash and serving with a smile. And you can bet I will be writing about it.

Rejection is universal. And creativity is fragile. We all need to be gentle with ourselves and each other—and strong as hell. You are not your rejections. Dig deep and find your faith in yourself, your message, and your book. And yes, you and I *are* going to laugh about this one day! (If only you could see me snorting at my desk as I type up some of these stories.)

16

The Bitch of Comparison

When Everyone Else Hits the Big Time

"I'm very much about letting other people shine
because it makes us all shine brighter."

~ Chelsea Handler

Jealousy—a universal emotion. Perhaps you've felt it. Lost a lover to a best "friend." Started a business with employees who left for a startup with more social media followers. Had a bestie stop taking your calls when success garnered her all sorts of sparkly new friends.

Writers are, by nature, sensitive. Today we have the clapback of Twitter, which makes us think twice before we overreact or misbehave. But history is filled with stories of longtime author feuds, rivalries, and jealousies:

Ernest Hemingway vs. William Faulkner
Ernest Hemingway (again) vs. F. Scott Fitzgerald
Ernest Hemingway (sheesh!) vs. Wallace Stevens
Mary McCarthy vs. Lillian Hellman
John Keats vs. Lord Byron
John Updike vs. Salman Rushdie

Truman Capote vs. Gore Vidal

A. S. Byatt vs. Margaret Drabble (sisters!)

I could go on and on. They'd write scathing reviews of each other's work, spit on their reputations—even spit on *each other* (Richard Ford on Colson Whitehead at a party over a bad review, because—"You spat on my book!").

My parents were relentless cheerleaders, telling my sister and me daily that we could be or do anything. "You're so smart, special, funny, beautiful (fill-in-the-blank), and everyone loves you." The subtext? The Universe is abundant; its favorite word is YES. Okay, Mom was dead, and Dad was freaking us out with his new Match.com dating addiction trying to replace her—*oh my God, too many yeses!*—but that's beside the point. Huge dreams were always manifesting. They just weren't yet mine.

But feeling maligned, misunderstood, or discarded hurts, no matter your upbringing. Being human in our modern-day world, where everyone is a "brand" vying for space at the top, is hard. Odds are, someone you love will go riding off into the sunset without you—*don't forget the little people*! In La La Land, especially, everyone's got a sob story. What hope do our shatterable hearts have as we endeavor to cheerlead ourselves? Plenty, thank goodness.

Miracle of miracles! A letter arrived from Leeza Gibbons. She'd heard about Mom's death and had reconsidered. "If you'd still like me to do an interview for your book, I'm all yours." Plus, she offered to consider promoting *Lives Charmed* on her national talk show! I wiped a grateful tear from my eye and held the letter to my chest. *Thank you, Mom. I know this was your doing.*

My agent had recently perked up thanks to the badassery of another mom—Diane's.

"Why don't you interview Arnold Palmer?" Sue Brodie said, taking the phone from Di's hand. "He's one of the nicest celebrities I know." I wanted to scream. The legendary golfer had been on my wish list since my book dream. Di's dad, John Brodie, a former quarterback with the San Francisco 49ers (yep, how very déjà vu all over again), had left his job as an NBC football commentator to play on the Senior Golf Tour. I knew he and Arnold were friends; I'd been trying to work up the courage to ask Sue for an intro, but I kept hearing the refrain "never mix business and friendship" in my head. I'd lost one mom; I couldn't bear to lose another.

"Oh, Linda. It was *so* easy," Sue said after the fact. "Arnie was getting his hair cut in a tent at the tournament. With your letter in my purse, I walked right up and gave it to him. He was so gracious."

"He was gracious because it was *you*, Sue," I said. "He's invited me to his home in Bay Hill next month! You've just done more for me and my future than anyone else could."

"Linny!" Di squealed. "Who doesn't like Arnold Palmer? Your book is practically guaranteed to sell now!" I hoped she was right. Now I just needed to convince Jesse to fund my flight to Florida.

Dan called me right back.

"Great job!" he said. "Let me know once you've written up Leeza and Arnold Palmer's chapters, and we'll be about ready for a new round of submissions. Just one more big name should do it, Linda!" *One more?* It was always one more.

Thankfully, I was getting my energy back following Mom's death. Without her, my world had tilted on its axis, and nothing had quite looked or felt the same since. But the torrent of tears that hit like a passing monsoon every day had lessened. This morning, no tears. Instead, an idea! *It's time to reach out to Meredith.* Her album would be out soon, I guessed. I figured she could use a friend about now, someone who'd been there "before." Maybe she could be that "one more" big name Dan wanted? Either way, I owed her a congratulatory letter and popped my long-overdue amends in the mail. I hoped she still lived at the same address.

A month later, I still hadn't heard back from Meredith. But in my truck on Highway 64 about to cross the historic Gorge Bridge to Taos for groceries, I heard her. Over the radio were the familiar licks of her signature guitar. Then, this explosion: *"I'M A BITCH, I'M A LOVER, I'M A CHILD, I'M A MOTHER . . ."*

Oh my effing God! It's Meredith! I could never mistake that voice! I'd known this was coming, but the sound of her still stunned.

Steven Pressfield 🌿

I try to find really unsuccessful friends. I just seek out losers and then hang out with them. I feel much better. And if they aren't losers when I meet them, I do everything that I can to make them losers.*

Jillian Lauren 🌿

Oh, gosh. I'm envious all the time of everyone's everything! I'm an artist, so I'm like, *How come she gets that? How come she's better at that? How come she gets more? If I were a man . . .* It's nonstop. Oh, and this one: *If I only had this or that, I'd be happy.*

That stuff is totally there, and I try to recognize it for what it is, which is it's not a crime. It's just human. Do I let it define my sense of self-worth? Not on my good days. I try to be very conscious of it. With envy and doubt, I try to preserve a little part of myself that is watching, able to say, "Hey, wow, look at you. You're really envious right now. Isn't that interesting? How curious." That becomes useful to me because I'm writing about people with human emotions. I'm writing about the real stuff we all feel. If I was in a spiritual place where I'd transcended all of that, that would be an opportunity lost to be better able to write about envy creatively in a character or in myself.

I pulled over to the side of the road, cranked up the volume, and danced in my seat. Even my kneecaps had goosebumps! Sitting with my engine idling and the radio blaring, I was back to being a true-blue *fan*.

"That was Meredith Brooks," the DJ blared, "with 'Bitch.' Sounds like a cross between Alanis Morissette and Sheryl Crow, doesn't she? This one's going

---

* In case it's not obvious, Steven's kidding.

to be HUGE, folks, and you're going to want to call in because we've got a whole box full of her new album—*Blurring the Edges*—to give away tonight."

Tears of joy trailed down my face. "Girl, you effing did it! YOU DID IT!" I screamed. "I'm so happy for you!" Feelings of fear and sadness and loneliness started to bubble up, too, but I pushed them aside. Right now, it was all about seeing the dream and celebrating it. Chew on that, naysayers! And, if Mer could do it, maybe I could too? Maybe we all could. I was sitting on the bench, but I knew all the plays!

Meredith's album got rave reviews, soon going platinum in many countries and selling twelve million albums. "Bitch" was a number one worldwide hit that was nominated for eighteen major awards (including two Grammys—for Best Female Rock Performance and Best Rock Song) making her the toast, hell, the crème-filled croissant of the red carpet for the MTV awards and People's Choice Awards.

"Well, I sure was wrong about that one," Paul Williams said the next time I saw him, shaking his head in disbelief. Several years earlier, I'd made him sit and listen to her demo cassette, hoping he'd help her. (This was *after* I'd snuck her into his house and made her hold his Grammys and the Oscar to visualize her future.) "She's going to be massive, Paul," I'd said, to which he replied that while he liked Meredith, especially her guitar playing, he wasn't sure he saw what I saw.

"At this point, I'd be lucky to have her ask me to sing with her!" he now said, laughing.

Elizabeth Lesser 🌿

There's an incredible meditation practice that helps me be creatively courageous. Think of images you see in religious iconography—like Buddha statues or Joan of Arc on her horse, or Mother Mary, sitting tall with her veiled face, her heart aflame. In all those images, you have this being with a very straight back.

Now, imagine yourself sitting on a horse. Let's just be Joan of Arc right now. She's got this strong back, but her heart is open.

She's vulnerable. The same with the Buddha. He's got a strong back and a big, fat belly that's relaxed and tender. That, to me, is the essence of creative courage. You develop this straight back, this sense of, "I belong here. I'm riding through my kingdom on my horse with a straight back. I am noble and dignified."

But before you get too full of yourself and turn into an asshole, you keep your chest open and your belly soft. You support your vulnerability with your strong back. You won't turn into an arrogant person because of your soft front. I would say that's the essence of true courage—not phony courage that leads to aggression and violence. Do whatever you can do to strengthen your backbone and keep yourself open and vulnerable.

As the months passed, I sat in wonderment, seeing Meredith pictured smiling in *TIME* magazine and reading about her foundation's work, bringing music into inner-city schools. *She's saving the world!* Soon she was opening for bands like the Rolling Stones and touring with Sheryl Crow and Sarah McLachlan, headlining the groundbreaking female lovefest Lilith Fair tour.*

From news clips, I was certain I could see Carrie-Anne and Janet in the front row on their feet and belting out the words as we used to do as a group, only now my nose was pressed to the window a thousand miles away. Every time I saw Janet flying through the air in Mer's "Bitch" music video, wearing a cheeky cheerleading outfit, I felt positively left out of the ultimate cool-girls club.

"Linda," my agent Dan said over the phone one day. "I've got a very interested editor, but she thinks you need bigger names." Dead air. I counted to five before he broke the silence. "You've got no platform whatsoever. You don't do

---

* Fun fact: Meredith's team tried to keep "Bitch" on alternative rock radio, but it left the genre within a week, shooting up to Pop's #1 song. Watching this, I was convinced that some things simply can't be held back. Then, just as remarkably, the Lilith women (and just about every female alternative artist), flipped from alt-rock to pop, where women ruled for the first time in history. Talk about a cool time to be a female artist or fan!

any public speaking; you don't teach or write articles; you're not on the radio, and you've never been on TV." Ouch. *Isn't this the kind of thing we should have talked about a year ago?* "If you were writing fiction, it wouldn't matter so much. But for nonfiction, she thinks you need more of your own star power. That, or bigger names. Don't you know anyone else you can interview?"

"I can't think of anyone. I used to be close friends with Meredith Brooks, but I wrote to her, and—"

"Yeah! Her! *She* would be great!"

Tomi Adeyemi

Once you believe you are capable, you are no longer jealous. Before reading Sabaa [Tahir]'s *An Ember in the Ashes*, I didn't believe that. I was still hiding from sixty-plus rejections. My writing goals were this dirty secret. When I read *Ember*, I had this incredible experience: "Okay, this is now a textbook for me. I am going to study it until I understand why it made me feel this way." I asked how it was created. What inspired this author? And then, "Oh, wow! This author got this amazing book deal. That's my dream. Let me look more into that." Even though I'd tried getting published and failed, I had gotten close enough to feel confident in the fact that it wasn't impossible. I just need to get better.

If someone feels confused, I usually ask them, "Who are you jealous of?" Jealousy is your best compass. They're doing something you want to do. Study them! I just watched *Jojo Rabbit* last night, and I loved everything about it. I'm so curious how it was created. Now my YouTube queue has ten *Jojo Rabbit* videos. People do all the thinking for you. Learn from it. Figure out what works for you, like adding tools to your toolbox.

An Ember in the Ashes taught me you could have an epic fantasy, and have it comment on something happening in our present day, and you could weave your culture in beautifully. I didn't know a story like that could exist until Sabaa created it. Once I knew that, she became my mentor, long before I ever talked to her. Don't think you need to DM Sabaa or me to understand how we're working. It's out there. It's all on the internet. Just a couple of Google searches and an intentional mindset can help you get that Masterclass lesson.

Sabaa Tahir 🌿

One of the things I love most about Tomi [Adeyemi] is how comfortable she is in her skin and in her work. She's such a confident writer—that's such a rare and beautiful thing. I also love how she turns the things she learns into help for others. I was not nearly as put together when I was gently stalking her and others. Like when I met Laini Taylor, who was one of my heroes, at Comic-Con. I blabbed to her endlessly, and then I was really embarrassed. I think we look at jealousy negatively, but I try to sort of flip the word *jealousy* into something else from my culture.

There's this concept of "nazar" in Muslim and Pakistani culture. It's the evil eye. When you're actively jealous of someone who you care about, you can accidentally put the evil eye on them. I don't want to put that on anyone, so I feel this weird burden. If I'm jealous of someone, even if it's someone I don't like, I don't want to curse them. I really try to flip it and think, *Okay, maybe this person has something I like.*

When I was first starting out, I was complaining to my mother, saying, "I just feel like I'm never going to get my book published." She said: "Eyes on the road ahead of you. If you look at other people, you're going to nazar them, and that's really bad. Don't do it." And then she said, "And don't nazar yourself."

"Want to join us at the Telluride Film Festival?" my newish friend Janet Yang asked, offering her condo and a hoedown at Oliver Stone's horse ranch.

Okay, this works! As Stone's producing partner, Janet was responsible for bringing one of my all-time favorite books to the screen, Amy Tan's *The Joy Luck Club*. We'd completed Janet's interview for my book a few months back and I was delighted she wanted to be girlfriends. What a wonderful distraction!

"Can we go, Jesse?" I squealed. "We hardly ever take family vacations, and we've never seen Telluride. And who knows who we might meet—for both our careers."

When we pulled up to Janet's condominium—*surprise!* The famed director Milos Forman greeted us at the door. Milos and Janet were about to film the movie *The People vs. Larry Flynt* with Woody Harrelson. Janet's dark eyes lit up as she showed us our room, and I had a sense this was her way of introducing us to people who could hire Jesse or give me an interview, all without saying so. I'd heard Janet described as an "immovable force with a smile" around Hollywood, and I was all about it.

"Woody's on his way over," Janet said. *Holy mother.* Mr. Hemp? The most organic, eco–movie star alive! Could this be it? If he agreed to an interview, my final "big name" would be an environmental activist. My teeth clenched at the thought of pitching Woody here, now, but what had Dad said? *It's just a number's game. Yeses come from asking.* And I'd been reading about how hemp, one of Woody's favorite plants, made up 90 percent of paper until the late 1800s. Wouldn't it be fun to publicize that it's one of the strongest and fastest-growing natural fibers on the planet? And, if the stars were *really* aligned, maybe Woody would notice that he and Jesse were separated at birth and cast him as his kin in a film? Suddenly a ball of nerves, I felt protective. This was big energy for any "journeyman actor" to hold. Would Jesse be okay around these heavy hitters?

Jesse seemed right at home with the moviemaker who'd won an Academy Award for *One Flew Over the Cuckoo's Nest* and a second for *Amadeus*. Of course, Milos hadn't seen Jesse's horror film death scenes, but I hoped his eye for talent could appreciate that my man wasn't showing any signs of shyness, insecurity, or spontaneous bleeding.

Just then . . . enter Tosh, stage left. Our five-year-old dervish who'd been roughing it in the country and attending a school where the average annual family income was $15,000 (subsidized with hunting, backyard chicken coops, and vegetable gardens) couldn't fathom the bounty before him. Young enough that he didn't remember the upscale homes we'd lived and worked in, his only comparison to this modest townhouse was our unfinished cabin.

"Mom, Dad!" Tosh yelled at top decibels as he ran full throttle into the hallway. "They have bathrooms here!"

We'd forgotten to explain to our son that most people in the "real" world don't use outhouses. Tosh screamed with glee as he ran to the sink and turned on the faucet, full blast.

"Ooooohhhh! They have running water!" Leaving the faucet gushing, Tosh raced to turn on the faucet in the adjoining sink before whipping around. "And they have a shower here too!" he exclaimed, banging on the glass door, and then heading off full speed into the nearest bedroom.

"Closets! And *caarrppet*!!!" We heard him dart up the stairs to a world of foreign appliances—hollering at the sight of a dishwasher, microwave, coffee maker, and garbage disposal. They might as well have been specially wrapped Christmas presents just for him.

Jesse looked at me, eyes wide. Janet smiled ear to ear. Milos, whom I'd remembered reading had parents who were murdered in Nazi concentration camps and who'd been raised by relatives and friends of his parents, didn't flinch. But even if he had, to me, Tosh's hullabaloo was the heart-meltiest, cutest thing I'd ever seen. We'd be leaving in forty-eight hours and, outside of Janet, we'd probably never see anyone from this weekend again. Our son's joy, and our time together, was everything.

Maria Shriver 🌱

I was sitting around with all my brothers, and we were like, "Can you believe our parents did this?" and, "God, Mommy did that!" and, "Daddy did that!" I was like, "Wait a minute! We're all five best friends. We're all sitting here together in their house. We all depend on each other. They must have done something *really* right."

Telluride, which sits in a box canyon surrounded by steep forested mountains and dramatically high cliffs, turned out to be magical, with a bad-boy flair. The old mining town's infamous past as the site of Butch Cassidy's first bank robbery and a former favorite stop for drug runners seemed like the perfect place to pull off a heist with Mr. Woody Harrelson. All I had to do was corner him around Oliver Stone's campfire that night and tease him about his mostly fruit and marijuana diet. Oh, and promise him final editing approval of his chapter so he wouldn't think I was some tabloid stalker.

I was mesmerized by Woody's bright and vivid blue eyes. Much has been written of these eyes. Oliver Stone says that he sees violence in them, but there was no evidence of that the next day as he and Jesse played an aggressive one-on-one basketball game. Not even after Jess beat him in the last seconds, proving that white men really can jump and that my husband was a blockhead. "Why couldn't you let him win? Don't you want him to hire you?" I said, only halfway teasing once out of earshot.

Woody was nothing if not adorable. Well, until I had that bright idea to prep for a yoga class he was teaching.

"Linda! Be my partner," Woody said, pointing to the mat beside him. I was so delighted earlier in the day that he'd invited me to his private class that I'd slathered myself in fake tanning lotion to turn my New Mexico pallor into a warm California cocoa. My tan didn't look too fake, per se, but I smelled to high heaven. Even I couldn't stand myself. I kept my distance from Woody, hoping he wouldn't catch a whiff.

"Is that as low as you can go?" Woody asked, walking over to watch me fail to touch my forehead to my knee, something he'd done seconds ago effortlessly. "You're not very limber, are you?" he said, grinning.

"Um, I haven't done yoga since having Tosh," I answered. He smiled. Then he led the ten of us through a few stretches and poses before . . .

"Okay, everyone, it's going to get a little hot in here, so don't be freaky," Woody announced. Everyone laughed.

Woody sat behind me to help me with the next pose, wrapping his arms around me from behind, his nose up against my neck. My very smelly neck. *Oh, kill me now.* Woody, the guy who rails against chemical companies, took a big breath in . . . and instantly dropped his arms, scooting backward on his backside, where he promptly started another pose without another word to me until I went up to him at the close for a formal goodbye. Good thing I had his assistant's info! At the end of the day, it's all about the gatekeepers.

My career goals still looked mostly delusional. At night I dreamed about building America's first alternative paper mill (it had never been done in the US), starting GASPP—Global Alliance for Sustainable Publishing Practices (I built the website, but my time and finances weren't sustainable), and going on *The Tonight Show* to somehow make green topics fun and hip in a cute black organic cotton dress (funny, they never called).

Our renunciation of the material world continued as the months rolled on, and my comeuppance kept coming up. My former support group friend Janet Gunn got the lead in the latest cable TV hit, *Silk Stalkings*, racing across the screen as an undercover crime fighter, driving fancy sports cars, and striding through luxurious locales in slinky designer clothes. Next, I learned that Carrie-Anne was training to make her A-list movie debut with Keanu Reeves and Laurence Fishburne in a little Space Age cyber-fantasy called *The Matrix*. Maybe you've heard of it. Carrie-Anne Moss was to be the female heroine—Trinity.

As the years rolled on, even after I was published, it felt like I couldn't go anywhere without their success finding me. I'd be minding my own business, driving down an empty country road, when, boom, Dick Clark would announce on the radio, *"And now, the hottest song in America, by the woman everyone is talking about, Meredith Brooks!"* I'd walk past the televisions in Walmart and hear Mary Hart from *Entertainment Tonight* yell across the aisles, *"Our top story is* The Matrix, *the highest grossing R-rated film of the year . . ."* Meredith, Carrie-Anne, and Janet's bigger-than-life images looked down on me from billboards, across from magazines racks at dentist offices and salon visits, even making occasional appearances in my dreams. *Lovely.* Twice, strangers mistook me for Meredith and once a man asked if I was related to Carrie-Anne.

Spirit family, Guru had said. What did it all mean? One day, to feel part of the family, I tried to buy Carrie-Anne's action figures—plural—but was told that "the most popular miniature dolls in the world" were all sold out.

And it seemed like everywhere I turned were stories of bestselling authors whose eager readers stood for hours in line to attend signings. Their books were selling in the hundreds of thousands, even millions, and being adapted for the small and large screens. Was I not disciplined enough? Committed enough? Had Guru—*my guru*—taught everyone something I'd missed? As I devoured success stories that weren't mine, my heart sank into my stomach.

"Papercut comparisons," Danielle LaPorte calls them.

> **Dani Shapiro** 🌿
>
> If you have awards and acclaim, X, Y, and Z—which I'm incredibly grateful for—it makes absolutely no difference when I'm facing the blank page.

> **Sarah Manguso** 🌿
>
> I'm going to speak in general, but really, I'm talking about myself. No matter how much one strives and how many goals one sets and achieves, there is always an infinity of goals above. Everything is relative. There are just as many people I would love to match in terms of the number of perfect sentences written or the number of books sold, but then there are uglier moments. I have many good conversations with my agent about this precise thing. Whenever I start feeling kind of greedy and acquisitive, needing that "next thing," he reminds me that everybody has this "one person they're constantly looking up to." Then he starts naming the most famous white guy, novelist, who wins all of the prizes. He says, "I guarantee that so-and-so is looking at so-and-so and wanting what he has. And that guy is looking at so-and-so and watching what he has." He then says, "And there are young writers who write to me, saying that they admire you, Sarah." At its best, this is a circle of inspiration. At its worst, it's a circle of raw envy.

Fortunately, I eventually got tired of feeling sorry for myself. One morning I walked outside, hugged my circle of trees, talked aloud to Mom, and felt oddly free. The letters I'd written to Mer, and Carrie-Anne, too—both unanswered (for a long while, but not unappreciated once they stopped traveling and could catch up, as they'd tell me later)—had helped free something within me. It was as if by sending out my olive branches of love, by honoring our past and sharing my joy at how their hard work had paid off, I'd cleared some safe place within me. Unleashed a reservoir of goodwill. With great relief, I watched as my thinking finally righted itself.

She's saying everything I want to say—but better. That means I can get better too.

I'll never have the audience they have. I'll find my OWN audience.

Why keep going when their voices are so powerful? Because we're a choir, and the world needs all our voices.

I called Woody's assistant, who had taken a liking to me. "I'll lasso him to the ground for you until he cries 'uncle,'" she promised. Phew. At least she hadn't forgotten and was still picking up her phone. I'd hold off on telling my agent until his interview was done, but I was more hopeful. I was learning to step off the roller coaster, to redirect my thoughts every time they strayed to the lunacy and dashed expectations of fake tans, wayward rock stars, and comparisons to the overtly "charmed," all of which had become thinly veiled excuses to cease doing my work. Embarrassment and jealousy may be universal emotions, but I was done allowing them to make me their bitch.

In her essay collection, *300 Arguments*, Sarah Manguso writes, "The trouble with comparing yourself to others is that there are too many others. Using all others as your control group, all your worst fears and all your fondest hopes are at once true. You are good; you are bad; you are abnormal; you are just like everyone else."

"Everyone else" makes me think of social media—where "everyone" hangs out. I don't think we can discuss comparison without addressing social media.

I treasure the sense of connection (and entertainment!) I experience daily from my social media accounts. I post musings, "microblogs," on writing and publishing nearly every morning—sometimes multiple times a day. The life-affirming lovefest includes favorite book recommendations, podcast quotes, cheering on cherished clients, and, of course, a zillion funny and sweet pics and videos of my pups and horses. (Follow me and join the love, and revisit lines from this very book!)

At first, I resisted social media mightily. I didn't have enough time for my real friends, much less a bunch of "fake" ones. Plus, as you've seen, I'm not above comparing my real life to someone else's perfectly crafted one and I was not looking forward to the pangs of jealousy I'd feel. (Can you imagine what a mess I'd have been spying on my former support group members had we all had accounts? For the love of God.)

I quickly learned that with the healing work I'd done inside and out, those instances of jealousy are temporary and the benefits of connecting through social media far outweigh the drawbacks. Social media, for me, has been a wonderfully life-enhancing, friendship-expanding, business-building, and information-gathering bonanza. Maybe that's how you found your way to these pages!

If you're not already well versed in the world of social media, there are shelves of books on the topic. As you know, being connected makes it so much easier to spread news of your book with readers, which is why publishers prefer that you come with a ready-made "following." But if your social media reach doesn't go far beyond your friends, family, your college roommates, and gym buddies, take heart. I've had many clients land traditional book deals with small accounts (fewer than two thousand followers)—the most recent being a gal who got a million-dollar deal with a top-five publisher. The key? Write a book (and book proposal!) they can't put down.

You've got to forge your own path when it comes to building a social media presence. It's okay to start slow, with one account on a platform that tickles your gag reflex less than the others. We all begin with zero followers. Take time to watch writers you admire and see how they share graphics and pictures and snippets from their lives and books. If you're like me, intimidation will give way to creative bursts and even eagerness. Rather than forcing yourself to post on a rigid schedule, wait until it feels right. You'll learn the difference between excitement in your belly and legitimate fear warning you to take a different tack. Trolls, Twitter clapback, and being virtually spat upon aside (ignore 'em all, they don't deserve your energy!), my guess is you'll come to see that enough "strangers" become beloved friends and readers to justify jumping in.

If you're currently feeling forsaken or jealous, rather than give up your dreams or dim your light, redirect that frustrated energy into rocket fuel. Realize that, as bestselling author and speaker Mel Robbins says, "Jealousy is simply blocked desire. If you flip that jealousy into inspiration, the block will disappear."

I hope we've convinced you that you are beyond compare, that your beautiful sensitivity means that your dreams matter, and that you've got all it takes to do you better than anyone. (Everyone does—sweet, right?) To channel my mom and dad—which I imagine they positively love right now, wherever they are—"You're so smart, special, funny, beautiful (fill-in-the-blank)—and everyone loves you." The Universe is abundant; its favorite word for you is YES!

Be your most relentless cheerleader. Then write for you, from you, as you.

17

Hook 'Em Narratives

Your Life Is Your Best Content

"Nothing is ever really lost to us as long as we remember it."
~ L.M. Montgomery

You've heard the old maxim: "Write what you know." Whatever you're scripting—fiction, memoir, academic research—your life and experiences will color and inspire your books.

You've also heard this popular refrain: "Truth is stranger than fiction" (Mark Twain, 1897). Doesn't it make sense to keep a record of your oh-so-bizarre and fascinating life? Many authors are meticulous diarists. Some legendary examples include Virginia Woolf, Henry David Thoreau, and Anaïs Nin—who kept a diary from age eleven until her death at seventy-four. Oscar Wilde said he never traveled without his diary because "one should always have something sensational to read in the train."

To best mine and keep track of the gold of their lives, most authors I know don't stray far from their notebooks, voice recorders, or cell phones, immortalizing the picture, audio, and video evidence of their one and only experience. Some keep drawers of journals, files bulging with memorabilia, and searchable digital notes on their computers, updated to the minute for access from any device.

Don't stress if you're one of the holdouts writing in longhand on yellow legal pads—a practice good enough for Charles Sailor, Neale Donald Walsch, and Hillary Clinton. Or, perhaps, like my sister and our mother, you've got a photographic memory and don't need to store anything outside of your noggin. Lucky you! I'll say this. Without long-ago mastered capture-and-conquer habits, I could *never* have re-created some of the dialogue you're about to read from one of the most entertaining and impactful conversations of my life.

"Next up," the ESPN announcer blared from the living room. I was in the kitchen making breakfast, but the gravity of the voice caught my ear. "Arnold Palmer has prostate cancer."

"Nooooo!" Jesse and I yelled in tandem. We stood before the TV in stunned silence as the host shared cryptic details—the beloved athlete's prognosis unknown, the timeline uncertain. I mouthed a silent prayer, first for Arnold. Then for my book.

Please let him get better soon and keep our interview!

Woody Harrelson still hadn't reappeared, although his assistant continued to crack me up with her candid details of struggling to wrangle the Woodster. "I will pin him down for you if it's the last thing I do," she promised. Oh, how I hoped she wouldn't quit or get fired before then.

Hoping for a lift, I called my friend Amelia Kinkade, a former horror-film actress turned LA pet psychic who was getting her minister's license while working on a book about talking to animals. I was seeking three things: 1) compassion from a fellow as-yet-unpublished author, 2) advice on how to look at my fears and losses more spiritually, and 3) ideas for up-leveling my career. Not surprisingly, she had no truck with my carefully catered pity party.

"You're delusional! Get the eff over yourself!" Amelia thundered.

"What?" I cried. "I'm trying to be such a good person. I don't understand why publishers won't sign me!"

"My Lord, girl," she said with her Texas drawl and throaty laugh. "Being a good person doesn't have a thing to do with it! Step away from the crack pipe! Hollywood and New York reward people for *skill*. And *talent*. You don't get to be a concert violinist because you're a nice person or want to save polar bears! If you have that job, it's because you're a kick-ass violinist. The Universe is not judging one's goodness or badness—people get paid because they do their job better than anyone else. God didn't give Meredith that record deal because she was a good little girl, and she deserved it. That 'Bitch' song kicks ass! *She effing ROCKS!* God doesn't care if Carrie-Anne is a nice person! Her acting kicks ass!" I pictured Amelia's bright red curls tossing while she wagged a finger at her dunce friend. "Are you waiting for heaven to reward you for being a good little girl, Linda? If you are, it's not gonna work."

"I don't know. Maybe. I think so," I said, wincing. This was embarrassing.

After I put out the fire in my cheeks, Amelia's words felt strangely empowering. Editors were saying I needed bigger stars because I needed BIGGER stars. It wasn't a judgment call from God, personally punishing me for being a shitty friend. If I send out a manuscript that sucks and I don't get a book deal, it's not because God is punishing me. I could cry, "But I've worked so hard on it. I've spent six years!" No one *cares* how hard or how long I'd worked or how charitable my intentions.

Amelia softened. "Who's your hero, Linda? The celebrity above all others who ignites your passion and sets your soul on fire?" She explained a part of prayer called "reaching the passion in the treatment" in the church she attended. It's when you want something so badly that you convince yourself that you already have it, allowing a huge river of gratitude and excitement to bring the thing you want rushing to you like a magnet. In full-on déjà vu, I was back in Meredith's studio, hearing her say, "Perhaps it's like putting the cart before the horse emotionally and generating all these thrilling feelings first so that the thing you want can't help but be drawn to you."

"Come on!" Amelia prodded. "Who do you admire more than any star in the world? And don't settle for any of these no-talent wannabes. Frogs and whistles; skip the middle ground and go straight to God Almighty!" *Where does she get this stuff?*

"It's Seal," I said, chuckling. "He's been at the top of my wish list for years."

"Well, then, let's manifest Seal! Let's access the God power within you to create what you *really* want. And remember, Linda. You can have a thousand things go wrong, but that doesn't mean it's not meant to be—that God's trying to stop you. It means you've got to be stubborn and hang on like a tick, mother-f-er!"

Alrighty then . . .

I had to start visualizing. I'd gotten out of the habit, but it was time. I sat back in my chair, closed my eyes, and . . . there was Seal! Seeing him before me was the easy part. Everything that followed—anytime I tried—not so much. Between Seal's stiff arms, my awkward laughter, and his one-arm back slaps, my visualizations were a forced mess. And yet, as God is my witness, Amelia pulled down lightning bolts.

Rhonda Britten

My entire life changed when a friend dared me to tell my story. The REAL story. Not the pretend-it-didn't-happen version I showed people. Abandonment, rejection, and embarrassment were the only things I had ever felt when someone knew what happened to me. That's why I never mentioned it. Not ever. But she kept pressing, telling me I'd hook into people's hearts with the truth of my story.

"Okay, I will take on your dare," I said. "I have two events coming up. I will wear the same suit. Give the same keynote. Use the same PowerPoint. The only thing different will be I will tell my story to one audience and not the other."

Event number one: After my passionate ninety-minute talk to one hundred people, two women and one man came up to tell me how my talk impacted them and ask a question or two. I was pleased. Event number two: I did the same talk except, awkwardly, blurting out my story about the day my father killed my mother in front of me, and then turned the gun on himself.

When I left the stage, I was convinced I'd proven this to be a horrible idea. *I didn't set it up right. No one wants to hear this depressing story. Oh, good job, Rhonda, adding in your three suicide attempts.*

As I entered the main hall, I knew that my speaker table, where I'd be selling my wares, would be deserted. I was ready to tell my friend that she was wrong and I was right. Then I saw something I'd never seen in the two years I'd been speaking. A line. A long line that went around the entire auditorium. A line waiting for ME!

I don't recall how I stumbled through, as woman after woman gushed to me how I had changed her life with my story, or begged me for an autograph, or signed up for my next workshop. I didn't have words. I had never hugged, held, or been loved on by so many people in my entire life.

That was when I knew my story wasn't meant for just me anymore. I knew my parents' deaths on that fateful day were meant to help open the world up to forgiveness, innocence, and fearlessness. I would no longer hide my story. I shared it freely from that point on, knowing it would open hearts and minds and give my audience and students hope.

Your life is your best content. And the worst day of your life will be the greatest gift you give to your readers.

Did you happen to notice, dear reader, what I've done in this chapter to try and "hook" you? I used vivid dialogue unique to Amelia, making my fiery, female Yoda come to life. Hopefully, you see her as I do in real life—a likable and memorable character. (And animal savior! Look her up.)

Robert McKee, in his book *Dialogue: The Art of Verbal Action for the Page, Stage, and Screen*, explains what it means to say an author has an "ear for dialogue." He writes, "Each of his characters speaks with a syntax, rhythm, tonality, and most importantly, word choices that no one but that character would use."

Robert McKee ❧

It's really a question of hooking and holding [readers'] interest and satisfying and rewarding their interest in the last pages. As long as they're interested, time flies. They're utterly unaware of the passage of time. But if they're not interested, time becomes oppressive and you want to start yelling, "Cut cut cut!" That interest often comes down to empathy. If two intelligent, sensitive people go to the same film or read the same novel, one loves it, one hates it. It's got nothing to do with the novel or the film.

The person who loved it felt empathy with the characters, and therefore their curiosity was acute, and they couldn't wait to see how it turned out. The person who hated it could not empathize with those characters and therefore, it was drudgery to read or watch it. But it's the same book. If you don't gain their empathy, they're not interested, and it doesn't work. If you gain their empathy and create a beautifully told story that holds their curiosity as well, then it's a success.

We have to learn to distinguish the difference between attention span and interest span. People say, the young people have low attention span. I don't believe that. For people to suddenly not have an attention span would require a change at the genetic level. What people don't have today is the kind of politeness, where they used to pretend to pay attention to something when they really weren't interested. People today, if you don't interest them, they turn off. The same person that somebody says has a brief attention span will binge twelve or fifteen hours of a long-form television series over a weekend. I mean, what kind of attention span does that require? If you're turning the pages of a novel, the length of the novel is irrelevant.

Do I have an especially good ear—enough so that I'm able to recall conversations with popping clarity years later? Sometimes. But more often than that, my talent comes in recognizing heightened moments of a discussion and grabbing a pen or hitting RECORD on the Voice Memo app on my iPhone or Zoom. (Back in the day, it was a palm-sized Sony cassette recorder I carried with me like an emergency backup appendage. On my call with Amelia, I added a RadioShack adapter, as I did for my follow-up calls with interviewees.)

Even today, when the energy's crackling between a friend and me at dinner or between my man and me in the car, I'm not above asking, "Mind if I tape this?" Sometimes I get an eye roll or an actual, "Not on your life." But often, the person I'm with smiles, sits a little straighter, and turns up the humor—and the volume. Because they, too, enjoy what's coming out of their mouth.

Tom Hanks

I always have a notebook and a pen. I've tried to go with little Dictaphone recordings. I do that when I'm in the car; I can just pick it up and hit RECORD and I can remember something. It's never-ending, because if you don't land on it, if you don't write it down, it could be lost forever.

In one of the stories of the book [Uncommon Type], I write about an immigrant man who escapes communist Europe by ship and ends up sleeping in Central Park. The character is based on Papou, my father-in-law. Papou won the lottery the day he came to America.

He was a bartender. He paid for his house—the house my wife was born in—with the nickels and dimes and quarters he got in tips being a bartender at the racetracks and various hotels. He did the work himself, by hand. That's why the plumbing is so screwed up in the house.

One day, our son had been born, and we were together because when a baby comes into a Greek family, everybody moves in and stays there for forty days. Papou was up early. I was up early. Everybody else was sleeping. I said, "Hey, Dad, how did you come to America anyway?" He spoke with a Bulgarian accent, and he told me a story that is very much like the story in the collection in the book.

I thought I was really brave because I once drove across America in a Volkswagen all by myself. "Oh man, I got stuck in a snowstorm in Steamboat Springs—the high country!" Instead, [Papou] told me how he escaped from the old country and helped a friend escape, too, where they were tortured by the communists. For the better part of an hour and a half, I was both riveted and amazed.

Samantha Bennett

Writers are recyclers. One of my all-time favorite things about writing is getting to use weird little bits of information I've picked up. Odd facts and helpful tips often work their way into my writing. And I lovelovelove borrowing other people's turns of phrase.

My friend once had a boss that would say, "Nevertheless, we must endeavor to excel," which is a line I've now put in a play. I love using character traits of people that I love, like creating a character with a passion for needlepoint, like my grandmother had, and me too! Or sharing my mother's parenting tips like, "Never argue with a child about food." I love folding in details from my life, like my abiding fondness for English muffins, which led me to write one of my all-time favorite lines of dialogue ever: "Toast. It's good anytime!"

I once helped write a comedy song called "70% Off" based on one of my rants about the joys and pains of discount shopping. And then there are the tidbits I've squirreled away to use in the future. For example, my cousin hates the word *lips* and I think that's hilarious. I can't wait to use that sometime.

In one of my favorite sections of *Your Big Beautiful Book Plan*, my co-creation with Danielle LaPorte, we write that you never truly start from scratch. Your life is your content. There's a good chance that part of your book (or speech or product) is hidden in plain sight—in your client session audio files, blog interviews, scandalous email chains, coffee shop convos, that one post that went viral, your teenage journal, your vision boards, or your workshop materials. Traipse through the treasure trove that is your life and capture and conquer!

I thank my lucky stars I was able to tape Amelia's rant that day and relive it for you here.

Martha Beck

When I was fifteen, my high school English teacher asked her students to keep a "writing journal" for stories and poems, as well as descriptions of life events. I had no ideas for stories or poems. But I did occasionally have life events, and these I began to pencil into a slim black composition book.

I never dreamed this journal would become the most important single object in my life, but that is what happened.

As an anxious and neurotic teen, I probably should have been in therapy. Turns out that a notebook can perform many of the same functions, while charging far less. Recording my thoughts in my black book felt like lancing and dressing a wound; it would ease the pressure in my psyche by holding my problems on pages, so I could briefly let them go.

By the time I started college I had many composition books, all full of my earnest, purple adolescent life. I wrote about everything that happened to me and everything I felt. Eventually, even the highly anticipated poems and stories began creeping out onto the pages. But mostly I just wrote down what happened, and this practice kept me (barely) sane.

As a young adult I noticed there were other people in the world and stopped journaling quite so much. But when I was twenty-five and my unborn child was diagnosed with Down syndrome, I knew just what to do: Go out and buy yet another slim black composition book.

Between my son's diagnosis and his first birthday, I filled nineteen journals. I worried that someone might find them and read my most vulnerable feelings, until I realized that anyone on Earth would rather be burnt at the stake than read nineteen stream-of-consciousness volumes about someone else's daily woes. But it occurred to me that if I just took my journals and boiled down the good parts, they might be made into something people *would* want to read.

The first book I pulled from those journals, *Expecting Adam*, became a national and *New York Times* bestseller and launched my career. I still write in journals. Trust me, my entries are boring as dirt. But I've found that sometimes, somewhere in the dirt of a detailed journal, just waiting to be panned out, are nuggets of pure gold.

Catherine Oxenberg

I wasn't writing to write a book. I was writing to protect myself because I was getting threats [for going after the cult that was holding her daughter hostage]. For some reason, I was extremely careful to keep notes in my journal to the tune of five hundred pages by the time I handed them over to my co-writer.

There were two parts to the book. Part one, which was much harder to write because it had to do with establishing my childhood and the early years with India. The memories were harder to reach, a lot dustier. It takes a lot of energy to go and dive into those memories, to reawaken them, and flesh them out, and make them three-dimensional.

The second part was extremely easy because I kept copious notes. From the moment I was told India was in danger, I wanted to make sure that I had a very accurate and detailed record of what was going on. To transcribe that with my writer, because it was so detailed, was a breeze. And then the third part of the process was writing in real time. As the story was unfolding, we were transcribing it up until the last moment when we went to press. The paperback's coming out. Coincidentally, literally ten days after Keith's guilty verdict. So, it just keeps going. It's this crazy synchrony.

Tosca Lee 🌿

I don't start the story or outline until I've researched. Part of the research, as often as it can be, includes traveling to the place. Taking pictures informs the story for me. I wish I could share that with the readers, so I like making Pinterest boards online. I can describe it—that's my job. I write about it. But I think it's really cool, a fun extra, if they're able to see the actual people, places, and objects.

Sarah Manguso 🌿

When writing 300 *Arguments*, I wrote about how, when I was twelve, I realized that photographs were ruining my memory. I'd study the photos from an event and gradually forget everything that had happened between the shutter openings. I couldn't tolerate so much lost memory, and I didn't want to spectate my life through the viewfinder, so I stopped taking photographs. All the snapshots of my life for the next twenty years were shot by someone else.

By contrast, I kept a daily diary for twenty-five years. Skipping a day was unthinkable. I wrote in hospitals, on buses, everywhere. There was absolutely no way to cross over to the next day without having fully analyzed or documented what had happened the previous day.

My book *Ongoingness* is about the end of a diary. I try to narrate what exactly is happening to my experience of memory and time that so utterly, and so quickly, and so shockingly to me erased that basic anxiety that I needed to document, and document, and document.

Dani Shapiro ✎

In *Hourglass*, I was writing about marriage, my marriage. From inside of it, the white-hot center of it. But in a way, it wasn't a story that I was telling. It was an exploration of time and memory and marriage and what it is to meet our younger selves through time. The structure of the book is mosaic-like, so there's a space between each passage. It wasn't like there was momentum carrying me along. I had to pause. I had to be mindful. I had to stop and think about what the white space was even doing between these two ideas and where the next passage was taking me.

One day I woke up, and I thought, "You know what! I need index cards, and I need them now!" As I'm driving all the way to Staples—I live in the country in New England and it's about half an hour from my house—I'm thinking, "Have I lost my mind? Why do I need to take ninety minutes in the middle of my day to buy index cards?" They turned into the centerpiece of my process. Every time I thought about something that I thought would belong in *Hourglass*, I scribbled it on an index card. I kept this big fat stack of cards with me as I was working, and when I was stuck, or I didn't know where I was going next, I would shuffle through them, almost as if it was the *I Ching*.

Guru Singh ✎

Towards the beginning of my book *Buried Treasures*, I relive one of my three near-death experiences, where a woman from another dimension talked to me. This was some of the most powerful content of my life, which is why I opened the book with it. She said, "Don't live your life logically. Live it mythologically."

Those words meant to me that I am a mythological character in the play of history. And just like any mythological character, I have magical powers. My life's work is to then realize my magical powers, just like the quest in any mythological tale is always about the hero's journey. Looking and searching and going through great challenges to find those magical powers that we all possess, because life is magical. Anyone who has given birth knows that.

But I'm not saying don't be logical. There are times when I'm driving a car, if I'm not logical, if I'm being mythological, then every other car had better get off the road. But when I'm living my life and thinking about what I want to be and do with my time here, I had better add some tremendous mythology to my logic to access my best life, my greatest content.

I hope this chapter inspires you to record and mine what makes your world uniquely yours and to bring it to the page. You may not have an Amelia in your life—*please, take mine!*—but there's no need to flog yourself for thinking, however unconsciously, that you're special and deserving and that life is a meritocracy and the harder you work and the more prayers you put up, the bigger your results should be. That's a trap that's been around since the dawn of time—so you and I wouldn't be the first to exhibit this brand of magical thinking. I mean, a writer has got to perform as many Hail Marys and Hindu Mantras and Eye of Newt rituals and affirmations as she needs to before she realizes that the best path forward is to get really fucking good at what she's doing. It takes as long as it takes.

18

Edit, Edit, and Then Write Some More

Fun Fact: Writing Is Rewriting

"Writing without revising is the literary equivalent of
waltzing gaily out of the house in your underwear."

~Patricia Fuller

So, you think you're almost done? *One more edit should do it!* You've made sure the blue eyes on page 46 aren't brown on page 220 and that Uncle Grady's southern accent doesn't come and go. Done and done!

Think again. You might benefit from eight more rounds, beta readers, a professional proofreader, or a digital typo fixer (they make apps for that!) before pressing "send" on your query.

Ahh. Editing. That little thang. As dearly as you might *want* to be finished or meet your self-imposed deadlines, I caution you against rushing. "Writing is rewriting" isn't just a saying on a nerdy bumper sticker. Once you've written what you know, and your stranger-than-fiction story lines sound plausible, it's time to take out the scalpel. To edit the hell out of yourself without losing your book's essence.

You'll be okay. It's enchanting, this practice of stringing the right words together in the "right" order. You just might learn to like it. For your sake, I hope so. I can usually tell which of my retreat clients will get book deals and who won't—and it comes down to their attitude about editing. The "pros" are willing, even hot, to take the magnifying glass to their manuscript, yet again. The shortcutters skim over clunky bits while trying to convince me why they're ready. (They're the same people who say things like, "I've been writing for ten years," "I don't want to market myself," "I'm going to hire someone else to do my social media," "I hate book proposals," "My psychic says . . .")

I've had clients argue that not *everyone* has to edit. They cite those famous few exceptions like Mozart, who was rumored to never make a change to a single note, or mega-bestseller Lee Child, who admits in this chapter to rarely editing a sentence of his *Jack Reacher* thrillers. My sister falls into this category. Born on Mozart's birthday, even, Carol sneezes out her wildly popular newsletter—thousands of them by now, sent to her hundreds of thousands of subscribers—in minutes with hardly any edits. The audacity. Okay, I say. If you can figure out how to take constant and unerring dictation from the gods, be my guest. But there's only one Mozart or Lee Child or smug little sister named Carol Allen. Some people are phenoms. The rest of us must learn to edit or pay someone who can.

In this chapter, we'll break down the different kinds of edits and editors and how to use them, from the initial writing phase all the way through to publication. And in case you're feeling like you're the only one the Universe is toying with, I'll include a few outrageous chopping-block stories behind some of your favorite books.

"Every writer needs a freelance editor!" said the flyer at Brodsky Bookshop. *Really? Everybody?* I hadn't considered hiring out. I had a New York agent who was sending my proposal to publishers. But that wasn't working, yet. Maybe I could up my game! If a freelancer could catch things Dan and I hadn't and make my manuscript stronger, wasn't it worth an hourly investment? I called the number promising PhD-level support for $35 an hour.

Deborah Susswein, a former English major who wielded *The Chicago Manual of Style* as if it were Lady Liberty's torch, became my spiritual advisor. It no longer mattered that my agent still wasn't the most communicative or that I hadn't booked additional marquee names. I was being proactive, drinking from the chalice of liquid language, and I was a delighted drunk. They say the best editing is hidden, and maybe so, but not to me. This woman's skillful nips and tucks turned me into a full-blown convert of the Church of Craft. *The difference a few tweaks make!* I'd been lost—or, rather, my pages had been—but over glasses of iced tea at an outdoor café under the shade of cottonwoods, they were becoming found.

Deborah was training me to better identify grammatical errors, break up long sentences for shorter ones, and use the active voice over the passive. She taught me the importance of reading a completed draft of a chapter or manuscript in its entirety before executing line edits. I'd make a day of these visits to Santa Fe, stopping on the way home for empanadas and ten-dollar Navajo turquoise earrings on the sidewalk of the plaza square. During my trek back to Jesse and Tosh, I'd offer prayers of thanks, a sort of amends to my parents, myself, the teachers who'd tried and failed to hold my attention: each mile in gratitude to my mission and my muse.

Just like years before, my writing improved every day. Little did I know how much the skills I was learning through these sessions would inform my manuscript for the most important interview of my career so far. Or how blessed I was to have found a literary love match out of the gate in my freelance editor. Not only was Deborah a tree hugger who drew little smiley faces and trees in the margins of my pages where my interviewees talked about saving the environment, but she knew how to make me laugh. "Just one more celeb!" she'd say, echoing my agent and bending down in a pretend stance to avoid getting hit. But I felt her genuine faith in the book, which made me double down in my commitment to making my chapters stronger.

Patricia Cornwell

I'm always trying to learn new ways to get better at this. It's about polishing. Constant polishing. I don't care how brilliant a writer you are or how great your story is. If the architecture stinks, the house is going to fall down.

Carol Allen ✒

When I wrote my first self-help relationship book [*Love Is in the Stars*], I had many early readers give me feedback—colleagues, teachers, mentors, therapists, clients, writing coaches—everyone I could think of to help assure the book was truly helpful and "ready." And although I'd put it through endless rounds of edits, I wanted it to be perfect, so I hired a line editor.

"I just want you to make sure my i's are all dotted and my t's are all crossed," I told her. "I've had this fully pre-screened and pre-qualified and don't want any editorial feedback at all. Just stick with grammar and punctuation." She agreed. Weeks later she turned it in with perfect line editing, but she couldn't help herself . . . All over it were the very comments I'd feared, of those internal voices that had kept me from attempting to write a book in this genre before. Comments like, "We've all heard this before," "John Gray already says this in his books," and "Everyone knows this," were scribbled all over the sides in her blue ink scrawl. And to think I was paying her! The very first stranger to read my work didn't have a single kind thing to say.

I was enormously grateful to be forty, and experienced, and well-loved and encouraged for decades by wonderful people before she came along, so her words didn't slow me down. And they didn't stop me from sharing that book with the world—a book that became the foundation of an entire business and career in which I've helped thousands of women with their relationships. But they could have, and I shudder to think of the many writers stopped by the criticism and feedback of people they think are on their side.

Seth Godin

Different people need different kinds of editors. We need to distinguish between line editing, copy editing, and project editing. A copy editor is somebody who makes sure you don't use semicolons the wrong way. I have one of those. We've never met, and I don't use her for my blog, but for the books I've written recently, it's been a pleasure. You send a Word file to someone, and it comes back with the little things fixed.

A line editor is much harder to find. A line editor is somebody who can think the way you want to think and say, "Let's rearrange these six sentences." If you can find somebody like that, who you trust, you should work with them forever.

A project editor is priceless. They might deserve more of the project than you get. The project editor is the person who says to Jerry Lewis, "Don't make that movie about the clown." That one sentence is worth, what, $10 million? I'm always on the search for that. I've been lucky to have a couple of partners and semi-partners through the years that have been insightful enough and wise enough, and kind enough to speak up about the projects, but in general, you will be disappointed. It's really hard to do that for someone else, so you'd better get good at doing it for yourself.

There he was! Woody Harrelson, hoisted two hundred feet up in the air on cables, hanging off the Golden Gate Bridge. Jesse'd hooked our TV up to our new solar panels and I couldn't look away from the unfolding drama. Traffic was at a complete halt for hours in both directions; swarms of police cars and media trucks looked as plentiful as ants. Like an eco-criminal mastermind from a superhero blockbuster, Woody was putting his life and career on the line to save a sixty-thousand-acre redwood grove from a scheduled clear cut. I was riveted.

I no longer cared if he didn't want to do the interview. He was doing it, damn it. I called his assistant, told her it was time, and she agreed, laughing about how patient I'd been. Woody met me for lunch at his favorite raw-food restaurant in Santa Monica for the first of several interviews, and over hummus wraps and green tea, we chatted like we'd been best buds all along.

"Be careful not to forget your environmental ideals when you become successful, Linda," Woody warned me, eyes unblinking.

"Thank you. I hear you. You have my word," I said, returning his stare.

"It makes me crazy sometimes, being so concerned with environmental issues," he said. "I really ingest the world's problems. A lot!"

"Ditto," I concurred, hoping he didn't recall my use of toxic tanners. As Woody talked about going to see the Headwaters redwood forest in Northern California, where sixty thousand acres of forest, mostly "magical" redwoods, some as old as two thousand years old, were marked with blue paint, signifying which ones were to be cut down, I lost my appetite. My mind was already organizing his chapter. People had no idea. I'd need to be courageous; my future publisher too.

"The area I was in no longer exists today," he said, nostrils flaring. "It was completely destroyed. Over half of the sixty thousand acres is stump fields now, heavily logged. A lot of ancient trees go down, and even the smaller trees are often killed because when the big trees are taken down, their huge mass kills the trees in their path." I cried in the car ride back to Carol's house, loving and hating humanity.

Nia Vardalos

The writing process for screenplays is that you write a screenplay and then you're in a room with people that you hopefully trust, and they give you feedback. Whether we take the idea or not, it's good to air it out, to talk about the work. The process brings us closer together. Because if someone gives me an idea and I don't like it, in debating why I don't like it, I will realize what I do like and end up doing that.

Lee Child

I do very little, almost no rewriting. I have a kind of nervous habit, which is that these books have got to be pacey. They've got to be fast. You get the feeling when you're writing them that you're burning through stuff at such a pace that the book is going to be way too short. There are usually two paragraphs in there that are just rubbish, just rambling. But I leave them in, for the time being. I leave them because I'm thinking, *I can't make this book even shorter.* But then, when I get to the end, it's perfectly long enough, everything is fine. So, I go back, and I take out those two baggy paragraphs. That's the only rewriting I do.

It's a peculiar thing for me. I promise you I'm a completely normal, sane person. But when I'm writing, I feel like the action's really happening. It *is* taking place. You can't go back and change that. It's like life itself. In real life, if something happens that we don't necessarily love, it happened. We can't change that afterward. That's how I feel about the story.

I live for the story. If I knew what was going to happen, then I'm done. I'd want the next story. If I knew what was going to happen, I would be bored sitting there for six months typing it out, and I think that would show through. I've also learned to love rabbit holes. If you write in an uncontrolled manner, then you just randomly come up with great stuff. I feel that if it was outlined, I would have to ignore those, and that would feel like wearing a straitjacket.

Next, Arnold Palmer's cancer was in remission! Hallelujah. Our interview was back on. In the weeks up to my trip to Florida, everyone had the same refrain: "He's the nicest. One of the greatest people in sports. You'll looooove him!" Arnie earned his reputation as a sweetheart from a billion charitable acts, ready smiles, jokes, and photos taken with the public. As the "John Wayne of sports" since the fifties when he'd taken golf from the realm of the rich and brought it to the masses, his army of fans, who still called themselves "Arnie's Army," were so loyal they'd kick his wayward balls back onto the greens. Such a rock star to his rowdy galleries, Arnold was the only player to require state troopers to keep the peace on a course. And as the first sportsman to endorse products (totaling over a hundred), he'd grown to popularity at a time when television was new and needed heroes. No bigs. He'd only given something like twenty thousand interviews.

But what if the 20,001st one wasn't the charm? Was it a sign that my plane landed amidst hurricane warnings, the rain coming down in sheets as I white-knuckled my gutless rental car through the slick roads? *I've come so far; just please get me there in one piece!* I was hot and starting to sweat—was it because of the thick humidity or nerves? I was about to meet a legend, and inside his freaking house! Arnold wouldn't know me to look at me, and I'd never walked his dog—*does he even have a dog again?*—but before too long, there it was: the driveway to Arnold's home, white buildings set against grand foliage and swaying palms.

"You can call me Arnie," he said to my "Mr. Palmer." His handshake was firm, his gaze warm. But I soon sensed an undercurrent of . . . was it boredom? "Tired for it," as Tosh used to say as he'd torpedo green beans to the floor of a crowded restaurant, demanding candy. Arnie wanted candy; I could see it in his eyes as he glanced longingly out the windows at the growing green swampland that was his lady love.

Being professionals, we both faked it. He looked as if he was doing his best to appear interested, but his answers were short, without elaboration. I stayed chipper and light, unlike the weather. And then it came. Every cell in my body could feel the futility of this exercise. *Arnold hates this. I'm only here for a favor. Change the energy to engage his higher nature, or the interview's a dud!*

"Does the wastefulness of modern society bother you?" I asked, proud of the hours of research behind that question. Arnold was born the month of the start of the Great Depression. He detested two things: wearing hats in restaurants and our throwaway culture.

Arnold froze as if I'd just put my feet up on his desk, his eyes steely, glaring into the frigid air-conditioned space between us.

"Does the wastefulness of modern society bother me?" Arnold shook his head, bit his upper lip. "What in God's name would you know about that?"

There it was. He loathed that I was here. I stared right back, refusing to be intimidated. I didn't come this far to be treated like the asshole I wasn't. With nothing to lose at this point, I went for it.

"I know a lot about that," I said, making my own eyes steely and sucking air into my lungs. "I had my baby at home with a midwife after a thirty-six-hour labor without drugs and breastfed him until he was three and a half. By choice, I live in a cabin on 365 acres of raw land in northern New Mexico that we saved from tree poachers. I use an outhouse in freezing temperatures. We don't have running water or electricity or even insulation; our cabin runs on solar power. I chop up dead wood for heat and lug water in jugs to do dishes. This book I'm interviewing you for is heavily focused on saving the environment because I personally think humans are a plague on the natural world, and the wastefulness of modern society is killing all of us."

Arnold was quiet for a few beats. Then he let out a huge belly laugh. "No kidding!" he bellowed, his cheeks rosy. "Hot damn! I thought you were some rich Beverly Hills brat!"

"Nope," I answered. "At one time, I had a dog-walking business in Beverly Hills, but we left because, frankly, all the wealth and shallowness freaked us out."

For the next hour, Arnie explained that in rural Pennsylvania, where he was raised, his father wasn't allowed to use the pool at the country club for which he was a greenskeeper. "Nothing made me happier than buying that golf course," he said, chuckling. Then he explained at great length how to shoot rabbits for food—not that I ever could—in case Jesse, Tosh, and I ever went hungry living so far from civilization. We compared outhouse notes, laughing about the racket hail makes on the ceiling when you're trying to do your business.

In the weeks that followed, as I edited Arnold's chapter, again and again, I felt grateful and proud that I'd been stubborn enough to stick with the book long enough to warrant his involvement. *Please, let his chapter be Arnie-approved!*

Another prayer answered.

"Linda!" Sue Brodie said with excitement weeks later. "I just saw Arnie at a tournament, and he said that his interview with you was one of the best of his life. Maybe even *the* best."*

---

* Tip! When someone raves about you or your work, even in passing, act quickly and ask permission to use their quote for your book and/or marketing materials. Arnie didn't want to hurt anyone's feelings by choosing me over them. But he did give me carte blanche to quote

Sabaa Tahir

Oh my God. If you could see my first drafts, you'd think, *Sabaa doesn't know what she's doing.*

There's a whole draft section of *The Writer's Home Companion* about how Elizabeth Bishop rewrote the poem "One Art" over and over and over again. I remember reading it—my brother got me the book when I was thirteen, and it was life-altering. It put me on this trajectory because there's an entire chapter that's just about her many, many drafts of one of my favorite poems, showing how bad some of the early drafts were. You read them and think, *Wait, but she made this publishable?*

That's also something I saw in the news a lot. We had reporters at the *Washington Post* who were Pulitzer Prize–winning reporters. I'd seen their first drafts, which was so enlightening. To know that these people who were considered the top of their game would sometimes turn in garbage. Then, they would get it to where it needed to be over the course of days or weeks. What a wonderful thing. Kind of a reprieve for our souls, to know that it's possible. I wish more young writers knew that this is the process, the real process. It's not just that you come up with these magical things. They're iterations.

Arianna Huffington

I used to be a painfully slow writer and constantly second-guessed myself. And then I realized that I would often give a speech for an hour without notes, so I thought, why not use that ability to produce the first draft? So I started writing by dictating, which has dramatically improved my productivity. And then I can edit, which I love to do.

him saying our interview was "one of the best." Score! That blurb lives forever on the back cover of *Lives Charmed.*

Danielle LaPorte
Part of packaging is keeping it concise. If I think I have wasted your time with an overly flowery sentence or a paragraph that didn't need to be in there, I'm mortified. I worship at the altar of word economy.

Being a writer was like living on a roller coaster—one of the rickety old wooden ones that look as if it might not last another day or tear you up, limb from limb, but instead gifts you with the ride of your life. (Witness: When Dan *finally* did get me a book deal, one of the most vocal Team Linda executives at my publisher just happened to be a long-term die-hard member of Arnie's Army.)

With the addition of a world-class icon, it was time to ensure my sample chapters and proposal were world-class. I had to further "kill my darlings"—a famous editing term.

The expression first appeared in a Cambridge lecture in 1913 by author and critic Arthur Quiller-Couch, who instructed writers to "murder your darlings"—that is, be ruthless in the elimination of things you adore but that don't help your story. (Like any truth that hits a collective nerve, the idea's been adapted many times and attributed to a handful of authors, including William Faulkner, Oscar Wilde, Allen Ginsberg, Chekov, and Stephen King—who wrote, "Kill your darlings, kill your darlings, even when it breaks your egocentric little scribbler's heart, kill your darlings.")

Not an easy task when everything that came out of my new best friend Arnie's mouth was darling to me. I had forty pages of transcripts and hundreds of pages of research to condense down to the twenty or so book pages I'd allotted each celebrity. I longed to make his chapter at least forty pages, but if I gave in to my whims, it could upset the book's balance, and make manufacturing more costly for my eventual publisher. Fortunately, I'd been on a murderous rampage for years already. I could do this!

I'd been collecting personal photos for every chapter, and Arnold gave me carte blanche to use as many pictures from his life as I chose. I *wanted* to use twenty, but again, in thinking about the book's balance and costs (images are expensive to publish—who knew if I'd be allowed), I settled on five: Arnold with his dad, Deke; playing golf as a kid with his little sister, Lois Jean, holding the bag; Arnie and Jack Nicklaus walking in a tournament; Arnold's 1964 Master's victory at Augusta; and a pic with his wife, Winnie, their daughters, grandchildren, and *dog*. I made sure I had permission in writing from each photographer and triple-checked the spelling of all photo credits.

As I'd done with each interviewee, I gave Arnold final editing approval of his chapter. For most journalists, this is a big no-no. Can you imagine the disaster of working for a newspaper or a TV network and giving your interviewee the chance to vet everything? You'd never get a true news story! But this wasn't news, and no one was on trial—and there were several points that needed clarification. But doing so was risky. Anyone could change their mind once seeing our words in black and white. Being such a fan of all of my interviewees, I also never wanted to turn anyone off if what I sent made me sound like a sycophantic kiss-ass.

My fears disappeared with Arnold's final approval. Breathing easier, I made the agonizing decision to cut the last non-celebrity interviewees. Carol was worried. "You've spent hundreds, maybe thousands of hours on those chapters. Are you okay?" I was. I wasn't disappointed for the book's content, which had only increased in value in my eyes with the addition of each well-known personality. What I hated was letting those worthy unsung storytellers down. I'd been passionate about sharing details of their work with the world and my heart and my arm felt heavy picking up the phone for those calls. But this was business. I wasn't going to let my emotions hinder my chances of being ready for market.

On the plus side, no writing is ever wasted. I'd been building my editorial skills with every hour spent. Do concert pianists, presidential portraitists, or Olympic ice skaters regret their hours of practice? I rest my case.

Jenny Lawson
Not to say I don't rewrite stuff a million times. But if I sit down to write something, and it's not the way I want it the first time—it's not funny and it doesn't sing to me—then it's dead. It's

dead information. Dead material. I will almost never go back to try and make it funny.

Laura Munson

I'm about to go out on book tour with a novel. I've got two books I'm working on, so it's a little like I'm leaving them hanging. But I have to believe that when we're so close to our work, we memorize it like a song, and it actually might not be harmonious. It might even be discordant. I think it's important to leave our work so that we can un-memorize it, come back, and read it fresh to see if it really sings.

A month before *Willa's Grove* was due to my publisher, I decided to cut a hundred pages and rewrite them. I don't recommend doing that, but if you're a true writer, let the book give itself to you. Sometimes that means working until the very end. And then you have to let it go.

Mary Karr

I threw away 1,200 finished pages. I threw away the equivalent of four finished books before I turned in the final manuscript to *Lit*, so it was very agonizing for me. At one point, I considered selling my apartment and giving all the money back. I despaired of ever finishing it. But none of my books has been particularly easy to write.

When I threw those pages Away with a capital A, I knew how crummy they were, or else I would have saved them. They were terrible. Trust me. If somebody says, "How do you know?" I'm like, "I know. I know for a living. I've been teaching for thirty years. I know what bad writing looks like." Everybody generates tedious work. It stands between you and the truth—it's brush you burn before you put the garden in.

When I was at my nadir, I had a wonderful moment when I had finally thrown it away. It was my third sort of pass, and I had thrown away my last hunk of it—a big hunk, several hundred pages. I sat at home and wept for five days. I walked around in my underpants, and I didn't see anybody but the guy who delivered curry. I just wept and watched *Oprah*. I just didn't know what to do. Finally, I called Don DeLillo, whom I'm lucky enough to know. I was snubbing and wiping my nose on the back of my hand.

He said, "What's the matter?"

I said, "I've written a really bad book. It's terrible. You can't believe how bad it is."

And he said kind of the perfect thing. He said, "Well, who doesn't?"

I thought, *This is arguably the greatest English language novelist alive, and he's saying, "Well, of course, we all write bad books."* I was able to exhale for the first time in seven years.

After whittling down the remaining interviews in my manuscript, killing darlings left, right, and center, I sent the whole shebang back to Deborah for polishing. "You can fix anything but a blank page," says Nora Roberts. Well, at least I had PAGES! Through friends, I also enrolled a few people I didn't know—who would therefore not be biased—to read the book and offer feedback. Nowadays, there are places where you can hire these "beta readers"—people in your target market who will give you a detailed written assessment of your project. (I've used one company for this book and loved the thorough report. See BookMama.com/BWBookLinks for recommendations.)

Tomi Adeyemi

Very few people write good first drafts. Those people are so few and far between that they don't matter. Assume yours is bad and that you can make it better.

Overwhelmed by writing and editing? Every writer you love has been there. They found their way. You will too. I didn't know it when I started, but there are several levels of editing. Developmental editing saves many a writer from the time suck of falling down deep story rabbit holes from which they may never emerge. How incredible it is to have help with your big-picture thinking, as in: What are your book's themes? How should it be organized? What's the narrative arc?

After the developmental editing is done, you can commend your manuscript to the very capable hands of a copy editor, whose job is to make sure that grammar and spelling are correct. (Deborah Susswein was my freelance copy editor.) After the book is set into type at your publishing house, the copy editor hands off the eagle-eyes job to the proofreader, who checks carefully, word by word, line by line, that the manuscript has been typeset correctly. If you're planning to self-publish, it's a good idea to hire both a developmental editor and a copy editor who can also pinch-hit as a proofreader.

Some writers have the good fortune of getting a crack editor's eagle eye as part of a publishing deal. For all of us, however, I recommend hiring that outside help before you or your agent submits your manuscript to publishers to better the odds of getting a book deal. My in-house editor friends tell me that lousy grammar and punctuation are grounds alone for rejecting a proposal; publishers are concerned that this kind of sloppiness and laissez-faire attitude toward accuracy can leak into the book in other ways.

These days, before sending my work off to my freelance editor Betsy Rapoport, or Vy Tran, my editor at BenBella, the publisher for this book—or my sister, who jokes that everyone should have an early reader who was actually *there* and will write over your shoulder—I copy and paste my chapters into Grammarly.com or ProWriter. This is not an ad (maybe it should be—I need to work on monetizing my work!), but I love editing apps. I'm an obsessive editor, but I'll never be the grammar or punctuation master that Deborah was or that Betsy and Vy are. I don't have to be. There are apps for that! That doesn't mean this step is always foolproof, however. AI is fallible. And finding the right editorial support is not unlike dating. You wouldn't want to marry upon first glance, and you might need several dates before finding the right editing partner. Maybe test your compatibility with a chapter or two versus a whole book.

Lastly, it's good to know that agents are not editors! Sometimes you'll get lucky with one that can do double duty, but make it your priority to turn in clean copy.

Rosie Walsh

I rewrote forty thousand words, completely scrapping what had come before, not using a single word. I could tell that nothing about what I had honored the pace of the first two-thirds. I sent it to my UK editor anyway, hoping she'd say, "Yeah, it's fine," and I wouldn't have to work on it anymore. She didn't say that.

I'd gotten my UK deal on a partial manuscript because she'd fallen in love with it early, which was lovely. But then I delivered an ending she wasn't happy with. I felt terrible; she'd taken a risk buying a book on a partial manuscript—a big leap of faith for any publisher—which is exactly why they don't do it. In many ways, I found it more stressful because of disappointing her, just obsessing, "She's got to be thinking, *My God! Why did I buy this bloody author? She's terrible!*" Of course, that's not what she was thinking, but rather, *I want to make this book outstanding.* Instead of emailing me her thoughts, she emailed: "Are you free to talk on the phone?" *Shit.* Needless to say, her feedback was that it didn't work. She said it very nicely, but firmly.

I rewrote it again, completely scrapping those forty thousand words. She sent another email: "Free for a phone chat?" The same thing happened. I rewrote it for a third time. Once again, there was maybe a couple of hundred words in that forty thousand I could salvage (not including the ten thousand my US editor, Pamela Dorman, would later chop out, in addition to all of the other words I'd chopped as an author when making my own previous passes). There are about three novels' worth of outtakes if anyone wants them.

We have to find ways of not caring. The reluctance to give up and start again is paralyzing. The horror we experience ditching our hard-written words is intense. I owe my UK editor, Sam Humphreys, a huge debt of gratitude because I don't think *Ghosted* would have sold around the world had she not sent me back to the drawing board again and again.

Pam [Dorman] was everything I had hoped for and more. I learned more with my initial six-week edit with her than I had in eight years of writing full-time. She is incisive and thoughtful, with an incredible ability to drill down to the core and cut out all the surrounding crap, which never feels like crap. "Clean" is the precise word; it felt so clean once she was finished. Like there wasn't a word out of place.

It doesn't matter what your intentions are. Sometimes your best-laid plans are appalling. There were many details that got scrapped. I thought they added dramatic tension. But they, like other ancillary characters, were unnecessary. They detracted from the tension, whereas when I was plotting the book, they felt so important. The first time I saw entire chapters being crossed out by my UK and US editors, my heart was in my throat. I thought, *Oh my God! What is she doing?*

"Just try it. See how it reads," I said to myself. Surprise, surprise, it read well.

My writing partner said, "I can't believe you're so willing; some cuts seem so brutal." But when I look at myself, who has completed five novels, and then I look at Pam, who's edited hundreds of novels, many of them global bestsellers, I think she's more on the money than I am. That's my rule. Give it a go. Leave it for a few days. If you cannot stop thinking about it, put it back in.

Gabrielle Bernstein

I was a speaker and hired an editor to clean up after me. I suddenly knew exactly what to do because there was somebody sweeping up and reorganizing and restructuring my sentences, fixing the grammatical errors. I didn't have to be afraid of writing and could let myself be free.

I had recently befriended [a famous author]. I said, "Lady! What did you do? Did you know how to write a book? How did you do it?"

She said, "Call Bonnie B. She's a writing coach, and she'll help you get your outline together, find your voice, and help you get organized."

I worked with Bonnie for four months. She was an angel sent from heaven with a southern accent. She said, "Darlin', I don't know why, but I think I need to work with you," and I was like, "All right, whatever it takes." I sent her a check and said, "Let's go."

Bonnie taught me how to write an outline. She said, "You know what, Gabby, just write, and I will clean it up after you." She didn't want me to edit myself. She was brilliant. She set me up to win as a writer. She said, "Write how you speak." I was so comfortable speaking. After the first chapter, I was off to the races. I knew exactly what to do because there was somebody editing behind me.

I found so much freedom in that process. That was my first book, *Add More Ing to Your Life*. In the five books that followed, I worked with another editor, Katie, who has become my writing companion. Katie doesn't ghost. I write every word of my books, but she cleans them up. She sweeps up the chapters behind me. I will write a chapter, and let me tell you a little secret, I won't even read the chapter, and I'll send it to Katie to edit. Then I go on to the next chapter. Once she sends it back, I'll go back and read that first chapter and start moving things around.

I write the whole book. Then I have Katie clean it up a little bit more, and then I send the book to my husband, who reads the book to reorganize. He's a really good writer, much better than I am. He'll read for content to make sure things are making sense. He pushes back and moves things around. By the time I submit to publishers, I have maybe five line edits. It's done, so clean. Any one of my editors will tell you this—that they get the cleanest manuscripts from Gabby Bernstein. And they're always on time.

Cheryl Strayed

It's interesting to hear the perspectives of others. If it's an editor I trust, I try hard to listen to that person—my editor, Robin Desser, for example. She always has really wise things to say. I don't do everything she suggests. Some of it I take, some I leave, and some I make into something else. But across the board, I try to hear what people have to say and respond to the extent that I can. But I also recognize that there's no accounting for taste. There's no book or script that anyone has ever written in the history of books or scripts that everyone loved or that everyone hated.

Subjectivity is part of art. It's my own subjectivity—*I think that sentence is good that way, instead of that way*—versus somebody else's idea of that, where I've learned to either stand my ground and say, "No, this is the best way," or "Oh. You know what? You're right. Thank you."

Thank goodness for editors. I love editors. We are not working against each other. When I think about the first draft of *Wild* versus the final draft, I feel nothing but gratitude for Robin, who weighed in mightily. I did all the work. I did all the writing. But she really helped me think about some very important things, large and small.

Not every writer likes sitting alone in a room staring at a screen. Many agree that it's more fun to have written a book than to write one. But as my sister says, "Better right than rushed. Better WRITE than rushed." I wonder who she plagiarized that from?

An unexpected benefit of so much rejection for *Lives Charmed* was that I'd had the space and motivation to edit my book a jillion times. Make it as clean and tight as I could.* Those efforts paid off. When Matthew, my eventual editor at my first publisher, sat down to clean up my manuscript, he said there wasn't really anything to do!

Imagine that. The girl with the C+ average in high school didn't need no fixin'. With my biggest interview yet now in the can—edited to perfection, I must say—and my first of two Woody interviews done, I was excited. Ready for even BIGGER things. Surely, they were coming—maybe even to our little forest, such a magical location. I'd put in the time. Followed directions, both internal and external. And become a good student. I'd done everything right, right? My sweet book project felt positively magnetic.

---

* Trust your readers. Resist overwriting. (Despite what you may have heard, the masses aren't all asses.)

19

Slippery as a Seal

The Gifts of Surrender

"The currency of real networking is not greed but generosity."
~ Keith Ferrazzi

On your path to authorship, there's something or someone you believe you need, a piece of the puzzle that still eludes you. You can see the outcome, even *feel* it, but you're not 100 percent sure how to attain it. So, you plan and scheme, plot and pray, only to find out that something remains beyond your reach or perhaps you're not as bright as you thunk you were.

This is where being married to a specific outcome can really jack you up. Perhaps you misread the situation? You wanted a result so badly that you temporarily didn't recognize yourself when things went sideways? Maybe you tried to force something and face-planted? There's a better way: surrender. There's opportunity in loosening your grip, pivoting, in the shifting of gears. Warning: You might have to drop something—an idea, seven chapters, your ego, a person, some comfort—along the way. I didn't say this was going to be easy, people. But I did promise an adventure! And, trust me, your loved ones will be entertained by all the cuckoo crap you do. You will be, too—once you're far enough out to feel gratitude for the madness.

"I thrive on chaos and things falling apart," Leeza Gibbons told me during our interview. "I always have a plan, and I always know it's going to be fine. But I expect that things will happen to derail my plans every single day." So, it wasn't just me—constantly diving and dodging mayhem?

I hoped Leeza didn't notice my eyes shifting every ten seconds to the insanely green backdrop behind her. *How's it so lush? What's her water bill? It's like the San Diego Zoo!* Once owned by the Mommie-Dearest wire-hanger-hating actress Joan Crawford (talk about chaotic!), Leeza's sprawling Hollywood Hills estate felt nothing but peaceful with its rolling lawns, massive trees, swing sets, fishpond, lap pool, and tree house. I couldn't fly here fast enough when I got her message. It had been two years since that ridiculous dinner on my living room floor, and I'd risked coming off as even more of an amateur by sending Leeza occasional updates about my book's progress. No pressure intended. Just a Pollyanna hope that the inclusion of other interviewees or a new testimonial or media connection would impress her enough to change her mind. *I know.*

Then again, here I sat—turning the tables and interviewing the Emmy-winning interviewer with Leeza treating me like a girlfriend and her butler bringing me iced tea and shortbread. I guess persistence paid off! I imagined us sitting next to each other like this on her talk show. *Please, for all that is good and holy, let her follow through on that!*

Back in New Mexico, I ran into Thomas One Wolf at the gas station.

"Linda, I talked to Angela this morning. She said to tell you that she's bringing Seal to meet us this Sunday."

"She's bringing Seal HERE?" I yelped, leaping off the ground in my muddy cowboy boots. "Holy shit!" Angela, a model and actress, was Guru's longtime client. We'd become friendly after he introduced us a few years back, and she'd stayed with us a couple of times while visiting the land. During Guru's recent visit, he told me the beyond-belief news that she was dating Seal. I was dying to pitch him for the book, of course. But I'd been stalling, hoping I'd stop wanting to hurl every time I thought of calling Angela about her boyfriend.

And yet, even with my lackluster attempts at visualizing meeting him, where Seal's arms were stiff or limp at his sides during my mental hugs, it still worked!

"Angela's thinking about buying some land while she's here," Thomas said. "I'll drive them over to that eighty-acre plot between you on Star Hill and the teepee on Chewena."

Man, the Universe was really outdoing itself! I could see where this could go. *Seal joining us for a sweat lodge. Seal singing by the bonfire. Seal counting shooting stars from our porch. Seal marrying Angela on Sacred Land. Seal—*

"They'll come to my cabin first," Thomas said. "Eat dinner at your house around 4:00 PM and then head out early. Seal has to be on a plane the next day, so it'll be a quick trip."

"Okay. Sure!" I said, hoping/knowing Seal would change his plans once he felt the peace in our secluded corner of the world. I'd make the one meal everyone, even Twinkie-loving Thomas, raved about—my penne pasta with goat cheese and olives, to which I'd begrudgingly add organic chicken, just in case. Maybe Guru would come too. Guru and Thomas had become like long-lost brothers. My two spiritual mentors under my roof, the vegetarian and the meat-eater, one lighting up incense, the other Marlboros.

This was it! Once I'd gotten twenty-plus soulful pages of interview stories from this superstar, my agent would finally have what he needed to get me out of literary limbo. These were the pre-Google days, so I paid a researcher at the Screen Actors Guild Library to rush me fifty pages on Seal, where I learned that his full name is Henry Olusegun Olumide Adeola Samuel and that a childhood bout of lupus left him with his distinctive facial scarring. Hmmm, not as exotic as the African tribal scarification rumor I'd heard and swallowed, but good to know, even if I was the last.

Everything was going exactly according to plan. I was hardly even missing Meredith and Carrie-Anne anymore. There was enough room in this big, beautiful world for all our dreams.

From the sliding glass door of my second-story office, I watched the full moon bathe our sage in golden light. I looked over to the stand of pines where Mom's ashes lay buried and said a prayer of thanks. I'd faced the impossible losing her, and yet miracles were still finding their way to our door.

Sue Monk Kidd 🌿

In *The Book of Longings*, there is a character, Aunt Yaltha, who I want in my life, wherever she may be. She had this moment with my character Ana, where she basically said, "All shall be well. That doesn't mean life won't bring you tragedy. It just means life will be life. But there is an inviolate place inside of you where it will not harm you."

I find that true. Terrible things happen, but there is someplace inside of me where I will be well in spite of it—no matter what. That gives me courage to know that we can face life and still have this inviolate place inside. It's a matter of finding our way there sometimes. That's part of life too.

One of the more painstaking processes of writing a book involving celebrities was getting them to sign off on their interviews. It's not that they'd been exceptionally high maintenance. On the contrary. "It's fantastic!" "Bravo!" "Do I sound that good in real life, or did you make me smarter in post?" *Um, er, ah-em.* (Yep, we edit those fillers out!)

But I was glad I'd taken the time to ask for help fact-checking. Thankfully, faulty details were easy enough to detect and correct, mostly a result of the casual nature of our chat fests. But a single phone call scared the hell out of me.

"Linda. My wife loves your book!" one of my interviewees said.

"Is there a problem?" I asked, sensing it in his tone.

"Yeah. Her mother has some issues with a few of the things I told you. Details too personal to publish. I'm sorry. They'll have to go." I gritted my teeth. Tried not to panic. Took a deep breath, my mind whirling through his text, wondering where.

"It'll be okay," he said. "We'll work it out." I nodded, not realizing he couldn't see me, which was a blessing.

Fortunately, he made good on his promise and replaced his deleted stories with other fabulous mom-friendly details that in some ways I liked even better (guilt can be a beautiful thing). Which personal stories were too sensitive? I'd have to kill you if I told you—or more of my "darlings"—and we can't have that.

Aditi Khorana

I never know how my novels are going to end, which is a nightmarish way of writing. I don't recommend it. The end I have in mind is never the actual end of the book. I do an outlining process, plotting until the last couple of chapters. Sometimes it takes a couple of months. I have to sit on it for a while.

I'm not above making myself crazy. I once thought, "Oh my God. I have four hundred pages of a novel, and now I have to scrap the whole thing." But once you sit on it, you realize that if you plotted well, the conclusion will make sense. It's already organically in there. You just have to find it, excavate it. It becomes like an archeological experiment where you do all the legwork, all the technical stuff, and then the magic comes in.

On the Sunday morning of Seal's visit, I awoke to a cacophony of squawking crows, whom I'd come to see as dreaded harbingers of fire, nearby hunters/poachers, or overall bad energy for how many times their alarms had preceded chaos. Thomas called the inky black birds "shapeshifters," believing they existed in more than one place at once to portend the future. But not in this sunny sky. Today they were just silly, noisy, glorious birds. "Hello, lovelies!" I sang out the window. Seal would be gracing our front stoop in less than nine hours!

I scurried around the house, dusting, washing windows, and making pasta sauce. Tosh wandered downstairs, clutching his little-kid Sony tape recorder with the bright-colored buttons.

"Hi, Mommy," he said, giving me a quick kiss. "Is *Space Jam* Man still coming today?" Tosh was obsessed with the film *Space Jam*, the "bestest animated movie ever," and its title song—Seal's remake of the famous Steve Miller hit "Fly Like an Eagle."

"For sure!" I answered.

Tosh's forehead wrinkled. "Mommy, do you think *Space Jam* Man will like us?"

"What a funny question, Bug," I answered. "Of course, he will! Remember—his name is Seal. He's mommy's favorite singer."

"He's my favorite singer too!" Tosh said with a kindergartner's loyalty. He walked over to the TV and pushed PLAY on the VCR for the hundredth viewing of his beloved movie, coincidentally starring none other than my elevator buddy, Michael Jordan.

By a quarter to four, the house was immaculate, the dogs were brushed, Tosh's hair was combed out of his eyes, and I was decked out in my best jeans and boots, notes on Seal's illustrious accomplishments fully memorized. Jesse was out back chopping wood, and Tosh had plopped himself at the base of the front window, eyes focused straight ahead on the horizon.

"Angela's car, Mommy!" Tosh shouted. "Come quick! *Space Jam* Man is here!" I headed down the front steps to greet Angela and Seal as they climbed out of her dark green Range Rover.

"Mama!" I said, forcing myself to connect with Angela before meeting Seal. She looked exhausted, her hair as lifeless as her mood. Seal looked exactly like his photos, only without the sparkle or the tight black leather (bummer . . . he was dressed in khakis and a baggy tee). The air around them felt tense.

"Hi, hon," Angela said flatly. "Nice to see you." Her eyes avoided mine; I wondered if the drive had worn her out? She didn't make a move to introduce me to her man, so I turned to Seal on my own.

"Hey, Seal! Great to meet you. I'm Linda," I said, coming in for a hug.

"Hello," he replied, his smile lackluster. He hesitantly opened his arms, and we embraced half-heartedly. Just then, I heard faint music from the top of the driveway.

Seal, singing about wanting to fly like an eagle to the sea, wafted through the trees.

Heaven help me: Tosh's tape recorder! I looked to see Tosh's little Power Ranger tennis shoes sticking out from behind the back wheel of our truck. My painfully shy boy was crouching behind the car, holding his music player speaker face out for our listening pleasure.

Only Seal, his face expressionless, didn't appear to find it pleasurable. I couldn't tell if he heard it or not. After two minutes of Tosh's serenading, Seal hadn't so much as glanced in Tosh's direction. Instead, he was making small talk with Jesse as if nothing out of the ordinary was happening. Even Auntie Angela, who'd typically be wrapping Tosh in a hug by now, was non-responsive. Jesse shrugged his shoulders at me as if to say, "Don't look at me, babe. I got no ideas here."

The music continued until I couldn't stand it another second. "Oh my God! Listen to that!" I trilled. "It's so funny!" No one so much as smiled. *This is so not funny.* "Our son's favorite movie is *Space Jam,* and he's been *obsessed* about meeting you! He must have taped your song from the soundtrack, and now he's playing it for you while he hides behind the car tire. Do you hear that?" I asked, laughing nervously and pointing toward Tosh. "*Isn't that the cutest thing?*"

"Anyway," Seal said to Jesse as if I'd cut him off mid-sentence, and he was finishing his thought, not bothering to look my way. "It's been a busy couple of days. Is that a trampoline?" He walked toward our giant trampoline at the far end of the driveway. He slipped out of his shoes, clambered onto it, and began bouncing up and down. Tosh, who loved his "tramp" even more than cartoon movies, turned off his recorder, placed it gently down in the dirt, and walked nervously up to me, grabbing my leg as his eyes locked on Seal's every move.

"Sweetie, do you want to jump too?" I asked. With my encouragement, Tosh hopped onto the trampoline and began bouncing next to his idol. Seal quietly acknowledged him. *Finally.*

"You havin' fun, babe?" Jesse whispered at me with a smirk.

"Yeah, a blast. Like drinking warm asparagus juice."

"You've put too much pressure on this meeting," he whispered. "Try and relax."

I squinted at him and slunk inside to finish up dinner.

"Great Spirit," I whispered under my breath, "can you please pull the wagon for me here? I can't do this by myself!" As I stirred the goat cheese into my simmering marinara, watching it bubble around the olives and artichokes, I wondered how on Earth was I supposed to get Tosh's crestfallen face out of my mind long enough to serve a man I now felt like poisoning? Intellectually, I knew better than to be attached to outcomes by this point. But my emotions hadn't made peace with the fact that reality was not measuring up to my carefully plotted plans.

Ann Patchett 🌿

I made such a mistake in a novel I had written. Two-thirds of the novel I thought were terrific, but it was all building up towards a plot twist that completely failed. I did not believe it on any level. It was so interesting to hear other people's responses when I said, "I wrote this book, and it's no good, and I'm going to have to start over again." There were some friends who looked at me like I had just told them I had pancreatic cancer, while others said, "That is so badass of you. I am so proud of you. You're gonna make something amazing now."

To me, the thing I was happiest about was that no one else had read it. I wrote this book. I finished it, I read it. I knew exactly what I had done wrong, and while I was reading it, I kept thinking, *I've just got to get it to the point where Maile can read it.* Maile Meloy is my best reader. And she's such a great editor. By the time I got to the end, I was thinking, *Oh no! No! I do not have to waste Maile's time. I am perfectly capable of knowing what I've done.*

It was like burning a cake. You make the cake, and you burn it, and you think, *Oh, fuck! Man, I burnt the cake. Wow, I am going to have to make the cake again. Okay, okay. I'm going to take my fingers and scrape out the fluffy stuff in the middle and just stand over the sink and eat it.* It cannot be saved. It's a burnt cake. But it's not a dead child, you know?

I remember when I was young, there was a prologue on *Bel Canto* that I had worked on for six months. Whenever you spend six months writing thirty pages, it's because it's crap. When I realized that I was going to have to throw that out, I sat at the breakfast table and wept. I was so crushed to think that I had lost all that time, and now I can look at this book and just think, *Oh, well. You know what? I'm just so glad I didn't waste anyone's time.* It made me feel very lucky. I don't sell my books or show them to anybody until they are absolutely 100 percent done.

"Dinner's almost ready!" I yelled, popping my head out the door. As everyone came wandering in, I dared to hope the food would shift the energy. Maybe so! Suddenly Seal was the most generous, affectionate, and loving man you'd ever want to meet—to our dog! Adobe, a rescue hundred-pound shepherd mix, became the object of Seal's passion as he lay on the floor and hugged her until we were ready to sit down.

Is it weird to be jealous of a dog?

"Oh no!" Seal said as he pulled up a chair, eyeing a piece of French bread on his plate next to a hefty serving of pasta. "I'm allergic to wheat. Is this all made from wheat?"

"Um, yes, it is," I said, careful to control my tone. "You can't eat any of it?"

"No, I can't," he said. No one breathed. "Well, I guess I can pick out the chicken," he offered with reservation and began to poke his fork around his plate.

Jesse saved the moment by bringing up *SportsCenter*—never thought I'd be happy to hear that. Until ten minutes later, when that was still ALL they could talk about. Football. Rugby. More rugby. *Are you guys kidding? Jesse doesn't even watch rugby. Nor do Tosh, Angela, or I. And how about paying attention to what's right under all our noses? Entire forests of aspen and pine are dying from beetle kill because western temps no longer get below freezing for more than ten days in a row—which you could mention in my book to help get the word out!*

Heat was now rising up my neck and into my hair, my scalp prickling with sweat. Good grief. I looked over at the glow of the woodstove and regretted adding that last log.

"What's your favorite European team?" Jesse asked our guest. *Oh, for fuck's sake.* I waited for a beat and then couldn't help myself from butting in.

"What are you working on these days, Seal?"

"A new album," he said. Surprise, surprise.

"Oh! With your producer, Trevor Horn? He's incredible!" I blathered, to which Seal gave me a slight head nod before nibbling on a bite of chicken. I hoped and prayed he'd return the favor and ask about *my* exciting career. No dice.

The long, downward spiral persisted as our dinner dragged to its finish. I felt Seal and Angela disconnecting further from each other and our family with each passing breath. Sensing a swift exit was imminent, I stalled for time.

"Dessert?"

"No, thanks." Seal was watching the door.

"More chai tea?"

"No, we're full," Angela said.

"We've got to be getting on the road," Seal declared. *Great, I never even had a chance to ask him for an interview, and my agent's going to lose faith!* Dan had been counting on this so that he could get me sold. He'd been trying to sell me for over a year; I was terrified his patience would run out. I'd made it sound like the interview with Seal—my most current and biggest star I'd had access to yet—was practically in the bag!

Charles Sailor 🖋

When *Second Son* came out, I had an opportunity to meet a lot of people in the business I hadn't met before, one of which was director David Lean, who said that *The Second Son* was the best story to come out of Hollywood in fifty years. When I met director John Huston, he said, "You're not the guy who wrote *The Second Son*, are you?"

"Yes, I am," I said.

"I really love your book, a lot. But prepare yourself. It's gonna be a long journey."

"What do you mean? MGM has bought the screen rights. All these people [Stallone, Redford, Newman] want to star in it."

"Yeah, I know," he said. "But I had *The Man Who Would Be King* for twenty years before I could get the financing. *Second Son* is a big canvas story like *The Man Who Would Be King*, so plan on at least twenty years." Then he said, "Chuck, I really love your book. But you're not Rudyard Kipling."*

Arianna Huffington ❧

I had to surrender my old ways of doing things. The wake-up call was that one day I collapsed at my desk, hit my head, and broke my cheekbone. I was so sleep-deprived that I just passed out. After that, I made it my mission to help other people avoid painful wake-up calls, some of which are much worse than mine. And from a creativity standpoint, nothing increases our creativity more than being fully recharged. When running on empty, I was disconnected from the deeper and wiser part of myself.

"Linda?" Seal said as he looked at me with a genuine interest for the first time.

He knows my name! "Yes?" I answered, heart thudding.

"Can you point me in the direction of your outhouse?"

"Oh, sure," I stammered. I grabbed a flashlight that hung near the door and led him through the darkness like a seasoned tour guide as Jesse and Angela headed to the car.

There we were, Seal and I, wandering through the night under a slivered moon with the ominous wail of coyotes howling in the distance. A tired superstar on his way to unleash whatever didn't agree with him at dinner (plenty, I'm guessing), and me, a frazzled celebrity chaser, nipping at his celebrated heels all the way to the shithole. *This is fantastic. When I'm old and gray, I'll revel in sharing this feel-good moment with my proud grandchildren.*

Seal grasped the handle of the outhouse and disappeared inside while I waited fifteen paces away. This was it; he'd be gone in three minutes.

---

* Fun fact: Chuck's big canvas story is STILL being optioned by major Hollywood producers. The riveting play-by-play is part of our podcast episode.

What if I never saw him again? What if this was my only shot? Okay. I'd ask him now while his pants were around his ankles. He'd be too shocked to say no. But I couldn't! There'd been no rapport whatsoever, and I was going to look certifiable! But then again, he'd be glad he said yes when he saw the good we'd do . . .

I heard Angela's car start up. *NO! I've got to keep my agent! Keep my husband from losing hope! Help the trees!*

"Seal?" I yelled. *Oh. My. God. I can't believe I'm doing this!*

"Yes?" he answered from behind the outhouse door, sounding more than a tad irritated.

Please, God . . . forgive me for being the biggest dingleberry ever. But my Golden Goose is about to leave with all my eggs!

"Um, this is really uncomfortable for me. But I have to ask you something."

"DON'T DO IT!" he yelled.

"What?" I said, hoping he was kidding. "Don't do what?"

"DON'T ASK!" I froze. The air around me perfectly still. "If you don't ask, you won't be upset if I say no!" he shouted.

Jeez! What's with this guy? It's not like I haven't interviewed a bunch of amazing people. I'd lived with an Oscar winner with platinum records on the wall, interviewed English aristocracy. Princess Diana had sent me a lovely letter. (Sure, it was a *rejection* letter, but the office of her Royal Highness took the time to write.) God, I was so totally puzzled and out of my depth with this guy that nothing computed. *Oh, wait! Of course!* Angela must have told him about my work on their way here. He knew this was coming and armored up. Now I was not only embarrassed but also hurt. Seal couldn't give one little interview to help a girl's mission? I couldn't wait for him to leave. *Remember to thank the crows tomorrow for their warning!*

After another uncomfortable minute, I could no longer hear Seal moving. *Is he just sitting with his feet up, hiding from me?* Oh, I could play this game. I'd wait him out. *This is my yard, buddy. You're my guest. You'll have to come out of there sooner or later.*

Without warning, the door to the outhouse flung open with such force that it ricocheted with a crash against the wall. Seal, newly energized, made a run for his waiting car—more like an all-out sprint. As I watched him pump his arms as if he were competing in the hundred-yard dash, I didn't even bother to paint a fake smile on my face as I offered a scant courtesy wave goodbye as he and Angela careened off into the night.

"Did he even say goodbye?" Jesse asked when all we could see was the red glow of taillights.

"If he did, I didn't hear it. Nor a thank you," I said. "It's like he thought I was stalking him."

"In our own driveway?" Jesse said. We laughed and headed inside, with plenty of time to make tea and get ready to watch Meredith singing on *The Tonight Show*. Her duet performance of "Lay Down" with Queen Latifah for Jay Leno, backed up by a world-class gospel choir, was so good that I didn't have time to feel sorry for myself through my jazz hands.

Patricia Cornwell ❧

I say go boldly. When I was coming along, if I wasn't bold, I wasn't going to get anything.

You get a certain desperate energy about yourself. If you're the reporter and there's a sniper on the roof, you're going to climb up that ladder. I did stuff like that. 'Cause if I don't get that story, [it's] someone else's, and now I'm screwed. I stayed up all night chasing down three death row inmates that had hacksawed their way out of a prison in Georgia and ended up in North Carolina after killing one of their compatriots and dumping his body in the Catawba River.

I'm running around because I got a tip from the police. I'm going to find these guys and I'm in a staff car and I'm screeching on the brakes.

"F that, Patsy! What are you thinking, you fucking idiot! What are you going to do when you catch 'em?" I mean, they tortured one of their people to death. Fortunately, I didn't find them before the police did, but, but you know, you've got to be like that. Don't let somebody tell you no. Just don't do things that are wrong."

Van Jones

I've always been trying to figure out some way to deal with what I call the "least of these": the people who are left out, locked out, left behind—to be a good voice, a good advocate, a good champion for people, causes and constituencies that frankly most people don't care a ton about.

That's been the big calling. I've tried to use public speaking. I've tried to use television. I've tried to use writing for that purpose. And inside of that, you can make a ton of mistakes. Early on, it's just about being so self-righteous and being so didactic and reductive that the only people who agree with you are your roommate and your ex-girlfriend, and everybody else is like, "Get this person away from me." It's just too shrill and too extreme and too over-the-top.

I feel like I've come full circle. You start off as a bomb-thrower in your twenties, and by the time you get to your late forties, where I am now, you wind up realizing the world needs bridge builders too. And sometimes, the best bridge builders are the people that used to be the bomb-throwers. I used to be the loudest guy in the room, the most belligerent in trying to make my points for my cause.

The day after their visit, Angela called to apologize, explaining she and Seal had been breaking up that night. Our dinner was their Last Supper.

My God. Even if Seal had been the right person for the job, my timing had been all wrong. My mission had fallen on deaf ears primarily because I'd been blind.

Abby Wambach

I think making "failure a fuel" has been a skill I've been learning my whole career. I was going to work with ESPN, which is the next common step, or trajectory, for most former professional athletes capable of speaking their mind and who've reached a certain level of fame or popularity inside of their sport. I thought: *All right. This is great. I'll give it a shot.* ESPN paid me a lot of money to work for them. But I didn't understand how much preparation went into commentating. I didn't know much about the men's international game in terms of the players and the background of some of these guys. Though I loved playing for Team USA for many years, soccer isn't something where I think, *I can't wait to watch the game.* I didn't grow up watching soccer. I grew up *playing* soccer. Those are very different things.

So, I found myself with the red light turned on, and everything I knew about myself as a human being went out the window. I had no idea of what the hell I was doing! I was a rookie, I sucked at it, which is normal. There's no reason why I should have been good at it. But I think that if it didn't go quite as badly, I probably would have tried to keep commentating. I would have continued down that road.

Pivoting is the most important part of this story. Sometimes we find ourselves in a situation where we've made this one decision, but we didn't read the signs right. We get sick, or the world isn't opening up, or there's a big sign that you're not on the life path you need to be on. I have a great passion for wanting to change the world in a positive way, especially for women. So, I did some real digging, and I figured out specific ways to do that.

Geneen Roth ❧

Losing our life savings to Bernie Madoff taught me something I would never exchange, even if I had the choice. Two months later, I knew that if somebody had come to me and said, "You could turn back the clock and get back your thirty years of life savings back—would you?" my answer would have been, "No. I will not turn back the clock."

Before we lost our money, without realizing it, I had been living with a low-level anxiety. Not just about possible loss, but about not having enough. There was a sense that I wasn't enough, and we didn't have enough. Then in one phone call, it was all gone. After I peeled myself off from the shock and the shame of having invested everything in one place, I realized I had so many good friends. Two, in particular, said to me in one form or another: "Nothing of any value has been lost." I wanted to smack them. *Oh, come on. How can you say that?*

And then, I realized that they were right. If all those years of meditating meant anything at all, this is where the rubber met the road. I realized that it was my mind going off the cliffs. It was the stories I was telling myself about the situation, not the situation. So, we lost our money. But every day, I started focusing on what I hadn't lost. I would not let my mind start in on the fear, the shame, the terror, the not-enough stories. Because of that vigilance of bringing my mind back every single time it wandered, I started feeling happier than I had been in years.

"You did whaaaat?!" squealed Amelia the next day. "Holy cow, Linda. That's hilarious!" I wasn't laughing, but she kept right on going.

"Imagine you're a massive, world-renowned celebrity, and everywhere you go, people want a piece of you. You're exhausted and only have one measly little day off, and your girlfriend drags you out to the boondocks on your miserable last day together to meet a bunch of hillbillies when what you need is alone time. You get to their cabin, and their kid's a pest, playing a song you're so sick of you want to die. It turns out that the hostess is a needy press person—the very last soul you want to come across, and she's so busy worrying about getting her story that it never occurs to her to ask ahead of time if there's anything you can't eat, so she makes all the shit that makes you sick."

Now I was the one feeling sick. In her verbal ass kicking, Amelia explained that had I taken their cues, saying something like, "Hey, Seal. You look like you need some rest. Do you guys want to lie down? And what do you like to eat? I have a choice of things 'cuz I didn't know what you'd be in the mood for," our night together could have been far more bearable. I cut Amelia off before the pet psychic could point out that Seal went up to the one being in our household who was authentically sending him love and didn't have an agenda: our dog. Or that I'd yelled at the singer while he was in the shitter!

Samantha Bennett ❧

I once did a lot of work for L.A. Theatre Works, which produces live, full-cast recordings of plays for the radio. We often got celebrities to participate, so I met and worked with a lot of famous people, almost all of whom were totally down-to-earth and delightful.

When we produced *A View from the Bridge*, Ed O'Neill played the lead, and he was marvelous. I knew he was famous, of course, but I'd never really watched *Married . . . with Children*, so to me, he was just another ferociously talented actor. One night we went out for a beer, and I called him the next day to thank him for buying me a drink. We chatted for a minute, and then he said, "So, what can I do for you?"

I was a little taken aback and said, "Huh? Nothing! I was just calling to say thanks and nice to see you and stuff."

"Oh," he said, sounding surprised. "That's nice." And I thought, *Jeez, this poor guy. He's got a life where he kind of has to assume that everyone wants something from him.* In that moment, I promised myself that I would never ask Ed for anything. And he's been one of my closest friends and most trusted advisors for almost twenty years now.

Oh. Wait. Now I need to ask Ed for his approval to share this story. Crapsies! Thanks a lot, Linda. Way to break my streak. Luckily, he said, "Fine." Because that's what good friends do.

Amelia was right. If I was ever going to make it in bigger arenas, I'd have to be sensitive to people's worlds (and establish that human connection Maria Shriver would later tell me about). Seal was a big star, and I made several big assumptions. Like believing that because he was coming to my house, he owed me. Or that my desires and those of my spellbound kid and hubs in need of a break superseded his. Or that because the natural world was dying, he alone could help put it on life support—all the while legitimizing my mother's unrealized green dreams—by handing me a bigger megaphone.

Good God, why would anyone *ever* want to be famous?

I still believe, of course, that God works through people. I just try and remember to stop and think about what those people want and need before I go forging a connection. *How can I make them happy to run toward me—rather than desperate to flee from me?* I've been to a few fancy-pants charity events in my day, and one thing I've learned is that everyone, no matter how high up the celebrity food chain, is always climbing toward a goal. You can bloody well bet there's someone, something, or an outcome they're attached to in that room—even if it's to be left alone. If my goals aren't a match, so be it. There are other elbows to rub. Other hearts to touch.

So, the next time you think your life's going one way and it pulls a 180, or your mission craps out entirely, or you're writing one book and it becomes a completely different story, remember that although Seal wasn't the star of my book, as I'd hoped (in fact, he didn't even get a mention in the pages of *Lives Charmed*), all I had to do was hang tough for twenty-six years for him to be one of the stars of this one. Ha! Not helpful? Never mind.

Terry McMillan

Everything doesn't always work out. But you don't have to feel regret. When you know what you're doing and why you're doing it, do it! When you get married, you don't say, "Gee whiz, is this going to last five years, ten years, or twenty? What will I do if it doesn't work?" When you start thinking that, it's a form of self-sabotage. You'll step on your own toes. Yet, that's what some writers do. They're already thinking, *What if I don't get published? Or what if I do? What's going to happen?* Be IN your story. The work should be more important than the outcome. And ultimately, if you do it the way that—if you put your heart into it—it's going to work.

Books are like beings that have their own life force. Isn't that what makes the adventure of writing or life suspenseful and exciting? The pieces of the puzzle that eluded you fall into a design you couldn't have imagined, showing you that it's not always up to you or your planning to save the day.

Sometimes the story has its own conclusions and sense of destiny. Sometimes the story writes itself.*

---

* I'm tempted to send this chapter (and the previous ones that raved about him) to Seal and see if he'd like in on the joke. Maybe even schedule an appearance on the podcast with Guru Singh. (They're still great buds—Guru's song "I Am," with Seal and Friends, is divine.) Seal could tell his side of the story of our absurd evening those many years ago. Share his thoughts as he ran from me and my outhouse.

Seal, if you read this, I really wanted to, but my editor and my inner conscience talked me out of asking when they both reminded me to "recall his 'DON'T ASK!'" To "respect the 'Don't ask.'" In any case, I still adore your music, and I'd love to have you on the show. You're welcome anytime.

PART FOUR

Birthing the Baby

Putting Your Work Out into the World

We're almost to the finish line—your book's birthday! Before we celebrate, however, you could find yourself in need of some support to slide you into home—and you might be surprised where it comes from!

And then . . . At last. Your name on the spine! Your book baby makes its blessed debut on bookstore shelves, phones, tablets, computers, and TV screens everywhere.

Take a bow, you. Bravo, beautiful writer. All of your work has paid off. Rest those weary eyes. You're an author! Many paths lie before you now.

20

Nature Leaves Clues

Life Really Does Conspire to Help You

"Every leaf speaks bliss to me."
~ Emily Brontë

In Cherokee lore, Great Thunder has two sons, the Thunder Boys, who dress in lightning and rainbows. Prayers to them bring rain and other blessings (and sometimes mischief). Spirituality and everyday life are braided together; the physical world and spiritual worlds are one and the same.

"Fire was the medium of transformation, turning offerings into gifts for spiritual intercessors," writes Peter Nabokov in his book *Where the Lightning Strikes: The Lives of American Indian Sacred Places*. Fire was cleansing, illuminating, the great giver of gifts. For some native tribes, those gifts came via steam from the fire used in the sweat lodge ceremony. Mother Earth's "womb" was a place to heal, hope, give thanks, prepare for war, bring questions, and receive visions.

Creatives have long looked to nature for awe and inspiration, seeking mystical messages or signs of support, otherworldly confirmation. Some writers flee to the sea to cure writer's block, find a-has in the crack of summer lightning, or see poetry within the colors of a rainbow in the calm after a storm. My friend Thomas One Wolf bowed to the four directions while singing his prayers to the

Great Grand Mother and Grand Father. For this part of my journey, I took my directives from the sky.

May this chapter allow magic to inform everything you do, its inspiration energizing all you hold dear in writing and life.

Every living thing in our forest in New Mexico—human, animal, plant—was on edge. It had been an eerie year without rainfall, a record of frightening proportions. With fires a constant threat, our "enchanted" state felt hexed. Even Governor Bill Richardson called on his citizens to pray for rain and asked all Pueblos across New Mexico to organize emergency Rain Dances.

"Disconnection from deep knowing is the road away from Nature," Thomas said. We would go toward knowing—into the lodge to pray and listen.

Jesse, Tosh, and I walked through the thirsty trees in bright sun to the Inepi lodge, where Thomas One Wolf, Grampa Pete Concha, and neighbors had gathered to lend their voices to the collective invocation. I opened the flap to the dark circular womb, knowing prayers were readily answered here.

The steam hit my face with a blast, but the fragrance of lavender and sweetgrass transported me like a portal to a scented utopia. Thomas offered his prayers in his native Suquamish and sprinkled herbs on the heated rocks, sparks popping like aromatic fireflies.

Toward the end of the forty-five-minute ceremony, our ears were stunned by a loud CRASH in the distance. *Could that be . . . thunder?!* Another boom followed.

"Listen to the thunder voices," Thomas said.

Then, the liquid music our ears had been aching for: Pelting rain!

The dozen of us knee-to-knee inside the circle all hooted and hollered at once.

"It wasn't even cloudy when we got in here!" our neighbor Dallas said, throwing open the flap to reveal the entire length of the sky roiling with inky charcoal clouds unleashing their lifeblood on parched soil. Joyous laughter and tears erupted from the lot of us.

"That's unbelievable, Mommy," Tosh said.

"I know, babe. Magic, huh?"

"The Great Grand Mother has heard our prayers," Thomas said.

The vibe indeed felt charged; if there was ever a time to ask for guidance, this was it.

"Grand Father, Earth Mother, how can I be of service?" I whispered. Thunder vibrated the ground beneath us, and nature continued her sound and light show. With each full-throated crash beyond our blanketed walls, I felt as if I was being commanded to follow an order. *But what?*

Dallas dropped the flap closed and we resumed our ceremony. Thomas sang his ancestral songs, and, in a flash, I had a vision—a full-bodied, sweeping picture show on the screen of my mind. It was even more dramatic than the only other waking vision I'd ever had—where I'd seen my dog-walking business, back when I didn't know that was a thing. That had turned out pretty great, as visions go.

Boom! Crash! I saw unknown faces. Friendships far into the future with bestselling authors and friendly media. Influence and good works. Books and more books—way past *Lives Charmed*. Environmental titles. *Whoa! There are others?*

Patricia Cornwell 🌿

There are only two words that will define what you're asked of while you're here. Just two words: Be willing. Just be willing [when] it picks you—whatever it is that you're supposed to be doing.

I'll tell you my little quick, weird story: I remember being twelve, and my mom was walking me through a shopping mall in North Carolina. As we passed a bookstore, I looked, and I had this vision that the window was filled with books that had my name on them. I thought, *That's really weird. That's really strange.* I wasn't even interested in doing that. I wanted to be a tennis player.

I didn't tell my mother. I didn't say anything about it, but I never, never forgot.

I believe everything is about physics, even things that seem "magical." Energy fields are drawn together. The thought in physics these days is that there is no beginning or end to space or time. As Einstein said, without time, everything would happen at once. I don't think we really know what "reality" is. That's why storytellers, people like all of us, quite frankly, are so important because we help define what life is and who we are and what we should become. Otherwise, you've got no GPS.

Was I seeing something that was going to happen in the future, or had it already happened in a universe where there's no beginning and no end? I do think we are "picked" [to do things] for reasons. And if we're willing to do them, it's the way it ought to be. That doesn't mean it's always easy or happy. But at least for me, there's an inner peace that I'm doing the best I can at what I think I'm supposed to do.

A dirt path unfurled, with forest on either side. As I began walking forward in my mind's eye, I could see that this was a journey of service, one on which I'd only started. *The path won't be easy,* I heard. I cringed. When had it ever been? *I didn't have to take the challenge,* the voice informed me. *There'd be no penalty.* Oh, but yes there would be, if only to my heart. Then a pang of worry hit. What if I didn't have the resources? The road ahead felt L O N G. But a sense of calm came over me. Mom would be my standard- and light-bearer. She would give me the courage she didn't have; I would help her complete what she'd regretted not doing.

"I wasted my life," she'd said on her deathbed. *The hell you did, Mom.*

My vision shifted to the perspective of the smallest creatures outside of the Inepi. Of how terrifyingly real the dangers of the land and sky had become for them. At least with this rain, I for once wouldn't have to fill the water bowls sprinkled throughout our property that the chipmunks and birds and God knows who else had come to depend on.

Jane Goodall 🌿

The most intense experiences I've had in nature have been quite unexpected. They've come sometimes when I'm alone, once when I was with chimpanzees. Suddenly, it's as though you are no longer yourself. You're not there. You are not present, and you feel nature in a completely different way. There's no way I can explain it; it's just being there without self. And it makes everything seem different. Then you come back to Earth and it's a very, very strange feeling. I've written about it, in *Reason for Hope*.

A fly once settled on me. I looked at it, and I thought, *It's a fly*. Then I thought about how we love to label things. I started looking at it as this extraordinary little living being—it was the most exquisite colors. I've never seen another fly like it. It was almost as though it was sent to teach me something. Taking away labels enables you to see something for what it truly is—its being-ness. But we do characterize: "That's a fly, that's a wasp, that's a mammal, that's a butterfly, that's a bison," instead of just feeling their being-ness.

As the storm ebbed and we left the Inepi lodge for our cabins, my feet felt heavy, but my spirit light. I would stay on this writing and tree-hugging journey for life. I had my marching orders—sort of—as mystical as they were practical.

Bronwyn Saglimbeni 🌿

I'd been doing PR for many years in San Francisco, where I lived. I was so burned out. I hated it. I'd been thinking about going to graduate school, about moving to DC or New York, but I didn't know what the hell to do with myself. I spent the afternoon in the park staring at the clouds, watching leaves blow in the breeze, filling up and tuning in, trying to hear my heart.

That night I had a dream. In it, I was looking at a wall covered in cursive handwriting. As I leaned in to see what the writing was about—and I can still see it as clear as day—it was the story of my life. It was like somebody had been watching *everything*. Every inch of my life was recorded in such loving, tender observations on this huge wall. My heart was exploding, and I thought, *Oh my God, I've never been alone. I've never been alone!* It was so beautiful. Then, I got to this one section of the wall that said: "Don't go anywhere. You are exactly where I want you."

I thought, *Well, I'm not moving to DC or New York. I'm going to stay in San Francisco.* I just surrendered and decided to listen to spirit, God, the Universe, whatever. *I will absolutely follow Your lead and do whatever the next step is.*

Within a year and a half, I met the man I would marry and have three kids with, my beloved Sal. A year later, I started my own business that's brought me so much joy. I think, sweet Jesus, had I not put myself in nature and had that dream, I might have gotten some degree I really didn't want. It was one of those moments where I thought, *Oh, thank God mine aren't the only oars in the water.*

Martha Beck ✎

At a time when everything in my life was falling apart—my body, my finances, my family—I got onto a plane and sat down in a window seat. The shades were down to keep the Arizona heat out of the plane. Sitting there with nothing to do, overwhelmed by panic and sorrow, I rummaged in my travel backpack for gum and found a little meditation book someone had given me on a previous trip.

I opened the book to a random page and found instructions for a visualization to use in hard times. The first step was to close my eyes and imagine a circle of light around me. It sounded pretty generic, but it couldn't hurt. I did it. The next step was to imagine that the light around me was my favorite color. *But I love ALL the colors*, I thought. So, I imagined a rainbow around me. Then the plane took off. As we rose through a layer of clouds, I felt a sudden urge to open the window shade. What I saw through the window was a rare weather phenomenon known as a "glory," where the shadow of a plane is surrounded by a huge, circular rainbow.

Following my vision in Thomas's Inepi, I was more committed to writing than ever. But conflicting rejection letters from publishers who'd seen *Lives Charmed* left me scratching my head. The names in the book were cutting-edge. The names were old news. My writing was fresh and unique. My writing didn't offer anything new. The green angle was important. The green angle wasn't sexy. (That last one came from the boss of an editor who'd dreamed about dolphins jumping over her head and found my proposal on her desk the following morning, a picture of a dolphin jumping over Wyland's head inside. She loved it. Her boss did not.)

If only I had the energy and know-how to self-publish. But I knew I didn't have it in me. I would hold out for my team, my people.

But one afternoon, the weight of swimming with my stories in a darkened sea while securing the pages from getting wet threatened to drown me. I was at the desk of my trailer office, head in hands, when Carol called.

"Oh, honey, you've got to be delirious by now," she said. "You've been through seven zombie apocalypses, crawled out of the grave, and put your intestines back in your body seventeen times. Your dream with your nine-month publishing goal was over six years ago, and you're still up every night with freezing fingers. I'm so proud of you. I really believe you're almost there."

What would I do without my little sister? Lose my mind, that's what.

Driving back home, nearly asleep at the wheel and with tears rolling down my cheeks, I prayed aloud:

"God, please! I know this book was Your idea. You're the one who gave me the dream. The people I'm meeting, the things I'm learning are the greatest gift. I would write all day long for free. But writers need readers, and I can't reach them without a publisher. I don't know what else to do. Am I wrong to believe I can earn a living doing the work I love most in all the world? If not, I need Your help!" My hands gripped the wheel as my pickup thump, thump, thumped over the hardened dirt ridges on our irritatingly long road.

Thomas One Wolf's words rang out in my mind:

"If you pay enough attention, all of nature will conspire to help you and show you the way. She brought you here, and She knows who you are. A mother takes care of her children, especially those who show her great kindness." In regular instances, Thomas's logic here would make zero sense to me, with violence aimed at environmental activists worldwide top of mind. But not now. Faith was all I had. My singular focus was as urgent as a wildfire.

ALL OF NATURE!

I looked up at the peak of Wind Mountain and felt an overpowering urge to pull over. I got out of my truck, left the door ajar with the engine running, and fell to my hands and knees, laying my forehead on the warm powdery clay as Thomas had shown me to do.

"Grandfather, Earth Mother, I come to You, Your humble daughter. Thank You for this good way and this good day. *Please*, I need Your help. I'm bone tired. I will do whatever it takes to hold on. But I need a sign. Pretend I'm a five-year-old and spell out Your answer so that I understand. Please, God, *who will publish this book?*"

I looked up, scanned the bright blue sky, and sighed. *Anything? Please? Give me the slightest clue to go on—a bird, a dust devil, a cloud animal—I'll figure out what it means when I see it.*

Nothing.

I waited.

Suddenly, and without a trace of a discernible breeze, every visible white puffy cloud in a primarily cloudless blue sky—from east, west, north, and south—began moving toward the others as if in time-lapse photography. Unblinking, I watched stupefied as the small puffs merged into one massive clump cloud, like a ball of Play-Doh, before being flattened with a rolling pin on a bright cerulean table. Then, unbelievably, in a flash, my clump cloud sped into two skyscraper-sized, soaring thin white letters—distinct, clean, and as perfectly formed as if on a license plate: **H C**.

There wasn't so much as a wisp of a cloud left anywhere on the horizon. *And, no, in case you're wondering, I've never done a single hallucinogen in my life.*

"HarperCollins!" I squealed as I dropped back to the ground in shocked humility. HarperCollins was famous for publishing wildly popular spiritual titles. The Universe was more magical than I could fathom!

I hoisted my teary, giddy self back into my truck and drove home, overflowing with gratitude. There was nothing to do now but keep my eyes down and fingers moving as I anticipated the happy call from my agent.

Having Carol's support and seeing the magical dance of those clouds combined with the utter absurdity of getting those up/down rejection letters had flipped a switch for me. *Screw it! It's all subjective. It's all opinion. I will bring forth my vision; write the book I want to read. My publisher—HARPER FREAK-ING COLLINS—will share my mission, period.*

Rhonda Britten ❧

I worked for a brilliant man, Paul, ramping up his public relations yet somehow began running his entire business. Due to my new role, I found myself listening to him as he rambled on one bright sunny morning in Los Angeles.

That's when it happened: something so unexpected, so otherworldly, I had to call it a miracle.

I noticed a big fluffy white cloud appeared on the ceiling of his condo. I remember just staring at it for a second shocked that a cloud was inside his house.

A thick book loaded with thousands of pages appeared to pop out of the cloud. The book opened, and the pages flipped furiously as if the wind was whipping through them. In that instant, I knew all the answers to all the questions I'd ever asked.

"Now, you must go and share this with others," I heard. The book slammed shut, and as quickly as it had appeared, it and the cloud had vanished.

Paul was still talking, oblivious to the cloud. I turned around to see who could have possibly been the recipient of the download—the book, the pages, the answers, the call. *It couldn't have been for me!* I was an orphan who dabbled in suicide attempts, drank herself silly for years, ended up arrested and in jail after three DUIs. There was no way. I must have seen it by accident!

Within twenty-four hours, I was in front of my minister, explaining how the vision couldn't have been for me. And if it was, I had to finish those lousy three credits I'd left undone in college so I could get my bachelor's. If I even thought I was supposed to listen to the cloud, well, then I also had to get my master's and a PhD. Then, I would write a book, I said. I mean, who would listen to me without a PhD and a book?

Reverend Joan Steadman interrupted my chorus of "I can'ts" and said, "If you got the call, you're ready."

I reiterated why I could never be worthy of the cloud, the book, the pages, the answers, the call.

"If you got the call, you're ready," she repeated.

It was a painstaking six months of back and forth. *Should I? No way. Really? Me?* But then, one day, I decided to believe what I'd seen. I wrote my first book, *Fearless Living*, which contained many of the answers I received. Not all. But some.

Two days later, my agent called.

"You have a book deal!" Dan said.

"Whaaaat? Really?! Who with?" I asked, a huge smile overtaking my face. Of course, I knew the answer.

"Health Communications," he said.

Wait—*what? Huh? Nooooo! Not HarperCollins? Who is this Health Communications? I love health. I'm a freak for health. But not for a publishing house!*

"Is this Health Communications any good?" I asked, not downplaying my disappointment in the slightest. *This can't be! What about the clouds? How could I have been so wrong?*

"They're the publishers of the *Chicken Soup for the Soul* books," Dan cooed. "Huge sellers, Linda." I looked across the room at my bookshelf, the one holding two *Chicken Soup* titles.

Whoa . . . I had an offer from an honest-to-God publishing company that moved millions of books! Okay. This was really happening—the phone call I'd hoped for and rehearsed more than any phone call of my life. And . . . Oh. Oh? *Ohhhhhhh!* Holy guacamole . . . I looked down at the initials I'd just scribbled on the pad in front of me. Health Communications. There it was: an H and a C! *But they're the wrong H and C.* I looked out the window. I'd read enough spiritual books and been to enough seminars and listened to enough preacher-speakers to know that a more extensive plan could be at work here (and that, apparently, God and Mother Earth knew how to spell).

"See! You really *do* have God's phone number," Dad said when I called with the news. Didn't we all? How did we forget so easily? The evidence was all around.

Martha Beck ❧

For us to not destroy the ecosystems for which our lives depend, humans must go through some sort of personal and individual transformation, which will then sort of fractalize into a different way of living in the world. Adam, my son with Down syndrome, was one year old, and I'd been doing speech therapy with him. I knew he'd never speak clearly—*he didn't say a word the first four years of his life*—but I worked with him desperately hard, almost out of guilt, because I had this feeling he'd never speak. Before falling asleep next to him, I said, "Just tell me why you're even here." I wanted to understand the point of someone who may never speak or think with this blighted life, which I thought he would have.

I had a dream I was in a room with a young man who gave me a piece of paper. On it was moving images of animals. I didn't know it, but all were African animals. There were penguins, which threw me off because I'd never been to Africa, and I didn't realize there were penguins in Africa. But I knew I was talking to my son's spirit.

The dream was about the restoration of the world and animals. Adam told me he isn't even here for human beings in the way I think of things. He's really here more for the earth itself, which totally baffled me. At the end of the piece of paper he'd given me, the drawings all turned into a line of text in a language I'd never seen. But I remembered it in English when I woke up. I didn't dare say it out loud. I didn't even write it down for many years because it freaked me out. I still worry that people will think it's bizarre. But the text said this:

"The Earth cries like a child, and the blood of the animals is the blood of innocence. You, having lost your innocence, cannot hear the cries of the blood as it beats in your own ears. It is to answer those cries that I have come as I have come."

And let me tell you, Adam tells me about the animals in the forest! I put up camera traps around my ranch in California, and he came and told me, "There's a bear in the forest that wants you to take those down. He says it nearly blinded him last night."

I went out and got the chip, and it turns out this young black bear had come right up to the camera, and a little red light goes on. You see his nose. And then he puts one eye up, and then the other eye right up to the light and staggers away completely blind.

So, there are ways I can check to see that Adam's not just blowing smoke. This kid works from a different language.

I bought a pair of boots that weren't mud-encrusted and went off to meet the wizards Peter Vegso and Gary Seidler, my two publishers at Health Communications, Inc., who'd seen something in me the others hadn't. They'd driven to Deerfield Beach, Florida, from Toronto in a Volkswagen Beetle following their own marching orders years earlier. Their version of taking on the system from outside of New York was to peddle drug addiction recovery pamphlets until they jump-started the codependency movement with Janet Woititz's *Adult Children of Alcoholics* and John Bradshaw's *Bradshaw On: The Family*, which popularized terms like "inner child" and "dysfunctional family." By the time they met Jack Canfield and Mark Victor Hansen, the authors of the *Chicken Soup for the Soul* series, Health Communications, Inc. was facing bankruptcy. But by thinking differently than 144 publishers before them ("no one buys feel-good short stories!"), they took a gamble and won. Theirs was now one of the largest—if not *the* largest—paperback publishing companies.

If only I could encourage them to change their paper sourcing! *One thing at a time, Linda. Remember, it's a long path.*

Tosca Lee ✒

I put off writing *Iscariot*, my first-person novel about Judas Iscariot, the infamous betrayer of Christ, for a long time out of sheer terror. I was cowed by the amount of work it would take, afraid how the first-person story would be received by savvy readers of historical fiction, students of scripture, and people of faith. I was not a theologian, historian, or religious expert. Just a woman struggling with her own questions and disillusionments, a working author worried about sinking her burgeoning career. But everything in my life—including many people around me—seemed to indicate I should write it anyway.

I compensated by researching full-time for a year and a half. I built a wall of protective knowledge around myself. And then I over-wrote the book by 130,000 words. My first draft was more than nine hundred pages. I had a monster on my hands. Somewhere in all that erudite, intricate detail, I'd lost sight of the most important thing: the human and divine mystery at the heart of the story.

I thought back to my time in Israel where I stood on the shores of Galilee, sat in Capernaum's synagogue, and explored the theater of history. I had learned so much. But as I entered Jerusalem, I was bereft. Ascending toward the Dome of the Rock that day, steeples and mosques and temples crowding the horizon like so many hands reaching for God, I realized I had not *experienced* one moment of mystery. I fought back tears on my way up the stairs and distracted myself by stopping to give an old beggar woman a few shekels. The moment I did, she grabbed my hand in both of hers and I nearly fell to my knees. *Here* was God. And I knew without a doubt I had traveled all the way to Israel just to hold her hand.

In the end, I threw out three theses' worth of historical detail and returned to mystery and human connection.*

After receiving what resembled a hero's welcome in the lobby of my publishing house, a swarm of people and their giddy smiles took me on a behind-the-scenes tour of what felt like my personal book/chocolate factory.

"Here's where *Lives Charmed* will be printed," they chimed. "And here's where your boxes will be stored before being shipped to bookstores around the country." I was awestruck. With so much of the business of printing now off in China, I'd never expected to see manufacturing controlled from start to finish here in the States.

Next, we filed into six cars to a bountiful feast surrounded by my new publishing family. I now understood why publishers are called "houses." I felt truly home.

"Our entire team, over twenty people, voted for your proposal in a unanimous vote," Matthew, my editor, said, beaming at me over his Kung Pao rice. "That's highly unusual for us. It almost never happens."

---

* Fun fact: *Iscariot* won Christian Book of the Year in fiction the following year.

"We see you as our next *Chicken Soup for the Soul* series," Gary, the cofounder, added. "We love you." My advance was teeny—a mere $5,000, which wouldn't even cover the postage I'd already spent—but my dream had come true! And they were going to hire an expensive top outside publicist to work with their in-house team, adding to the dream.

I couldn't believe how the energy had shifted, and I wanted to keep the momentum moving. I racked my brain trying to come up with a way to show these folks the depth of my gratitude. I called Arnold Palmer's assistant, and he had Arnie personalize a photo for the office, which got rave reviews. Next, I framed collages for much of my team, complete with photos, funny handwritten notes, and signatures from many of the celebrities highlighted in the book. One by one, the thank-you letters arrived. Never, ever, they reported, had they received such a cherished gift from any author. The next time I visited, I saw my collages hung on office wall after office wall.

True believers fill history with tales of their best prayer practices. Did I get an answer so clear from those clouds because I'd had such total faith that I would? Benjamin Franklin said, "Work as if you were to live a hundred years, pray as if you were to die tomorrow." I suppose my begging-on-hands-and-knees prayer was a die-tomorrow prayer. You could argue the same about Jesse's "go-fuck-yourself" prayer from chapter eight. We certainly didn't phone those in. I was, however, relieved that our family had graduated beyond the F-bomb variety.

As we've discussed, writers are empathetic. Highly sensitive. We perceive things others don't. Sure, some are highly insensitive. *Clouds, what clouds?* (Don't try to change those folks, by the way. I've tried.) We are who we are, and everyone has their unique stories to tell.

When poet and highly sensitive creative Joy Harjo was on my podcast, she mentioned living in New Mexico during the years I'd lived there. Talk about receiving gifts out of nowhere! I'd been wanting to be sure I'd remembered Bill Richardson's statewide call to pray for rain accurately and had been doing exhaustive online searches but had come up with nothing. Joy had named her daughter Rainy Dawn; maybe she could provide the confirmation I needed?

"I do remember when that happened!" Joy said. "Anyone that's lived in New Mexico, and I've lived there most of my life, knows that when the Pueblo people dance for rain, well, here come the clouds! It's communication. It's about developing that kind of communication. It means that you have a respectful relationship. And like a relationship with anyone, you must *build* that relationship. You can't just assume it, because with every relationship comes responsibilities."

The pandemic had just begun when Joy and I did our interview. Thomas and Grampa Pete were gone by then, and I was so sad that I couldn't call them and ask their take on the pandemic—remembering all the times they'd told me their prophecies, about the dark times coming to our physical and political worlds.

I had a sense that Joy, who's been communicating with Mother Nature and reading Her cues since birth, would have a fascinating take on Covid-19. Did she ever.

Joy Harjo 🌿

We all needed to stop. A lot of us had the sense we were working towards this, but we didn't know exactly what form it would take. We knew it would be something related to the earth's body. We were getting the messages very clearly. We have been getting the messages very clearly for a long time. That it came this way was a surprising vehicle for the stoppage, but it's what we needed.

The first time I went to the Battle of Horseshoe Bend, where my grandfather and many other relatives fought against Andrew Jackson and the illegal move where there was a massacre, I got bronchitis. I had never had bronchitis before or since. Since then, I've almost died twice from pneumonia. The lungs are major processors of grief. Maybe what's happening here [with COVID-19] is that we're processing our own grief. Certainly, we have grief as a nation. We have grief in this country, in the history of this country.

But we also have grief as citizens of this Earth body. If you think of every human being bearing a set of lungs (or one lung for some people), maybe what we are here to do for the earth is to help clean the earth. Maybe our lungs, all working together, are helping the earth's grieving?

I'm getting older, and the people that I always went to for the answers with a capital A or for insight, for that deeply spiritual insight you won't find in books or anywhere else, they're all gone. But their insight is still here; they planted it. It's available, but again. Like communicating with the spirits who bring rain, there's a relationship that must be cultivated.

Whether you're highly sensitive or not, I believe now more than ever that we must take the time to, as Joy Harjo noted, "form a relationship" with nature. To hear Her messages, for us, and about what *She* needs—for both our sakes. It's enlightening to pay attention to the world around you and to cultivate a more direct connection with forces and guides seen and unseen.

My cinematic vision in the Inepi that stormy day was true to life. My path would be a long one. Only now are some of the details I saw that day finally coming to pass. But like any worthwhile journey, there were joyous wins along the way—events that would make every bit of doubt and effort worth it a hundred times over.

21

Divine Timing and Dreams Realized

Now All Those Delays Make Sense!

"Art can't be hurried. It must be allowed to take its course.
It must be given its space—and can't be rushed or checked
off a to-do list on the way to something else."
~ Ryan Holiday, *Perennial Seller*

Despite all the delays, naysayers, deleted files, money woes, sleepless nights, and writer's block, *many* books are born every year. Millions, actually. Think about how many books you've read in your lifetime. If you were to try and count every book currently in existence, you'd be looking at eye strain of galactic proportions with around 134,021,533 unique books!

Though it's not easy to write a book or get it published, the process *is* simple. There are steps and plans, and a whole world of people who take those steps and follow those plans and end up with a book with their name on it. And guess what? There's always room for one more! We will never stop wanting riveting stories, memorable characters, or life-changing information. We're insatiable. Stories give our lives meaning. Our brains are literally wired for them—it's how we experience being human.

Countless hours of dreaming and praying and inexhaustible reading and writing time preceded my "charmed" delivery and the books of those of every author I know or have interviewed. I love hearing their voices crack or watching their eyes light up or water as they remember what it was like seeing their titles on the shelves or in the trades for the first time, and other big "firsts" that forever changed their lives.

"*Eat Pray Love* has taken very good care of me," Elizabeth Gilbert says. Amen to that.

And it's not just books that bless us when they're born, but so many other dreams that spring up with them. Speaking and teaching. TED Talks. Radio shows and podcasts. Media of all kinds. Friendships far and wide. Nourishing community. Crackling conversations. Domestic and international travel. Newspaper and magazine articles. Expanded businesses. Follow-up products. Growth and healing. Rave reviews. Cash, too—all topics we'll cover in Book 2. For now, know this. KEEP GOING. Writing and publishing won't always feel glacial. When things heat up, you'll be grateful for the prep time. Your book has its own destiny, and splendid surprises await.

"Congratulations!" Kim Weiss, the publicist from Health Communications, Inc., said as she handed me my finished book at an event in Los Angeles, my beaming father standing at my side. There it was—all 321 pages of it. The title, *Lives Charmed*, just as I'd dreamed it over seven years before. The HCI colophon proudly stamped on the spine. My name in huge type on the front. Color photos of my star interviewees and blurbs on the back.

Holding it for the first time, I thought: *Hello, you. I know you . . . I think.* But I'd expected to feel jubilant at this moment, over the moon even. Instead, I felt an odd (fortunately fleeting) sense of melancholy, as if they'd accidentally handed me someone else's child. With the hurly-burly surrounding publication, I was surprised to discover that after all those years of work and expectation and focus and rejection, the hefty object I held at long last felt . . . foreign. I'd heard mothers exclaim that they looked at their newborn babies and thought, *Who are you? You're not my child!* I hadn't experienced that with Tosh, but I wondered if I was feeling a kind of postpartum book blues?

Tom Hanks

It's a very personal thing. You just sit there, and you hold the book, and you look at it, and you think, *Has this been created out of thin air? Has it been beamed to me? Look at all the molecules that went into this hardcover and these pages.*

But the celebration of it was extremely quiet, and it was all by myself. Look, I'm not saying time didn't stand still. It did. I might have just been standing in my office over my desk. Was I there for two and a half hours just staring down at this thing in my hands, or was it 2.2 seconds? I don't know. Either one would have made sense to me. I think it's because it's yours. It's a beautiful baby. You hold it in your arms, and you think, *Look at the spine on this kid. Look at the beautiful lettering.*

Tosca Lee

The first time I saw my name and book title in *Variety* or *The Hollywood Reporter* reporting a film or TV deal in the works, I remember thinking, *Huh?! Wow! That's really weird.* But then, at the same time, you've been trying for this for so long and the conversations were happening for so long. So, in a way, it's kind of like when you see your name on your book for the first time. It's like, "Okay, wow, this is really real. It's so cool. I'm holding it!" You went through all these edits, and you read through all these galley proofs, so you've already envisioned it and seen it happen a million times.

Thankfully, my mood quickly lifted before traveling to Chicago the following week for BookExpo America, the largest publishing conference in North

America. By the time my editor, Matthew, and I strolled down Michigan Avenue on our way inside, I adored the look and feel of my book.

"Matthew, thank you for being my champion. I'm so grateful."

"My total pleasure," he replied. "You're going to do great today. Are you ready?"

"Um, yeah!" *Only seven years ready.* * Matthew led me through the maze that was the McCormick Place Convention Center. Twenty-five thousand booksellers, publishers, authors, and fans were gathered at booths for signings, meetings, and discussions. I was now part of the literary community that included authors around me like Alice Walker, George Stephanopoulos, Peter Jennings, Tom Wolfe, and Catherine Coulter.

"Close your eyes," Matthew said as he led me around a corner by my elbow. When I opened them, I gasped. The folks at Health Communications had erected a huge backlit blow-up of my cover, my beautiful cover—the one Jesse and I had helped design with a picture he'd taken 35,000 feet up in the air. We'd been on our way home from his acting gig on the island of St. Martin when I looked out the window of the plane to see the pinkest purpliest puffiest cloud formation I'd ever seen. Now that image was illuminated in lights with my name in big, bold letters like something my mother would have crafted in heaven.

Peter, my co-publisher, came up and gave me a big hug. "There's our star!" he said. "You look beautiful, Linda. Have a wonderful signing. We're so glad you're here!"

And with that, Kim, our publicist, led me to a long table, gave me a pen, and began handing me books from several tall stacks. The line of smiling faces went on and on. I didn't recognize anyone but wanted to hug every single sweet soul. Except one face stood out—the Chicken Soup man himself, standing in my line! One of the more surreal moments of the day was signing a copy to Mr. Jack Canfield as part of the house that *Chicken Soup for the Soul* built.

I wished like hell my mother were alive to celebrate with me. But something told me she wasn't far from view.

---

* Your own timeline could be long or short. I've had clients who've had an idea for a book, written a quick proposal, signed with an agent, and sold their manuscript in less than a year (while I was still on chapter 2—ha). It's not done until it's done, but do yourself and your book a favor and keep it on your calendar and atop your to-do lists.

Just a little over two years prior, I'd been outside gathering kindling on my first birthday since Mom passed, bawling my eyes out, missing her like the ground misses the rain. Princess Diana had died that morning, and the entire world, including myself, was in mourning. As I doubted that my special day would ever feel special again, a helium balloon floated over my head from the south. I was standing thirty-five miles from the nearest store, with no houses in that direction for as far as the eye could see, the words HAPPY BIRTHDAY bobbing above me dancing in the wind. I wiped the snot from my face and laughed out loud. For all her environmental leanings, Mom was a birthday balloon person. I still have a bag of them she'd ordered with Dad's name printed on them that I'd found amongst her things.

Standing in my publisher's booth—*my publisher!*—I sensed that Mom, the biggest reader I'd ever known—was smiling down on this whole book-lovin' scene.

Elizabeth Lesser

The power of writing memoir for me is that I'll always remember things that I otherwise would've forgotten. I forget everything. So, writing about an intense experience is like a memory-booster. In writing the story of my sister's death [*Marrow*], I feel like I'm walking with my sister's soul linked with mine. We shared our blood, our marrow, and then we did what I call in the book our "soul marrow transplant," and that's forever.

I do feel that she's with me and helping me walk strong in the world.

Arielle Ford

My late sister, Debbie Ford, had her team of angels, her muses that talked to her and helped her write. They'd wake her up in the middle of the night to write, and sometimes she would loan them out to me. No kidding! They would wake her with a message for me, and she'd have to be the translator, telling me what they were saying.

Jennifer Rudolph Walsh ✒

A story can crisscross the globe. Look, I'm crazy about ideas which come and go, but tell me a story and I will never forget it. Tell me a story about something that's happened to you in your life or something that happened to somebody you love. Somebody who thought things were going to go one way, but then they went a totally different way. That leaves a tattoo on my heart. That's what moves me beyond. I think ideas are extraordinary. I'm an ideas junkie, but it's a bit like junk food—good in the moment but isn't going to nurture or sustain you in the long run. But story-telling has the ability to transform us at our very core; what we believe about ourselves, what we believe about each other, what we believe about the world, and what we believe is possible for the future.

Jodee Blanco, the outside publicist HCI had hired, was making magic happen.

"You're going on *Extra*, Lin! That's so unbelievable!" screamed Diane.

"I know! It's a miracle!" I said. "We're shooting a day at Paul Williams's house, and then at Catherine Oxenberg's."

"I'm freaking for you! What are you wearing?"

"I have no idea!" I was so punch-drunk tired/nervous that I started laughing like a lunatic . . .

Di said, "Get yourself together; you're on *Extra* in two days! You can't wear your country duds on TV! And you need a new hairstyle. Granola's great for the forest, but not for TV!" ("Granola" was our code word for *Don't you dare go out in public like that!*)

Swooping in to save the day, Di overnighted a box of clothes from Atlanta, where her husband, Chris Chandler, was still playing for the Falcons. Di hired her favorite LA hairdresser to meet me in Los Angeles for, miracle of miracles, my *Leeza* show taping. Leeza had made good on her promise and was dedicating most of an episode to my book, including interviews with Catherine Oxenberg, Paul Williams, and me. Paramount Studios sent a limo, and Jesse; Tosh; Carol; and her husband, Bill; and I got all dressed up and piled in. I felt adored onstage as Paul held my hand and he and Catherine and I laughed about old times. The night before, I'd had a dream of a one-liner I "should" say onstage. With relief, I'd remembered it during the taping. When the perfect moment presented itself, I let 'er rip:

"Can you believe it, Leeza? I lived with them. I worked in their homes. And they still like me!" Cath, Paul, and the audience laughed. Then Paul said, "No. We *love* you."

Chris Chandler, who I'd included in the book, was patched in over satellite. Leeza raved about my book and me, and Paul closed out the show singing "The Rainbow Connection."

Someday we'll find it. The rainbow connection. The lovers, the dreamers, and me.

I would never, ever regret being a dreamer. Sure, my path had been hard, but whose wasn't?

Tom Bergeron

I was thinking about the nature of what we each do. For me, I love live television. I love that instant reaction. If something occurs to me in the moment on the dancing show or wherever, and you have seven hundred people burst into laughter because something just occurred to me and I said it, that's a bit of a rush. It really is. I think the split personality part for me is that I never watch what I do. For all the years that *Dancing with the Stars* has been on, I've only seen one episode. I like the moment of doing it, and then I am often surprised when people recognize me because I have to remind myself, *Oh, that's right! I did it on television.*

Aditi Khorana

I had basically tied my fate to the first manuscript, and I received requests for the full document from almost every agent I sent it out to. But one by one, the rejections came in, and each one felt like a blow to my psyche. Rejection is such a primal sort of pain.

In the end, I racked up something like sixty rejections. What made it all the more terrifying was that I had quit my job to write and within a short time period after quitting that job, my relationship of nearly a year ended, and I had moved out of my home. Nobody told me that this is sometimes what it looks like. You take a risk, and what you see as failure is actually your whole life coming undone to make way for a new one.

After a period of mourning, I wrote another book, what would become my debut novel [*Mirror in the Sky*], in just three months and sold it for a significant deal. But before I could write that book, I had to be stripped of so much of the conditioning I had grown up with that I couldn't do it. I wasn't talented enough. I didn't have the work ethic. I didn't have the drive. I was sensitive. How would I live through failure and rejection? I was invisible; how would anyone see me? Immigrant people of color like me don't get those kinds of opportunities. People like me don't get big book deals. Who the hell am I to think I can have this? People like me don't make a life writing books. I was wrong. I did it. And I continue to do it every day.

My books deal with the issues I've always grappled with: being an immigrant, being the child of immigrants, being the grandchild of refugees, and a global citizen of a colonial legacy, being a woman, a feminist, a person of color. I also write about how narratives shape our collective notions of ourselves and our society and how these very narratives can be changed for a new global order. As such, in this world, there are still difficult days. There is still failure and doubt. But what's changed is *me*. My writing, the work I did on myself. All that failure stripped away anything that's false.

In its place came quiet confidence in my skills and talents. In my persistence and drive. In my ability to subvert any idea that wasn't working for me. I have never loved any job more than this one. It's not a job. It's a devotion, the thing I am most dedicated to, the thing I would do anything for. And I couldn't have learned that if the path had been swift.

Elie Wiesel said that books, just like people, have a destiny. Some invite sorrow, others joy, some both. I'll never understand how the bits of a book's destiny organize themselves for maximum impact.

For example, one of my mother's best friends, Kay, stood in for Mom by throwing me a book party at her high-rise condo overlooking the water in San Francisco following my Barnes & Noble signing at Fisherman's Wharf. Was it my book's destiny that someone happened to plan a massive fireworks display off the bow of a freighter in the October night directly outside Kay's floor-to-ceiling windows just as I walked through her door to cheers? Was it my mother, coincidence, or destiny that timed such a bigger-than-life event, as if putting exclamation points on my special celebration?

How about being invited to be a speaker at Page Turners, at Stanford University, the book club my mother co-founded? Sitting in a cozy living room in Palo Alto, in a home full of women who'd spent a night a month for thirty years with my mother, I read from my book. As they voiced their enthusiasm and we shared stories of Mom, we all cried together. *How did this happen?*

Then, standing at the podium at the Bodhi Tree Bookstore for my LA book party, I looked out over a packed house. (Hint: Order food and drinks for launches in LA. All those hungry out-of-work actors, dancers, and even media folks, show up for a free meal.) Someone raised their hand and asked, "What drove you to interview these out-of-the-box thinkers?"

"I had an amazing teacher at USC," I said. "I still haven't graduated, but my Community Psychology professor changed my life by teaching me to look at society holistically. To think about what it takes to build a better world. This book is my attempt to build that better world through extraordinary conversations."

"I'm here!" I heard a man yell from the back of the crowded room. "I'm here!" I looked over the sea of heads, and there he was, Milton Wolpin, my beloved USC professor whom I hadn't seen or heard from in over twelve years, waving both his arms in the air above his head.

"Whaaaat?" I yelled and ran across the room straight for him. We bear-hugged, and the room erupted into cheers. I was laughing and crying with such joy that I wasn't remotely worried about my melting makeup. What kind of magic could orchestrate such a celebratory, full-circle moment?

"Did you know I'd be here?" I asked him.

"I saw the advertisement for your signing and had to come," he said.

Destiny. Do books have a destiny?

Call me a believer.

Dani Shapiro

When *Devotion* came out, a lot of good things happened. But Oprah didn't call. I never actually walked around thinking, *Oprah's going to call me*, but had I figured it, this would've been the time. I did a lot of traveling and speaking for the book in different places—from churches to yoga studios, to temples, bookstores, and people's backyards. Then I wrote *Still Writing*, which was about to come out. One day I was in New York, and I was going to be teaching that night, and my phone rang. I saw that it was my agent calling, but I was in such a bad mood that I thought, *Ugh. I'm sure this is going to be bad news, so I'm not even going to answer it.*

She called a couple of times, and I was like, "I just don't want to deal with whatever this bad thing is." Then, right when I was about to go in and teach at a place called The Center for Fiction in Manhattan, I thought, *Let me just get this over with.*

She said, "Where have you been?"

"What's wrong?" I said.

"Well, I have some good news, actually. I heard from the people at *Oprah* today, and they're very interested in having you as a guest for *Super Soul Sunday*." And that's how that began. Three years after *Devotion* had come out. And it was completely not connected to my new publication of *Still Writing*. I don't even think they knew I had a new book coming out.

When I finally spoke to the wonderful producer, the first thing she said to me was, "You've been on our radar for a while." Which I think is an excellent lesson because we don't know those things. I think all we can do in life, in general, is keep our heads down and put one foot in front of the other and follow our instincts and our sense of what's right and what's next and allow whatever happens to happen in its own time.

And, you never know *who* will read your work!

"I loved your charmed book," Carrie-Anne Moss would say to me at a get-together at Guru Singh's home. I couldn't believe my ears. *I* loved *The Matrix*. Of course, I'd seen it—everyone had. It never once occurred to me that Carrie-Anne would be interested in my art or read my work. Wow, it was so good to see her again! She was as centered and spiritual as I'd remembered, and I had a sense as I watched her speaking later with Guru that she, too, would be some kind of teacher beyond the big screen.*

Carrie-Anne thoughtfully shared several of the ways in which my life had had a positive impact on hers, and I was struck by how easy it is to deny our own value, and how once again, Guru and the spaces he created were a source of profound healing.

---

* Fun fact: Carrie-Anne Moss is the founder of AnnaPurnaLiving.com, a robust community that guides women to their wisdom by giving them tools to empower and transform their lives. Articles, free tools, and stunning online courses build community for support, create conversations to empower, and give women strategies to turn the simple into the majestic. High vibrations, all the way.

Jillian Lauren

My favorite thing about releasing a book is the life it takes on of its own. In allowing your work out into the world and really giving your work to the world, you've given it, it's gone. It's not yours anymore. I love when my work starts to breathe, and people talk about it and tell me things about my book that I didn't see. That is my favorite part; that the story transforms when it goes out. It's also the hard part because I don't have control over it anymore. But it is really freeing and often very beautiful and *very* rewarding.

Another Guru Singh gift! This one through the death of his beloved mama, Tidi, whom everyone adored. When I arrived at her Celebration of Life service and sat down, Meredith and Janet were sitting just to my left. Through hushed conversation, we fell into an immediate heart space, as if we were back in Mer's dining room sharing the details of our lives—the most important of which was that Meredith had recently had a baby boy! And I was invited to the baby shower at—of all places—Dr. Phil's estate.*

On the way to the shower, I stopped at Pottery Barn and bought a lovely box of wooden alphabet blocks. Unlike the $250 pink faux fur rocking horse I'd lugged into a past Beverly Hills shower, I paid $28 for the blocks. Meredith had never been snobby about labels or price tags, and I doubted that had changed. Besides, I was in no financial position to try and impress anyone, so my simple offering would have to be good enough.

What's my intention for the party? I asked myself.

For the first time in years, I didn't have an agenda heading into a VIP event. I decided that my sole reason for showing up was to support Meredith at this treasured time. To be of service. Love was my only scheme.

"I'm going to Dr. Phil's house," my friend Susan said on my way over. She'd been trying to get on Phil for his book for a year and was dying to ride shotgun.

"Too bad you're gonna get on his show. You'll sell a ton of books."

I really agree, what with all the shenanigans I'd pulled that

---

* Fun fact: Meredith had recently written "SHINE," a new theme song for Dr. Phil's talk show.

Jenny Lawson 🍂

So often, I will feel like, "Well, I pretty much just wasted the last five years of my life. I've read some books and I've binge-watched a lot of TV, and what else has happened?" But being able to write it down in a book and have these chapters, I'm able to say, "Oh, actually. I did accomplish life!" Sometimes that accomplishment is just surviving and just getting by. Sometimes that can be such a celebration. A lot of times, when I start to feel like a failure or a loser, I will go back, and I will reread my books. Even though they're ridiculous, about getting a bag of dicks at the post office, or these mortifying, ridiculous, dumb stories, they're all entertaining and I can laugh when I look back at them.

When I first started writing about mental illness, I was very afraid of how people would respond. I worried that they would run away. Instead, what they said was, "Me too. I thought I was the only one who felt like this."

I started getting letters from people who said that they were actively in the process of planning their suicide and decided instead to get help. Not because of what I wrote, but because they saw thousands of people in the comments section of my blog saying, "Me too; I'm worthless too." They thought, *Well, that can't possibly be right. And if it's not right for them, maybe it's also not right for me.*

When I read those letters, I think, *Maybe my words do make a difference.* Then I share more, and then other people share because of that.

"You're going to Dr. Phil's house?" my friend Susan said on my way over. She'd been trying to get PR for her book for a year and was dying to ride shotgun. "Oh my God! You've got to get on his show. You'll sell a ton of books!"

You'd think I'd readily agree, what with all the shenanigans I'd pulled thus far.

"I don't believe so," I said, pulling onto Beverly Drive and scanning side streets for the entrance to the talk show host's famed driveway. "Doesn't feel right. Today needs to be all about Mama and Baby."

"Really?" she said. "Don't tell me you've finally lost your nerve!"

"Maybe so," I answered before closing my BlackBerry and catching a reflection of my smile in my side mirror.

Joy Harjo ✍

I think every poet is a kind of ambassador for poetry. I had a new book coming out, *An American Sunrise*, and I got an email from a man I'd known a long time who runs the national book festival. He also runs the Poetry and Literature Centre and oversees the Poet Laureateship, but it's appointed by the Head of the Library of Congress.

He said, "Are you available for a call?" Then he wrote back a PS: "It's just a quick question."

I was not prepared at all; I had no idea. On the call, I heard him say, "Wait a minute, we're on speakerphone, and here's Dr. Carla Hayden." Then they said: "We want you for the twenty-third US poet laureate." It was like lightning, so much energy moving through.

It was a celebration, but it was also a big responsibility. What was especially exciting for me was that it was the first time a Native person had been in this position. It has done so much for Native people. There was a study recently done by a group called IllumiNative, who's been gathering data on images of Natives in the public, and in one of their studies, they found that a large part of the population of the US think we're dead—that after the cavalry left, we disappeared. Our culture has disappeared, and we're no longer Native. Little do they know, we're over five hundred tribal nations. We have different languages and cultures—we're extremely different from each other.

What's cool about this position is seeing Native poets all over this country. I just got the galley of our anthology of Native poets, a new book called *When the Light of the World Was Subdued, Our Songs Came Through: A Norton Anthology of Native Nations Poetry*. So, it's changed my life in ways that become clearer every day.

Dr. Phil's estate was a five-minute walk from Kirk Douglas's, a route I'd traveled a thousand times with Kirk's dog and mine. Just as ultra-luxurious as I'd expected, photographers—*paparazzi? I wasn't sure*—were in tents, set not so conspicuously around the perimeter of the yard to capture, I supposed, images of the most popular amongst us. I gave my keys to the valet and entered.

Guests were falling all over themselves to schmooze with the good doctor—talking loudly. Laughing with that added kick. Angling to be in the shot. I understood why. I'd lived for years thinking my entire life was dependent upon access and participation of the famous and fabulous like him. And that without that, I'd never have the success or influence I hoped for. Ten minutes with Dr. Phil could get your book written up in *People* and in the "Hot Deals" section of *Publishers Weekly* or in *Vanity Fair*'s "Hot Type." But with the six-foot-three life strategist two feet away, even I was amazed that I didn't feel the need to introduce myself. On the contrary, after a quick kiss to Meredith, I turned and walked to the far side of the yard and sat down at the "after-thought" table with the normal-looking, non-glitzy folks: Meredith's neighbors, a makeup artist, and two lesbian childhood friends of Mer's who were entertaining as hell, doing a comedy act for our table about their vibrating super-sized Harley-Davidson "sex toy."

"We're honest to goodness dykes on bikes!" they joked.

I loved them. I loved this day. How glorious not to have a care in the world a million miles away from the celebrity table.

Laura Munson 🌿

I remember when I finally got my big dream—my first book deal, with fourteen unpublished novels in my drawer—and I was going to my first reading. It was on the upper east side of Manhattan. I was in a limo, with all these publishing-world demigods, and I looked out the window, and I thought, Gertrude Stein is right: "There's no there . . . there."

For so many years, I had told myself the story that my self-worth was completely contingent on being published to wide acclaim. All of those essays and short stories sent to *The New Yorker*, all of those books sent to agents and publishers. All of those rejections...all taken so personally. What an exhausting way to live your life! So I turned to the head of marketing and publicity for Penguin Random House and said, "As much as I am grateful for all that you are doing for this book and its message—and I will be a tireless messenger—I just realized that this whole success thing that has driven my life is a myth. And that means that if success is a myth, then failure is too." I felt this levity. My shoulders dropped five inches. I said, "So, that means the only thing we can control is doing the work. And that's good news."

That's a nugget for every writer. If you're a writer, it's about doing the work and creating a writing practice that works for you based on who you are, nobody else. We have to have butterflies in our stomach for this thing; there has to be a payoff, or we're not going to do it.

Rhonda Britten 🌿

Don't go begging for a deal. You heard me. Do. Not. Beg. You, beautiful writer, are the prize. Your book is filled with heartbreak, tears, and triumphs. Don't give it away so easily.

You're the one who spent long lonely nights praying over the keyboard with no food in sight. Exhausted. Exhilarated. Frustrated. You're the one who spent years accumulating the wisdom that you'll be stuffing into every page, worried you're not giving enough because you want to give it all. You're the one who had the courage to hear that still, small nudge whispering "write this" and followed it with no guarantees.

That effort. That commitment. That confidence. That's attractive. And that book you put your heart and soul into deserves to be partnered with a publisher who gets it. Who loves it. Who is willing to bid for it. And gets you! That's why when it was time to send my proposal out to publishers, I knew I would either find a publisher who understood my message or do the "unthinkable" and self-publish.

Out of the thirteen publishers my agent sent my proposal to, we had twelve meetings. (Nine would go on to bid on my book, *Fearless Living*, during a four-day auction.) In the end, three publishers were left standing, all offering $200,000 for a first-time author, an unknown in California.

Here's how it happened: As we sat down to meet the Simon & Schuster team, one of the executives broke up the chitchat to let us know he'd be leaving early. I nodded in understanding and thanked him for letting us know. Then, I took out the ten questions I asked every publisher in every meeting. They went like this . . .

1. What was your favorite part of my book?
2. What was it about my book/proposal that made you decide to schedule a meeting?
3. How does my book relate to what matters to you?
4. Share one of the successes you've had with a book in my genre.

Right about here, I noticed the executive who said he'd be leaving early wasn't going anywhere. I motioned to him and said, "I thought you had to leave?"

His reply? "I've never been in a meeting with an author like you before. I can't leave."

5. I'm looking for a home for my books. Not a printer. How do you see my book fitting into the long-term strategy you have for your imprint?

6. How would my book, *Fearless Living*, support you in your life?

And on I went. I didn't ask for their approval. I wasn't looking for them to gush all over me (though it's nice when they do!). I was looking for a publisher who understood my mission, wanted to join me in transforming fear, and was willing to roll up their sleeves. Too many authors had told me of their disappointment. Most had handed over their books, praying their editor (and sales team) were miracle-workers. They're not. Your editor is probably worried about their career and could use all the help you can give them to get your book in the hands of the most people.

Here's a tidbit I didn't know. The sales team only cares about your book based on the pitch your editor gives them. If your editor can't inspire and doesn't really understand your book, the sales team will put your book on the back burner. That's just a fact. So, my motto was: I'm here to help you help me. That's what I told every publisher.

My promise was that I would continue to speak day in and day out. I would sell books at every stop. I would blog and post and do all I could do to get my book out there. I have an email list this big and email frequently. "Now," I said, "what will you do to add to my already extensive operation?"

Your publisher can be just a big ole printer, or they can be a partner.* In truth, you'll be the one deciding what they are based on how you see them and treat them. Always remember that the publishers you meet need you. They're desperately looking for the next bestseller or that unique voice. And, my dear beautiful writer, you're it. Act like it.

When it came time for Meredith to open her presents, I moseyed up to the crowd around her on the patio. She glanced at a few of the bigger, obviously expensive gifts and, eyes shining, landed on mine. Mer took the "U" block from the twenty-six letters and started singing a magical unicorn song she sang to her baby every night—a four-minute lullaby about how he was brought to their waiting arms by virtue of a celestial unicorn. Meredith began to cry, as did I. In fact, I'm not sure there was a dry eye in the yard.

Meredith looked at me, whispered, "Thank you," and put her hands to her heart. Later, as I was leaving, she said she could feel my heart and would love to hang out. We talked for hours on the phone and had lunch the following week at her new house, where we discussed possible books to collaborate on. (That's where I was given the gift of seeing the past five years through *her* eyes—traveling through up to three countries in one day, having friends feel slighted because calls home from Japan or Europe cost $300 and were reserved for her mother, and having no idea I'd never felt anything but a member of her treasured circle. *Jesus.*)

"And, Linda?" Meredith said.

"Yeah?"

"Thank you for being so chill and peaceful at my shower. Your presence was so calming."

I laughed out loud. *Calming?* I could get used to the sound of that.

---

* Brian Tart, the Editor in Chief of Dutton, would win the bid for the proposal Rhonda and I crafted together over a year. He made Rhonda's choice easy by basically writing her a love letter about her book. Rhonda went on to publish three other books with Brian.

Without strategy, not trying to control the universe had become my new goal. I'd begun this journey because writing was my favorite activity. There was a simplicity, a purity in my belief in the words, in my mission. All things were possible when I showed up to the page. Now, years later, many of the large and small dreams I'd pined for were coming true. But Thomas's wisdom was proving prophetic yet again. What was making me happiest was becoming the person I wanted to be.

Joel Stein ❧

Nothing has been as good as when I first got paid to write. That was the best moment. I didn't have enough confidence to do freelance gigs that I probably could have gotten because people said that I could write things and I didn't have the confidence, so I never got it done. But my first paid writing gig was a job with health insurance and a desk and all the adult stuff I needed to survive.

I'd gotten paid on other things, but something felt different about this being like a job. Whereas this wasn't a side gig. This was me actually maybe being able to survive from writing. That felt amazing. Nothing's ever felt that good.

Rosie Walsh ❧

It was a dark January evening in the UK in the middle of winter. I was heavily pregnant and took a walk, ending up at a convenience store to get some water. I'd been thinking earlier that day that I had sent my manuscript to Allison, my US agent, weeks before after making all the changes that she'd suggested, but I hadn't heard anything. I thought, *Oh well. I guess nobody wanted to buy the book.*

At the counter, I checked my phone. Allison had sent me an email entitled, "Oh My God." It said: "I sent your book out last night because we're having a snow day in New York today. I told editors that if they were going to be at home all day tomorrow, they needed to read this book because it's going to be massive." I was stunned. The email continued: "I've had editors emailing me since 2:00 AM. They all want to talk to you. They're super excited. When can you get on the phone?"

I had just enough change to pay for my water and read it again, realizing it was REAL. I started typing back to say, "Now! Now! Tell them to call me back now!" And, of course, at that moment, my phone ran out of battery.

It took me forty minutes to shuffle home. When I finally plugged in my phone, I already had three or four more emails saying, "Oh my God. So-and-so at so-and-so publishing house wants to talk to you. We're going to have to set up a schedule." I spoke to three editors that night, one a legendary editor; I couldn't believe I was on the phone with her. Allison and I were FaceTiming constantly since our phone deals wouldn't let us connect internationally, screaming at each other in between calls.

We had four more phone chats to go that evening when she FaceTimed and said, "I've canceled those because we have received a preemptive offer that we just can't possibly ignore. This is the stuff of dreams. You need to sit down." She told me the number and I didn't talk for ages. I was like, "Yeah, but what do you mean?" She kept repeating the amount of money, and I was like, "Yeah, but what do you mean?" I could not take it in. It was so completely preposterous that this would happen to me, this chubby, pregnant woman shuffling around Bristol without her wallet.

Meg Wolitzer

There's a little bit of the Snoopy dance when I finish a book. A sense of real pleasure and excitement that I actually finished this thing. Sometimes when you see the end in sight, you speed up and run toward it. The runs are often shorter than you thought they'd be. The minute you turn the corner, it's like when you see the destination you've been driving toward and race toward it. I definitely get excited: speed up, finish the book, and order Chinese takeout. I always think I'm not going to look at the book then. I'm going to give myself a break. But the minute we shut off the light for bed, I'll lift the lid of my computer, just to look at those pages again. It's like you can't let go.

Then, it's a long process of not letting go when it goes to copy editing. You're still making changes, but it feels really, really good. I sometimes say to my editor, "I can't even believe I wrote that whole thing." It's like, I can't believe I ate the whole thing!

I can't believe I wrote the whole thing!

Years later, while I was working on *this* book, the women of my support group and I reminisced about the past and our individual journeys.

"Seriously? Had I known that publishers wanted you to have bigger names for your book," Meredith Brooks said, dumbfounded, "I would have helped!" And when I told her how I felt left out of the fun during filming of her "Bitch" music video, she said, "God, Linda! You and Tosh with your bouncy happy energy would have been the perfect 'Bitch' random dancers!"

Guys! Love bugs! My dear, beautiful readers! Promise Mama Linda that you won't put unnecessary roadblocks in your path to creative freedom. For heaven's sake, reach out to your friends and contacts at some point during your writing journey. I can't promise your vulnerability will pay off. But I can say with experience that the support you think won't be there may, in fact, be waiting for you to join the party.

My dear friend and mentor of many years, Betsy Rapoport, a former executive editor at Random House, always asks her writing workshop participants, "How many lives would your book have to change for you to feel all your effort was worthwhile?" She says people typically hem and haw, then finally admit, "I'd be happy if it changed one life."

"Great," she tells them. "What if that life was yours?"

We both believe that the point of writing isn't to hit bestseller lists; it's finding your voice and embodying it fully. When you can do that, what part of your life won't get better?

Even if it looks foreign at first, it's a magnificent thing to hold your printed book in your hands or see it on bookstore shelves or glowing in full color on screen. It changes you; it heals pieces you didn't even know still needed healing. It may be a quiet feeling, but one still worthy of celebration.

The smoothness of the cover, the page numbers, the accent font, your name. On. The. Front. It's enchanting, mesmerizing, like any newborn. And then it seeps in. This is *your* work. Your life's work. Your big idea. Maybe even your bread 'n butter. Many thousands of words coherently strung together to influence somehow, someway, someone, somewhere. You did it! Pop the champagne. Or the carrot juice (in a champagne glass, my pick). Take a deep breath. Enjoy the ride.

When that moment comes true for you, or even if it already has, consider taking a picture or a video of yourself with your book in your hands and tagging me when posting. Use the hashtag #BeautifulWritersBook or #ImaBeautifulWriter and I'll celebrate with you and maybe share it! To keep yourself and others motivated during the journey, you can also post yourself *in-process*, doing the work. Again, tag me and use the hashtag #BeautifulWritersatWork. You never know which fellow world-changing word wranglers you'll connect with and inspire. (That reminds me of another motto I live by: #FriendsDontLetFriendsWriteAlone.)

Lives will change. Even if there's no big money, or the publisher doesn't wine and dine you or come with a publicist, or you self-publish. The fireworks may all be internal, but no less valid. Yes, you, Beautiful Writer, are the prize.

CONCLUSION

Sometimes I Forget
I'm a Writer

"Write what should not be forgotten."
~ Isabel Allende

Lives Charmed came out in the fall of 1998, and I kept at it. By 2016, I'd been working on a memoir about Jesse and my divorce, stealing minutes and hours whenever possible while running my retreat and ghostwriting/editing business. Too close to my own material to see when enough was enough, I'd amassed over two hundred thousand words. Painstakingly and too urgently, I edited out half, believing and hoping—but not at all sure when I let my mind go there—that it was finally time for "The End."

Streamlining is intoxicating. Killing your darlings, a high for an organizational freak like me. But pieces were lost in the frenzied pace—some of the heart, the raw emotion, the essence of what I'd started out to share. In trying to do too much, I'd shortchanged the whole. I no longer loved her. But it was too late to back out. My agent had already scheduled meetings with publishers later that week. As I packed my bags for LAX, for a book I no longer believed in, my friend Martha Beck listened to my concerns and echoed my hesitation. "Don't even go," she warned over the phone. "Cancel your trip!"

Remind me not to ignore Martha's advice in the future.

"I *love* the publishing stories," one CEO/publisher exclaimed. "I want more of those!"

"But it's not a writing book," I said. "I put those stories throughout to highlight the struggle of two artists trying to make it, but this is really a divorce memoir."

The editor sitting to her left was going through her own messy divorce and didn't want me to close the book with a love story. "I want you alone in the end," she said. (Challenge: I'd just gotten engaged to my now-husband.) "Can you write less of the happy-ending stuff and more of those writing debacles?"

Holy fuckballs.

On the same day across town, a second publisher said, "Cut the writing stories. I'm dying for more divorce details! Can I see a picture of Jesse online? He's so bad-boy cute!" Four of us stood around a computer and looked up pictures of my old family. Surreal much?

Reminiscent of past rejections for *Lives Charmed* ("You need more famous people!" "You need more unknowns!"), none of this made sense. Gutted, I called Carol, Diane, Betsy, and Danielle sobbing on my way to LaGuardia.

When you can't see the forest through the trees, get the hell out of the forest. It was hot and dry and dusty in there, and I couldn't smell the sky. Over the next few weeks, my feelings of disappointment turned to an ache to look up, away from the page and the screen. To feel the clouds across my face and see new vistas and old friends. And sometimes . . . often . . . to do absolutely nothing.

Nothing. Why didn't anyone tell me how nice it is doing nothing? Soon, days went by without thinking about my book. There was a lot of sitting under trees, watching insects fly, napping. To my shock, I'd somehow let go, given my book back, at least for now, to God, my muse, the ethers—whatever. *You guys figure it out and then let me know. Or don't. I'm good.*

"You mean that thing you've been working on *forever*?" friends said.

"Yep. If I'm happy anyway, maybe that's the point." And then I poured myself another glass of hibiscus tea for my next appointment of feet in grass. No one knew what to say, which was also lovely. Sometimes not planning or knowing feels like floating.

The dogs dug it. Our walks were twice as long. Diane didn't even try and hide her glee. Our phone chats rambled without adherence to a watched clock. With Tosh in college, my time was freer than it had been since our teens.

My sister, Carol, of course, had the best response. The one I sometimes hear myself tell a client: "No writing is ever wasted. It's healed your divorce. It's healed your kid. It's healed you. It's made you a better storyteller. It's made you a better teacher, a more compassionate person. Trust that." Even when Carol whispered, "Perhaps its job is done," I agreed. Perhaps so.

And then I felt even lighter. Daily. Hourly. Pretty much all the time. Was this the answer all along . . . to not write? To not give a flying fuck? To lose the thing you think you need more than air itself to find your breath? I didn't know this unattached, wordless Linda existed. But I liked her very much. Her free-wheeling self hung around and made my life awesome for half a year.

Ernest Hemingway said that there was nothing to writing: "All you do is sit down at a typewriter and bleed." Without the words and open wounds, I figured the new me might be here to stay, which had become A-OK by me.

Then one day, a thought floated through: *I used to be a writer. Is that passion gone forever? Because I think I'm starting to miss her.*

I'd forgotten. But I was remembering.

Then one morning: *Why am I awake at 5:00 AM? That's my old life. The girl who never slept. Because she was wired and WRITING.*

That's when I heard them. The words. Followed by others. They were back as if they'd never left. And the odd thing was . . . they felt good.

Oh. Oh? Oh! My. Lord. There you are! You're here! And I'm here! And I'm not bleeding or tired! *God, it's good to see you. But . . . listen here. If this continues, we're going to go to bed early and play by some new rules because that old no-sleep thing and no-time-for-friends thing . . . that was crackers, and we're too old for that!*

I was grinning, though. Real wide. I almost stopped to ask the words where they'd been, but I was already headed for my desk. They could keep their secrets. My desire to write was the only why I needed. Grateful they'd been gone, I was elated they were back. I couldn't wait to find out what they had to share. It seemed I had some stories to finish.

I lit a candle. Took a deep breath and thanked the muse. Then I entered the trees. And I started again.

THANK YOU for spending your precious time with me, with us! What a fantastic surprise it was for me that morning to find that the divorce memoir I thought I was returning to was, in fact, the impetus for the book you hold in your hands.

Sometimes we need time away to let the pieces—and even the universe—fall into place. Many of the clawing-my-way-to-the-middle writing stories I've shared here were originally scripted for that memoir of my divorce and subsequent midlife mess. When *Beautiful Writers* stepped forth and introduced herself, I loved her right away. I hope you love her too.

Trust your delays. Creativity is mysterious. "Until it's done, it's not done," says your book. Writing time *is* never wasted time. With space and patience, the chaos and confusion and blind alleys you run down start to make sense. You're better for all the back-and-forth. Blessings in hindsight.

Lives Charmed had some stellar successes, but it did not become a runaway bestseller. That's a roller-coaster tale for the next book. (You didn't think we'd go gently into that good night, did you? My bestselling author friends—some from upcoming episodes!—will be back to share the magic and mayhem of our journeys *after* publication.) But the process of giving life to my first book opened countless doors and utterly transformed my world. For starters, I got to leave the toilet scrubbing job I'd taken at Trader Joe's market on an extended stay in Los Angeles while promoting the book. As much as I appreciated going from $12 an hour to a writer's living wage, I would come to miss those customers. In a surprise plot twist, the constant stream of people in my checkout line was so dear I found that I deeply loved humanity after all. Another lesson I'd have missed had I not published.

Birthing that book radically altered how I saw me—what I was capable of—and how others saw me. Through publishing, I was embraced by a loving national media, befriended authors whom I'd long idolized, and became the features editor for a magazine for years, where I had the profound pleasure to write celebrity cover stories through the same spiritual and environmental lens I'd been using. It wasn't long before I was ghostwriting bestsellers for world-changers, a hard (*omg!*) but fun gig. And, Lord, did those connections and that financial stability come in handy when Jesse fell in love with someone else and bailed, and I had to save the kid and the "farm." I crawled back to my favorite childhood place, Carmel, and launched my retreat business. Once again, in helping others tell their tales, I was the one who was saved: kid, farm, and all.

Along the way, I've lived, loved, published a green book, released a top iPhone dating app because, well, that seemed logical, and spoken on the TED-Women stage (about said app). And, of course, I stumbled into hosting a podcast that has led me straight to you.

As I look back on it all, I still get teary-eyed thinking of the scared college dropout I once was who was terrified that she'd let her parents down. Still, to this day, when a writer with her master's or PhD looks to me for support, I think, *How on God's green earth did I get so lucky?*

Because I had the ache, I had what it takes. And so do you.

One of the things I'm most grateful for is how *Lives Charmed* led me out to the forest of New Mexico, where I befriended Thomas One Wolf.* Writing that book taught me how to channel my power and launched my voice as a megaphone for Mama Earth, the cause dearest to my heart. I've since had the privilege of meeting, working with, and interviewing inspiring people who are changing the world thanks to their words. In helping magnify their voices (often influencing them to add environmental themes to their books), I've found that the power of our pens has supercharged ink. How often have we heard that "the pen is mightier than the sword"? Never doubt that your words have the power to travel far beyond the confines of two covers.

In closing, the book in your hands is printed on Forest Stewardship Council® paper made from sustainably managed forests. Choosing BenBella Books as my publisher was the easiest decision—in great part because of their

---

* Thomas is no longer with us. But I recently discovered (and fell in love with) a treasure of a coffee table book, *Spirit Walk,* by Julie Morley devoted to Thomas One Wolf's wisdom.

enthusiasm for my desire to print on FSC paper and to joint-donate a portion of our royalties to FSC's tree-saving foundation. The most exciting call of my life came recently when my contacts at FSC, a group I'd watched for many years from afar, asked me to be an FSC Ambassador. Within twenty-four hours, they'd loaded my picture and bio onto their website and told me that one FSC lead had been so motivated after our call that he'd been awake most of the night. Imagine that. The brainstorming we did together to help save forests caused him to lose sleep. I didn't see that one coming. But you know what? It may take half a lifetime to find your people, but they're out there. It takes as long as it takes.

I hope you'll follow my tree-hugging adventures on social media and over on BookMama.com. And that you'll consider publishing your books on FSC paper or other eco-friendly options. I look forward to hearing about your journey.

For now, I'll close with a question.

Do you sometimes forget you're a writer? Ahhh. Unclench your stomach. Breathe into your gut. And know that anytime you need encouragement, my writerly friends and I are here on the page and on the airwaves, ready to remind you of this heartfelt truth: You are a B.E.A.U.T.I.F.U.L. writer. Full stop.

Your stories are alive. Your desire has purpose. And your soul knows the song. Follow what you know, one small step at a time. It's my hunch that one day you will likewise wake up with all of the clarity you'll need.

Write on!

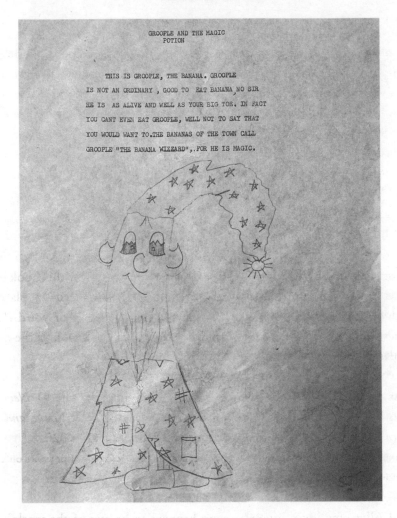

"What an astonishing thing a book is. It's a flat object made from a tree with flexible parts on which are imprinted lots of funny dark squiggles. But one glance at it and you're inside the mind of another person, maybe somebody dead for thousands of years. Across the millennia, an author is speaking clearly and silently inside your head, directly to you. Writing is perhaps the greatest of human inventions, binding together people who never knew each other, citizens of distant epochs. Books break the shackles of time. A book is proof that humans are capable of working magic."

~ Carl Sagan, scientist, astronomer, author

FEATURED AUTHORS

Unless updated after the fact, the celebrity author excerpts in this book come directly from our interviews on my *Beautiful Writers Podcast*—a place for up-close conversations with your favorite authors. In the event you'd like to listen (please do, wherever you download your podcasts), you'll find the names of their episodes below, alongside their brief bios.

Tomi Adeyemi, Nigerian-American novelist, and author of the #1 *New York Times* bestsellers *Children of Blood and Bone* and *Children of Virtue and Vengeance*, and a *TIME* magazine 100 most influential person of 2020.
Beautiful Writers Podcast episode: "Tomi Adeyemi & Sabaa Tahir: YA Superstars on Living & Writing Heroically."

Carol Allen, my bossy little sis—who happens to be one of the world's best relationship coaches and Vedic Astrologers, and the author of *Love Is in the Stars: The Wise Woman's Astrological Guide to Men*. Her entertaining newsletter has been read by millions.
Beautiful Writers Podcast episode: "The Late Debbie Ford's New Book (w/ her sister Arielle Ford & my sister Carol Allen)."

Martha Beck, *New York Times* bestselling author, life coach, and *O* magazine columnist. Her books include *Expecting Adam*; *Leaving the Saints*; *Finding Your*

Way in a Wild New World; Diana, Herself; and her 2022 Oprah's Book Club selection, *The Way of Integrity.*
Beautiful Writers Podcast episodes: "Jenny Lawson & Martha Beck: Seriously Funny + Broken (in the best possible way)," "Abby Wambach & Martha Beck: Wisdom from the Wolfpack," "Geneen Roth & Martha Beck: Messy & Magnificent," "Elizabeth Lesser & Martha Beck: Creative Courage," "Glennon Doyle & Martha Beck: Beautiful Love Warriors," and "Martha Beck: Shortcuts to More Magic."

Rob Bell, *New York Times* bestselling author of many books—including *What We Talk About When We Talk About God, Love Wins, What Is the Bible?,* and *Everything Is Spiritual*—and award-winning podcaster of *The RobCast.*
Beautiful Writers Podcast episode: "Rob Bell & Charles Sailor: On Creativity & the Bible."

Samantha Bennett, popular speaker, creativity/productivity expert, founder of the Organized Artist Company, and author of *Get It Done* and *Start Right Where You Are.*
Beautiful Writers Podcast episodes: "Best-Of Birthday Mix: Expert Top Tips" and "Seth Godin & Samantha Bennett: This Is Marketing!"

Tom Bergeron, funny man, and Emmy Award–winning host of three of the most popular TV shows of all time: *Dancing with the Stars, America's Funniest Home Videos,* and *Hollywood Squares.* His memoir, *I'm Hosting as Fast as I Can!,* is about being Zen and staying sane in Hollywood.
Beautiful Writers Podcast episode: "Lee Child & Tom Bergeron: Writing & Righting Wrongs."

Gabrielle Bernstein, #1 *New York Times* bestselling author of *The Universe Has Your Back,* and many other bestsellers, including *Super Attractor, May Cause Miracles, Judgement Detox,* and *Happy Days.*
Beautiful Writers Podcast episodes: "Gabby Bernstein: On Judgment & Bestsellers" and "Dani Shapiro & Gabby Bernstein: Divine Duo."

Rhonda Britten, Emmy Award–winning life coach on NBC's *Starting Over.* She is the founder of the Fearless Living Institute and author of four bestselling

books: *Fearless Living, Change Your Life in 30 Days, Fearless Loving*, and *Do I Look Fat in This?*
Beautiful Writers Podcast episode: "Best-Of Birthday Mix: Expert Top Tips."

Lee Child, creator of the *Jack Reacher* series, with over 100 million copies sold, is the "strongest brand in publishing," according to *Forbes* magazine. As of this writing, *Reacher*, Child's binge-worthy TV series, has just been greenlit for its second season.
Beautiful Writers Podcast episode: "Lee Child & Tom Bergeron: Writing & Righting Wrongs."

Deepak Chopra, author of ninety-two books, including *Quantum Healing, The Seven Spiritual Laws of Success*, and *Metahuman*, and Fellow of the American College of Physicians.
Beautiful Writers Podcast episode: "Deepak Chopra & Arielle Ford: Metahuman & Infinite Creativity."

Patricia Cornwell, one of the world's most prolific authors, selling over one hundred million copies in her *Scarpetta* thriller series alone. She's been described as a real-life female James Bond, and penned the first forensic thriller (*Postmortem*), paving the way for an explosion of entertainment featuring all things forensic across film, TV, and literature.
Beautiful Writers Podcast episode: "Patricia Cornwell & Tosca Lee: Thrilled to Death & Destiny."

Taylor Dayne, singer, songwriter, memoirist (*Tell It to My Heart*), and one of *Billboard*'s Top 60 Female Artists of All Time (#35 in 2018), with eighteen top-ten hits and over seventy-five million albums sold.
Beautiful Writers Podcast episode: "Taylor Dayne & Bronwyn Saglimbeni: Tellin' It From Her Heart."

Arielle Ford, bestselling author of many books, including *The Soulmate Secret* and *Wabi Sabi Love*. Former book publicist to Deepak Chopra, Marianne Williamson, Wayne Dyer, and Neale Donald Walsch.

Beautiful Writers Podcast episodes: "Best-Of Birthday Mix: Expert Top Tips" and "The Late Debbie Ford's New Book (w/ her sister Arielle Ford & my sister Carol Allen)."

Marie Forleo, author of the #1 *New York Times* bestseller *Everything Is Figureoutable*, based on her concept from Oprah's SuperSoul Sessions. Founder of the online business program B-School, MarieTV, and *The Marie Forleo Podcast*. *Beautiful Writers Podcast* episode: "Elizabeth Gilbert & Marie Forleo: Behind the Bestsellers."

Leeza Gibbons, Emmy Award–winning talk show host, celebrated radio host, Hollywood correspondent on *Entertainment Tonight* and *Extra*, and author of two *New York Times* bestsellers, *Take 2* and *Fierce Optimism*. *Beautiful Writers Podcast* episodes: "Maria Shriver & Leeza Gibbons: They've Been Thinking" and "Leeza Gibbons: Embracing Fierce Optimism."

Elizabeth Gilbert, *New York Times* bestselling author whose works include the genre-exploding *Eat Pray Love* (becoming a movie starring Julia Roberts), *Committed*, *Big Magic*, *The Signature of All Things*, and *City of Girls*. *Beautiful Writers Podcast* episodes: "Elizabeth Gilbert: The Big Magic of Creative Living" and "Elizabeth Gilbert & Marie Forleo: Behind the Bestsellers."

Seth Godin, author of twenty bestsellers, including *This Is Marketing*, *Tribes*, *Purple Cow*, and *Linchpin*, as well as teacher and marketing whiz. *Beautiful Writers Podcast* episodes: "Seth Godin: Tribes, Blogs and Book Biz" and "Seth Godin & Samantha Bennett: This Is Marketing!"

Jane Goodall, PhD, DBE, is the founder of the Jane Goodall Institute and UN Messenger of Peace. Jane Goodall is best known for the groundbreaking research into the lives of wild chimpanzees in Gombe, Tanzania, now spanning more than sixty years, and has written many books for adults and children, including *The Book of Hope*. *Beautiful Writers Podcast* episode: "Dr. Jane Goodall & Keely Shaye Brosnan: Power of the Pen to Heal Mother Earth."

Kelly Noonan Gores, writer, producer, director, and star of the award-winning *Heal* documentary, host of *The HEAL Podcast*, and author of the book *Heal: Discover Your Unlimited Potential and Awaken the Powerful Healer Within*.
Beautiful Writers Podcast episode: "Anita Moorjani & Kelly Noonan Gores: Miraculous Healing."

Tim Grahl, managing partner and publisher at Story Grid Universe and author of *Your First 1000 Copies*, *Book Launch Blueprint*, *Running Down a Dream*, and the young adult novel, *The Threshing*. As a marketing whiz, Grahl shot to acclaim supporting five clients onto the *New York Times* Best Seller list at the *same* time.
Beautiful Writers Podcast episode: "Steven Pressfield & Tim Grahl: Slaying Creative Dragons."

Tom Hanks, typewriter-obsessed Renaissance man (Oscar-winning actor, screenwriter, director, producer, and musician). He's published essays in the *New York Times*, *Vanity Fair*, the *New Yorker*, and his first book of fiction, *Uncommon Type: Some Stories*.
Beautiful Writers Podcast episode: "Tom Hanks: Uncommon Type."

Joy Harjo, three-term Poet Laureate of the United States, musician, playwright, author, and member of the Muscogee Nation. Her writing includes nine books of poetry, two award-winning children's books, and memoirs *Crazy Brave* and *Poet Warrior*.
Beautiful Writers Podcast episode: "Joy Harjo: Poet Laureate of the United States."

Arianna Huffington, founder and CEO of Thrive, founder of the *Huffington Post*, and author of fifteen books, including instant international bestsellers *Thrive* and *The Sleep Revolution*.
Beautiful Writers Podcast episode: "Arianna Huffington: Revolutionizing Sleep for Creativity (. . . and everything else)."

Van Jones, CNN commentator, lawyer, activist, founder of The Dreams Corps, and *New York Times* bestselling author of *The Green Collar Economy*, *Rebuild the Dream*, and *Beyond the Messy Truth*.
Beautiful Writers Podcast episode: "Van Jones & Glennon Doyle: Beyond the Messy Truth."

Mary Karr, award-winning poet and author of the critically-acclaimed and *New York Times* bestselling memoirs *The Liar's Club*, *Cherry*, and *Lit*, as well as *The Art of Memoir*, and five poetry collections, most recently *Tropic of Squalor*. She's a sought-after speaker, songwriter, and the Peck Professor of Literature at Syracuse University.
Beautiful Writers Podcast episode: "Mary Karr: Write the Next True Thing."

Valarie Kaur, civil rights leader, bestselling author (*See No Stranger: A Memoir and Manifesto of Revolutionary Love*), and founder of the Revolutionary Love Project. She has won national acclaim for her work in social justice on issues ranging from hate crimes to digital freedom. Her speeches have reached millions worldwide and inspired a movement to reclaim love as a force for justice.
Beautiful Writers Podcast episode: "Valarie Kaur & Chris Jackson: A World-Changer and Her Superhero Publisher."

Aditi Khorana, former news journalist, and film marketing executive for Hollywood studios. *Mirror in the Sky* was Aditi's first novel, followed by *The Library of Fates*—a feminist historical fantasy, set in ancient India.
Beautiful Writers Podcast episode: "Rosie Walsh & Aditi Khorana: Ghosted. A Publishing Phenomenon."

Sue Monk Kidd, *New York Times* bestselling author of *The Book of Longings*, *The Invention of Wings*, *The Mermaid Chair*, *Dance of the Dissident Daughter*, and *The Secret Life of Bees*.
Beautiful Writers Podcast episode: "Sue Monk Kidd & Ann Patchett: Longings—In Writing & Life."

Dean Koontz, one of the world's most highly paid writers, having sold over half a billion books, has authored numerous suspense thrillers that incorporate horror, fantasy, science fiction, mystery, and humor. Most of his titles have appeared on the *New York Times* Best Seller list, with fourteen hardcover and sixteen paperbacks reaching #1.

Beautiful Writers Podcast episode: "Dean Koontz & Robert McKee: Masters of Suspense."

Anne Lamott, author of one of the most successful writing books ever, *Bird by Bird*. Her other bestsellers include *Operating Instructions*, *Almost Everything*, *Help Thanks Wow*, *Grace (Eventually)*, *Dusk Night Dawn*, and *Traveling Mercies*, as well as several novels.

Beautiful Writers Podcast episode: "Anne Lamott & Glennon Doyle: Hallelujah Anyway."

Danielle LaPorte, Oprah *Super Soul* 100 Leader, cofounder of the *Beautiful Writers Podcast* and my co-author on *Your Big Beautiful Book Plan* is also the author of *How To Be Loving*, *The Desire Map*, *White Hot Truth*, and *The Fire Starter Sessions*.

As my co-host from October 2015 through June 2016, Danielle can be heard on each of the first sixteen episodes. In addition, she comes back to record these *Beautiful Writers Podcast* episodes: "Danielle LaPorte & Book Mama Pod Reunion, Post Deadline Truth Tellin'," "Tom Hanks: Uncommon Type," and "Danielle LaPorte & Dani Shapiro: White Hot Truth-Tellers."

Jillian Lauren, novelist and author of the *New York Times* bestselling memoirs *Everything You Ever Wanted* and *Some Girls: My Life in a Harem*. The STARZ TV series *Confronting a Serial Killer* depicts the story told in her latest book, *Behold the Monster*.

Beautiful Writers Podcast episodes: "Jillian Lauren: Writing the Hard Stuff" and "Paul Williams and Jillian Lauren: Hitmaker for Generations."

Jenny Lawson, author of the *New York Times* bestsellers *Let's Pretend This Never Happened*, *Furiously Happy*, *You Are Here*, and *Broken*. Proprietress of the Nowhere Bookshop. Jenny's popular blog, *The Bloggess*, "is mainly dark humor mixed with brutally honest periods of mental illness."

Beautiful Writers Podcast episode: "Jenny Lawson & Martha Beck: Seriously Funny + Broken (in the best possible way)."

Tosca Lee, *New York Times* bestselling author of eleven historical novels and thrillers, including *The Queen of Sheba*, *The Progeny*, *The Line Between*, and *A Single Light*.
Beautiful Writers Podcast episodes: "Tosca Lee & Hayli Baez: Writing the Perfect Thriller" and "Patricia Cornwell & Tosca Lee: Thrilled to Death & Destiny." (Tosca's snippet about loglines and sections she includes in her fiction book proposals comes from our interview in *Book Proposal Magic*.)

Elizabeth Lesser, *New York Times* bestselling author of *Broken Open* (and several other bestsellers: *Cassandra Speaks* and *Marrow*), and cofounder of Omega Institute. She's given two popular TEDWomen talks and is one of Oprah Winfrey's Super Soul 100—a collection of leaders using their voices and talent to elevate humanity.
Beautiful Writers Podcast episode: "Elizabeth Lesser & Martha Beck: Creative Courage."

Sarah Manguso, Guggenheim Fellow, writing professor, and author of eight books, including the novel *Very Cold People* and nonfiction titles *The Two Kinds of Decay*, *The Guardians*, *Ongoingness*, and *300 Arguments*.
Beautiful Writers Podcast episode: "Sarah Manguso: When Writing Heals the Writer."

Robert McKee, legendary lecturer of *STORY.* Award-winning author of *STORY, DIALOGUE*, and *CHARACTER.* USC professor, whose students have earned over seventy Academy Awards and three hundred nominations.
Beautiful Writers Podcast episode: "Robert McKee: Story Is Everything" and "Dean Koontz & Robert McKee: Masters of Suspense."

Terry McMillan, #1 *New York Times* bestselling author of *Waiting to Exhale* and *How Stella Got Her Groove Back* (both made into hit films starring Whitney Houston and Angela Bassett, respectively), and eight other bestsellers. Former tenured English professor.

Beautiful Writers Podcast episodes: "Terry McMillan & Dani Shapiro: Novels, Memoirs, & Films—Oh My!" and "Terry McMillan & Laura Munson: The Sisterhood of the Traveling Novelists."

Anita Moorjani, international speaker, and author of the *New York Times* bestseller, *Dying to Be Me*, which chronicles her spontaneous total cancer healing following a near-death experience, plus *Sensitive Is the New Strong*, and *What If This Is Heaven?*
Beautiful Writers Podcast episode: "Anita Moorjani & Kelly Noonan Gores: Miraculous Healing."

Laura Munson, *New York Times* bestselling memoirist (*This Is Not The Story You Think It Is*), author of the bestselling novel *Willa's Grove*, and writing coach. The flurry of comments on her 2009 essay, "Those Aren't Fighting Words, Dear," published in the *New York Times*'s "Modern Love" column (leading to her memoir deal), crashed the *Times*'s website.
Beautiful Writers Podcast episode: "Terry McMillan & Laura Munson: The Sisterhood of the Traveling Novelists."

Catherine Oxenberg, actress, screenwriter, royal, and first-time author of *Captive: A Mother's Crusade to Save Her Daughter from a Terrifying Cult*.
Beautiful Writers Podcast episode: "Catherine Oxenberg: Rambo Princess Diaries."

Ann Patchett, bookstore co-owner (Parnassus Books) and Pulitzer Prize finalist (*The Dutch House*), is also the winner of a PEN/Faulkner Award and author of seven other novels as well as assorted nonfiction and children's books.
Beautiful Writers Podcast episodes: "Ann Patchett: Unplugged" and "Sue Monk Kidd & Ann Patchett: Longings—In Writing & Life."

Steven Pressfield, author of *The Legend of Bagger Vance*, which Robert Redford turned into a film. He's also the author of *Gates of Fire* (taught at the US Military Academy) and many books on creativity, including *The War of Art*.
Beautiful Writers Podcast episodes: "Steven Pressfield: Resistance and Invoking the Muse" and "Steven Pressfield & Tim Grahl: Slaying Creative Dragons."

Geneen Roth, the first to link compulsive eating and dieting with deeply personal and spiritual issues, has authored ten books, including the *New York Times* bestsellers *When Food Is Love*, *Lost and Found*, and *Women Food and God*.
Beautiful Writers Podcast episode: "Geneen Roth & Martha Beck: Messy & Magnificent."

Gretchen Rubin, author of several books, including the blockbuster *New York Times* bestsellers *Outer Order, Inner Calm*; *Better Than Before*; *The Happiness Project*; *Happier at Home*, and *The Four Tendencies*.
Beautiful Writers Podcast episode: "Gretchen Rubin: Creativity-Saving Habits."

Bronwyn Saglimbeni, communications coach, blogger, podcaster, and speaker, who has written, directed, and produced more than 175 TEDx, TEDGlobal, and TED talks. Host of the *20 Minutes with Bronwyn* podcast.
Beautiful Writers Podcast episode: "Taylor Dayne & Bronwyn Saglimbeni: Tellin' It from Her Heart."

Charles Sailor, *New York Times* bestselling novelist of *The Second Son* and *The Man Who Rode the Tiger*. Former actor and Hollywood screenwriter for TV shows like *Kojak*, *The Rockford Files*, *CHiPs*, and the debut of *Charlie's Angels*.
Beautiful Writers Podcast episodes: "Charles Sailor: Hollywood Rebel" and "Rob Bell & Charles Sailor: On Creativity & the Bible."

Nell Scovell, TV comedy writer, producer, director, and collaborator on the #1 *New York Times* bestseller *Lean In*. Her memoir, *Just the Funny Parts*, documents her decades writing for, among others: *The Simpsons*, *Late Night with David Letterman*, and *Sabrina, the Teenage Witch*, which she created and executive produced.
Beautiful Writers Podcast episode: "Nell Scovell: Just the Funny Parts & Then Some . . ."

Dani Shapiro, bestselling novelist, author of *Still Writing*, and the memoirs *Devotion*, *Slow Motion*, and the *New York Times* bestseller *Inheritance*. Dani's also a writing teacher and the creator/host of the wildly popular *Family Secrets* podcast.

Beautiful Writers Podcast episodes: "Dani Shapiro & Gabby Bernstein: Divine Duo," "Jennifer Rudolph Walsh & Dani Shapiro: Agent & Writer on Togetherness," "Danielle LaPorte & Dani Shapiro: White Hot Truth-Tellers," "Terry McMillan & Dani Shapiro: Novels, Memoirs, & Films—Oh My!" and "Dani Shapiro: Behind-the-Scenes Writing."

Maria Shriver, mother and grandmother, award-winning journalist, writer, former First Lady of California, Alzheimer's advocate and activist, and author of numerous *New York Times* bestselling books, including *I've Been Thinking*, *Ten Things*, and *And One More Thing Before You Go*.
Beautiful Writers Podcast episode: "Maria Shriver & Leeza Gibbons: They've Been Thinking."

Guru Singh, revered teacher and third-generation yogi, spiritual leader, and author of many books, including his memoir, *Buried Treasures: The Journey from Where You Are to Who You Are*.
Beautiful Writers Podcast episode: "Guru Singh: Buried Treasures Revealed."

Joel Stein, humorist with former columns in *TIME* magazine, the *LA Times*, and *Entertainment Weekly*. Stein's latest book, *In Defense of Elitism*, is his decidedly not-so-snobby attempt to wrestle back honor to the intellectual elites from the populists.
Beautiful Writers Podcast episode: "Joel Stein: A Funnyman's Defense of Elitism."

Cheryl Strayed, #1 *New York Times* bestselling memoirist (*Wild*, made into a movie starring Reese Witherspoon) and author of *Tiny Beautiful Things* (now a hugely successful stage production), plus *Brave Enough* and *Torch*.
Beautiful Writers Podcast episode: "Cheryl Strayed & Nia Vardalos: Answering the Biggest Questions That Stump Writers."

Sabaa Tahir, #1 *New York Times* bestselling author with two titles on *TIME* magazine's 100 Best Fantasy Novels of All Time list: *An Ember in the Ashes* and *A Torch Against the Night*. Also, the first Pakistani-American to hit the YA *NY Times* bestseller list for both fantasy and contemporary.

Beautiful Writers Podcast episode: "Tomi Adeyemi & Sabaa Tahir: YA Superstars on Living & Writing Heroically."

Nia Vardalos, actress, Academy Award–nominated screenwriter (*My Big Fat Greek Wedding*), and author of the *New York Times* bestseller *Instant Mom*—with all proceeds going to adoption groups.
Beautiful Writers Podcast episode: "Cheryl Strayed & Nia Vardalos: Answering the Biggest Questions that Stump Writers."

Jennifer Rudolph Walsh, editor of *Hungry Hearts: Essays on Courage, Desire, and Belonging*; founder of Together Live, former board member and global head of Literary, Lectures, and Conferences at William Morris Endeavor (WME), representing luminaries like Oprah, Brené Brown, and Dani Shapiro.
Beautiful Writers Podcast episode: "Jennifer Rudolph Walsh & Dani Shapiro: A Top Lit Agent & Writer on Togetherness."

Rosie Walsh, British documentary producer and author of six novels, including the *New York Times* and international bestsellers *The Love of My Life, The Man Who Didn't Call* (in the UK), and *Ghosted* (in the US).
Beautiful Writers Podcast episode: "Rosie Walsh & Aditi Khorana: Ghosted. A Publishing Phenomenon."

Abby Wambach, soccer legend (GOAT), two-time Olympic Gold Medalist, and #1 *New York Times* bestselling author of *Wolfpack, Wolfpack (Young Readers Edition)*, and the memoir *Forward*.
Beautiful Writers Podcast episode: "Abby Wambach & Martha Beck: Wisdom from the Wolfpack."

Paul Williams, Songwriting Hall-of-Famer, actor, Oscar-winning composer, president of ASCAP, *New York Times* bestseller of *Gratitude and Trust*, co-authored with Tracey Jackson, and recovery advocate—sober now for thirty-two years.
Beautiful Writers Podcast episode: "Paul Williams & Jillian Lauren: Hitmaker for Generations."

Marianne Williamson, political activist, spiritual thought leader, and author of fourteen books, four of which have been #1 *New York Times* bestsellers, including *A Return to Love* and *Healing the Soul of America*.
Beautiful Writers Podcast episode: "Marianne Williamson: From Tears to Triumph."

Meg Wolitzer, *New York Times* bestselling author of many novels, including *The Female Persuasion, The Ten-Year Nap*, and *The Wife*, which was made into a critically acclaimed movie starring Glenn Close and Jonathan Pryce. Wolitzer also writes for young readers, and her picture book, *Millions of Maxes*, was published in 2022.
Beautiful Writers Podcast episode: "Meg Wolitzer: Blockbuster Novelist."

Laura Yorke, avid horsewoman and literary agent (and ex–veteran book editor and publisher at three Simon & Schuster imprints before moving to Putnam, co-founding the Golden Books Adult Trade division, and acting as editor at large of ReganBooks/Harper Collins).
Beautiful Writers Podcast episode: "Laura Yorke: What Agents Really Want."

ACKNOWLEDGMENTS

To Carol Allen (aka Bossy Little Sis), my person since the day you were born. Fortunately, Mom gave you her acerbic wit, eagle eyes, and photographic memory, and I'm the blessed beneficiary. Endless thanks for recalling the details I didn't, for injecting your smashing spin on the mayhem, and for your "I'm so sorry, it's just not good enough yet" annoyances. Every writer should be so charmed with the stubbornness and years it takes to gain your approval. Thankfully, you're the biggest-hearted person I know. And that husband of yours? So many of the blessings I've experienced came through brother Bill (Allen)! To quote Dad, I'm the luckiest.

Betsy Rapoport (aka Best Editor of All-Time). If Carol and I could choose a sister, just think—the three of us could argue about storylines in the same house! Lol. More cooks in the kitchen! From the time I sent you 600 pages of rambles in 2004 to now, you've been my publishing soulmate, holding my heart and my words in your loving, darling-killing hands. Bless you for honoring my naiveté and grandiosity. Seeing as how I wasn't willing to do what you did and work desk-to-desk with publishing greats in Manhattan all those years, what a gift it's been to receive your endless patience, good humor, and dedicated mentorship. I'd never have the career I have if it weren't for your confidence and care. Thank you for always making me better. "I love you" doesn't half cut it.

We writers are nearly all too close to our stories to be objective, hence why we need help! We ache to find our publishing Dream Teams, like my lovable group of ride-or-dies—including my agent, Rachel Ekstrom at Folio Literary Management. Sister, you found the missing format piece of the book puzzle that eluded us all, bringing, finally, thousands of hours of work together. After brainstorming with some of the most beloved agents in the biz—they know who they are, and I cherish each one of them!—it was your vision that made the difference. And to have your tree-hugging heart expand my world with your connections at BenBella—wow!

BenBella, you're a dream. Rachel and I say it all the time: We cannot believe how ON IT y'all are. Is that how things go down in Texas? From the speed with which you designed ten gorgeous book covers to choose from (how?) to your timely and thorough detail, combined with your eco-vision (FSC paper for the win!), we're consistently blown away. I'm so grateful you found me, Glenn Yeffeth—and that you've brought together this powerhouse team to whom I bow down, including: Sarah Avinger, Sarah Beck, Ross Burlingame, Jennifer Canzoneri, Morgan Carr, Aaron Edmiston, Aida Herrera, Alicia Kania, Adrienne Lang, Monica Lowry, Dayna Lupica, Raquel Moreno, Susan Welte, Alyn Wallace, Tanya Wardell, and Vy Tran.

Dearest Vy. I've written for a lot of publishers, but our alliance is the one that most makes me cheer at my desk. Every time you send me an email, I know it will make my day. Your edits are world-class, and this book is far better for your vision. Thank you for choosing me (and not killing my word count!). I hope this is just the beginning.

To my Forest Stewardship Council (FSC) family. YOU. It's always been YOU, the tree-huggers whom I've long admired. Thank you for embracing my work and investing your lives to safeguard healthy forests—so we may all live more beautifully. I cherish all of you, starting with Lou Raiola, Chris McLaren, Maggie Abel, Jenna Mueller, and Aubrey McCormick.

Van Jones told me that writing a book is a team sport. You don't say. So many team players have been invaluable. Matthew Tower and Aditi Khorana, my heaven-sent brainstorming VIPs. From our calls and lunches in Carmel, Matthew, to those three days in a hotel in West Hollywood, Aditi, where you read through 2,000 pages of podcast transcripts to help me wrangle my first actual outline in 2018, no amount of thanks can suffice.

Guru Singh. I simply cannot. This book is a testament to my deep and abiding admiration. Thank you for your prophecy and your belief. It's inspired my every move. Ditto to you, Paul Williams—my life-changer. Watching you write hit songs in five minutes in your kitchen was magic. And my "Uncle" Chuck Sailor (and Barbara George!), my first author role model—you made writing and publishing feel real because, for you, they were! Kay Sprinkel Grace, your endless love and powerful female role modeling inspire me still. Sue Brodie, I worship you, Mama.

To Meredith, Carrie-Anne, and Janet. (No spoilers; last names are for storylines.) You three beauties have taught me more about femininity, perseverance, fame, focus, and what success and friendship really are than I can articulate. Endless love to you, sisters. Danielle LaPorte. For two solo players, we've had one hell of a creative partnership. From meeting at that café in Santa Fe in our muddy boots before either of us was published to now, I love what we started together and how you've helped me ride without training wheels, never far from reach.

To my sweet Bay Area family. LOVE you so. To my Los Altos crew, how blessed we were to grow up where and when we did. I heart you, even those who took a little heat in a few of these pages. We were young, it was funny, and I hope you feel my heart. Joe Parente, to me, you'll always be the writer of the two of us. Pat Johnson and Kathleen Feigelman, I miss you! Ditto to Gina, Sally, Missy, Margot, Kathi, Lisa, Carol, Diana, and so many others. I'll hug you this fall at the reunion that John won't let me miss.

To every "Carmelie" retreat participant who's listened to and offered feedback on pieces in this book at lunches and dinners over the years, I thank God for you! (Mama needed permission and feedback as much as anyone!) I was keeping track to name you here, but it got ridiculous. Too much gratitude for a few sheets of paper. Forgive me and please know that your support has meant everything, and I work every day to be worthy of you.

Thank you to every author who's been on my *Beautiful Writers Podcast*. You light the way. (Due to contractual obligations, a few guests couldn't join us on these pages. If you're missing them, revisit their episodes or their beautiful books!) Thank you to all of my interviewees for your kindness and, in many cases, friendship. There are waaaay too many to list here (and, honestly, you're all my favorite in one way or another). But I want to offer a special early adopter shout-out to Dani Shapiro, Liz Gilbert, Steven Pressfield, and Martha Beck, who went above and beyond for the podcast and this book. To Tom Hanks, who approved his excerpts on location on the first day of a movie shoot! To Van Jones (and Gus!), who also granted their sweet support amidst a zillion other deadlines while traveling. (Writers be busy, y'all.) To Martha, my dearest Martha, comin' in with terrific additional text to a last-minute ask while also getting ready to tape her Oprah Book Club appearance. And Ter . . . (Terry McMillan). I don't know how I got so lucky and still pinch myself every time you call or pick up my calls.

Boundless love for my desk-jockey girlfriends. What a blessing it is, doing this writerly life with you. Even when we don't talk, my days are far lovelier knowing you're there. I could write a book of gratitude all about you, but word count (ugh): Amy Ahlers, Heide Banks, Laura Belgray, Samantha Bennett, Janet Bertolus, Rhonda Britten, Amanda Burkman, Chellie Campbell, Victoria Loveland-Coen, Anese Cavanaugh, Taylor Dayne, Sharon Van Epps, Jessica Fein, Ali Flint, Arielle Ford, Lauren Francis, Anne Friedman, Kim Fulcher, Barbara George, Leeza Gibbons, Jaclyn Goldis, Kelly Noonan Gores, Patti Hall, Robin Hammer, Allison Hill, Adrianne Hillman, Steph Jagger, Amelia Kinkade, Lisa Lai, Jillian Lauren, Tosca Lee, Janice MacLeod, Rowan Mangun, Natalie Kottke Masocco, Erica Mather, Julia Mathison, Abby Lowe McNeil, Laura Munson, Elizabeth Murray, Elise Museles, Justine Musk, Linda Northrup, Kate Northrup, Catherine Oxenberg, Nadia Prescher, Andrea Quinn, Nancy Rainford, Diane Reed, Dina Eastwood Ruiz, Bronwyn Saglimbeni, Tanmeet Sethi, Diane Danvers Simmons, Jenn Sutkowski, Maia Toll, Sarah Vermunt, Andrea Vieira, Leanne Wood, and Laura Yorke. To borrow a play out of Jenny Lawson's playbook, if I forgot you, please add your name here: _____, and know that despite my mental hard drive being full (deadlines are intense!) I ADORE you!

Hugs to my Beautiful Writers Group members, some of whom have been with us since 2015, when Danielle and I started our group and podcast. The years have flown by, but you've made it a blast with your talent, commitment, hilarious quips, and unrelenting faith. Cheerleading each other on is LIFE. #FriendsDontLetFriendsWriteAlone

Jules! Beautiful Julia McPherson, of Innerspace Marketing. You've been the right arm of my business for the past seven years, and I'd be lost without you. Thank you for your can-do-everything, savvy BS detector, beautiful designs, and laughter. I love, love, love you. Lucie Balassone-Mosny: Jules and I kiss the ground upon which you walk. Talk about the best attitude! And dear Kevin Baker of Red Room Sound: Every podcast episode has been a joy with you at the editing bay. Bless you and your sunny disposition and nuts mind-blowing work ethic. To my Carmel home-away-from-home crew at the La Playa Hotel and the Wild Plum Café, including Sammy Ramos, Tracy Hunter, and Pamela Burns. You. Are. Beyond.

Larry. I honor that you're shy and not one for the spotlight. So, I'll keep this short except to say that whenever I prayed for "my guy," I saw a strong, ethical man with a daughter with dark hair. You're not going to get off that easy because our storyline comes into play in future stories. But for now, I'll say that my family was too small with the death of my parents. You and Mom, your siblings and their families, and your beautiful Hayli (and Rick Baez, and our grandbabies Hazel and Hunt!!!) have given my heart a home.

Diane Chandler, Di Di. My girl. My alter-ego. The always-sunny, fun one who was out whoopin' it up in college while I was back at our apartment or sorority house with a book. I will always live through your exploits and write about us—my way of putting my love for you in a forever time capsule. I still remember looking out my front window as a girl as you and your glamorous sisters walked to town, wishing I was cool enough to be your friend. I felt that way as roommates at USC, and I'll feel the same way into our nineties. It's going too fast, baby. But we've surely got time, as in lifetimes.

To Tosh, my fiery, fabulous, soulmate kid. You, your dad (hey, Jesse James!), and I came in wired differently. But even when we diametrically disagree, I appreciate your passion and always feel your heart. There's no greater joy in my life than hearing you call me Mom. (Or "Maaa! You got any food up in this bitch?!") As my dad said to me, "Thank you so much for choosing me this time around." You're the light of my life, T.

To my forever Angels, missyouloveyoualwaysandforever: Thomas One Wolf, Grampa Pete Concha, Joanne and Al Tisch, Gram Marian Tisch, Marilyn Traynor, Vy Metter, Etta Sivertsen, and Miss Merry Fuzz Buckets, who was at my feet or in my lap as I wrote many of these pages.

And to you, my beautiful readers and fellow tree-hugging dreamers. I love you. I feel you. I am you. Write on. xo

INDEX

INDEX

ABOUT THE AUTHOR

Michael Higgins Photography

Linda Sivertsen, "Book Mama," is in LOVE with books—reading, writing, and selling them. Her titles have won awards and hit all the lists as an author, co-author, and former magazine editor and ghost-writer. But her driving force has been to publish sustainably. Naïve and optimistic enough to believe in magic, she's on a mission to save forests via her role as a Forest Stewardship Council (FSC) Ambassador. When she's not fostering literary love matches on her *Beautiful Writers Podcast* (a favorite stop for writers on tour) or midwifing books at her Carmel or virtual writing retreats, Linda can be found on the back of a horse or running with her dogs. She and her husband live on their ranch in Scottsdale, Arizona.